THE GREATER PLAINS

THE GREATER PLAINS
Rethinking a Region's Environmental Histories

Edited by BRIAN FREHNER *and* KATHLEEN A. BROSNAN

University of Nebraska Press
Lincoln

© 2021 by the Board of Regents of the University of Nebraska

All rights reserved

Publication of this volume was assisted by the National Science Foundation.

Library of Congress Cataloging-in-Publication Data
Names: Frehner, Brian, editor. |
Brosnan, Kathleen A., 1960– editor.
Title: The Greater Plains: rethinking a region's environmental histories / edited by Brian Frehner and Kathleen A. Brosnan.
Description: Lincoln: University of Nebraska Press, [2021] |
Includes bibliographical references and index.
Identifiers: LCCN 2020051246
ISBN 9781496225078 (hardback)
ISBN 9781496226471 (paperback)
ISBN 9781496227058 (epub)
ISBN 9781496227065 (mobi)
ISBN 9781496227072 (pdf)
Subjects: LCSH: Human ecology—Great Plains. | Natural history—Great Plains. | Great Plains—History. | BISAC: HISTORY / United States / State & Local / Midwest (IA, IL, IN, KS, MI, MN, MO, ND, NE, OH, SD, WI) | NATURE / Ecosystems & Habitats / Plains & Prairies
Classification: LCC GF13.3.G6 G74 2021
DDC 304.20978—dc23
LC record available at https://lccn.loc.gov/2020051246

Set in Minion Pro by Laura Buis.

CONTENTS

List of Illustrations . . viii
List of Tables . . x
Acknowledgments . . xi
Introduction . . xiii
BRIAN FREHNER AND KATHLEEN A. BROSNAN

Part 1. Indigenous Grassland Adaptations over the *Longue Durée*

1. Before the Horse: Indigenous Food Systems on the Plains, 1300–1680 . . 3
   NATALE ZAPPIA

2. Travois Trails: Mobile Lifeways of Nineteenth-Century Plains Indian Women . . 28
   LEILA MONAGHAN

3. Bison Hunters and Prairie Fires: A View from the Northwestern Plains . . 48
   MARÍA NIEVES ZEDEÑO, CHRISTOPHER ROOS, KACY HOLLENBACK, AND MARY HAGEN ERLICK

4. To Know the Story behind It: Indigenous Heritage and Buffalo Hunting on the Northern Plains . . 66
   GENEVIÈVE SUSEMIHL

Part 2. Animals on the Great Plains

5. Kinscapes and the Buffalo Chase: The Genesis of Nineteenth-Century Plains Métis Hunting Brigades . . 89
   NICOLE ST-ONGE AND BRENDA MACDOUGALL

6. Fauna and Flux on the Plains' Edge: Animal Kinship, Place Making, and Cherokee Relational Continuity . . 114
CLINT CARROLL

7. Bison and Bookkeeping: Accounting for an Environmental Imagination in Great Plains Trading Posts . . 138
GEORGE COLPITTS

8. An Uncommon Nuisance: Cattle Feeding, Nuisance Complaints, and Legal Remedies on the Southern Plains . . 156
JACOB A. BLACKWELL

Part 3. Modern Agriculture and the Transformation of the Plains

9. Measuring Expertise: Ralph Parshall and Watershed Management, 1920–1940 . . 179
MICHAEL WEEKS

10. A "Plow to Save the Plains": Conservation Tillage on the North American Grasslands, 1938–1973 . . 202
JOSHUA NYGREN

11. From Wheat to Wheaties: Minneapolis, the Great Plains, and the Transformation of American Food . . 230
MICHAEL J. LANSING

12. "Nature Rarely Establishes Sharp Boundaries": Settler Society Agricultural Adaptation in the Great Plains Northwest . . 253
MOLLY P. ROZUM

Part 4. Energy Landscapes

13. Energy Heartland: How the Midcontinent Pipeline System Fueled and Fouled the Great Plains . . 279
PHILIP A. WIGHT

14. Places of Overburden: Strip Mining and Reclamation on the Northern Great Plains . . 300
RYAN DRISKELL TATE

15. Encountering Oil Cultures in a Prairie Town .. 320
JONATHAN PEYTON AND MATTHEW DYCE

16. Blows Like Hell: The Windy Plains of the West .. 340
JULIE COURTWRIGHT

Contributors .. 363

Index .. 365

ILLUSTRATIONS

1. Map of the Great Plains . . xxix
2. *Women with Travois Digging Roots* . . 37
3. Illustration of painted rawhide bags . . 43
4. Blackfoot demonstration of how to start a prairie fire . . 53
5. Stranglewolf bison jump . . 57
6. Spring Coulee bank profile . . 58
7. Jacques Berger contract . . 96
8. Map of the Berger kinscape . . 97
9. Pierre Berger graph . . 100
10. Map showing cattle-feeding concentrations . . 158
11. Map showing cattle feeding has diminished . . 159
12. Ralph Parshall next to a Parshall Flume . . 183
13. Colorado-Big Thompson profile map . . 188
14. Parshall ideal water supply . . 191
15. Vortex tube under construction . . 196
16. Bellvue Irrigation Lab . . 197
17. Two of Duley and Russel's early V-sweeps . . 209
18. Oscar H. Will & Co. 1951 annual catalog cover . . 254
19. Walter Prescott Webb's map of land regions of the United States, 1931 . . 264
20. Walter Prescott Webb's map of agricultural regions of the United States, 1931 . . 265
21. Mr. Hardy Pioneer Hybrid, Will Co. logo, Oscar H. Will & Co. catalog, 1955 . . 267

22. Will's Bismarck Seed House 1961 annual catalog cover . . 268
23. Contemporary U.S. and Canadian crude-oil and petroleum-product trunk lines . . 281
24. An Aermotor windmill pumping water into a reservoir . . 345
25. Lesley's wind wagon . . 356

TABLES

1. Cheyenne waterway names . . 32
2. Arapaho place-names in Colorado . . 33
3. Resources mentioned by Jim Blood . . 35

ACKNOWLEDGMENTS

This book has been made possible in part by support from the National Science Foundation (NSF): Science, Technology, and Society. Matt Corpolongo and Kayla Griffis-Molina ably helped in the research and writing of the application and Tina Smith of the University of Oklahoma (OU) Office of Research graciously guided us through the submission process. We also are grateful to NSF program director Frederick Kronz who was generous with his time and wise in his recommendations for our application. Christa Seedorf at OU and Hannah Hohenstein-Flack at the University of Missouri–Kansas City administered the grant on behalf of our institutions.

The NSF grant allowed us to host a three-day conference with the book's contributors. The OU libraries, Department of History, and Office of the Provost provided financial support for our efforts. We want to thank Tara Carlisle, Courtney Buchkoski, James Hart, and Kyle Harper in particular. Conference participants benefited from tours at OU's Fred Jones Jr. Museum of Art and its Sam Noble Oklahoma Museum of Natural History led by Mark White and Daniel Swan, respectively. Daniel Swan and Robert Rundstrom provided invaluable insights with their commentary on papers.

We ended the conference with a visit to the Joseph H. Williams Tallgrass Prairie Preserve and the Osage Nation in Pawhuska, Oklahoma. We are grateful to Bob Hamilton for granting access to the preserve and for allowing us to use conference facilities where we workshopped papers. We also thank Samuel D. Fuhlendorf, Regents Professor and Groendyke Chair at Oklahoma State University, who shared his research on fire and bison grazing at the Tallgrass Prairie Preserve. A highlight of the conference was our visit to the Osage Nation Museum. We are extremely grateful to the Osage Nation and all of the people who welcomed us and worked to assemble a panel of speakers who explained the rich history of the Osage people and their lands. In particular, we thank Chief Geoffrey M. Standing Bear, Sheryl Decker, Jason E. Zaun, Hallie Winter, Jackie Rodgers, Jann Hayman, Eddy Red Eagle, Ross Walker, Shane Rencountre, Everett Waller, and the Wah Zha Zhe Youth Council.

Finally, we are deeply indebted to John Buchkoski whose hard work helped make the conference a great success. John arranged transportation, meals, and museum visits, coordinated our internet broadcast and social media, and handled all publicity. A talented historian who has published his own research on the plains, John was integral to the conference and this book.

We want to thank Bridget Barry at the University of Nebraska Press for a superb job shepherding this book through peer review and publication as well as all of the other staff at the press who helped with copyediting, page proofs, images, and publicity. We thank them for their enthusiasm, expertise, and patience. And of course, we thank the anonymous reviewers for their extremely helpful critiques and suggestions.

Being part of *The Greater Plains*, both the NSF-supported conference and this book, has been a rare intellectual gift and a rewarding personal experience for all involved. We are indebted to everyone who made it possible.

Any views, findings, conclusions, or recommendations expressed in this book do not necessarily represent those of the National Science Foundation.

INTRODUCTION

BRIAN FREHNER AND KATHLEEN A. BROSNAN

The North American West is moving eastward. Some 140 years ago John Wesley Powell of the U.S. Geological Survey famously identified the 100th meridian, which slices through much of the Great Plains, particularly in the United States, as the rough dividing line between the arid and humid sections of the continent based on the amount of annual rainfall. In the twenty-first century, climate scientists argue that "a sharp aridity gradient still exists, but that it's now centered around the 97th meridian."[1] While scholars long debated the appropriate boundaries of the Great Plains and now contemplate how the phenomenon of climate change may alter historical definitions, the denizens of the states and provinces popularly viewed as part of the region have simply begun to adapt. Shifting climatic conditions, for example, have prompted some Oklahoma farmers to abandon tilling the soil and focus on raising cattle; a herd of Angus requires less water than food crops.[2] In Canada the Prairie Adaptation Research Collaborative examined the potential impacts of climate change on activities ranging from agriculture and forestry to tourism and recreation and outlined potential responses from crop diversification to infrastructure conservation and floodway reengineering.[3] Such transitions are the latest human adjustments to the Great Plains ecologies. Across centuries technological adaptations—to the region's distinctive water, grass, animal, and energy systems—have guided its environmental history as much as, and arguably more than, the ecological disasters that too often have formed the overarching narrative of the Great Plains. These adaptations provide a starting point for this volume and the unifying theme for its essays.

As the field of environmental history found its intellectual footing in the 1970s, Donald Worster's *Dust Bowl: The Southern Plains in the 1930s* (1979) emerged as a foundational text. Placing humans' relationships with nature at the core of the regional story, Worster built on the work of earlier scholars, such as Walter Prescott Webb and James Malin.[4] Webb and Malin provided important antecedents to the contemporary field by making the environment integral to their arguments about region and culture. Webb, however, also espoused a perspective rooted in environmental determinism that environmental historians found less tenable. Webb argued, for example, "the Great Plains environment . . . constitutes a geographic unity whose influences have been so powerful as to put a characteristic mark upon everything that survives within its borders."[5] He identified the 98th meridian as a fault, noting that "the Great Plains have bent and molded Anglo-American life, have destroyed traditions, and have influenced institutions in a most singular manner."[6] While Malin recognized that humans needed to adapt to the ecology of the plains, he did not believe that the environment circumscribed their activities. He emphasized social conditions, cultural values, and the pioneer's "contriving brain and skillful hand." Malin concluded, "People are more important than the physical environment. People can make choices."[7]

Like these predecessors, Worster focused on the interconnected relationship of social and environmental change, but he rejected the predetermined conclusions of Webb's narrative and critiqued Malin for his faith that the grasslands were resilient enough to withstand capitalism's damage—a faith that led to Malin's dismissal of New Deal management policies.[8] By contrast Worster offers a harsh indictment of capitalism and the system of farming it spawned. "On the plains the elements of risk were higher than they were anywhere else in the country, and the destructive effects of capitalism far more sudden and dramatic. There was nothing in the plains society to check the progress of commercial farming, nothing to prevent it from taking the risks it was willing to take for profit. This is how and why the Dust Bowl came about."⁹

If Malin perhaps overstated both the transformative power of human ingenuity and restorative power of the environment, Worster's groundbreaking study and many of the works that followed have focused on environmental declension and episodes of disaster such as the Dust Bowl, emphasizing negative interactions between people and their surroundings. This collection of essays represents an attempt to move beyond degradation and exploitation as the defining ecological narratives of the region by examining the Great Plains through the interrelated themes of water, grasses, animals, and energy. In no way does this volume seek to minimize the very real limits and constraints the Great Plains imposed upon the people who live or lived there. However, people did not interact with their surroundings in a singular way or live from disaster to disaster. Instead they often adjusted their methods of resource use through technological developments. Certainly, humans' reliance on technology resulted in exploitation as the authors presented here show, but this project will consider a variety of alternative narratives, including the role of technology in adaptation, persistence, preservation, and sustainability. Humans' capacity to alter their behavior in response to changed environmental circumstances is a theme that demands the world's attention now more than ever, and it is the primary idea that drives this volume. This collection asks readers to envision "A Greater Plains," that is, a region where human adaptation to changing environments advances our understanding beyond dust, drought, and declension.¹⁰

Through these essays we cover many subregions of the U.S. and Canadian plains and integrate multiple disciplinary perspectives. Thus, the geographic and methodological scope of the project is large. To achieve these ends, we sought and received funding from the National Science Foundation for a workshop in Norman, Oklahoma, a collaborative gathering from which this volume emerged. Contributors presented first drafts of their research and received critiques. With internet broadcasts and social media, we engaged as wide an audience as possible. Visits to museums and archives on the campus of the University of Oklahoma would inform their revisions. On our final day we loaded into several vehicles and drove toward Pawhuska, Oklahoma. Along the way we traveled through different environments that embodied many of the technological adaptations that have occurred for centuries across the plains. We passed through densely populated urban and industrial environments such as Oklahoma City and into grasslands burned by wildland fires in the preceding months. On the prairies pump jacks bobbed up and down, as they have for decades, to extract oil from the earth. As oil fields faded from view, we traversed miles of rolling hills populated with new "farms" where turbines captured the energy of the wind. The Tallgrass Prairie Preserve outside Pawhuska offers thousands of acres of grasslands, a remnant of an ecology that once dominated much of the plains. Some 2,500 bison roam the site, descendants of a species that once populated the region from Canada to Texas in the millions. We learned about the ways humans have employed "controlled" fire in this ecology as a technology to feed themselves and as an often futile means to suppress more dangerous fires. At the Osage Nation Museum, tribal members explained their experiences living on this land and the adaptations they and their ancestors have made over the centuries, from burning prairies to embracing oil extraction in the twentieth century.

Consequently, the NSF-sponsored workshop allowed contributors to immerse themselves in some of the landscapes that make up the larger region known as the Great Plains. What constitutes the region we call the "Great Plains" is, of course, a question with a complicated history. Yet we believe there is value in a regional approach. Regionalism has multiple meanings within the field of American environmental history. First, it referred to a specific movement originating in the interwar years that offered a counterpoint to modern urbanity. The term suggested that regionally scaled projects were more harmonious with the environment and thereby sanctified traditional societies. Its proponents included Webb, noted polymath Lewis Mumford, and southwestern nature writer Mary Austin. After World War II environmentalists adopted from regionalists a set of ideas prioritizing place as a factor in both history and planning for the future. Regionalism, they contended, offered an intimate connection between place and culture.[11] Places, viewed at various scales, have distinct characteristics that differentiate them from other places. Historical understanding depends on finding the appropriate scales, even while using notional entities such as the Great Plains. The history we write is profoundly shaped by the spatial frame we choose. The regional approach inherent in this collection allows us to probe the dialectical engagement between the local, the national, and the transnational.[12]

The Great Plains, as a region, is both a physical reality and a cultural construction defined by complex relationships. As historians Edward L. Ayers and Peter S. Onuf explain, regions are "places where discrete, though related, structures intersect and interact in particular patterns. The region *is* climate and land; it *is* a particular set of relations between various ethnic groups; it *is* a relation to the federal government and economy; it *is* a set of shared cultural styles. But each of these elements, even the influence of land and climate, is constantly changing."[13] Not all historical accounts of the Great Plains have emphasized the role of change and adaptation in defining the region. Agricultural historian R. Douglas Hurt calls the plains "the big empty," a place "where most of the cities skirt the fringe of the region and distance betrays time. It is a region of isolated inland communities."[14] If there is some truth to Hurt's description, particularly looking backward from the twenty-first century, we believe that there is much to challenge it from a historical perspective across multiple centuries. Our exploration of "regionalism" with regard to the Great Plains considers not only whether there exist specific issues and characteristics that separate the area from places west of the Rocky Mountains, or east of the Mississippi River, but whether past interactions reveal complex, constantly shifting adaptations to an equally complex ecology. By focusing on such adaptations, this volume complicates earlier narratives of the plains as a region prone to ecological disaster.

People have lived on the plains for millennia, and their adaptations to sometimes dramatic environmental change often constituted the norm rather than the exception. Collectively, the contributors argue that the way to understand the region is through the technologies they employed to survive and, at times, thrive. This understanding must come from an analysis of the methods that succeeded and failed along with such technological developments that altered the landscape in both intended and unexpected ways. Such a perspective illustrates that human interactions with the environment were never one-dimensional, nor were they ever strictly positive or negative. Technological developments on the plains demonstrate the complexities that are inherent in the history of peoples' experiences in the region.

As we contemplate these adaptations, the four themes of water, grasses, animals, and energy serve to organize the essays in this volume. Each author explores the complicated intersection of two or more of these elements, allowing us to discern concepts and issues that are distinctive in the region. The theme of *water* allows contributors to engage with water usage over time and the struggle between people and the region's variable climate, including harsh cold winters, hot humid summers, and periodic droughts. Water not only provides the source of life, as it does in any region, but poses specific challenges for people on the Great Plains. Through an examination of water on the plains, the volume's contributors can assess the other three themes as corollaries, as water provided for grasses, which fed animals that provided energy as food. Whether through a lack of water, or flooding, humans grappled with how to use water wisely, while ensuring that it continued to exist for such use. Construction of New Deal hydroelectric dams in Oklahoma and the formation of reservoirs in western Kansas illustrate more modern technological adaptations, but humans employed a wide variety of methods to control and utilize limited water resources over the centuries. Competition for water throughout the region, and especially in Texas for hydraulic fracturing versus agriculture, epitomizes how technology can intensify competition for resources among differing constituencies.

Grasses provide an opportunity to think about plains soils and vegetation and how they reflect human activity in the ecosystem.

Grasses such as those on the Tallgrass Prairie sustained a variety of fauna, most notably the North American bison, which allowed for the flourishing of Indigenous tribes in the region and sustained the ecological balance of the plains. Native flora as well as introduced crops, such as wheat, have defined the region and influenced how people have subsisted and produced food. Grasses are defined broadly so as to integrate, for example, new species of wheat to battle diseases and insects, marking an important technological development in the adaptations of plains' residents. In addition, the native grasslands of the Great Plains provided an effective barrier to erosion and soil loss, which facilitated the introduction of various economic staples. Changes to the ecosystem made by people settling the region resulted in the alteration or total disappearance of native grasslands. The presence or absence of grasses due to erosion, excessive harvesting, or drought reveal how the boundaries or definitions of the region might have changed over the centuries from a biological and ecological perspective. The study of grasses is, therefore, vital to this edited volume.

The theme of *animals* offers insight into how people produced and consumed food and radically changed the composition of native fauna in the region, particularly in the case of the North American bison.[15] Animals are essential to the flow of energy in any ecosystem, and this volume will assess their role in the human and environmental history of the region. Although the near extinction of the bison is indeed a pivotal occurrence in American environmental history, humans found many symbiotic ways to interact with animals and create lives in the region. Indigenous peoples adapted to their environment through their domestication and use of the horse on the plains for transportation and, sometimes, for intertribal commerce. European settlers introduced livestock including bovines, swine, and poultry to the region, which demanded the further use of grains, grasses, and the land itself. Cattle provided the basis of the ranching economy on the plains but simultaneously competed with the bison for limited food supplies. This, ultimately, also made life for Indigenous tribes more precarious. And after World War II, feedlots constituted another adaptation that accelerated the industrialization of cattle and other animals. Reintroduction of bison and the creation of preserves illustrate how humans recognized and responded to technology's sometimes adverse impacts.

Finally, contributors use the category of *energy* to examine how people established the means to manipulate their technologies over the course of nearly five centuries. The term "energy" evokes images of oil derricks and twenty-first-century controversies involving wind turbines and pipelines, all important historical topics this volume will examine. However, energy in other forms has a long history in the region and has shaped how humans have altered environments. For example, the biota of the plains provided vast stores of caloric energy for Indigenous people.[16] The introduction of the horse and firearms allowed them and Euro-Americans to exploit this energy source at unprecedented levels, dramatically altering different peoples' interactions with the environment.

Through these themes the contributors engage with the concept of "regionalism," some more explicitly than others, to show how people formed cultural relationships with the environment to live on the plains. The four themes we have identified allow for a more complex, interconnected, and thus complete analysis of the Great Plains region than would focusing on select historical events that could be construed as moments of crisis and decline. Using these organizing themes, the volume brings historians, geographers, archaeologists, anthropologists, and specialists in Native American studies together in an interdisciplinary forum—scholars whose paths do not generally cross at professional meetings—and allows them to build on each other's contributions to tell a more fully integrated story of the Great Plains environment and of the people who survived and thrived on this often challenging landscape through social and technological adaptations.

While we believe the essays in this volume engage academic communities, we also think they serve a larger public by offering a starting point to begin thinking about how adapting to such a large, sprawling environment has shaped the lives of people living throughout the region and the lives of those who preceded them. We define technology broadly as the practical application of knowledge gained through education but also through experience and experiment, allowing us to cast a much longer chronological net. A recasting of the plains as a region with technology as a primary feature of its past will allow people to conceptualize their own interactions with this environment in the present and future and to recognize that such relations need not end in disaster and decline. A deeper understanding of the region's past will offer a powerful case for further adaptations including technologies that would limit water usage or inform research for carbon-free energy sources, while also providing cautionary tales about the limits of such adaptations. Our multidisciplinary focus enhances the larger scholarship in environmental history, a field that has long embraced interdisciplinarity with diverse theories and research methodologies.

In addition to informing a broad public audience, this volume has the potential to influence policy makers' decisions about social and environmental change throughout the region and on both sides of the national border. The plains, geographically and ecologically, includes a portion of Canada. The themes that inform this collection of essays appear elsewhere in the western United States and Canada. Therefore, the scholarship we present may guide legislators and other public officials who craft laws and policies in response to the introduction of new technologies that affect environmental change and that defy national political boundaries. Many of the essays in this volume alter definitions of the Great Plains and complicate traditional conceptions of the region. Therefore, we believe that local, state or provincial, and federal governments will benefit from thinking across political boundaries in their efforts to implement and regulate technologies they intend to combat ecological and social challenges. Perhaps scholarship of the sort in this volume may prompt policy makers to fashion ideas in the spirit of environmental adaptation, protection, and preservation rather than with a declensionist mindset that sees only irreparable environmental despoliation.

The four topical themes of water, grass, animals, and energy provided useful categories for contextualizing these sixteen essays, but other themes emerged as contributors revised their work and read each other's contributions. First, the issue of mobility runs throughout many of the essays and comes in many forms. The need to traverse the enormous spaces contained within the Great Plains required adaptations in transportation systems that humans developed to move across its many bioregions. The technologies they fashioned put many different cultural and racial groupings in contact with one another. Animals too moved throughout the plains, and mobility complicated the history among and between humans and animals, as reflected in many of these essays.

The issue of mobility informs the first cluster of essays that examine Indigenous adaptations to the Great Plains' grassland environment over the *longue durée*. Natale Zappia argues that food networks crafted by Indigenous people on the Great Plains throughout the period from 1350 to 1850 present an alternative historical chronology that deemphasizes a narrative framed around colonialism and Spaniards' introduction of the horse. Although the spread of horses throughout the Great Plains certainly served as a key moment in which humans' relationship to the environment changed, native people crafted relationships with the land through technologies and networks of activity in order to feed themselves and strove to protect systems of food production they assembled over centuries. Fire provided the most effective tool for Indigenous people to engineer the northwestern plains, and according to María Zedeño and her fellow authors, bison hunters cultivated a symbiosis with fire that aggregated human population, increased the land's capacity to feed people, and served as a mechanism of social control long before Europeans arrived. Together, these essays emphasize human adaptation to environment as a consistent pattern over the *longue durée*. Their insights provide important context for understanding contributor Leila Monaghan's study of Cheyenne and Arapaho women whose mobility and labor practices accelerated and intensified when men shifted to mounted hunting practices, requiring women to carry horse-drawn travois loaded with hides, children, and older family members over long distances. Females experienced the environment differently than male counterparts, and they recorded testimony of their experiences on tipis and leather bags known as "parfleches." The process of bison hunting over the centuries so epitomized and symbolized human adaptation to the environment that an Indigenous hunting locale in Alberta, Canada, has been designated a provincial, national, and world heritage site. As told by Geneviève Susemihl, the archaeological, historical, and ethnographical significance of this heritage site, called the Head-Smashed-In Buffalo Jump, serves as an outstanding example of the subsistence hunting techniques of Plains nations and narrates their stories to a global audience.

As the first four essays suggest, human mobility occurred often in conjunction with animals, a subject that describes the next four articles in this volume. Cultural change among Indigenous and non-Indigenous groups reveals how people integrated animals into their lives and into their understandings of the region. Clint Carroll explains how the Cherokees fostered kinship ties with deer and panthers during the post-Removal era when settler encroachment into Indian Territory prompted a partial shift from a matrilineal clan system of governance to a more centralized political authority. Carroll concludes that animals played a significant role as teachers, messengers, and mediators in Cherokee culture during this transitional time up to the present. The Cherokees' relationship to animals contrasts markedly with the financiers and operators of industrialized cattle feedlots in the 1950s and 1960s who created "An Uncommon Nuisance," as described in the essay by Jacob Blackwell. The economy of scale that enhanced the efficiency necessary to feed tens of thousands of cattle on the southern plains created tons of manure that fouled the land, air, rivers, and streams and precipitated environmental regulations and threats of nuisance lawsuits. Feedlot operators mostly succeeded in defending their practices by influencing state legislators or by winning legal challenges. These industrialists rationalized cattle to maximize efficiency but so too did employees of the Hudson Bay Company in creating an elaborate system of accounting technology to quantify bison, effectively abstracting the animal by representing it in statistical form. George Colpitts argues that bookkeeping throughout the nineteenth century acted on the human imagination by privileging information that framed traders' understanding of bison and of the Indigenous people who hunted them. Thus, culture influenced how Indigenous and non-Indigenous humans comprehended animals, but the animals themselves had the capacity to influence human culture and social dynamics. Nicole St-Onge and Brenda Macdougall make this point clearly in their study of the Plains Métis hunting brigades. Descendants of French-Canadian voyageurs and native women, the Métis drew upon a web of kinship ties throughout the northern Great Plains to construct commercial bison-hunting brigades and military alliances that empowered them, both north and south of the U.S.-Canadian border. Military defeat in 1885 fractured their system of transregional alliance, but the near total disappearance of the bison population was the factor that most undermined their strategic social and cultural alliances and pushed them to shanty settlements on the edges of towns and cities. Collectively, these four essays show that humans had complicated relationships with animals on the Great Plains and that their interactions proved pivotal in shaping the environmental history of the region.

Perhaps more than any other human activity, agriculture as practiced on the Great Plains has shaped our understanding of the region, and the resultant story is often one of environmental decline. Examples abound of human folly demonstrated by farmers who attempted to subdue a volatile environment subject to extreme fluctuations of heat and aridity. Donald Worster's *Dust Bowl* stands out as a classic example of this theme. Worster transformed our conception of the region's limits, and essays in this volume add new layers to the story. Michael Weeks argues that a federal presence was indeed palpable in northern Colorado irrigation efforts but, he warns, federal presence "cannot be confused with power." Decisions about how to employ research generated by federal water engineers were made at the local level by members of mutual irrigation companies. Elsewhere on the plains local interests mattered too but existed in an uneasy tension with federal technocrats. When officials at the USDA Soil Conservation Service advocated new forms of tillage to conserve cropland, they operated within a network of private and public interests and reflected a "conservation-industrial complex" that, Joshua Nygren contends, characterized agricultural practice throughout much of the region. Agriculture and capitalism relied upon human faith in technology to adapt to the plains environment, a point Worster made clear. Indeed, private companies such as General Mills proved adept at using technology to harness rivers and to power mills, transforming wheat into flour and providing a key ingredient for cereals such as Wheaties. This story of food production, Michael Lansing argues, is also a story in which industrial agriculture linked cities like Minneapolis to their rural hinterlands and to the stomachs of consumers throughout the region and world. Agricultural production functioned as a source of regional identity for Indigenous and non-Indigenous groups alike, particularly in the northwest portion of the Great Plains. Using a North Dakota case study, Molly P. Rozum examines the northern grasslands to suggest how the struggle for agricultural adaptation in the settler society resulted in changing regional conceptions, from the Northwest to the northern Great Plains and the Middle West. Tribal methods of food production initially shaped at least one man's vision for an adapted settler society agriculture, but this vision did not survive the science and technology that transformed settler society commercial agriculture after World War II. Agriculture proved highly contested for Indigenous and non-Indigenous people alike, and these essays reveal their stories as fundamental to the region's history.

Beneath the agricultural economy that buoyed many plains communities sat rich deposits of oil and gas, and alongside them blew abundant wind, all of which were potentially lucrative resources that connected the region to outside interests. Oil resources in particular had the potential to transform people's lives in both the United States and Canada, but Jonathan Peyton and Matthew Dyce relate a history in which southwestern Manitoba's oil economy created ambivalence, as some people experienced financial loss and witnessed environmental ruin due to others' hubris-fueled visions of fantastic wealth. We must look for multiple "oil narratives" within these communities to see that oil extraction left ambiguous legacies of accommodation, adaptation, state intervention, and small profits. They argue that the transition from farming to an oil economy possesses symbolic significance on both sides of the national boundary. Pipelines present another example of a technology at the center of economic and energy transitions in the communities through which they run. Philip Wight demonstrates how the Standard Oil Company linked Great Plains' oil resources to the broader U.S. economy with its construction of the six-hundred-mile Kansas-Indiana pipeline. This transportation corridor provided a template for energy transportation and transformed how people understood the environment. Technology played a similarly powerful role connecting coal-rich communities in Wyoming, Montana, and the Dakotas to the rest of the nation but with dire environmental consequences. Ryan Driskell Tate shows that the 1973 oil crisis precipitated a rush of energy conglomerates into these states and that their gigantic "earthmovers" stripped away surface ecology, dramatically transforming a place that Edward Abbey once called a "land of almost painful beauty." Thus, the history of extracting energy resources like oil and coal involved multiple narratives depending upon where one stood in relation to the environment and its resources. This point applies equally well to Julie Courtwright's essay that historicizes how people experienced powerful wind currents that shaped their sense of place living in this region before and after technology made wind power viable as a potential source of energy.

Environmental transformation resulting from technology on the Great Plains began rather slowly, but industrialization accelerated the pace of change by the end of the nineteenth century. Much of the soil and many of the grasses that comprised the plains ecology disappeared or diminished, giving way to massive crop harvests and oil and gas production by the 1930s. Industrialization introduced new technologies that changed the scale of agriculture, enhancing harvests with the use of motorized plows, reapers, and combines. The introduction of grains and new scientific research allowed farmers to use nonnative grasses and other vegetation to fight pests by altering natural flora that had been ravaged by insects. Standing water, in some areas, was replaced with additional plant species to fight malarial infestations. In these ways science and technology enabled some people to build their lives on the plains, and their decisions created an abundance of resources for the United States and Canada. These human adaptations forever changed the region's history. In addition, oil and natural gas extraction expanded greatly into the twentieth century and perpetuated social, economic, and environmental change. As hydraulic fracturing technology became more prominent and oil transported through transcontinental pipelines intensified, there has arisen a greater need for analysis of the ecological impact of these developments on the region. Navigating the energy future may be informed by a greater understanding of the past, and we hope that this volume may contribute to the decisions that will be made.

Notes

1. Harvey Leifert, "Dividing Line: The Past, Present, and Future of the 100th Meridian," *Earth*, January 22, 2018, https://www.earthmagazine.org/article/dividing-line-past-present-and-future-100th-meridian.

2. Joe Wertz, "The Arid American West Marches East, Changing Climate and Agriculture," *StateImpact Oklahoma*, July 19, 2018, https://stateimpact.npr.org/oklahoma/2018/07/19/the-arid-american-west-marches-east-changing-climate-and-agriculture/.

3. Norm Henderson and Dave Sauchyn, eds., *Canada's Prairie Provinces: A Summary of Our State of Knowledge* (Regina SK: Prairie Adaptation Research Collaborative, 2008), 11–15, https://www.yumpu.com/en/document/view/25141975/climate-change-impacts-on-canadas-prairie-provinces-a-summary.

4. Donald Worster, *Dust Bowl: The Southern Plains in the 1930s* (New York: Oxford University Press, 1979).

5. Walter Prescott Webb, *The Great Plains* (1931; repr., Lincoln: University of Nebraska Press, 1981), n.p. (preface).

6. Webb, *The Great Plains*, 8.

7. James Claude Malin, *The Grassland of North America: Prolegomena to Its History* (Lawrence KS: privately printed, 1947; repr. with addenda and postscript, Gloucester MA: Peter Smith, 1967), 44. Also see Robert Swierenga, "Theoretical Perspectives on the New Rural History: From Environmentalism to Modernization," *Agricultural History* 56, no. 3 (July 1982): 499–500.

8. Worster, *Dust Bowl*, 205–6; and Donald Worster, *Nature's Economy: A History of Ecological Ideas*, 2nd ed. (New York: Cambridge University Press, 1994), 242–51. Also see Richard White, "American Environmental History: The Development of a New Historical Field," *Pacific Historical Review* 54, no. 3 (August 1985): 318–20.

9. Worster, *Dust Bowl*, 6.

10. The concept of a "Greater Plains" was articulated by Jack Seitz, a doctoral student at Iowa State University. See Julie Courtwright, "Great Plains," in *The Routledge History of Rural America*, ed. Pamela Riney-Kehrberg (New York: Routledge Taylor & Francis, 2016), 82, 85n60.

11. Robert L. Dorman, *Revolt of the Provinces: The Regionalist Movement in America, 1920–1945* (Chapel Hill: University of North Carolina Press, 1993), cited in Lisa Powell, "Regionalism and Bioregionalism," in *Encyclopedia of American Environmental History*, ed. Kathleen A. Brosnan, vol. 4 (New York: Facts on File, 2011), 1111–12.

12. For a discussion of spatial analysis see Richard White, "The Nationalization of Nature," *Journal of American History* 86, no. 3 (December 1999): 976–86.

13. Edward L. Ayers and Peter S. Onuf, "Introduction," in *All Over the Map: Rethinking American Regions*, ed. Edward L. Ayers, Patricia Nelson Limerick, Stephen Nissenbaum, and Peter S. Onuf (Baltimore: Johns Hopkins University Press, 1996), 5–6 (emphasis in original).

14. R. Douglas Hurt, *The Big Empty: The Great Plains in the Twentieth Century* (Tucson: University of Arizona Press, 2011), xii.

15. For additional literature on Great Plains bison see Dan Flores, "Bison Ecology and Bison Diplomacy: The Southern Plains from 1800 to 1850," *Journal of American History* 78, no. 2 (September 1991), 465–85; Andrew Isenberg, *The Destruction of the Bison: An Environmental History, 1720–1920* (Cambridge: Cambridge University Press), 2001. See also Geoff Cunfer, *On the Great Plains: Agriculture and Environment* (College Station: Texas A&M University Press, 2005).

16. With respect to the caloric energy of animal species, see Richard White, *The Organic Machine: The Remaking of the Columbia River* (New York: Hill and Wang, 1996), chapter 1 passim.

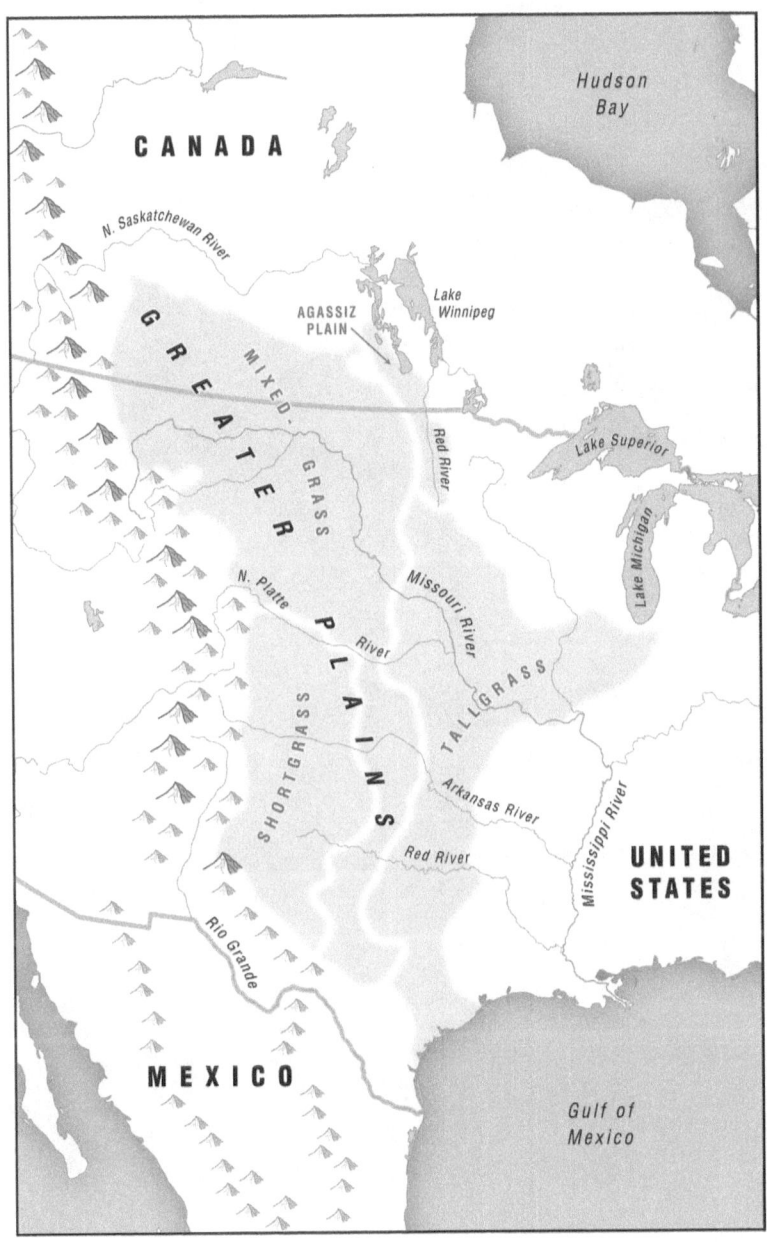

FIG. 1. Map of the Great Plains. Created by Erin Greb Cartography.

THE GREATER PLAINS

PART 1

Indigenous Grassland Adaptations
over the *Longue Durée*

1

Before the Horse

Indigenous Food Systems on the Plains, 1300–1680

NATALE ZAPPIA

> These [people] of Quivira have an advantage over the others because of the houses they have and because they plant corn.
>
> —FRANCISCO CORONADO, 1540

In 1541 a Wichita (or possibly Pawnee) trader approached the eastern plains village of Kirikurus.[1] It may have been several years since he visited this town filled with dozens of homes and extensive fields of maize, beans, and squash stretching for several square miles. The Spanish conquistador Francisco Vásquez de Coronado and a force of thirty others (Spanish, Pueblo, and Mixtec) accompanied him. As they entered town, Coronado's group may have recognized the piles of bison hides and baskets of pemmican on display at Kirikurus—commodities they first encountered at Pecos Pueblo on the opposite edge of the plains. Located north of the Arkansas River somewhere between present-day Kansas and Oklahoma, the residents of Kirikurus greeted this Native traveler by conversing in a sign language commonly used throughout the plains—also something that impressed Coronado. Their silent hand gestures moved so quickly and fluently, in fact, that it seemed "as if they were talking."[2]

His real name remains unknown, but the Spaniards called him Ysopete. Standing beside Ysopete, Coronado anxiously attempted to decipher this exchange. Earlier that year he organized a large army of roughly five thousand to head out onto the Great Plains. As with his fellow conquistadors across the Americas, Coronado sought to find promised riches in a place mistranslated as "Quivira."³ Another Wichita (or Pawnee) captive at the Pecos Pueblo in eastern New Mexico—named "El Turco" by Spaniards—fueled this speculation and convinced Coronado to sojourn out into the plains with El Turco as a guide.⁴

After a month of aimless wandering, depleted food reserves, and mixed results at hunting bison, Coronado's army grew increasingly desperate and impatient. By the time they reached Kirikurus, Coronado realized El Turco's real plan: to lure Spanish forces out into the disorienting grasslands and toward likely starvation. Furious with this deception, Coronado reshackled El Turco and then relied on Ysopete (who may have tipped off Coronado to El Turco's plans) to guide them to Kirikurus. To Coronado's dismay, though, none of the treasures they hoped for materialized at Kirikurus, and after securing corn and pemmican from their hosts, the thirty remaining soldiers from his expeditionary force (most had already turned back weeks earlier due to lack of food) returned to New Mexico.

The archives are unclear as to the fate of Ysopete. Perhaps he was able to remain in Kirikurus or resume trading back and forth across the plains. Or perhaps he ended up sharing El Turco's demise—ferociously garroted with an iron collar and strangled to death. Thousands of other victims like El Turco no doubt felt the frustrated blows of perpetrators such as Coronado. Such was the violence that crisscrossed the region during the early modern period. But the deceptive nature of the plains—seemingly empty, flat, depopulated, and bereft of valuable commodities—nonetheless stymied Spanish efforts at colonial domination.

Scholars have retraced Coronado's disastrous journey many times, devising new analyses along the way: the limitations of Spanish colonialism, relative autonomy of Indigenous captives, and the violence of borderlands slavery. This historiography has combed through numerous sixteenth-century accounts of conquistadors obsessed with seizing gold and silver.⁵ But these colonial documents also reveal a remarkably productive and elaborate foodscape—not unlike the Mediterranean world that resonated with Spaniards. Thus, while Coronado complained about "savages" and the lack of any riches, he simultaneously remarked that Kirikurus cultivated the "best land" he had seen since his arrival in Mexico and marveled at the plums, grapes, and mulberries reminiscent of Spain. One of Coronado's companions on the journey, Castañeda de Nájera, penned the most detailed account of the expedition. His writing frequently described the productive landscapes of the plains:

> [Quivira] is heavily populated . . . this land was seen to be very much like the [land] of Spain, in regard to its types of plants and fruits. There are plums like the ones in Spain, grapes walnuts, blackberries, rye grass, oats pennyroyal, oregano, and flax in great quantity . . . in its environs there are other very populous *provincias* with large numbers of people.[6]

Alongside this agricultural description, Nájera further offered a vivid account of bison processing:

> Across these plains travel people in pursuit of the bison, hunting and curing hides in order to take them to the settled areas to sell during the winters. . . . They dry their meat in the sun, cutting it thin like a sheet of paper. When it is dry, they grind it like flour in order to store it and to make porridge. To eat it they throw a handful into a pot. The pot is filled because the meat meal swells up considerably. They cook it with lard, which they always try to render when they kill a bison. They emptied a large intestine and filled it with blood. They slung [it] around their necks in order to drink when they were thirsty. When they have opened the stomach of a bison, they press the chewed grass to the bottom and drink the juice that remains on top. They cut open the bison along the back and cut them apart at the joints with a flint . . . tied to a small stick. . . . The speed with which they do [this] is something to see and observe.[7]

This chapter looks closely at the Indigenous history underpinning these scenes by asking: What relationships, technologies, networks, and systems did El Turco wish to protect? And how might understanding Indigenous food on the plains shed light on these networks? I utilize a food systems lens to highlight production strategies, storage techniques, and interregional Indigenous food commodity markets that moved along what Andrew Isenberg has called a "sea of grass."[8] Further, by exploring the period before the unleashing of horses on the plains (1300–1680), this chapter also asks historians to engage in deeper and richer interdisciplinary methodologies that may better understand the importance of continental North American history during the early modern period (1350–1850). Fortunately, such a reexamination is underway and offers a revealing portrait of "deep history" involving overlapping Indigenous political economies and ecologies that "sailed" rapidly across the vast plains along "pre" historic corridors. These earlier (and much longer) histories, in turn, created the unique set of cultural and environmental conditions that allowed the Indigenous Great Plains to navigate and even master the equestrian revolution of the seventeenth to nineteenth centuries on the plains. The "before," then, created the "after."[9]

For many scholars the dynamic history of interior spaces like the Great Plains only come into focus after the Age of Revolutions and the relentless expansion of white settler societies arriving from the shorelines of the East and West. Others focus on Indigenous power but almost exclusively within the evolution and expansion of horse cultures. The plains, no doubt, experienced its "hottest chronology" after the arrival of horses in the sixteenth century. New pastoral Indigenous state formation (even an empire, as Pekka Hämäläinen argues), points to perhaps the most formidable example of Indigenous techno-cultural engagement with the emerging world economy after these forces were unleashed during the Pueblo Uprising of 1680. In many ways this event fostered the pastoral revolution leading to the largest transformation of the plains since perhaps the end of the Pleistocene. Horses altered human migrations, shifted military power by enhancing a runaway gun trade, and most importantly led to the near-extinction of bison.[10]

In recent years this story has dominated Native American historiography while the dramatic ecological changes on the plains became the focus of some of our best environmental histories.[11] The *longue durée*, though, has received less coverage than the "hot chronology" despite the important ecological and economic integration crisscrossing the plains and only glimpsed at by Coronado.[12] The equestrian revolution, no doubt, served as a "big bang" that irrevocably altered the plains. But stretching and emphasizing the conceptual, temporal, and spatial boundaries of the plains in the period "before the horse" reveals the historical continuities that emerged and survived the period between 1300 and 1680.

Temporal Boundaries: Removing "Prehistory" from the Plains

To understand the period before the horse, we must remove the "pre" from prehistory. Fortunately, scholars of Native North America have increasingly looked to blurring or removing the line between "pre" and "post" 1492—the date most closely associated with the start of "history" in North America.[13] Afro-Eurasians of the sixteenth century chronicled as much when they waded haphazardly into the existing political-economic battles, rivalries, and networks shaping Native North America. In recent years more historians than ever before have employed interdisciplinary methodologies and sources long utilized by anthropologists to further understand earlier histories on the plains: archaeology, oral history, material/visual cultural, and ethnography.[14]

The physical sciences too have contributed to new interpretations of history before 1492. Climate and soil science, dendrochronology, starch grain analysis—all of these techniques corroborate changes in the food systems, migrations, and cultural geography in the pre-Columbian centuries. Thus, stretching the temporal boundaries of the plains allows for more historical angles to peer into El Turco's and Ysopete's actions in 1541. Climate change research on the phenomenon known as the "Little Ice Age," in particular, explains this history occurring not only in North America but also around the world during the earliest encounters between Natives and Afro-Eurasians.[15]

. . .

El Turco's subversive efforts in 1540–41 succeeded in shielding a vibrant, dynamic, and widespread Indigenous agropastoral system. Indeed, his sacrifice foiled early Spanish colonization efforts, which ultimately allowed for the rise of powerful Indigenous societies in the coming centuries like the Comanches, Osages, Lakotas, and Blackfeet.[16] This Indigenous network rested upon an equally dynamic food system that reached back at least five hundred years but also experienced recent innovations, thanks in part to the onset of the Little Ice Age starting in the fourteenth century. This climate pattern resulted in a global temperature dip that altered food systems across Native North America and perhaps nowhere else as dramatically as its continental grasslands.[17] Waxing and waning over more than four centuries, these effects included the expansion of glaciers and winters in the Northern Hemisphere, extensive drought, severe flooding, shrinking plant habitats, and shorter growing seasons. This led to the migration of people, plants, and other animals, sometimes resulting in the "ethnogenesis"—or better yet a "regenesis"—of new Indigenous cultures.[18]

Across the Northern Hemisphere, in places like western Europe, North Africa, and East Asia, cultivation acreage shrunk by as much as 25 percent as frost days crept further and further into the spring and fall. Drought plagued already-dry regions as well. Even more catastrophically, pandemic disease like the plague swept across Afro-Eurasia, striking close to 30 percent of the population.[19] In North America the great urban centers suffered similar fates as maize harvests along the Mississippi River Valley experienced extensive and frequent flooding. At Chaco, Casas Grandes, and Lower Colorado River farming centers in the Southwest/Far West, drought afflicted maize production, leading to mass migrations.[20] The plains (particularly the southern plains), in relative contrast, hosted cooler and wetter conditions nurturing grass and herbivore habitats. Bison herds grew and foraged in new pastures afforded by the Little Ice Age—but also thanks to increased prescribed burning (discussed further below). This once obscure climate era, then, has received copious coverage by scholars looking to connect human relationships with global environmental phenomena.

The very name "Little Ice Age" connotes ecological difficulty or hardship, evoking Pleistocene hunter-gatherers clinging to the edge of existence around campfires in caves. It certainly acted as a "disruptor," but the Little Ice Age also provided unique, even singular opportunities for humanity. It is more than coincidental, after all, that this period almost precisely parallels what is known as the early modern period: the age defined by the first true moment of globalization, expansion of empires, demographic explosions, and the industrial revolution. In Native North America, the Little Ice Age also provided extraordinary opportunities to innovate regional and continental food systems for all sorts of producers, traders, hunters, and foragers. This very dynamism that Coronado witnessed—"the best hunters and farmers" as he put it— was facilitated by the Little Ice Age and forged by a remarkably diverse network of Indigenous entrepreneurs that operated without a central political-economic or cultural "core" like those that existed between 900 and 1300—the era known as the Medieval Climatic Anomaly.[21]

These centuries experienced global warming that expanded food production around the world. In North America this led to a maize production revolution (sometimes associated with the "Cahokian big bang") that produced a medieval urban Indigenous landscape. Major urban centers included Cahokia, Toltec, Chaco, and Spiro—all dependent on maize cultivation.[22] After three centuries of ecological expansion, though, maize-based food systems reconfigured and even retreated as unpredictable weather patterns and growing seasons frequented cultivation areas. Urban centers in the Mississippian world shrank while other settlements along the edge of the plains grew in reaction to the Little Ice Age. Many of the communities that Coronado encountered, in fact, were descendants from these urban spaces who engaged in either farming or hunting or both, sharing ideas, technology, and overlapping foodways. The Osages, for example, incorporated Cahokian cosmology, urban grid design, and architecture in their Oklahoman/Arkansan settlements. Long after the decline of Cahokia, Osage leaders patterned their villages to mirror the abandoned

Cahokian landscape, dividing their clans between the sky people and earth people on an east-west axis, with the lodges of the sky and earth chiefs bisected by the path of the sun. Such a pattern replicated their view of the cosmos that they inherited from their urban descendants at Cahokia, and even directly correlates with an excavated Cahokian site known as "mound 72." The birdman tablet discovered here presents a stunning visual representation of Osage cosmology. Osage oral history further points to their earlier migration to a "new country" where they joined water, land, and sky. This settlement was a place "where the land was undefiled by decaying carcasses and where there were no visible signs of death."[23]

Osages were just one of a stunningly diverse array of communities engaged in the *longue durée* of the plains. Osages, Wichitas, Caddos, Pawnees, Kansas, Mandans, Arikaras, Hidatsas, Jumanos, Apaches, Shoshones, Utes, Pueblos, Blackfeet, Dakotas—all of these and many more cultures inherited the food systems built on maize but also experimented with other effective food production strategies. Indeed, these "prehorse" plains communities simultaneously "burned" and "built" their food systems. By *burning* I refer to pyrogenic landscapes created by Indigenous communities across the plains—strategies ably analyzed by Julie Courtwright and Stephen Pyne. Prescribed burning regenerated soil, kick-started seed dispersal and germination, kept forests at bay, and cultivated pastures for herbivores. But prescribed burners also integrated other food production strategies, include hunting and herding, agroforestry, selective thinning and pruning, aquaculture, and intensive foraging.[24]

Building refers to (primarily maize) cultivators but recognizes the particular set of techno-ecological relationships forged by Indigenous farmers during this time. Unlike wheat, maize planting required deliberate sowing with careful companion planting (beans, squash, sunflowers, tobacco) to help "build" the soil and maintain nitrogen levels, provided mulch, reduced compaction, and alleviated any need for plowing. This method of growing or building soil, as Jane Mt. Pleasant has recently argued, made maize a superior product that survived the ravages of the Little Ice Age and continued to thrive along the edges of the plains (indeed maize culture would ultimately dominate the global market).[25] Between roughly 900 and 1300 these strategies operated in parallel orbits aligning with the particular set of ecological parameters set by the plains and the fertile lowland river valleys. But during the thirteenth to sixteenth centuries, builders and burners broke ecological barriers to forge new food systems.[26]

Expanding Conceptual Boundaries: Historicizing Indigenous Food Systems

Reimagining farmers and hunters as "burners" and "builders" exposes another methodological bias employed by historians. Since the very first written histories, chroniclers privileged the events, fears, and dreams of those operating within monocultural food systems. That is to say, those living in largely sedentary villages and cities resting on singular staples like wheat, rice, sorghum, potatoes, and maize have captured the attention of historians while those living outside these landscapes (pastoralists, hunter-gatherers, nomadic herders, "barbarians," etc.) have largely been ignored—except when they threatened the umbrella of "civilization" where urban centers resided.[27] Within urban areas and their hinterlands, individuals across class, gender, race, and other social constructions held competing visions of their history—which many times violently clashed. But the primacy of the monocultural narrative and its dominant food systems was never in doubt. Emerging out of these systems, writing dominated, displacing other forms of history. To these chroniclers all of humanity's political, economic, and cultural complexity—any of it worth recording that is—was situated in monocultural societies that wrote on parchments, tablets, and paper.

Agriculture—defined as the practice of intensive farming—has served as the dividing line between history and "prehistory," "savage" and "civilized," complex and "primitive." Over the past five millennia, agricultural food systems steadily consumed land and infiltrated the cultural systems of 99 percent of humanity while other forms of food production became further isolated both in practice and history. For much of Native America outside of the maize heartland and its frontiers, documenting food production has remained part of anthropology rather than history.[28] Similarly, dieting fads have closely paralleled the romanticization of nonagricultural communities, reaching for a preindustrial palate (also known as "paleo") shunning carbohydrates and eating like hunter-gatherers who lived "close to the land" and "in balance with nature." Such distorted perceptions of Indigenous food systems have occurred frequently, especially since the nineteenth century in response to the rapid ascendance of imperial-industrial expansion that eviscerated many of these practices.[29]

But these food systems are also historical and contingent. In fact, they have dominated humanity up until very recently, or as Jared Diamond reminds us, up until "the world before yesterday."[30] Native America during the centuries leading up to 1492 is no exception. The vast majority of the North American landscape was indeed dominated by human-generated food systems, but just not those primarily reliant on maize monoculture. Of all of these, fire, in fact, defined food production across Native Americas. And on the plains, pyrogenic-generated food systems reigned supreme.

On the face of it, *burning*, of course, refers to purposeful ecological interventions through prescribed fire setting. Sometimes termed "slash-and-burn" agriculture—usually employed as a somewhat derogatory classification by scholars when compared with modern monocultural food production—or "pyrogenic" land management, prescribed burning reaches back to the origins of humanity. Its methods and practices are wide-ranging, diffuse, and deep. Fire-controlled food production far exceeds agriculture in its application by humanity.[31] It remains ubiquitous in almost all forms of land use and especially food production. Thousands of plants have evolved in response to these human and nonhuman interventions (on any given day eight million lightning strikes hit the earth).[32] The resulting relationship has been captured from satellites—a vivid global dance where fires advance and then retreat as plants reseed and counteradvance before repeating the pattern over and over again. Seen from space, it becomes immediately evident that fire is an essential ingredient for life on earth.[33] Much like other overlooked Indigenous agroethnic landscapes (for instance the Amazon rainforest, which is now recognized as the result of human intervention), the grasslands of North America—including the Great Plains, Desert, and Great Basin, and central California—owes its existence to pyrogenic management.[34]

On the plains fire bred ecological complexity and abundant foodscapes. Millions of acres of fire-generated prairies, flatlands, meadows, and other mostly treeless landscapes produced approximately three thousand species of plants (many of them forage for herbivores), and at least 120 edible species covered the plains. Over ten thousand years ago humans began figuring out how to mimic the spread of seeds to select for those that provided maximum carbohydrates. Agricultural landscapes thus emerged out of generations of observation, failure, practice, and luck. This process rested on human action passed through cultural knowledge—oral traditions, shared technology, and intellectual diffusion. Pyrogenic landscapes similarly resulted from an even more careful process of trial and error among human communities looking to encourage the proliferation of particular grasses, seeds, and fruit-bearing plants.

Ecologists today have finally recognized the importance of maintaining these alternative food systems. State agencies across the Great Plains and other regions with prairie ecologies (such as central California) have consulted with Native pyrogenic practitioners, employing traditional ecological knowledge (known by its acronym TEK) in grass management and agroforestry strategies. This new consultation not only recognizes the value of Indigenous knowledge but has also resulted in the repair of devastated habitats after decades of fire suppression.[35]

...

During the Little Ice Age Indigenous fire complemented other nonagricultural production strategies. Once seen as passive, intensive gathering, for instance, required (and still does in parts of the world) carefully trained experts to selectively weed, clear underbrush or add mulch, or pinch shoots, buds, and invasive growth.[36] This expertise required the same if not more dedication, precision, and training as monocultural maize production. Equally as important, gender dictated the means of production. In both monocultural and polycultural food systems, women and children determined many of the contours of the foodways. Situated on the "frontline" of food production, these practitioners determined the flavor, size, or frequency of all kinds of plant-based nutrients. Equally as important, they innovated storage techniques, technology, and proliferation. Grass management thus simultaneously provided predictable, energy-dense food as well as preserved it in the form of tightly stitched baskets—all overseen by women.[37]

The third component of the plains food system—meat production—served as perhaps the greatest innovation during the Little Ice Age. Much has been written about the relationship between Archaic big game hunters and Pleistocene extinctions. While the debate still continues, recent work by Edmund Russell emphasizes the outsized role of human-driven natural selection. Because of a human preference for bigger herbivores, Ice Age hunters paradoxically provided optimal conditions for smaller animals to successfully adapt by living in larger and larger herds.[38] Herding provided protection against apex predators (like humans), while smaller herbivore bodies allowed for fewer nutrient requirements. Thus bison, elk, antelope, and deer all evolved rapidly in response to human-induced ecological changes. Both reliant on grasses, herbivores and humans further interacted as changes in climate affected burning strategies, harvesting cycles, and growing seasons.

We tend to think of evolution as a long-term, glacially slow phenomenon, but modern-day examples of rapid shifts in natural selection can happen in as many as three or four generations (the rapid ascension of tuskless elephants is the clearest example).[39] With such shifts in rainfall and temperature variations, the delicate dance between humans, plants, and animals created new opportunities for innovations in food production. Thus, the delicate mix of pyrogenic intervention, climate change, a shift away from river-centered maize, and increased human migration to prairie landscapes all led to increased hunting (and even indirect forms of herding) of bison. As Nájera and others witnessed in the sixteenth century, bison products ranged across the spectrum, providing fresh meat and preserved nonperishable calories (in the form of pemmican—itself a multifaceted product brilliantly detailed by George Colpitts).[40] Hides, bones, and even dung further fueled interregional trade. Collectively, then, burning, gathering, and hunting/herding fed a population of as many as a million people across the plains by the sixteenth century.[41] This food system, though, also stimulated maize production on the edge of the plains, where "bison diplomacy" fueled the rise of new cosmopolitan centers where burning and building coalesced.[42]

Expanding the Spatial Boundaries: Early Modern Cultural Geography on the Plains

By the time the Wichitas of Kirikurus first encountered Coronado in the sixteenth century, the flat and expansive grasslands connecting every corner of the continent had undergone dramatic and sustained ecological transformations. Everywhere one looked—from the immense Great Plains, which stretched from Mexico to Canada, to the mixed woodland prairies of the Upper Mississippi to the Great Basin and Plateau of the Far West to the elongated strip stretching along interior California—human communities large and small experimented with intensive food production strategies. Not unlike the expansion of maize frontiers that exploded along the edges of the plains during the tenth century leading to the urban centers of Cahokia, Toltec, Spiro, and Chaco, so too did the trading centers of the Mandans, Hidatsas, Arikaras, Dakotas, Pawnees, Shoshones, Apaches, and Kalispels push against old ecological boundaries.[43]

New Indigenous food systems on the plains converged in what ecologists call an ecotone—edge environments harboring a mix of biota from different environments but also containing singular, unique habitats for certain plants and animals to thrive. Plains/prairie ecotones, then, also served as "food frontiers" for burners and builders. Historicizing the expanding "burner" food frontiers allows us to link seemingly divergent cultures, regions, and food systems in the period after the shift away from riverine urban landscapes. But it also incorporates the earlier worlds of Cahokia, Chaco, and others into this story. The societies that built cities of maize did not simply disappear. Reinvention certainly occurred, but so did continuous reliance on maize. A synthesis of nutrients, technology, and ideas unfolded. The cosmopolitanism of densely packed urban centers became subsumed by equally dynamic but far-flung interregional centers.

During this time burners and builders both experimented to reshape food frontiers. These new patterns, in fact, continued long into the age of Afro-Eurasian interactions and the age of globalization. Perhaps the most remarkable aspect of this period is the role of individual consumers, producers, and traders to shape food systems. The relative dip in maize production provided more options and a wider array of choice for kin and communities untethered from regional state power. This diffuseness fueled multiple links that moved especially quickly along relatively unobstructed grassland roads. Every twist and turn in the road created more choices and individual autonomy. For some, maize became even more important. For others, quite the opposite. The contingencies of history, then, shape this story. And perhaps no other story vividly conveys these choices as that of Maxi'diwiac.

. . .

The extraordinary oral history told by Maxi'diwiac (Buffalo Bird Woman) illustrates a common experience on the plains. In 1910 Maxi'diwiac shared with the anthropologist Gilbert Wilson how corn came to the Hidatsas, who for centuries lived along the banks of the Missouri River in present-day North Dakota. Over a period of several months, Maxi'diwiac divulged a meticulously detailed account of Hidatsa history, culture, economy, and food production. The ethnography continues to serve as a useful food production manual for Natives and non-Natives alike interested in small-scale agricultural practices largely reliant on the three sisters of maize, beans, and squash (Maxi'diwiac also includes tobacco and sunflowers as the foundational "quintet" in a Hidatsa or Mandan garden).[44]

Maxi'diwiac covers every seemingly possible topic, from seed selection to storage to fertilizing to fencing. Her deep knowledge of plant varieties, methods, and processing was encyclopedic—indeed remarkable. Yet as she conveyed it, this was common knowledge for her people since they began farming. In this, Maxi'diwiac's account shares similarities with all of the other maize-dominant societies that shaped the urban landscapes of precontact North America.[45]

Her food system paralleled, in some ways, those that unfolded in Cahokia, Toltec, Spiro, and Chaco. But Maxi'diwiac's history also revealed an important distinction that faced Native societies like the Hidatsas as the effects of the Little Ice Age shifted ecological landscapes. Indeed, in between the urban centers that alternated between expansion and collapse between 900 and 1600 along the river systems of the Mississippi, Missouri, Rio Grande, Colorado, and Arkansas, new centers—some of them urban in ways not unfamiliar to a typical Cahokian or Chacoan—gained power, influence, and control over interregional food systems.[46] Maxi'diwiac's descendants, for example, lived at one of these places (known at the Mandan-Hidatsa trade center) on the eastern edge of the plains between the fourteenth and sixteenth centuries. This center and surrounding satellite villages may have had as many as ten thousand residents.[47]

The Hidatsas emerged from the shoreline of Devil's Lake in present-day North Dakota. Like the Lakotas and other Siouan-speaking societies living on the northern plains, the Hidatsas cultivated small amounts of potatoes, onions, and ground beans in their villages. But most Native societies primarily managed perennial grasses rather than annuals (like maize). Unlike heavy feeders like maize, tallgrass perennials (such as bluestem, blue grama, buffalo grass, and western wheat grass) are 90 percent roots and 10 percent aboveground. Roots, rather than seeds, dictated survival and propagation.

But Maxi'diwiac's Hidatsa ancestors made a fateful choice sometime during the fifteenth century.[48] She relayed this vivid and singular historical moment to Gilbert Wilson:

> My people knew nothing of corn or squashes. One day a war party, I think of ten men, wandered west to the Missouri River. They saw on the other side a village of earth lodges like their own. It was a village of the Mandans. . . . It was autumn, and the Missouri River was running low so that an arrow could be shot from shore to shore. The Mandans parched some ears of ripe corn with the grain on the cob; they broke the ears in pieces, thrust the pieces on the points of arrows, and shot them across the river. "Eat!" they said. . . . The warriors ate of the parched corn, and liked it. They returned to their village and said, "We have found a people living by the Missouri River who have a strange kind of grain, which we ate and found good!" . . . a few years after, a war party of the Hidatsas crossed the Missouri and visited the Mandans at their village near Bird Beak Hill. The Mandan chief took an ear of yellow corn, broke it in two, and gave half to the Hidatsas. This half-ear the Hidatsas took home, for seed; and soon every family was planting yellow corn.[49]

After centuries as "burners," the Hidatsas chose to become "builders." To the ears of Wilson, perhaps, this Hidatsa story confirmed the assumption that food production moved along an evolutionary line from hunter-gatherer to farmer. Such a narrative also linked early ethnographers with nineteenth century Anglo reformers and even further to Spanish colonial missionaries espousing the advantages of "civilized" agricultural practices reflecting cultural evolution.

But many others, if not most of Maxi'diwiac's neighbors descending from the Oneota culture (itself influenced by Cahokian culture), actually chose the opposite direction, moving from intensive farming to full-time hunting.[50] Arapahos and Cheyennes made this switch, as did the most famous of the Plains nations: Lakotas and Comanches. Others still successfully bridged both worlds, including the Illinois, Pawnees, and Witchitas. Some of these societies did so only after the arrival of the horse, but others tapped into the resources and infrastructure of the plains beforehand. And the ones that joined in on horseback later did so in order to take part in the existing trade networks.

...

Take, for example, the discoveries at the Vore site in eastern Wyoming. Twenty-two stacked bison beds reveal an astonishing process of bison commodification that exploded by the fifteenth century. At least ten thousand butchered and processed bison remains have been excavated at Vore.[51] But bones are just part of the story. The site lies approximately equidistant between the Hidatsa trade center and the eastern Shoshone rendezvous. They also provide a window into the rapidly developing food transit hub that the Great Plains became starting in the fourteenth century. Perhaps the best way to think of the plains, ironically, is to again conjure up Isenberg's concept of a vast sea (which it once was millions of years ago). The first European explorers, in fact, viewed it this way. Part of this reflected a lack of imagination and understanding of the remarkable diversity of the grasslands, not unlike when English travelers remarked how New England forest all looked the same.[52] But the immensity of the plains was also punctuated by rivers, small lakes, and isolated mountain ranges (like the Ozarks and Black Hills) that acted as "islands" in the sea of grass. As Dan Flores has argued, the Rocky Mountains could also be understood as an island barrier between two great population centers harnessing the grasslands hugging the coast and the central plains.[53] More Indigenous people lived within interior California, in fact, than any other part of Native North America outside of Mexico.[54]

What seemed like an endless barrier to impatient Spaniards in the sixteenth century, though, proved to be a series of rapid and heavily trafficked roads linking the Mississippian Puebloan; Caddoan with Makah; and Pawnee with both Atlantic and Pacific.[55] Many of these networks, of course, existed and also thrived at points during the Medieval Warm Period. These roads also funneled groups migrating between and away from urban centers that shrank during the Little Ice Age.[56] Similarly, both time periods featured durable and most likely high-status material objects—turquoise, shells, baskets, and textiles. But more than anything else, two staples—bison meat and maize—acted as the primary commodities and form of currency linking the plains. If the Vore site is at all representative, the amount of meat processed is staggering.

Alongside favorable weather conditions for the bison-dominated food systems, the longer winters of the Ice Age also paradoxically intensified trade during the warmer months as advanced plains communities prioritized (women-controlled) bison processing and corn storage. Such an ecological paradox (harsh conditions leading to a proliferation in trade) also occurred simultaneously in the Far Southwest in the Mojave and Colorado Deserts.[57] On the plains, several new trading hotspots emerged. The Mandan trading complex served as the northeastern hub. At the southern edge sat the Caddoan and Jumano villages that linked traders further into the Aztec periphery. More than one thousand miles directly west sat the major trading hubs of Pecos and Zunis—themselves satellites to the Corazones trading center connected to Central Mexico as well as a terminal point for Mojave traders bringing coastal California trade.[58] Directly one thousand miles north sat the Shoshone rendezvous. It is from here that the Comanche empire would emerge two centuries later after the Pueblo Uprising of 1680. Finally, the Dalles trading center on the Columbia River connected the food systems of the Northwest coast with Blackfeet, Nez Perce, and Flat Head traders. The size and scope of trade during this time is vast: at least six major centers of several thousand people, another dozen smaller trading villages of several hundred, and hundreds of other smaller interregional villages along the edges of the plains.

Conclusion

In 1680 the Pueblo Uprising upended the nascent Spanish political order of the Southwest borderlands, removing outside colonialism for over a decade. Yet perhaps the most far-reaching consequence proved to be the proliferation of horse trading between the builders of the Pueblos and the burners of the Great Basin. Economic interactions suppressed by Spaniards quickly resumed according to the conventions of the plains economy. Utes and Comanches obtained herds, and a new era of raiding, trading, and Indigenous power unfolded across the plains. Yet these new pastoral landscapes depended upon the earlier food systems forged by the burners and builders of the plains during the fourteenth century. Reading between the lines of oral histories like Maxi'diwiac's, but also within and around the patches of fire, bison-processing centers, remnant orchards, intensive foraging areas, and tangled roots paints an entirely different patchwork that connected the plains of the fifteenth and sixteenth centuries. Over the course of the *longue durée*, Indigenous societies forged new food systems and ecological frontiers that would shape the hot chronology of horse-dominated plains.

Notes

1. Richard Flint and Shirley Cushing Flint, eds., *Documents of the Coronado Expedition, 1539–1542: "They Were Not Familiar with His Majesty, nor Did They Wish to Be His Subjects"* (Dallas: Southern Methodist University Press, 2005), 320.

2. Flint and Flit, *Documents of the Coronado Expedition*, 320.

3. Spanish explorers called the village "Quivira"—most likely a reference to the Arabic work "quivir" (big). The more accurate name (Kirikurus) stemmed from the Wichita vocabulary. See Frederick Webb Hodge, ed., *Handbook of American Indians North of Mexico*, 2 vols. (Washington: Government Printing Office, 1907); and Robert Julyan, *Place Names in New Mexico* (Albuquerque: University of New Mexico Press, 1996), 153.

4. Daryl W. Palmer, "Coronado and Aesop: Fable and Violence on the Sixteenth-Century Plains," *Great Plains Quarterly* 29, no. 2 (Spring 2009): 132.

5. A few of these studies include Lisbeth Haas, *Saints and Citizens: Indigenous Histories of Colonial Missions and Mexican California* (Berkeley: University of California Press, 2013); Pekka Hämäläinen, *The Comanche Empire* (New Haven CT: Yale University Press, 2008); Juliana Barr, *Peace Came in the Form of a Woman: Indians and Spaniards in the Texas Borderlands* (Chapel Hill: University of North Carolina Press, 2007); Brian DeLay, *War of a Thousand Deserts: Indian Raids and the U.S.-Mexican War* (New Haven CT: Yale University Press, 2010); Richard White, *The Middle Ground: Indians, Empires, and Republics in the Great Lakes Region, 1650–1815* (Cambridge: Cambridge University Press, 1991); Kathleen DuVal, *The Native Ground: Indians and Colonists in the Heart of the Continent* (Philadelphia: University of Pennsylvania Press, 2006); and James Brooks, *Captives and Cousins: Slavery, Kinship, and Community in the Southwest Borderlands* (Chapel Hill: University of North Carolina Press, 2002).

6. Flint and Flit, *Documents of the Coronado Expedition*, 423.

7. Flint and Flit, *Documents of the Coronado Expedition*, 423.

8. Andrew C. Isenberg, *The Oxford Handbook of Environmental History* (Oxford: Oxford University Press, 2014).

9. Exciting new reinterpretations of "prehistory" on the plains include Geoff Cunfer and Bill Waiser, eds., *Bison and People on the North American Great Plains: A Deep Environmental History* (Austin: Texas A&M Press, 2016); Robert Morrissey, "The Power of the Ecotone: Bison, Slaves, and the Rise and Fall of the Grand Village of the Kaskaskia," *Journal of American History* 102, no. 3 (December 2015): 667–92; and Adam Hodge's *Ecology and Ethnogenesis: An Environmental History of the Wind River Shoshone, 1000–1868* (Lincoln: University of Nebraska Press, 2019). See esp. chap. 3. New work on "pre" history includes Juliana Barr, "There's No Such Thing as 'Prehistory': What the Longue Durée of Caddo and Pueblo History Tells Us about Colonial America," *William and Mary Quarterly* 74, no. 2 (2017): 203–40; and Daniel Lord Smail and Shryock Andrew's "History and the 'Pre,'" *American Historical Review* 118, no. 3 (2013): 709–37. For a discussion of "pre" history, see below. Charles Mann's *1491* and *1493* attempt to make this point. See *1491: New Revelations of the Americas before Columbus* (New York: Knopf, 2005) and *1493: Uncovering the New World Columbus Created* (New York: Knopf, 2011); also see the seminal work by Colin Calloway, *One Vast Winter Count: The Native American West before Lewis and Clark* (Lincoln: University of Nebraska Press, 2003).

10. For a discussion of Indigenous empires, see Pekka Hämäläinen, *The Comanche Empire* (esp. introduction). For the Indigenous gun trade, see David Silverman, *Thundersticks: Firearms and the Violent Transformation of Native America* (Cambridge MA: Harvard University Press, 2016); Andrew Isenberg, *The Destruction of the Bison: An Environmental History* (Cambridge: Cambridge University Press, 2000); Dan Flores, "Bison Ecology and Bison Diplomacy: The Southern Plains from 1800 to 1850," *Journal of American History* 78 (September 1991): 465–85. Sarah Knott, "Narrating the Revolution," *William and Mary Quarterly* 73, no. 1 (January 2016): 3–36, explores the role of "hot chronology" at certain points in world history. For a recent reinterpretation of the Pueblo Uprising, see James Brooks, *Mesa of Sorrows: A History of the Awat'ovi Massacre* (New York: W. W. Norton, 2016), esp. chap. 4.

11. In addition to the scholars above, other seminal works include Theodore Binnema, *Common and Contested Ground: A Human and Environmental History of the Northwestern Plains* (Norman: University of Oklahoma Press, 2001); George Colpitts, *Pemmican Empire: Food, Trade, and the Last Bison Hunts in the North American Plains, 1780–1882* (Cambridge: Cambridge University Press, 2015); Elliott West, *The Contested Plains: Indians, Goldseekers, and the Rush to Colorado* (Lawrence: University of Kansas Press, 1998); Anne Hyde, *Empires, Nations, and Families: A History of the North American West, 1800–1860* (Lincoln: University of Nebraska Press, 2011); Elizabeth Fenn, *Encounters at the Heart of the World: A History of the Mandan People* (New York: Hill & Wang, 2014).

12. Fernand Braudel coined the term *longue durée* to describe deeper historical relationships between human communities and their environments over millennia.

See *The Mediterranean and the Mediterranean World in the Age of Philip II*, 2 vols. (1966; repr., Berkeley: University of California Press, 1996). For the *longue durée* in Native America, see Barr, "There's No Such Thing as 'Prehistory'"; and James Brooks, "Women, Men, and Cycles of Evangelism in the Southwest Borderlands, AD 750 to 1750," *American Historical Review* 118, no. 3 (2013): 738–64.

13. In addition to the scholars mentioned above, Daniel Richter makes a similar call to historians in *Before the Revolution: America's Ancient Pasts* (Cambridge MA: Belknap, 2011).

14. Some recent examples include Garrett Bailey and Daniel C. Swan, *Art of the Osage* (Seattle: University of Washington Press, 2004); Geoff Cunfer and Bill Waiser, eds., *Bison and People*; Colin G. Calloway, *One Vast Winter Count*; David C. Posthumus, "All My Relatives: Exploring Nineteenth-Century Lakota Ontology and Belief," *Ethnohistory* 64, no. 3 (July 2017): 379–400; Clint Carroll, *Roots of Our Renewal: Ethnobotany and Cherokee Environmental Governance* (Minneapolis: University of Minnesota Press, 2015). Similar work has advanced in the western plains and Great Basin. See Adam Hodge, *Ecology and Ethnogenesis*. Also see Ned Blackhawk, *Violence Over the Land: Indians and Empires in the Early American West* (Cambridge MA: Harvard University Press, 2008).

15. Recent works on early modern climate history include Anya Zilberstein, *A Temperate Empire: Making Climate Change in Early America* (Oxford: Oxford University Press, 2016); and "Manoomin: The Taming of Wild Rice in the Great Lakes Region," Environment & Society Portal, *Arcadia* (2015), no. 2, Rachel Carson Center for Environment and Society, https://doi.org/10.5282/rcc/6830. Also see "Forum: Climate and Early American History" in *William and Mary Quarterly* 72, no. 1 (January 2015): 3–159. For soil ecology and history, see Richard R. Drass, "Corn, Beans, and Bison: Cultivated Plants and Changing Economies of the Late Prehistoric Villagers on the Plains of Oklahoma and Northwest Texas," *Plains Anthropologist* 53, no. 205 (February 2008): 7–31; for starch grain analysis see Sonia Zarrillo and Brian Kooyman, "Evidence for Berry and Maize Processing on the Canadian Plains from Starch Grain Analysis," *American Antiquity* 71, no. 3 (July 2006): 473–99.

16. Silverman, *Thundersticks*; Isenberg, *The Destruction of the Bison*; and Flores, "Bison Ecology and Bison Diplomacy." For the Osage, see Bailey and Swan, *Art of the Osage*; Jeffrey S. Girard, Timothy K. Perttula, and Mary Beth Trubitt, *Caddo Connections: Cultural Interactions within and beyond the Caddo World* (Lanham MD: Rowman & Littlefield, 2014).

17. The Little Ice Age is having a historiographical "moment." Recent works emphasizing this period include Richter, *Before the Revolution*; Brian Fagan, *The Little Ice Age: How Climate Made History, 1300–1850* (New York: Basic Books, 2000); and William Foster, *Climate and Culture Change in North America AD 900–1600* (Austin: University of Texas Press, 2012).

18. Patricia Galloway, *Choctaw Genesis: 1500–1700* (Lincoln: University of Nebraska Press, 1998); Gary Clayton Anderson, *The Indian Southwest, 1580–1830: Ethnogenesis and Reinvention* (Norman: University of Oklahoma Press, 2009); Robbie Ethridge,

From Chicaza to Chickasaw: The European Invasion and the Transformation of the Mississippian World, 1540–1715 (Chapel Hill: University of North Carolina Press, 2010). For "regenesis," see Michael Witgen, *An Infinity of Nations: How the Native New World Shaped Early North America* (Philadelphia: University of Pennsylvania Press, 2013).

19. The historiography on medieval and early modern plagues across Afro-Eurasia is immense. For a recent study focusing on the plague that decimated fourteenth-century Europe, see John Kelly, *The Great Mortality: An Intimate History of the Black Death, the Most Devastating Plague of All Time* (New York: Harper Perennial, 2006); also see Dorothy H. Crawford, *Deadly Companions: How Microbes Shaped Our History* (Oxford: Oxford University Press, 2016).

20. Jane Mt. Pleasant, "A New Paradigm for Pre-Columbian Agriculture in North America," *Early American Studies: An Interdisciplinary Journal* 13, no. 2 (Spring 2015): 374–412.

21. Brian Fagan, *The Great Warming: Climate Change and the Rise and Fall of Civilizations* (New York: Bloomsbury Books, 2009).

22. Major studies on Cahokia and the surrounding Mississippian world include Timothy Pauketat, ed., *Medieval Mississippians: The Cahokian World* (Santa Fe NM: School for Advanced Research Press, 2015); Thomas E. Emerson, *Cahokia and the Archaeology of Power* (Tuscaloosa: University of Alabama Press, 1997); Timothy R. Pauketat and Thomas E. Emerson, eds., *Cahokia: Domination and Ideology in the Mississippian World* (Lincoln: University of Nebraska Press, 1997); Timothy R. Pauketat, *Cahokia Mounds* (Oxford: Oxford University Press, 2004); also see Robert Michael Morrissey, *Empire by Collaboration* (Philadelphia: University of Pennsylvania Press, 2015), esp. chaps. 1–2.

23. Bailey and Swan, *Art of the Osage*; Girard, Perttula, and Trubitt, *Caddo Connections*; and Jean Dennison, *Colonial Entanglement: Constituting a Twenty-First-Century Osage Nation* (Chapel Hill: University of North Carolina Press, 2012).

24. Julie Courtwright, *Prairie Fire: A Great Plains History* (Lawrence: University of Kansas Press, 2011); Stephen J. Pyne, *Fire in America: A Cultural History of Wildland and Rural Fire* (Princeton NJ: Princeton University Press, 1982); Thomas Vale, ed., *Fire, Native Peoples, and the Natural Landscape* (Washington DC: Island Press, 2002); and M. Kat Anderson, *Tending the Wild: Native American Knowledge and the Management of California's Natural Resources* (Berkeley: University of California Press, 2005).

25. Jane Mt. Pleasant, "The Paradox of Plows and Productivity: An Agronomic Comparison of Cereal Grain Production under Iroquois Hoe Culture and European Plow Culture in the Seventeenth and Eighteenth Centuries," *Agricultural History* 85, no. 4 (Fall 2011): 460–92.

26. Foster, *Climate and Culture Change in North America* (esp. chap. 5–6).

27. Several new works have begun to reassess the role of pastoral economies in world history. See Jack Weatherford, *Genghis Khan and the Making of the Modern World* (New York: Broadway Books, 2005); Pekka Hämäläinen, "What's in a Con-

cept: The Kinetic Empire of the Comanches," *History and Theory* 52, no. 1 (February 2013): 81–90; Matthew J. C. Cella, *Bad Land Pastoralism in Great Plains Fiction* (Iowa City: University of Iowa Press, 2010); Anne Porter, *Mobile Pastoralism and the Formation of Near Eastern Civilizations: Weaving Together Society* (Cambridge: Cambridge University Press, 2010).

28. For an excellent and exhaustive overview of Indigenous food systems, see Bruce David Smith, *The Subsistence Economies of Indigenous North American Societies: A Handbook* (Washington DC: Smithsonian Institution Press, 2011).

29. Ferris Jabr, "How to Really Eat Like a Hunter-Gatherer: Why the Paleo Diet is Half Baked," *Scientific American*, June 3, 2013. For colonizing diets, see Margaret D. Jacobs, "The Habit of Elimination: Indigenous Child Removal in Settler Colonial Nations in the Twentieth Century," in *Colonial Genocide in Indigenous North America*, ed. Alexander Laban Hinston and Andrew Woolford (Durham NC: Duke University Press, 2014), 189–207.

30. Jared Diamond, *The World Until Yesterday: What Can We Learn from Traditional Societies?* (New York: Viking, 2012). Also see Mann, *1491*.

31. Prescribed burning is now an established practice among commercial ranchers and farmers around the world. See John R. Weir, *Conducting Prescribed Fires: A Comprehensive Manual* (College Station: Texas A&M Press, 2009).

32. On the ubiquity of lightning strikes and its role in ecology, see Donald R. MacGorman and W. David Rust, *The Electrical Nature of Storms* (Oxford: Oxford University Press, 1998). For works on Indigenous food production through fire, see Anderson, *Tending the Wild*; Courtwright, *Prairie Fire*; Pyne, *Fire in America*; Charles Menzie, *Traditional Ecological Knowledge and Natural Resource Management* (Lincoln: University of Nebraska Press, 2006); Laurelyn Whitt, *Science, Colonialism, and Indigenous Peoples: The Cultural Politics of Law and Knowledge* (Cambridge: Cambridge University Press, 2009); Nancy Turner, *Ancient Pathways, Ancestral Knowledge: Ethnobotany and Ecological Wisdom of Indigenous Peoples of Northwestern North America* (Toronto: McGill University Press, 2014); and Beth Rose Middleton, *Trust in the Land: New Directions in Tribal Conservation* (Chapel Hill: University of North Carolina Press, 2011).

33. For a fascinating interactive map of global fires, see http://fires.globalforestwatch.org/map/.

34. In his book *1491* Charles Mann provides an excellent overview of these landscapes; see also Vale, *Fire, Native Peoples, and the Natural Landscape* and Anderson, *Tending the Wild*.

35. There has been a renaissance in Indigenous prescribed burning across Native America in recent years. One successful project includes the Osage and Nature Conservancy–managed Tallgrass Prairie Preserve. For an overview of similar overlapping initiatives occurring in Native Oklahoma, see Devon Mihesuah, "Searching for *Haknip Achukma* (Good Health): Challenges to Food Sovereignty Initiatives in Oklahoma," *American Indian Culture and Research Journal* 41, no. 3 (Spring 2018): 9–30.

36. Anderson, *Tending the Wild*.

37. Heidi Erdich, *Original Local: Indigenous Foods, Stories, and Recipes from the Upper Midwest* (Minneapolis: Minnesota Historical Society Press, 2013); also see Robin Wall Kimmerer, *Braiding Sweetgrass: Indigenous Wisdom, Scientific Knowledge and the Teachings of Plants* (Minneapolis: Milkweed Editions, 2015); Cynthia Fowler, *Ignition Stories: Indigenous Fire Ecology in the Indo-Australian Monsoon Zone* (Durham NC: Carolina Academic Press, 2013); James E. Sherow, *The Grasslands of the United States: An Environmental History* (Santa Barbara CA: ABC-CLIO, 2007).

38. Edmund Russell, *Evolutionary History: Uniting History and Biology to Understand Life on Earth* (Cambridge: Cambridge University Press, 2011).

39. Russell, *Evolutionary History*.

40. Colpitts, *Pemmican Empire*.

41. Sherow, *The Grasslands of the United States*; Kees Klein Goldwijk, "Long-Term Dynamic Modeling of Global Population and Built Up Area in a Spatially Explicit Way," *Holocene* 20, no. 4 (June 2010): 565–73.

42. Morrissey, "The Power of the Ecotone." Source: Raymond Wood and Margaret Liberty, eds., *Anthropology on the Great Plains* (Lincoln: University of Nebraska Press, 1980).

43. David La Vere, *Looting Spiro Mounds: An American King Tut's Tomb* (Norman: University of Oklahoma Press, 2007); Kathleen DuVaal, *The Native Ground: Indians and Colonists in the Heart of the Continent* (Philadelphia: University of Pennsylvania Press, 2006).

44. Gilbert Wilson, *Buffalo Bird Women's Garden: Agriculture of the Hidatsa Indians* (St. Paul: Minnesota Historical Society Press, 1987); Fenn, *Encounters at the Heart of the World*.

45. The "rise and fall" of Cahokia and fellow pre-Columbian urban centers along the Mississippi-Ohio River systems is hotly debated. For the "Cahokian diaspora" and possible cultural connections with Siouan-speaking societies, see Timothy Pauketat, *Ancient Cahokia and the Mississippians* (Cambridge: Cambridge University Press, 2004), esp. 153–55. Amanda L. Regnier argues that Mississippian societies became "blended" rather than "shattered" during the early Little Ice Age. See *Reconstructing Tascula's Chiefdom: Pottery Styles and the Social Composition of Late Mississippian Communities along the Alabama River* (Tuscaloosa: University of Alabama Press, 2014). Also see John H. Blitz and Karl G. Lorenz, *The Chattahoochee Chiefdoms* (Tuscaloosa: University of Alabama Press, 2007); Thomas E. Emerson, Dale L. McElrath, and Andrew C. Fortier, eds., *Archaic Societies: Diversity and Complexity across the Midcontinent* (Albany: SUNY Press, 2009); Meghan C. L. Howey, *Mound Builders and Monument Makers of the Northern Great Lakes, 1200–1600* (Norman: University of Oklahoma Press, 2012). For a critique of labeling pre-Columbian societies as "chiefdoms" or "systems," see Timothy Pauketat, *Chiefdoms and Other Archaeological Delusions* (Lanham MD: AltaMira, 2007). Mt. Pleasant also critiques assumptions about Cahokian drought and agricultural disruptions in "A New Paradigm," 403–8. Recent work points to increased flooding (rather than drought) as contributing to the decentralization of Cahokia. See Samuel E. Munoz, Kristine E. Gruley,

Ashtin Massie, David A. Fike, Sissel Schroeder, and John W. Williams, "Cahokia's Emergence and Decline Coincided with Shifts of Flood Frequency on the Mississippi River," *Proceedings of the National Academy of Science* 112, no. 20 (May 2015): 6319–24.

46. See Brian Fagan, *Archaeologists Explore the Lives of an Ancient Society* (Oxford: Oxford University Press, 2005); Suzanne K. Fish and Paul R. Fish, eds., *The Hohokam Millennium* (Santa Fe NM: School of Advanced Research Press, 2008); for the Lower Colorado Basin, Natale A. Zappia, *Traders and Raiders: The Indigenous World of the Colorado Basin* (Chapel Hill: University of North Carolina Press, 2014).

47. Fenn, *Encounters at the Heart of the World*.

48. Fenn, *Encounters at the Heart of the World*.

49. Wilson, *Buffalo Bird Women's Garden*.

50. See Thomas Edward Berres, *Power and Gender in Oneota Culture: A Study of a Late Prehistoric People* (DeKalb: Northern Illinois University Press, 2001).

51. See Ernest G. Walker, "An Overview of Prehistoric Communal Bison Hunting on the Great Plains," in *Bison and People*, ed. Cunfer and Waiser, esp. 122–58; Smith, *Subsistence Economies*.

52. William Cronon, *Changes in the Land: Indians, Colonists, and the Ecology of New England*, rev. ed. (New York: Hill & Wang, 2003), chap. 3.

53. Dan Flores, *The Natural West: Environmental History in the Great Plains and Rocky Mountains* (Norman: University of Oklahoma Press, 2001).

54. Kent G. Lightfoot and Otis Parrish's remarkable handbook, *California Indians and Their Environment: An Introduction* (Berkeley: University of California Press, 2009), reexamines Native Californian technology, demography, political-economy, and TEK across regions and cultures.

55. For Makah interior networks, see Joshua Reid, *The Sea is My Country: The Maritime World of the Makahs* (New Haven CT: Yale University Press, 2015); for larger continental networks, see Silverman, *Thundersticks*; Brooks, *Captives and Cousins*; Barr, *Peace Came in the Form of a Woman*; for Atlantic networks moving east, see Andrew Lipman, *The Saltwater Frontier: Indians and the Contest for the Atlantic Coast* (New Haven CT: Yale University Press, 2015); and DuVaal, *Native Ground*.

56. Robbie Ethridge and Sheri M. Shuck, *Mapping the Mississippian Shatter Zone: The Colonial Indian Slave Trade and Regional Instability in the American South* (Lincoln: University of Nebraska Press, 2009).

57. Zappia, *Traders and Raiders*, esp. chap. 2; Blackhawk, *Violence Over the Land*.

58. For Corazones trade, see William K. Hartmann, *Searching for Golden Empires: Epic Cultural Collisions in Sixteenth Century America* (Tucson: University of Arizona Press, 2014).

2

Travois Trails

Mobile Lifeways of Nineteenth-Century Plains Indian Women

LEILA MONAGHAN

Life was mobile for nineteenth-century Plains Indian women. Women and men traveled across thousands of miles of open prairie and through adjoining hills, mountains, and riverine landscapes. An anonymous Arapaho woman, speaking of her childhood, remembered, "As was the custom then, the Arapaho made frequent moves from place to place by means of ponies. The old women and children often rode in the travois; and sometimes heavier things were hauled."[1]

Travois are sleds made of poles attached to horses or dogs. Horse travois were made from tall tipi poles. When they needed to travel, women disassembled their lodges and used the poles to pull their goods from one campsite to another. The key parts of the landscape that made all this travel possible were the short-grass prairie lands that stretch from southern Saskatchewan, down through central and eastern Montana, eastern Wyoming, Colorado, New Mexico, and the Oklahoma Panhandle, and into central Texas. On the land around my home in Laramie, Wyoming, for example, the grass grows no higher than your knee, the ground is hard, and vegetation appears brown for most of the year. This dry land is ideal for pulling travois across long distances.

The current volume highlights the importance of water, grass, animal, and energy systems in the Great Plains. Women used the technology of the travois to cross the grasslands, access water and food for humans and animals, find wood for fires and lodging, and find myriad sources for other necessary materials. This was in part possible because shortgrass prairie lands are ringed by rough mountains containing a wide variety of resources. Just as boats make the barriers of rivers navigable, the technology of the travois, particularly after Plains groups acquired horses in the late eighteenth century, opened up broad reaches of territory.

The effect of the introduction of horses on men's lives has long been a topic of discussion. As early ethnographer James Mooney put it in 1898, "With the horse he [the Indian] was transformed into the daring buffalo hunter, . . . leaving him free then to sweep the plains with his war parties along a range of a thousand miles."[2] But the effect of horses and the new, heavier travois on women's lives has been less discussed. Women were the community members that were responsible for making camp, providing shelter and most food to others, and transporting materials across the great open spaces between camps. For example, in 1851 B. Gratz Brown, writing from a nineteenth-century Euro-American perspective, described the women present at the Fort Laramie Treaty proceedings as doing the "drudgery" of moving camp including putting "their lodges, camp equipage, children, and sometimes their dogs" on "prairie buggies" made from the lodgepoles of their tipis. Brown judged the men as contributing nothing to this process: "they regard it as a disgrace to do any kind of work." He did not see men's hunting as equal labor to the women's work of moving camp.[3] The typical horse and travois could carry two hundred pounds worth of materials and made traveling long distances with a variety of material goods possible. Travois transported small children, the elderly, and goods including buffalo-skin lodges, sleeping skins, food, and cooking equipment.[4]

This paper explores nineteenth-century Native women's use of shortgrass prairie lands. These women are the ancestors of the current Tsististas and Sotaa'e'o peoples of the Northern Cheyenne Nation of Montana, the Northern Arapaho Tribe of Wyoming, the Cheyenne and Arapaho Tribes of Oklahoma, and the Lakota peoples of South Dakota, North Dakota, Nebraska, and Minnesota.[5] Data such as Cheyenne river names and Arapaho place-names give a broad range for traditional territories. A review of the literature on Plains women's mobile lifeways, including the use of travois, shows how women made extensive use of the rich landscape assemblage[6] offered by the Great Plains. While writings on the Plains Indian Wars between 1864 and 1876 have usually focused on the men of the conflicts, primary documents about the war often included stories about the Native women as well. These sources reveal how Cheyenne, Arapaho, and Lakota women used travois to transport goods and even the wounded before, during, and after battles. They provide insight not only into the battles but also into the mobile lifeways torn apart by warfare. Analyzing illustrations of decorated leather parfleches collected by Alfred E. Kroeber in his 1899 expedition to Wyoming shows the importance of landscape to Arapaho women even after the Arapahos were forced onto the reservation.[7] Together, these approaches provide rich details for understanding the nomadic lifestyles of nineteenth-century Cheyenne and Arapaho women.

Rethinking Great Plains Territory and Resources

Past and present Indigenous inhabitants of the Great Plains share a broad view of the uses of the territory. Based on archaeological analyses of the western Black Hills of Wyoming, Marcel Kornfeld argued that prehistoric inhabitants of the northern plains from 10,000 BP to the beginning of the historical period "were broad spectrum subsistence strategists."[8] These foragers utilized large "regions through a pattern conditioned by characteristics of the landscape including resource structure."[9] They made extensive use of what I am calling here the landscape assemblage, the totality of landscape features including ecological resources such as water, grass, animals, energy, and mountains and the social resources of other Plains communities.

Plains Indigenous groups today continue to identify themselves as connected to a nomadic lifestyle that covered a large range of territory and made use of a wide variety of resources. For example, a significant number of tribes protested the Keystone Pipeline in South Dakota and Nebraska, including the Oglala Lakotas, and justified their rights to do so in terms of historical land-use patterns. In their 2014 position paper, the Oglala Sioux described the extent of their territory as encompassing "a landscape in the Great Plains region that covers part of ten present-day states as well as part of Canada." They also described the tribes' nomadic lifestyle. "Historically speaking, our people had annual purposeful travels from one seasonal camp site to the next, and we followed our brothers the buffalo through a pathway of life that supported our entire existence all within our aboriginal/ancestral homelands."[10]

Massey and Driver described the plains culture area as extending from "the North Saskatchewan River in Alberta nearly to the Gulf of Mexico in Texas and from the Rocky Mountains on the west to about the hundredth meridian on the east."[11] This area tracks roughly with the extent of short- and mixed-grass prairie lands that runs from Canada to Texas. Cheyenne and Arapaho place-names give one source for the extent of their territory within the larger plains area.

Cheyenne and Arapaho Place-Names and Plant Names

One proxy for the range that nineteenth-century Cheyenne people were familiar with is the Cheyenne river and stream names recorded by Grinnell in 1907. These names reflect a territory bounded by the Missouri to the north and east and the Red River to the south. The only major river named north of the Missouri is the Milk River of Montana. Many names refer to specific vegetation or animal life found near the rivers and creeks and give a good indication of resources important to the Cheyennes (see table 1).

TABLE 1. Cheyenne waterway names

Animals	Plants	Other useful resources
Mammals:	*Food:*	Coal/gun powder
Beavers	Hackberries	Moon shell (beads from traders)
Elk	Roseberries	Flint arrowpoints (a previously
Porcupines	*Trees:*	manufactured cache was found)
Turkeys	Ash	Pipe dance
Wild sheep	Box elders	Trading
Wolves	Cedar	Red paint/red clay
Birds:	Elms	
Crows	Lodgepoles	
Geese	Medicine wood	
Kingfishers	Red willows	
Owls	(a dogwood variety)	
Shellfish:	Willows	
Mussels	*Other:*	
	Greasy grass	
	Rushes	

Created by author from George Bird Grinnell, "Cheyenne Stream Names," *American Anthropologist* 8, no. 1 (1906): 15–22.

One of the reasons that the range of the Cheyennes is so large is that it includes the ranges of both the Southern and Northern Cheyennes, who were formally separated by the U.S. government in 1855 after fights over limited resources. The Southern Cheyenne and Arapaho Reservation in Oklahoma, established in 1869, and the Northern Cheyenne Indian Reservation in Montana, established in 1884, reflect the southern and northern extent of nineteenth-century territories.[12]

The Arapahos, who were living with the Cheyennes, also split. The Southern Arapahos currently share the Cheyenne and Arapaho Reservation in Oklahoma. The Northern Arapahos eventually separated from the Northern Cheyennes and were forced to settle next to the Eastern Shoshones in 1878 in what is now the Wind River Reservation in Wyoming.[13] As with Cheyenne stream names, Arapaho place-names can reflect historical events, natural features, or natural resources. A trail north of Estes Park, Colorado, is Hiseibooo, Woman's Trail, marking where women and children escaped

TABLE 2. Arapaho place-names in Colorado

Animals		Plants	Other material
Mammals:	*Birds:*	*Vegetation:*	Ceremonial paint
Bears	Crows	Brush	(blue, yellow)
Beavers	Eagles	Sagebrush	Game bags
Buffalo	Falcons	Pines	Guns
Coyotes	Sage chickens	*Food:*	Pipes
Dogs	(sage grouse)	Bullberries	Rawhide dishes
Elk	Sandhill cranes	White turnips	Shells
Mountain lions	White owls		Stars
Mule deer	*Insects:*		Stone hammers
Sheep	Ants		(for women)
Wolves	Flying bugs		Tipis
	Miller moths		Tipi liners
			Tipi poles

Created by author from Place Names, The Arapaho Project, Center for the Study of Indigenous Languages of the West, the University of Colorado Boulder, accessed June 1, 2020, https://www.colorado.edu/center/csilw/language-archives/arapaho-word-lists/place-names.[14]

from a battle. Table 2 shows a list of natural resources mentioned in a compilation of Arapaho place-names in Colorado.

The Arapaho list is similar to the Cheyenne's and includes mammals, birds, insects, and everyday objects. Both the Cheyennes and Arapahos list only two plant foods each—two berries for the Cheyennes and bullberries and wild turnips for the Arapahos. George Murdock's *Ethnographic Atlas* described the Cheyenne diet as 80 percent being provided by hunting and 20 percent by foraging, a finding supported by these Cheyenne and Arapaho place-names.[15] Overall, the names indicate how both groups recognized and used a wide range of resources, understanding the landscape as an assemblage of different environments consistent with the descriptions of Kornfeld and Osborn in *Islands on the Plains*.[16]

Naming a place after animals or plants is an act, in linguistic terms, of marking a source as particularly culturally significant. However, there were also plentiful unmarked plant resources. For example, in 1905 Grinnell listed nineteen medicinal plants in the collection of his Northern Cheyenne "mother," Wind Woman, including plants that prevented tooth trouble, vomiting, and nose bleeds.[17] John Moore's review of the 1880 census found eleven people named after plants (another marked category) of the "100 food and medical plant species" recognized by the Cheyennes.[18] The University of Colorado Arapaho dictionary found about "100 different plants . . . many having several different uses. There are also a number of other Arapaho plant names for which no actual plant can be identified."[19]

While current day Lakotas harken back to "our brothers the buffalo," river names and place-names reveal a range of important animals, and plant names reflect a deep knowledge of local natural resources. The gendered nature of buffalo hunting, with men traveling away from camps, meant that women and men had different territories. Men could have easily traveled through the deep scrub bush of what is now western Wyoming in search of buffalo while women more often traveled across the more eastern shortgrass prairie lands pulling a camp full of goods on their travois.

Travois Travel and Using the Landscape Assemblage

Nineteenth-century Cheyenne and Arapaho women traveled between resource-rich islands, setting up camps as they moved. Their horse-drawn travois were ideal for towing loads across relatively flat lands. Norman Henderson recreated travois travel with both a dog travois and a Hidatsa style horse travois in the Qu'Appelle Valley of Saskatchewan, part of the most northern stretch of the shortgrass plains.[20] Describing travel with the dog travois, he wrote, "The thick mat of dried grass blades gave a resilient spring to the dog's step and cushioned the travois poles. The effect was almost magical: a smooth, apparently frictionless, soundless glide."[21]

In other terrains travois are much less effective. In his horse travois experiment, Henderson found that the travois performed poorly in "even light bush (the projecting ends of the cross poles are liable to catch on anything)."[22] His horse, however, could pull both up and down hills and through dirt and mud. Henderson cites the Cheyenne Wooden Leg's 1931 description of movements

TABLE 3. Resources mentioned by Jim Blood

Animals	Plants	Landscape features
Antelope	Chokecherries	Cut Bank Creek
Bison	Cypress Hills lodgepoles	Cypress Hills
Blacktails	Gooseberries	Foothills of the mountains
Deer	Red willow berries	Lower Cut Bank Creek near
Elk	Serviceberries	horse corrals and cliffs of rocks
Moose	Sweetgrass	Marias (Bear Creek) River
	Tobacco	Milk River
	Wild plants and tubers	Pakoki (Bad-water) Lake
		Sweet Grass Hills

Created by author from Brandi Bethke, "Dog Days to Horse Days: Evaluating the Rise of Nomadic Pastoralism among the Blackfoot" (PhD diss., University of Arizona, 1990), 261–62.

in 1876 as clearly visible on the landscape. Groups with travois left trails "from a quarter to half a mile wide" on the open plains.[23]

In her study of northern plains Blackfoot uses of dogs and horses, Brandi Bethke found that ethnohistorical and archaeological data point to a shift from a bison-centered "'hunter-gatherer landscape' to a horse-centered 'pastoralist landscape'" after the introduction of horses during the Contact Period starting in 1700. Focus shifted from foraging to maximizing access for horses to water, forage, and shelter, as well as protecting them from theft.[24] This postcontact pastoralism featured band migration in a "generally cyclical pattern towards areas of known resources and sacred places."[25] Jim Blood, a southern Piikani Bloodfoot, recounted one year's travel to C. C. Uhlenbeck (1912). According to Blood, a year's travel took the group across varied terrain, including between islands of resources. While most of the travel is across easily traversed prairie land, some of it is across more rugged terrain including Sweet Grass Hills, Cypress Hills, and the rocky outcrops of Writing-on-Stone. While Robert Kelly estimates the traditional diet of the Blackfoot (Siksika) as being obtained 80 percent through hunting and 20 percent through foraging—the same ratio as the Cheyenne diet—the plant resources listed by Blood are more extensive than those mentioned in Cheyenne river names or Arapaho place-names, perhaps reflecting a broader diet in practice (see table 3).

While the rolling grasses of the plains were ideal for travel, the use of travois in rugged terrain has been documented by Steve Platt's work. His archaeological study documented travois trails through the Bighorn Mountains—two Sioux and three Crow trails. Trails through rugged territories followed more specific routes and sometimes left clear trail ruts. They were also marked by lines of cairns, stacked stones, to mark the way.[26]

Although there is no specific work on the use of travois among the Cheyennes and Arapahos, there are widespread mentions in more general ethnographic and historical works. Early Cheyenne sources tell of dog travois. George Bird Grinnell recounted one story from before the Cheyennes migrated from the Missouri River to the Great Plains that tells of the frequent moves the group had to make to find food. Men "reported that a certain lake was covered with water-fowl of all kinds; so the whole camp moved over to it, the dogs hauling the travois."[27]

Expectations that females were in charge of setting up camp and using travois to transport goods and people can be seen throughout descriptions of nineteenth-century Cheyenne culture, including in the play of children. Young girls "moved a little way from camp and there put up their little lodges [tipis]—made and sewed for them by their mothers—arranging them in a circle just as did the old people in the big camp." The boys did not help set up these miniature tipis, but they sometimes acted as horses and dragged the lodgepoles or hauled travois with the little babies on them.[28] There is also clear photographic evidence for the importance of travois among the Cheyennes even after reservation life.[29]

Unlike the Cheyennes, the Arapahos had a long tradition of pedestrian communal buffalo hunting precontact. After the introduction of horses, however, buffalo hunting became a male-oriented affair. Just as among the Cheyennes, Arapaho girls were exposed to travois work at a young age. One Arapaho woman recounted how girls had to take care of their personal playthings. They had "to bundle them up and to see that they were properly packed on the travois."[30] Girls were also in charge of unpacking their goods.

FIG. 2. *Women with Travois Digging Roots*, from the George Bird Grinnell collection, National Museum of the American Indian, Smithsonian Institution, (N13545).

Travois allowed women to move heavy camp equipment across long distances. On hard prairie lands, this travel was relatively easy, but travel was also possible on specific trails in more rugged landscape. The process for switching poles from being part of a travois to part of a tipi was complex. These processes, however, were learned early and done often by young girls and the women they became. Descriptions from the Great Plains Wars give some insight into some of the specifics of these routines.

Military Records

Because the major events of the Plains Indian War—the Sand Creek Massacre, the attack at Washita, and the Battle of Little Bighorn—were well documented, they offer a source of descriptions that can contextualize women's mobile lifeways.[31] In these tales of war and death, we learn about behavior under conditions of battle and can catch echoes of a more peaceful life. Grinnell's description of

Cheyenne girls' play shows how girls were trained in even peaceful times to react to attack. In play battles, if the girls "thought the battle was going against them, [they] would pull down the lodges, pack up their possessions, and begin to run away."[32] The women at Sand Creek (November 29, 1864) and Washita (November 27, 1868) had no time to pack their possessions. They just fled death and capture as best they could. From the many documents on Little Bighorn (June 25–26, 1876), however, we can glean a picture of ordinary life and the range of women's possible roles in battle.

There are no women's accounts of the Sand Creek Massacre, but the accounts of men with close connections to Cheyenne women reflect both the overwhelming brutality of the attacks and what women were able to do under the circumstances. Trader John Smith, husband of the Cheyenne woman Zerepta, testified that "all manner of depredations were inflicted on their persons."[33]

A letter from Edmund Guerrier, the grown son of Tahtahtoisneh, to the same congressional committee that Smith testified before showed both an ordinary night spent sleeping in a lodge and how one woman had escaped with a small herd of ponies.

> The [women] ... in my lodge looked out and then called to me to get up; "there were a lot of soldiers coming." ... [Artillerymen] began firing with their rifles and pistols ... I struck out ... I went to the northeast; I ran about five miles, when I came across an Indian woman driving a herd of ponies, some ten or fifteen. I got a pony. She was a cousin of mine—one of White Antelope's daughters. I went on with her to Smoky Hill.[34]

The lodge that Guerrier was sleeping in was not his own but belonged to one of his female relatives. His letter gives hints of how women lived together in a lodge and accepted male relatives as guests. His description of his cousin shows a skilled horsewoman defending essential property, her horses.

Many of the survivors of Sand Creek were not able to get to horses. George Bent, son of Owl Woman and American trader William Bent, described the night of the attack as the "worst night I ever went through." People had fled the camp with just the clothes on their back and with no buffalo robes or wood to keep them warm. Those who were able to tried "to keep the children and wounded from freezing to death" with small fires and covering them with piles of vegetation. They also "kept hallooing" to let others wandering the plains know where they were. Some went back to the site of the slaughter to try to find family and friends. "Few were found alive, for the soldiers had done their work thoroughly; but now and then during that endless night some man or women would stagger in among us, carrying some wounded person on their back."[35]

Travois would have been useful that bitter night, but one of their limitations was that there was little access to them without a formal dismantling of the camp. The poles to build the travois were left behind when villagers had to abandon their lodges and warm buffalo robes. Instead men and women had to drag the wounded back themselves.

George Armstrong Custer's attack at Washita followed the same early morning tactics that John Chivington and his troops had used at Sand Creek. The military quickly overran the Washita camp and caught most people asleep including Cheyenne witness Kate Bighead. In 1928 she described how, "It was early morning when the soldiers began the shooting. There had been a big storm, and there was snow on the ground. All of us jumped from our beds, and all started running to get away. I was barefooted as were most of the others."[36] Many of the women and children fled into the cold snow. Some tried to ford the icy river, with its waist- and chest-deep waters. The "razor edges of broken ice" cut people's feet and the river ran red with blood of people and horses.[37] "The ponies, after being shot, broke away, and ran about, bleeding, until they dropped."[38] The attack at Washita shows how the military was not only attacking people but an equestrian way of life.

Stories about Little Bighorn, because there were so many more survivors, give a fuller picture of Plains Indian life including the lifeways of Lakota and Cheyenne women. The Lakota woman Moving Robe told of digging wild turnips on a nearby hill before returning to camp at the sign of soldiers and then joining the battle herself after hearing of the death of her brother.[39] Women had time to do a proper move of households, something that had not been possible at Sand Creek or Washita. The camp was a temporary stopping place. According to Pretty White Buffalo, she and the other Hunkpapa women had worked through the night "to make ready for the march that we were to take up that morning," working to put together "many bundles" of her goods.[40]

Cheyenne Kate Bighead, who had barely escaped during the attack on Washita, did not fight like Moving Robe but did provide active assistance on the battlefield.

> I went riding among the Indians at different places on the battlefield, in search of [my nephew] Noisy Walking. . . . [I found him in a deep gulch]. I stayed with him while a young man friend went to the camps to tell his mother.
>
> Women from many families brought lodgepole travois, dragged by ponies, to take away the dead or wounded Indians. Some of the women, mourning for their own dead, beat and cut the dead bodies of the white men. Noisy Walking's mother and her sister came to get him. We put him upon the travois bed and took him across the river to our camp.[41]

Women were an essential part of the Battle of Little Bighorn. They finished what the Lakota and Cheyenne men had started by killing the wounded and offering support to the warriors in the form of songs and medical assistance. Woven in with this tale of death is a story about the versatility of travois when women had access to them. Travois were the ambulances and hearses of the battle.

While travois are associated with tipis, women built other forms of shelter when necessary. After the battle the Cheyennes and Lakotas needed to move quickly in order to avoid retribution by the U.S. military. Bighead described how a temporary camp differed from a permanent one. The "poles and skins" that women used to construct their big lodges were kept packed away. Instead, they "gathered willow wands and built little dome shelters, or the people slept that night without any shelter except robe bedding."[42]

Travois also allowed women to travel between Washita in what is today Oklahoma to Little Bighorn in Montana, sites almost 1,000 miles apart. This distance was traveled with horses pulling travois loaded with a mobile village complete with its household goods. According to Blood's description of Blackfoot travel, they moved a distance of roughly 150 miles or more in a year.[43] The distance traveled by Bighead and the Cheyennes was six times that. There is also evidence of the seasonality of travel. Little Bighorn, the most northerly of the attacks, occurred on a hot day at the end of June while Sand Creek, in what is now southern Colorado, and Washita in Oklahoma took place on cold days in late November. When you look at these sites in Montana, Colorado, and Oklahoma, you can see Little Bighorn and Sand Creek are both part of the shortgrass prairie region and Washita is just east of shortgrass lands in a region of mixed tall- and shortgrass prairie. It is also to be noted that most of the warriors, men in their prime, were away from the winter camps at Sand Creek and Washita, while they had gathered in large numbers before the June Battle of Little Bighorn.

This evidence shows how much work it took women to take down and erect tipis, and how women used travois in a wide range of different ways. Because travois poles were also the structure for their homes, women had to take into account this work when deciding whether to erect a tipi or to build a more modest willow dome. The long distances traveled and the seasonal nature of many resources, particularly plant resources, also gives us insight into the wide and deep knowledge women had about the environments they traveled through. At any particular time, this environment might or might not be shared by the men in their families. Women's awareness of the environment is also reflected in their artwork, as discussed below.

Arapaho Women's Perspectives

While military and historical records record men's accounts and some Native women's accounts of the Plains Wars through the filter of interviewers, they rarely give us insight into women's perspectives on the world. One source, however, women's leatherwork, can provide at least a glimpse of the construction of Arapaho women's perceptions of world, particularly how they viewed the spaces they inhabited. Alfred Kroeber collected a variety of women's artwork from the Wind River Reservation as part of the Jesup Expedition of 1899. A collection of forty-five painted parfleches and other leather bags in particular gives a rich view into women's perceptions of the world including a life lived in mountains, on the plains, on trails, and in tipis.[44]

Jeffrey Anderson argues that "Plains Indian women's art . . . has been historically overshadowed by attention to male art forms."[45] Anderson analyzed Arapaho women's quillwork, an art form no longer practiced by the Arapahos because of the interruption of tradition during the reservation era. Many of the traits found in quillwork, including movement and symbolic patterns, are also found in the parfleches collected by Kroeber. These bags reflect what Anderson describes as "the common designs of women's art that allow individual creativity."[46]

While Kroeber described the basic symbolism of the bags, he rarely connected the imagery to women's larger worldviews. For example, for the bag illustrated on the left side of figure 3, he gave a dry account of tents, tent poles and rivers.[47] If we take the analysis a step further, we can see it as an image of travel from the small winter camps at the bottom of the image (the three triangles with doors) to the large summer camp circle at the top (squares often represent circles in Arapaho iconography). The crosshatched line in the center represents a river, and alongside are parallel lines that could well represent travois furrows. While Western notions of home assume it to be a stable unchanging place, this image presents a world where travel and movement were the norm.

Images of mountains, tipis, trails, rivers, and other natural and human features abound in all the artwork collected by Kroeber and are particularly clear in the forty-five rectangular leather bags—parfleches, berry bags, feather bags, and bags for other uses—illustrated in his 1902 report for the American Museum of Natural History. Mountains are the most common feature, over 73 percent (thirty-three of forty-five) have one or more images of mountains

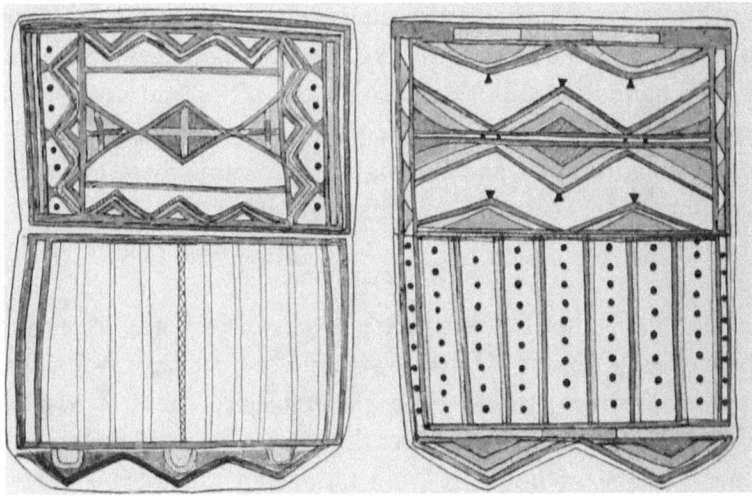

FIG. 3. Illustrations of painted rawhide bags by anonymous Arapaho women, pre-1900, American Museum of Natural History Library. Alfred L. Kroeber, "The Arapaho: General Description and Decorative Art and Symbolism" (The Mrs. Morris Jesup Expedition). *Bulletin of the Museum of Natural History* 18 (September 3, 1902): 127.

or hills. Tipis (called tents by Kroeber) feature in nearly half of the images and are made with the same triangular lines as the mountains. Rivers, land areas, and grass are all common, as are parts of tipis including pegs, poles, beds, and internal fire pits.

Animals, animal parts, and animal tracks are also featured. One bag has illustrations of multiple paths. "Enclosing the whole design are the customary lines or stripes. . . . Those of them that are blue represent buffalo-paths; the white, antelope paths; the yellow, elk-paths; and the red, deer-paths."[48] Almost all bags have multiple forms, some up to twelve. The most symbolic images the bags feature include representations of the world, life symbols, and sacred bear paws. One image of hills can be read as a metaphor for "periods of life," which Anderson defines as "childhood, youth, adulthood, and old age."[49] As a body of work, these decorated bags show women's deep connections to the landscape assemblages they inhabited. Women not only traveled the world but thought about landscape features in a range of productive and creative ways. This art is also quite different from men's ledger art from the same period, which often features images of men on horses fighting battles.[50] For woman, the entire landscape was a place they could make home by erecting their tipis, hanging quillwork from the poles, and lighting the fires within them, and they celebrated this in even their secular artwork.

Conclusion

Bringing together the very different sets of evidence presented here gives us a broad view of how nineteenth-century Cheyennes and Arapahos used the landscape assemblage of the Great Plains, including how they made use of the grasses, animals, water, and energy sources of the plains. Women and men had different understandings of the landscapes they inhabited. Women's view of the world was colored by their responsibilities for making and moving camps by the use of horse-drawn travois. Their constant travel gave them a rich sense of the mountains, rivers, and plains they inhabited, something that is reflected in their artwork. Men's understanding of the world was different. They moved across greater distances while hunting, including hunting buffalo, and raiding but did not need to transform new locations into a home base every night. Despite the slightly more limited range for women, mobility was built into every aspect of their lives. They were trained as girls to pack up and move camps quickly. The terrain became part of the women's symbolic understanding of the world including the Arapaho concept of the four hills of life.

Women of different Plains groups also had overlapping territories that reflected the ability of groups to move long distances, sometimes thousands of miles. As long as they had buffalo skins for the lodges, poles to structure their tipis and to use in their travois, and horses to draw them, women could make any part of the vast territory of the plains their home. They could also use the resources of the diverse landscape assemblage of the plains and adjacent areas—from buffalo, to wild turnips, to dozens of different plant species—to feed and clothe themselves and their families. This chapter points the way to further research including more work on women's art, ethnographic and ethnohistorical work on native plant species and collection practices, and the continuing reinterpretation of military histories.

Much of history is written from the perspective of settled people, but this preliminary examination shows the importance of movement in the lives of Cheyenne and Arapaho women. For Plains Indian women, the shortgrass prairie was a highway from Oklahoma to Montana and back. The travois made a mobile and relatively comfortable lifestyle possible. Home was not a place. Instead, a set of poles carrying goods, and the knowledge of how to quickly transform these objects into a weatherproof lodge, let women construct homes across the plains.

Notes

1. Truman Michelson, "Narrative of an Arapaho Woman," *American Anthropologist* 35 (1933): 596.

2. James Mooney 1898, quoted in George Hyde, *Life of George Bent: Written from His Letters* (Norman: University of Oklahoma Press, 1968), 17.

3. Brown, quoted in "Laramie," Correspondent to the *Missouri Republican*, October 3, 1850, dateline Fort Laramie, August 26. *Publications of the Nebraska Historical Society*, vol. 20, ed. Albert Watkins (Lincoln: Nebraska Historical Society, 1922), 237.

4. Norman Henderson, *Rediscovering the Prairies: Journeys by Dog, Horse, and Canoe*. (Victoria BC: TouchWood Editions, 2005).

5. Thank you to Yufna Soldier Wolf and Teanna Limpy for their helpful discussion of naming issues.

6. Thank you to Robert Rundstrom for suggesting that landscape assemblages would be a useful concept here and for providing a definition.

7. Alfred L. Kroeber, "The Arapaho: General Description and Decorative Art and Symbolism (The Mrs. Morris Jesup Expedition)," *Bulletin of the Museum of Natural History* 18 (September 3, 1902): 1–150, https://archive.org/details/cu31924089417103.

8. Marcel Kornfeld, "Pull of the Hills: Affluent Foragers of the Western Black Hills" (PhD diss., University of Massachusetts, 1994), 253. See pp. 26–32 for the archaeological chronology of the area.

9. Kornfeld, "Pull of the Hills," 138.

10. Bryan Brewer, "The Keystone XL Pipeline Is Not in the National Interest: Position Paper of the Oglala Sioux Tribe" (enclosure to March 5, 2014, letter from Oglala Sioux Tribal President Bryan Brewer to the Secretary of State John Kerry), 4, https://2012-keystonepipeline-xl.state.gov/documents/organization/249461.pdf.

11. Harold Driver and William Massey, "Comparative Studies of North American Indians," *Transactions American Philosophical Society* 47 (1957): 165–456.

12. Donald J. Berthrong, *The Southern Cheyennes*, vol. 66 (Norman: University of Oklahoma Press, 1963); Ramon Powers and James N. Leiker, *The Northern Cheyenne Exodus in History and Memory* (Norman: University of Oklahoma Press), 2012.

13. Virginia Cole Trenholm, *The Arapahoes, Our People* (Norman: University of Oklahoma Press, 1986), 147.

14. Thanks to Andrew Cowell for this and other Arapaho citations.

15. Murdock atlas, quoted in Robert Kelly, *Lifeways of Hunter-Gatherers*, 2nd ed. (Cambridge: Cambridge University Press, 2013), 42.

16. Marcel Kornfeld and Alan J. Osborn, eds. *Islands on the Plains: Ecological, Social, and Ritual Use of Landscapes* (Salt Lake City: University of Utah Press, 2003).

17. George Bird Grinnell, "Some Cheyenne Plant Medicines," *American Anthropologist* 7, no. 1 (1905): 37–43.

18. John H. Moore, "Cheyenne Names and Cosmology," *American Ethnologist* 11, no. 2 (1984): 298.

19. The Arapaho Project, "Plants and the Arapaho," accessed May 28, 2020, https://verbs.colorado.edu/ArapahoLanguageProject/RMNP/Plants/Index.htm. See also Andrew Cowell, "Arapaho Plant Names," in *Papers of the Thirty-sixth Algonquin Conference*, ed. H. C. Wolfart (Winnipeg: University of Manitoba, 2005), 135–71.

20. Norman Henderson, "Replicating Dog Travois Travel on the Northern Plains," *Plains Anthropologist* 39, no. 148 (May 1994): 145–59; Norman Henderson, "Replicating Horse and Travois Travel," *Prairie Forum* 21, no. 1 (1996): 137–48.

21. Henderson, "Replicating Dog Travois Travel," 154.

22. Henderson, "Replicating Horse and Travois Travel," 142.

23. Henderson, "Replicating Horse and Travois Travel,"143.

24. Brandi Bethke, "Dog Days to Horse Days: Evaluating the Rise of Nomadic Pastoralism among the Blackfoot," (PhD diss., University of Arizona, 1990), 305.

25. Bethke, "Dog Days to Horse Days," 260.

26. Steve Platt, "Trails and Aboriginal Land Use in the Northern Bighorn Mountains, Wyoming" (master's thesis, University of Wyoming, 1992).

27. George Bird Grinnell, "Some Early Cheyenne Tales," *Journal of American Folklore* 20, no. 78 (1907): 186.

28. George Bird Grinnell, *The Cheyenne Indians*, vol. 1 (New Haven CT: Yale University Press, 1923), 110–11.

29. Grinnell, *The Cheyenne Indians*, 96. See also figure 2.

30. Michelson, "Narrative of an Arapaho Woman," 596–98.

31. For a general discussion of foraging lifeways see Kelly, *Lifeways of Hunter-Gatherers*.

32. Grinnell, *The Cheyenne Indians*, 111.

33. U.S. Congress, *Condition of the Indian Tribes: Report of the Joint Special Committee, Appointed under Joint Resolution of March 3, 1865*, 38th Congress (Washington DC: Government Printing Office, 1867), A042, http://quod.lib.umich.edu/m/moa/ABB3022.0001.001?rgn=main;view=fulltext.

34. *Condition of the Indian Tribes*, A065–66.

35. Hyde, *Life of George Bent*, 157–58.

36. Kate Bighead, quoted in Thomas Marquis, "She Watched Custer's Last Battle," in *Custer on the Little Bighorn* (Hardin MT: Hardin Tribune, Herald Print, 1967), 35.

37. Red Black Bird, quoted in Richard Hardoff, *Washita Memories* (Norman: University of Oklahoma Press, 2006), 338.

38. Mrs. Lone Wolf, quoted in Hardoff, *Washita Memories*, 336.

39. Moving Robe, quoted in Richard Hardoff, *Lakota Recollections of the Custer Fight* (Lincoln: University of Nebraska Press, 1991), 93.

40. Mrs. Spotted Horn Bull, quoted in James McLaughlin, *My Friend the Indian* (New York: Houghton Mifflin, 1910), 166.

41. Bighead, "She Watched Custer's Last Battle," 40.

42. Bighead, "She Watched Custer's Last Battle," 40.

43. Bethke, "Dog Days to Horse Days," 263.

44. Kroeber, "The Arapaho," 106–36.

45. Jeffrey Anderson, *Arapaho Women's Quillwork: Motion, Life, and Creativity* (Norman: University of Oklahoma Press, 2013), 11.

46. Anderson, *Arapaho Women's Quillwork*, 135.

47. See figure 39 in Kroeber, "The Arapaho," 128.

48. See figure 2 of plate XIX in Kroeber, "The Arapaho," 109.

49. Anderson, *Arapaho Women's Quillwork*, 115.

50. For examples of men's art see Black Horse Ledger, Ayer MS 3227, Newberry Library, Chicago, ca. 1877; Rodney Thomas, *Rubbing Out Long Hair (Pehin Hanska Kasota): The American Indian Story of the Little Big Horn in Art and Word* (Spanaway WA: Elk Plain Press, 2009); Janet Berlo, *Plains Indian Drawings 1865–1935: Pages from a Visual History* (New York: Harry N. Abrams and the American Federation of Arts and the Drawing Center, 1996).

3

Bison Hunters and Prairie Fires

A View from the Northwestern Plains

MARÍA NIEVES ZEDEÑO, CHRISTOPHER ROOS,
KACY HOLLENBACK, AND MARY HAGEN ERLICK

Introduction

Since the end of the last glaciation, fire has been essential to the return and expansion of grasslands on the northwestern plains. Overwhelmingly, however, scientific explanations of grassland fires have revolved around natural phenomena, discounting the fact that Native Americans changed greatly the surrounding environment for their use and survival with fire.[1] Scars on old trees, charcoal particles in lake sediments, or postfire erosion in arid lands are generally attributed to natural fires given certain conditions such as episodes of global warming and dry climate: as G. W. Williams notes, "since the trees and sediments cannot document how the fires *started*, lightning becomes the easiest 'natural' explanation."[2] Yet, historical and ecological references to intentional use of fire under numerous circumstances and for a wide variety of purposes are growing fast. H. T. Lewis, long-term scholar of Native fires, recorded at least seventy different fire applications to manipulate vegetation. His and over three hundred other studies detail how fire was used to improve hunting grounds, manage crops, improve growth and yields of grasslands and pastures, fireproof key econiches from destructive wildland fires, collect insects, deter pests, signal strategically and combat enemies, manipulate the trade market, clear pathways, fell trees, and clean riparian areas.[3]

Fire in the North American grassland was a common occurrence throughout the Holocene.[4] Historical accounts of early travelers across the plains support the role of fire as important in creating and maintaining the prairie. Plains historians have debated the origin of fire for a very long time; Carl Sauer and Omer Stewart most effectively articulated the role of anthropogenic fires in the maintenance of a healthy grassland.[5] The climatic regime of the northwest plains, with its cold snowy winters and hot dry summers, favored the growth of fescue grass that would provide ample fuel for natural and anthropogenic fires. The most important uses of fire on the upland prairie near the Rocky Mountains involved the manipulation of bison herd movements and the renewal of nutritious grasses (especially around fall and winter hunting areas) so that the pregnant cows would remain in areas of fresh spring growth until they had calved.[6] Given the extent of fire use by historic bison hunters, one would expect that this practice originated far into the past.

There are a number of regions in North America (e.g., the Southwest) where anthropogenic fires have been recorded and dated through dendrochronology; unfortunately, the archaeology of ancient anthropogenic fires is still in its infancy.[7] When scholars indeed acknowledge prehistoric fires as intentional, explanations most often lean toward signaling, agriculture, settlement abandonment, and acts of war. Far less common are discussions of anthropogenic fires in the context of premeditated landscape and resource management in the past with the intention of obtaining specific future results; this gap is likely the result of methodological challenges in identifying ancient fires in certain contexts.

Modern pyro-archaeological studies have focused on various ecosystems (e.g., the Pacific Northwest, California, Southwest, and Southeast).[8] Prehistoric fires in grassland ecosystems, however, have received the least attention, even though fire is an essential component in grassland renewal. Through the analysis of grass phytoliths preserved in a sequence of buried soil horizons in the Lauder Sandhills in southwestern Manitoba, Canada, Matthew Boyd demonstrated that, as early as 2,400 radiocarbon years ago, hunter-gatherers deliberately burned the prairie.[9] In this pioneering study, he concluded that fire may have been used to make bison-herd movements more predictable and may have enabled higher human carrying capacities.

Boyd's study has huge implications for reconstructing how bison hunters in the past developed an understanding of the delayed effects of their immediate actions, which in turn allowed them to plan for the future. Beginning two thousand years ago, bison hunters developed architectural features for mass-harvesting bison and, a few centuries later, they adopted the bow-and-arrow technology. The combination of fire, permanent architecture, efficient hunting weapons, and millenary ecological knowledge created a snowball effect as indicated by exponential population growth and aggregation near large-scale communal hunting facilities during the last millennium.[10]

In this chapter we present the results of a pyro-archaeological study aimed at identifying evidence of intentional fire use by Late Prehistoric bison hunters (Old Women's Phase) who were the immediate ancestors of the historic Blackfoot. The ultimate objective of this study is to demonstrate how bison hunters incorporated fire into their annual calendar to promote grassland growth in bison milling areas in order to attract herds near their encampments at critical times of the year. First, we summarize historical evidence of fire uses by the Blackfoot. Then, we introduce the archaeology of Old Women's Phase bison hunting along the Two Medicine River, Montana. Third, we present and discuss the results of the pyro-archaeology component in the Kutoyis Archaeological Project. We conclude that the natural and cultural impacts of certain historical-ecological trends in the Great Plains, such as anthropogenic fires, are best understood and explained by applying a long-term perspective.

Fire among the Blackfoot

At the time of first indirect European contact (ca. 1730), the Blackfoot were specialized bison hunters whose territory extended from the North Saskatchewan River in Alberta to the northern shore of Yellowstone Lake in Montana, and from the Rocky Mountain

Front to the Great Sandhills in western Saskatchewan.[11] Late Prehistoric bison kill sites associated with the Blackfoot's immediate ancestors encompassed large areas of upland prairie where they built rock-lined funnels that connected bison milling areas to a steep bluff overlooking a river valley or to a wooden corral or "pound." Major drainages trended northeast from their source; these drainages had areas of broad valley floors lined with cottonwood and aspen forests as well as diverse understory vegetation. Bison "jumps" or kill sites associated with steep landforms were common along the upper and middle river valleys, whereas bison pounds were situated in gentler terrain toward the eastern part of their territory.

Defensible boundaries in the Blackfoot territory were first recorded by Henry Kelsey in 1691. He traversed central Saskatchewan and noted that the tribes inhabiting this region (Crees, Assiniboines, and Gros Ventres) recognized a boundary with the Blackfoot and knew that it was not to be crossed without consequence.[12] This is technically a prehistoric boundary as the horse did not arrive into the northern plains until 1730. As George Colpitts notes, by the early 1800s both the Blackfoot and their neighbors had resorted to keep burning the prairie along this boundary to deter intrusions and create a no-man's-land.[13]

One of the earliest fires recorded in Blackfoot country was deemed accidental by Hudson's Bay trader Peter Fidler, who saw a grass fire near the present town of Calgary in January 1792.[14] It was later noted that the Indians "deliberately started fires for ceremonial, superstitious, and other reasons, for example, as an offering for fair weather or the return of a war party. Fire was also used for war, signalling, hunting, and controlling the movement of wildlife."[15] Most eyewitness accounts of the Blackfoot use of fire are associated with territorial defense and warfare. The Blackfoot were noted for using fire to surround a hiding enemy party, as observed by Osbourne Russell in 1835: "They commenced setting fire to the dry grass and rubbish with which we were surrounded . . . in a few moments the fire was converted into one circle of flame and smoke which united over our heads."[16] Warren

Ferris also noted, in his trip to Big Hole Valley, Montana, in 1831 that the Blackfoot set fire signals at first sight of an approaching party. "We were now on the borders of the Blackfoot country and had frequently seen traces of small parties, who it was reasonably inferred might be collected by smoke, which is their accustomed rallying signal. . . . Clouds of smoke were observed on the following day curling up from the summit of a mountain."[17] In his trek across Montana in 1859, John Mullan further observed trails that had been cleared by fire in the Big Hole Valley.[18]

Only vague notes were made in the historical period about the Blackfoot burning the prairie for reasons beyond signaling, trade competition, and war. Yet contemporary Blackfoot people uphold traditions of prairie fires (see figure 4). Kainai (Blood) elder Andy Blackwater, for instance, noted that fire was held in great respect because of its power.[19] People used fire to clear undesirable brush and forest stands, to make room for useful plants, and to promote new grass growth in bison wintering areas. As well, fire was an essential tool in bison drives. Bison runners or scouts, often camouflaged in bison or wolf skins, would carefully observe the position of a herd relative to the intended jump or pound site. A small fire was lit behind the herd so that when the herd became aware of the fire they would naturally enter the stone-lined funnel and run toward the fall. Hunters would line along the funnel to push the bison forward and discourage escape. This aspect of the bison drive was imbued with spiritualism and ceremony, as were all other aspects of the relationship between bison and the Blackfoot.

It is important to note that, for the Blackfoot and many other Plains groups, bison hunting was not only a subsistence and trade economy; bison, in fact were (and continue to be) at the center of their spiritual and practical worlds. Fire, from this perspective, would have allowed the renewal of the prairie and, in turn, the renewal of the bison herds—a form of reciprocity for all the gifts bison gave to the Blackfoot people.

At a Kainai (Blood) encampment that Prince Maximilian de Wied visited in 1832, he observed that the act of setting fire for the bison drive was ritually reenacted during the Okan (Medicine

FIG. 4. Blackfoot chiefs demonstrate to photographer Harry Pollard how to set a prairie fire (1903). Provincial Archives of Alberta, P 467.

Lodge Ceremony) or Blackfoot Sun Dance. At the culmination of the four-day dance the Motoki or Buffalo Women Society came out of their lodge dancing as buffalo cows while the attending crowd stood in driving funnel formation in front of their lodge.[20] The Motoki lodge is a ceremonial representation of the bison piskun or corral.[21]

Given the prevalence and religious significance of the interaction between bison hunting and fire, it is reasonable to expect that prairie-burning activities left recoverable remains in the archaeological record. The Kutoyis Archaeological Project (KAP), which focuses on landscape-scale Late Prehistoric bison hunting organization in the Blackfeet Indian Reservation, Montana, has proven to be the ideal locale to ascertain this ancient interaction.

Bison Hunting on the Two Medicine River, Montana

Until Native Americans adopted the horse and amassed large enough herds to make mounted hunting a profitable enterprise, all communal hunting was done on foot. Europeans who first entered the northwestern plains toward the end of the eighteenth century were struck by the scale of pedestrian bison-hunting ventures among the Blackfoot. Working mainly as traders for the Hudson's Bay Company or the North West Company, these Europeans described in some detail the layout and construction of bison "parks" and the tactics of hunters who drove the bison by pushing herds into the parks and killing them with bows and arrows, axes, clubs, spears, and any other powerful weapon they could muster.

Eyewitness accounts of bison hunting during the Early Contact Period referred, for the most part, to facilities and events taking place in the periphery of the Blackfoot aboriginal territory. With very few exceptions (e.g., Peter Fidler's 1792–93 winter expedition to the foothills of southern Alberta), the fierce Blackfoot did not wish to have traders and fur trappers in their heartland and, therefore, the specific construction and topographic layout of Blackfoot hunting complexes located near the Rocky Mountains were largely unknown to Europeans.[22] Traders never failed to note fires burning, even through winter. However, the use of fire to manage bison and grassland was rarely, if at all, noted by these outsiders.

The glacial till–covered Rocky Mountain foothills provided hunters with unlimited amounts of stone to build permanent bison drives, lodge foundations, effigies, monuments, and so on.[23] As well, the foothills furnished ideal topographic features to build the jumps. Peter Fidler (1792, December 27–29) witnessed the pedestrian bison drives along the Alberta foothills; he noted that the Peigan hunters had built one or more connected pounds or corrals (known in Blackfoot as piskuns or "deep blood kettles") under a bluff or cliff.[24] They killed large numbers of bison by stampeding them until they fell stumbling into the pound.

European observers also took important note of the knowledge and skill possessed by the hunters. Wind, weather, season, ecology, topography, and astronomy all came into place when attempting to sight and attract a bison herd into the jump. This knowledge was passed down through generations, along with the rituals and "medicines" necessary to hunt successfully.[25] Prescribed fire was a critical component of their ecological knowledge. To take advantage of the foothills topography, the Blackfoot ancestors painstakingly built rock-lined funnels connecting bison milling areas and a potential kill site. Sometimes these funnels connected milling areas to water bodies, so that the hunters would be able to move a herd from one drainage to the next. The result was an intricate network of drivelines that crisscrossed the upland prairie strategically, to bring bison to their death. Yet another important piece of knowledge was the fat content of bison males and females at different times of the year. Hunters aimed at obtaining the greatest amount of fat and therefore targeted different sectors of the herd depending on the season.[26] Intricate drivelines helped hunters split the herd for this specific purpose.

The ideal jumps were located above broad valleys where the floodplain was wide enough to provide enough room for a processing camp. Proximity to water and fuel were also critical for processing large amounts of meat; communal hunts could yield thousands of pounds of meat. Hunters used jumps in the cold months of the year, which helped preserve fresh meat until it was dried and turned into pemmican. Pemmican was nutritious, lightweight, and could be stored for long periods of time.[27] Bison tongues, a sacred food, were dried for use in ceremonies and particularly in the summer Okan.[28] Jumps were rarely used in the late spring or summer, when only pounds or parks were built from wood to hunt for immediate consumption.

The central Two Medicine River Valley, with its lofty bluffs and broad valley floor, offered the ideal conditions for building multiple bison drives. As early as the 1890s Walter McClintock visited the Two Medicine River jumps in the company of Blackfoot bison runners.[29] They explained to McClintock that the construction of multiple jumps was strategic; it allowed hunters to drive herds in a certain direction depending on weather conditions and to change plans if these conditions changed. They also told him that the driving and jumping enterprise, along with processing, was a band-wide affair that necessitated all able hands. Wintering encampments of each band were also interspersed along the central valley in close proximity to the jumps.

Blackfoot Pyro-Technology

The KAP aimed at reconstructing the spatial organization of communal bison hunting dating to the Late Prehistoric through Protohistoric periods (1,000–250 cal BP) from a perspective that highlights architectural investment on bison-driving facilities along the Two Medicine River.[30] (See figure 5.) Zedeño and colleagues gathered information discussed here during a multiyear archaeological project, which focused on the geography of extractive localities illustrative of the bison-hunting complex of the ancestral Blackfoot (Old Women's Phase). A survey conducted by Thomas Kehoe in the 1950s revealed the existence of five driveline/jump clusters located on both banks of the river.[31] These clusters extended along the central and lower valleys. Since then, the fourth cluster has been destroyed by agriculture and the fifth cluster is only partially preserved. Nevertheless, we relocated ten jumps and mapped the corresponding drivelines and encampments. In total, we recorded twenty-six thousand stone features of which twenty-four thousand are part of the hunting complexes.

To assess the role of fire on Blackfoot land use and its relationship to the ecology of shortgrass prairies of the Rocky Mountain foothills, we used a spatially explicit geoarchaeological approach. Specifically, we used stratified records of fire and postfire erosion from terrestrial sediments near archaeologically documented driveline and bison jump complexes. We cleared, described, and continuously sampled alluvial sediments from two small fan terraces in the Spring Coulee tributary of the Two Medicine River (KAP 2 and KAP 3). Spring Coulee drains an area that includes the catchment basin for the driveline complex associated with the Two Med-

FIG. 5. Stranglewolf bison jump viewed from Magee bison jump, Two Medicine River, Montana. Photo by M. N. Zedeño.

icine/Schultz bison jump.[32] These stratigraphic sequences included interbedded overbank flooding deposits and colluvial deposits, with young soils overprinted on some deposits, especially at KAP 3.

We also partially cleared, described, and discontinuously sampled a thick sequence of colluvial deposits adjacent to the Stranglewolf bison jump and driveline complex (KAP 4). This fan collects sediments from a small drainage that overlaps the driveline basin. Both KAP 2 and KAP 4 contain discrete, fine-grained beds that are rich in charcoal and interbedded with colluvial (KAP 4) and fine-grained alluvial (KAP 2) deposits. To determine the age of these fire-derived deposits, we radiocarbon-dated aggregated fine charcoal from charcoal rich deposits at KAP 2 and 4, and non-fire-related deposits and soils at KAP 2, 3, and 4. Both the Two Medicine/Schultz and Stranglewolf bison jump sites have been radiocarbon-dated to the fifteenth and sixteenth centuries cal BP, although older deposits at both jump sites may not have been exposed in limited test excavations.[33] Radiocarbon dates from the Kutoyis jump site

FIG. 6. Spring Coulee bank profile, showing several burning episodes. Two Medicine River, Montana. Photo by Christopher Roos.

indicate that peak use may have occurred during the fourteenth, fifteenth, and early sixteenth centuries, but that earlier uses date to the twelfth and thirteenth centuries.

Interpretation

Radiocarbon dating was complicated by the fact that the source material for alluvial and colluvial deposits included glacial till that also contained charcoal; in this case the charcoal was from prior to the Last Glacial Maxima (ca. 26,000–18,000 years ago). This meant that many dates on aggregated charcoal were artificially too old because they included some of this ancient charcoal inherited from the glacial till. Therefore, we excluded dates in the sequence that are older than dates from deposits stratigraphically below them in our analysis.

For our oldest locality (KAP 3), all three radiocarbon dates are in stratigraphic order spanning the last 10,000 years. All three of these are from soils and not clearly from postfire deposits. At

KAP 2 eight of the twelve dates are in stratigraphic order. A basal date is Terminal Pleistocene in age and may date the basal colluvium; this could also be impacted by inherited ancient charcoal, as a second date from this unit was beyond the measurement limit for radiocarbon (>49,000 years ago). Five of the eight dates are on discrete charcoal beds. The remaining samples bookend the fire dates but are from non-fire-related deposits. At KAP 4 inherited charcoal was a more significant problem. Nonetheless, eight of twenty-eight dates are in stratigraphic order over the last 1,000 years, with two dates on basal alluvial deposits that are Terminal Pleistocene in age. Two charcoal beds from the stratigraphic sequence were undated, whereas five were directly dated. Three non-fire-related deposits were dated to bookend the sequence of charcoal-rich deposits.

Radiocarbon dates that are in stratigraphic order were calibrated using Bayesian algorithms in BCal.[34] In this way, we could use the stratigraphic order of the dated deposits to generate informed posterior probability distribution functions. This approach allowed us to estimate with 95 percent of statistical confidence the age of charcoal-rich deposits that were not directly dated.

Results

Charcoal-rich deposits at both KAP 2 and 4 indicate that peak fire activity occurred between roughly 750 and 350 cal BP, with evidence for postfire erosion extending to ca. 950 cal BP. These dates overlap with local radiocarbon-dated use of the Two Medicine/Schultz and Stranglewolf jump sites as well as dates from other jumps and campsites.[35] Furthermore, the non-fire-related dates on either side of the charcoal sequence and the lack of charcoal-rich beds at KAP 3 suggest that this period of fire and postfire erosion may have been unique in the entire Holocene.[36] It is important to note that there is no climatic reason to think that this pattern of burning should have changed in the seventeenth century; in fact, higher fuel production correlated to grassland expansion in moist conditions likely spanned the Medieval Warm Period (ca. 950–650 BP) as well as the Little Ice Age (ca. 750–140 BP). Fescue grasslands of the northwestern plains are fuel limited and require greater levels of moisture to produce abundant and continuous fuels in order to carry fires. Episodic decadal wet periods are equally abundant during 750–350 BP and thereafter. This observation further corroborates the inference that the period of enhanced fire activity between 750 and 350 cal BP was associated with the active use and maintenance of the driveline complex for intensive bison hunting.

Old Women's Phase bison kill sites on the Two Medicine River and vicinity generally exhibit two fire signals: one associated with the burning of the fresh bone bed, which results in patchy hot fires that turn the soil into brick, and another associated with heat features in the associated processing camp. Anthropogenic fires analyzed by the authors present yet a third, nonrandom, and very distinctive fire signal—it appears stratigraphically as episodic charcoal-rich deposits interbedded with noncharcoal deposits. This signal differs from natural wildfires in that it is directly associated with bison kill and processing sites. Likewise, radiocarbon age ranges for both sites and nonrandom fires match the beginning and end of human use of kill sites as well as the beginning and end of grassland burning practices. The analysis of burning sequences further indicates that hunters were burning the grassland near bison jumps in alternate patterns, so that some jumps were available for grazing and mass-harvesting while others were recovering from a recent patch-burning episode.[37]

There are two primary ways by which anthropogenic burning may have been used by ancestral Blackfoot hunters. One mechanism would have been to use fire to drive bison herds toward the jump. Alternatively, fire could have been used as a mechanism to manipulate the location of herds to attract them toward particular driveline complexes or to render other areas less attractive. Gerald Oetelaar favors the latter, which is in keeping with a growing literature on pyric herbivory.[38] Bison prefer recently burned patches of forage, so selective patch burning attracts bison to particular areas where they may more easily be manipulated into a particular drive lane. Alternatively, freshly burned areas that have not yet regenerated are unsuitable for forage and may repel bison from particular areas where they are not wanted. Based on the radiocarbon-dated charcoal stratigraphy alone, we cannot adjudicate between the fire-drive or pyric herbivory explanations. Nor are they entirely mutually exclusive. However, our sampling localities most closely correspond to fire-improved grazing areas than to driving initiation areas that are much farther away from the jump, often more than four thousand meters. Therefore, we tend to agree with Oetelaar that a pyric herbivory model for fire lighting during peak driveline use is most likely. In this sense, we can clearly think about Blackfoot hunters as ecosystem engineers in the fescue prairie province who possessed the particular technology associated with construction, use, and fire-optimization of driveline complexes.

The patch burning that would have been necessary to manipulate forage in this approach would have had impacts beyond the suitability and desirability of forage for bison. Patch heterogeneity created by this strategy would have had impacts on habitat suitability for small mammals, birds, as well as for botanical diversity in the grasslands. The decline in this patch-burning strategy, as seen in the cessation of the charcoal-rich deposits at KAP 2 and KAP 4 by 350 cal BP, is consistent with the temporary retreat of the Blackfoot to the north and, later on, their transition from pedestrian to equestrian bison hunting. We know from historical and ethnographic records that fire use, including pyric herbivory patch burning, persisted into the equestrian period.[39] However, the stratigraphic and ethnohistoric records suggest that it did not continue in the same kill localities as in the preceding centuries, although it certainly was ubiquitous around late-fall kill sites to the north, specifically on the Upper Oldman River in Alberta, Canada, as observed by Peter Fidler in 1792. Historic anthropogenic fire signals and their purpose may prove far more difficult to sort out than prehistoric ones, given the extent of fire use as a weapon in areas traditionally used for bison hunting by the Siksika and Kainai divisions of the Blackfoot Confederacy. Finally, the extensive growth of Blackfoot horse herds, combined with new bison-hide trade opportunities beginning in 1830, conspired to terminate the ecosystem engineering practices of the ancestors.[40]

Our records also suggest that the archaeological landscapes characterized by driveline complexes and bison jumps in the northwestern plains may have also been characterized by pyrogenic heterogeneity and biodiversity, even as economic inferences have emphasized the importance of bison. In fact, many of the ecological consequences of patch burning beyond hunting may not have had clear economic impacts for Blackfoot hunters. Nevertheless, in these landscapes the Blackfoot were key ecosystem engineers through their manipulation of fescue grasslands through patch burning to enhance their hunting productivity.

Conclusion

The antiquity of fire practices in the northwestern plains (2,400 years) is a testament to the unique relationship that bison hunters had with their prey and their environment. Early in the development of specialized bison hunting, fire was implemented as a tool for gaining control over the movement of bison and, as a consequence, increase the human carrying capacity of northern grasslands. The findings from our pyro-archaeology study reveal a direct correlation between human intensive communal hunting during the last millennium and prairie fires. Furthermore, geoarchaeology indicates that postfire erosion began and stopped in tandem with the construction and decommissioning of vast hunting complexes located along the Two Medicine River Valley, respectively. When combined with extensive evidence of meat processing for storage at the Kutoyis processing site, the record of anthropogenic fires in the valley's hunting complexes is further evidence of the ancestral Blackfoot's ability to transform their landscape in order to bond with their keystone species and plan for the future. As noted by Zedeño and colleagues, planning, which involves not only the development of a calendar but also the adoption of institutions of social control, in turn indicates that the ancestral Blackfoot society operated within a higher degree of organizational complexity than previously thought.

In sum, precontact fire use among northwest plains bison hunters constitutes an example of the combined effect of human agency and technological acumen on the manipulation of prairie ecology that led to great prosperity among these mobile people—prosperity that ended only with the demise of bison.

Notes

1. Daniel B. Botkin, *Discordant Harmonies: A New Ecology for the Twenty-First Century* (New York: Oxford University Press, 1990), 169.

2. Gerald W. Williams, "References on the American Indian Use of Fire in Ecosystems" (Washington DC: USDA Forest Service, 2005), 1.

3. Henry T. Lewis, "Patterns of Indian Burning in California: Ecology and Ethnohistory," in *Before the Wilderness: Environmental Management by Native Californians*, ed. Thomas C. Blackburn and Kat Anderson (Menlo Park CA: Ballena, 1973), 55–116; Williams, "References," 3; Robert T. Boyd, ed., *Indians, Fire, and the Land* (Corvallis: Oregon State University Press, 1999); George Colpitts, *Pemmican Empire* (Cambridge: Cambridge University Press, 2015); Stephen J. Pyne, *Fire in America: A Cultural History of Wildland and Rural Fire* (Princeton NJ: Princeton University Press, 1982); Thomas R. Vale, ed., *Fire, Native Peoples, and the Natural Landscape* (Washington DC: Island Press, 2002); Gordon G. Whitney, *From Coastal Wilderness to Fruited Plain: A History of Environmental Change in Temperate North America 1500 to the Present* (New York: Cambridge University Press, 1994).

4. Theodore Binnema, "Presettlement Rangeland Management on the Northern Plains," *Rangelands* 18, no. 6 (December 1996): 217–18.

5. Carl Sauer, "The Agency of Man on Earth," in *Man's Role in Changing the Face of the Earth*, ed. W. L. Thomas (Chicago: University of Chicago Press, 1956), 49–69; Omer Stewart, "Burning and Natural Vegetation in the United States," *Geographical Review* 41, no. 2 (April 1951): 317–20.

6. George W. Arthur, *An Introduction to the Ecology of Early Historic Communal Bison Hunting among the Northern Plains Indians* (Ottawa: University of Ottawa Press), 1975.

7. Stephen Nash, *Time, Trees, and Prehistory: Tree-Ring Dating and the Development of North American Archaeology, 1914–1950* (Salt Lake City: University of Utah Press, 1999).

8. Matthew Boyd, "Identification of Anthropogenic Burning in the Paleoecological Record of the Northern Prairies: A New Approach," *Annals of the Association of American Geographers* 92 (September 2002): 471–87; W. M. Denevan, "The Pristine Myth: The Landscape of the Americas in 1492," *Annals of the Association of American Geographers* 82, no. 3 (September 1992): 369–85; Christopher Roos, "Western Apache Pyrogenic Placemaking in the Mountains of Eastern Arizona," in *Engineering Mountain Landscapes: An Anthropology of Social Investment*, ed. Laura Scheiber and María Nieves Zedeño (Salt Lake City: University of Utah Press, 2015), 116–30.

9. Boyd, "Identification."

10. María Nieves Zedeño, Jesse A. M. Ballenger, and John R. Murray, "Landscape Engineering and Organizational Complexity among Late Prehistoric Bison Hunters of the Northwestern Plains," *Current Anthropology* 55 (February 2014): 23–58.

11. John C. Jackson, *The Piikani Blackfeet: A Culture under Siege* (Missoula MT: Mountain Press, 2000).

12. Charles N. Bell, *The Journal of Henry Kelsey: 1691–1692* [. . .]. Winnipeg: Dawson Richardson, 1928.

13. Colpitts, *Pemmican Empire*, 133.

14. Peter Fidler, "Journal of a Journey Overland from Buckingham House to the Rocky Mountains in 1792–1793." Typescript of Unpublished Journal, 1792–93, J. G. MacGregor Collection, Provincial Archives of Alberta, Edmonton; Bruce Haig, ed., *A Look at Peter Fidler's Journal* (Lethbridge: Historical Research Centre, 1990).

15. J. G. Nelson and R. E. England, "Some Comments on the Causes and Effects of Fire in the Northern Grasslands Areas of Canada and the Nearby United States, 1750–1900," *Canadian Geographer* 15, no. 4 (December 1971): 295–306, 297.

16. Aubrey L. Haines, *Osborne Russell's Journal of a Trapper* (Lincoln: University of Nebraska Press, 1965).

17. Paul C. Phillips, ed., *Life in the Rocky Mountains* (Denver: Old West, 1940).

18. John Mullan, *Report of Lieutenant Mullan, in Charge of the Construction of the Military Road from Fort Benton to Fort Walla Walla*. 36th Cong., 2nd Sess. (1861), House Executive Document, 44, 37.

19. Andy Blackwater, personal communication, 2017.

20. Stephen S. Witte, Marsha V. Gallagher, and William J. Orr, eds., *The North American Journals of Prince Maximilian of Wied: Volume 2, April–September 1833* (Norman: University of Oklahoma Press, 2008), 349.

21. John C. Ewers, *The Blackfeet: Raiders of the Northwestern Plains* (Norman: University of Oklahoma Press, 1958).

22. Fidler, "Journal of a Journey," 1792–93; Haig, *A Look at Peter*.

23. Ewers, *The Blackfeet*; George Bird Grinnell, *Blackfoot Lodge Tales* (Lincoln: University of Nebraska Press, 1962). Thomas F. Kehoe, "Stone Tipi Rings in North-Central Montana and the Adjacent Portion of Alberta, Canada," *Bureau of American Ethnology Bulletin* 173 (1960): 421–73; Thomas F. Kehoe, "The Boarding School Bison Drive Site," *Plains Anthropologist* 12, no. 35 (February 1967): 1–165; Claude E. Schaeffer, "The Bison Drive of the Blackfeet Indians," *Plains Anthropologist* 23, no. 82, pt. 2 (November 1978): 243–48.

24. Fidler, "Journal of a Journey," December 27–29.

25. Russel Lawrence Barsh and Chantelle Marlor, "Driving Bison and Blackfoot Science," *Human Ecology* 31, no. 4 (2003): 571–93.

26. James W. Brink, "A Hunter's Quest for Fat Bison," in *Bison and People on the North American Great Plains*, ed. G. Cunfer and B. Waiser (College Station: Texas A&M University Press, 2016), 90–121.

27. Brandi Bethke, María Nieves Zedeño, Geoffrey Jones, and Matthew Pailes, "Complementary Approaches to the Identification of Bison Processing for Storage at the Kutoyis Complex, Montana," *Journal of Archaeological Science: Reports* 17 (February 2018): 879-94, http://dx.doi.org/10.1016/j.jasrep.2016.05.028; Colpitts, *Pemmican Empire*.

28. Allan Pard, personal communication, 2013.

29. Grinnell, *Blackfoot Lodge Tales*.

30. Calendar years before present. Zedeño, Ballenger, and Murray, "Landscape Engineering."

31. Kehoe, "Boarding School."

32. C. I. Roos, M. N. Zedeño, K. L. Hollenback, and M. M. H. Erlick, "Indigenous Impacts on North American Great Plains Fire Regimes of the Past Millennium," *PNAS* 115, no. 32 (2018): 8143-48, figure 1.

33. The term "cal BP" will refer to "calendar years before present" throughout this chapter.

34. Caitlin E. Buck, J. Andrés Christen, and Gary N. James, "BCal: An Online Bayesian Radiocarbon Calibration Tool," *Internet Archaeology* 7, 1999, https://doi.org/10.11141/ia.7.1.

35. Zedeño, Ballenger, and Murray, "Landscape Engineering," tables 1 and 2.

36. Roos, Zedeño, Hollenback, and Erlick, "Indigenous Impacts," figure 3.

37. Roos, Zedeño, Hollenback, and Erlick, "Indigenous Impacts," figure 3.

38. Gerald A. Oetelaar, "Better Homes and Pastures: Human Agency and the Construction of Place in Communal Bison Hunting on the Northern Plains," *Plains Anthropologist* 59, no. 229 (2014): 9-37, https://doi.org/10.1179/2052546X13Y.0000000004; B. W. Allred, S. D. Fuhlendorf, D. M. Engle, and R. D. Elmore, "Ungulate Preference for Burned Patches Reveals Strength of Fire: Grazing Interaction," *Ecology and Evolution* 1, no. 2 (October 2011): 132-44, https://onlinelibrary.wiley.com/doi/pdf/10.1002/ece3.12; David M. J. S. Bowman, George L. W. Perry, Steve I. Higgins, Chris N. Johnson, Samuel D. Fuhlendorf, and Brett P. Murphy, "Pyrodiversity and Biodiversity Are Coupled Because Fire Is Embedded in Food-Webs," *Philosophical Transactions of the Royal Society B: Biological Sciences* 371, no. 1696 (2016), https://doi.org/10.1098/rstb.2015.0169; Samuel D. Fuhlendorf, David M. Engle, Jay A. Y. Kerby, and Robert Hamilton, "Pyric Herbivory: Rewilding Landscapes through the Recoupling of Fire and Grazing," *Conservation Biology* 23, no. 3 (June 2009): 588-98, https://doi.org/10.1111/j.1523-1739.2008.01139.x.

39. Oetelaar, "Better Homes."

40. C. I. Roos, M. N. Zedeño, K. L. Hollenback, and B. Bethke, "Pox, Pistols, and Ponies: Indigenous Fire Regime and Bison Hunting Change after 'Contact'" (paper presented at the 76th Annual Plains Anthropological Conference, San Antonio TX, October 27, 2018).

4

To Know the Story behind It

Indigenous Heritage and Buffalo Hunting on the Northern Plains

GENEVIÈVE SUSEMIHL

For thousands of years the environment of the Great Plains has been shaped by people's ingenuity and creativity. While humans adapted to the ecology of the plains through communal activities and technologies, they formed cultural relationships with their environment.[1] Hunting activities especially influenced people's social conditions and cultural values throughout millennia. In order to feed their people, the Plains hunters engaged in communal bison hunting, which not only provided critical supplies of food, but also served a number of social purposes. Applying their profound knowledge of bison behavior and biology, they developed highly sophisticated hunting methods to kill large numbers of animals, resulting in, according to archaeologist Jack Brink, "the most rewarding procurement of food ever devised by human beings."[2] Many places and landscapes on the Great Plains have become witnesses of these communal hunts and associated gatherings of the past. Having taken over a role of narrator, these heritage sites and landscapes are helping to foster an understanding for the complex relationships of people and past environments. To read and understand a site or landscape, however, people have to be able to make sense of the place and its features.[3]

Heritage sites and cultural landscapes have been shaped by many forces unique to place and time, such as natural, cultural, and historical processes and events, and legal processes of land division that imposed governmental and organizational structures on the landscape.[4] This "interrelationship between the natural givens and cultural manifestations is an axiom," however, that is not limited to a certain region or time, but has influences on the present and future of people who have been involved with the place.[5] An approach to sites and cultural landscapes is thus most valuable when it "recognizes the continuity between the past and present with people living and working on the land today."[6] The challenges are even more complex "when descendants of those who were inhabitants during the notable era are still living and have some knowledge of and interest in the landscape."[7]

Heritage is "our legacy from the past, what we live with today, and what we pass on to future generations"; it is an "irreplaceable source of life and inspiration."[8] For Indigenous people, heritage is essential to the restoration and permanence of their cultural distinctiveness. The inscription on the World Heritage list brings an increasingly global awareness of and attention to the site. Besides having a symbolically highly significant status, World Heritage informs and educates the community and the public not only about the past, but also about the present of peoples and societies and thus helps shape the future. Indigenous heritage sites—for centuries of tribal and local importance—have thus become global storytellers, and the stories they narrate and the information passed on are perceived worldwide.

The World Heritage Site of Head-Smashed-In Buffalo Jump in southern Alberta tells a story of nature and culture that immortalizes a memory. It presents complex issues as it deals "not just with a place, but with many activities that occurred on that place, several cultures that inhabited the region, as well as conflicts among those cultures."[9] The preservation and presentation of the site have been achieved through the creation of an interpretive center, framing the story of bison hunting in a historical context and within a popular Western story line. When discussing the site, a variety of narratives need to be considered, including the role of adaptation, persistence, preservation, and sustainability of Indigenous people. Examining the site of Head-Smashed-In Buffalo Jump and its interpretive center, I will look at the modes and contents of the site's storytelling. How is the story of the buffalo jump communicated to the public, and by whom? What narratives have been developed, and what has been omitted? Which community is being represented, and why? Besides reflecting on the relation between heritage and story line, I will consider the involvement of the Blackfoot as source community in the storytelling and the role of cultural heritage for them. Discussing different elements in the storyline of the site, I will argue that such aspects as ownership and community involvement have significant implications and consequences on the modes and contents of a heritage site's interpretive matrix and grand narrative, which in turn have considerable impact on Indigenous capacity building and community development.

The Site of Head-Smashed-In Buffalo Jump

The site of Head-Smashed-In Buffalo Jump is located in southwestern Alberta, about 170 kilometers south of Calgary. It is a place that tells of human imagination and shrewdness of the Indigenous people who invented and kept it alive for thousands of years, a place of memories and stories, and one of the most sacred sites within the traditional domain of the prairie people. It is also considered one of the oldest, largest, and best-preserved buffalo jumps in North America. Controlled and managed by the Government of Alberta, Head-Smashed-In Buffalo Jump (HSIBJ) had been declared a Canadian National Historic Site in 1968, a Provincial Historic Site in 1979, and—because of its extraordinary archaeological, historical, and ethnographical value, combined with its prairie setting and outstanding interpretive potential—a UNESCO World Heritage Site in 1981.[10] It is an outstanding illustration of the subsistence hunting techniques of Plains nations. Layers of bison bones buried up to eleven meters below the cliff represent nearly six thousand years of use of the buffalo jump by Indigenous people.[11] Covering 1,470 acres, the site is composed of four distinct components: the gathering basin, the V-shaped drive lanes, the cliff kill site, and the campsite and processing area. Each part has different archaeological remains associated with communal buffalo hunting, ranging from drive-lane cairns and projectile points to butchered bone and fire-broken rock. To the Blackfoot, it is one of the most important heritage sites, exemplifying the culture and society of the Plains Indians for many centuries before the European settlement of the region, representing a complex range of Indigenous identities, ideologies, and social relations.

Head-Smashed-In Buffalo Jump is one of many kill sites across North America where herds of bison were brought to their deaths. These sites can often be identified by rock cairns, bone fragments, stone tools, and artifacts from processing sites and camps that were always nearby.[12] At HSIBJ herds of bison were first driven over the cliff at least six thousand years ago—a time when no other buffalo jump in North America was being used. Later, the site was abandoned, possibly for as long as two thousand years, and historians are unsure when and why people walked away "from an ingenious trap, the tricks of which they had clearly mastered."[13] Later, about two thousand years ago, HSIBJ became "a veritable cornucopia of bison killing."[14] Indeed, according to Brink, "so rich in bones and artifacts are these more recent kill events that some have argued . . . that the great buffalo kills had evolved into 'factories,' producing bison products beyond the immediate needs of the people, products destined for trade to distant regions of North America."[15] Anthropologist and chronicler of the Plains culture George Bird Grinnell reported that even decades after the end of the buffalo hunting days, Blackfoot elders spoke "with enthusiasm of the plenty that successful drives brought to the camp."[16] There are also spiritual places nearby that relate to proper preparation and maintenance of this sacred landscape.

Reading a Place: The Significance of Stories

The site of Head-Smashed-In was named after a tragic event, the story of which has been handed down through generations of Blackfoot.[17] Once, when the buffalo were roaming the prairies and people had been living with them for time immemorial, the people were preparing a buffalo hunt at a precipice. A curious young boy, too young to join as a hunter, wanted to watch the spectacle and crawled beneath the cliff, just below where the great beasts would plunge over the edge. When he heard the thunder of the buffalo he braced himself against the rocks. The falling animals, however, hit him, and he was crushed by the weight of the buffalo piling up during the successful hunt. Only when the hunters removed the carcasses for processing did they find his body with his head smashed in.[18] To the Piikani, one of the four Blackfoot tribes, the place was only known as *piskaan* (buffalo jump), and some elders believe that the story of the boy refers to another, nearby site.

When Head-Smashed-In Buffalo Jump was named by government and museum officials, they were lectured many times by Blackfoot elders how they got the name wrong.[19] By naming the place, however, they started to develop a narrative for the place that reflected a Western, scientific approach that marginalized the Indigenous voice. The name is an essential part of the bearer's identity, and as names can be given by anyone who has the command of a language, the relationship among name, namer, and named is a complicated one involving privilege, ownership, and freedom.[20] In this sense the dynamic of "naming" becomes a primary colonizing process, because it appropriates, defines, and captures a place in language. The process of naming becomes, according to Ashcroft et al., a "step into the reality of place, not simply reflecting or representing it, but in some mysterious sense intimately involved in the process of its creation, of its 'coming into being.'"[21] As names always have a meaning, the loss or changing of names comes with a loss of identity, irritation, and struggle for belonging.

Place in that respect can be understood as a "complex interaction of language, history and environment," a "palimpsest which archaeologists can read and storytellers, historians and writers of fiction may form into chronological narratives."[22] Landscapes and places thus can be read like a historical text or a Lakota winter count.[23] In postcolonial discourse, place is characterized by a sense of displacement in those who have moved, and by a sense of "immense investment of culture in the construction of place."[24] This also means to acknowledge the presence of those who have lived there before and continue to live there, but have been marginalized and become almost invisible to the new settlers and to the visitors of a site. When the colonial map was drawn it effectively erased both the Indigenous map and the Indigenous knowledge it signified.

Indigenous people, however, relate to place and land through stories that structure the world, as the Canadian author Robert Bringhurst describes: "Stories are the first maps. . . . If we stop telling stories, . . . we won't find our way, not only because we don't have the maps that stories are for us, but because without the wisdom of these stories there won't be a world for us to live in any more."[25] We "place" ourselves "within the context of the land's story," states Jeannette Armstrong, and to the question "Kwtlakin, What is your place?"[26] her Syilx answer would not be "a specific location," but instead she would give the story of the "cultural location" that identifies her. This story, she argues, would not only be a story that relates "cultural practice identifiers" within her Syilx cultural heritage or language, but it would also be "a placement" of herself "on the 'storyscape' of the Syilx people" and thus of herself within her historical and cultural landscape.[27] For Indigenous people today the issue of land rights is of utmost importance, since the land codetermines who they are, in material and immaterial terms. When one culture, however, decides what is significant and worth protecting in the culture of another, there is always the possibility of injustice arising.

We relate to heritage the same way we relate to land—through stories. This has been acknowledged in the usage and interpretations of cultural heritage, heritage being characterized as the "contemporary use of the past."[28] While historical narratives of place and land have been dominated by white, Western male voices, excluding and marginalizing minority, ethnic, and gender groups, "postmodern interpretations of the past clearly favour plural histories over so-called 'grand narratives,'" as Smith states.[29] Heritage sites should therefore serve as places "where memories and histories meet, even collide," and interpretation of heritage might provoke reactions in its recipients which can lead to conflict and controversy among the stakeholders of the site. Questions of ownership and participation of the source community thus become central to the management of the site, where local people are an integral part, since the owner determines what and how a site is being protected and what stories are being told. Only when the local community and the people whose culture is represented are involved in the interpreting will the stories represent the respective culture. Head-Smashed-In Buffalo Jump serves well in the discussion of this aspect, as ownership, management, and community involvement play significant roles in the storytelling of the site.

Indigenous Buffalo Hunting on the Northern Plains

For tens of thousands of years, the American bison (commonly known as buffalo; *Iinnii* in the language of the Blackfoot) shaped the North American prairie ecosystem and linked Native peoples to the land. Acting as bioengineers, bison affected plant communities, transported and recycled nutrients, created habitat variability that benefited grassland birds, insects, and small mammals, and provided abundant food resources not only for species such as grizzly bears and wolves, but especially for the people living in the plains.[30] For them buffalo hunting was the primary subsistence activity, and their nomadic life was a consequence of their need to secure success in hunting. Since they completely relied on the buffalo, the Plains tribes developed highly efficient hunting techniques to obtain their livelihood, the buffalo jump being the most sophisticated technique to capture and kill bison. The knowledge and skill required to consistently use such devices despite regular fluctuations in bison movements is impressive, and as stories assert, they most probably acquired that knowledge through an older hunting collaboration with wolves.[31]

Using their excellent knowledge of the topography and of buffalo behavior, the people killed their prey by chasing them over a precipice. The carcasses were later carved up in the camp below. To encourage the buffalo to run to the desired point of the cliff, the hunters built drive lanes of piles of rocks or other materials, which converged from the jump-off point onto the plains in the direction of the gathering area. At HSIBJ these drive lanes extend more than fourteen kilometers into the gathering basin.[32] To locate and collect the bison, young men dispersed widely, urging the herd toward the drive lanes, which required several days. To start the drive, a "buffalo runner" would "entice the herd to follow him by imitating the bleating of a lost calf."[33] As the buffalo gathered near the cliff, hunters would circle the herd and alarm the animals by shouting, waving robes, and shooting arrows, thus starting a stampede that would force them over the precipice.

These hunts drove not merely dozens, but hundreds of animals, and even over one thousand buffalo were reportedly killed.[34] Depending on the quantity of meat, the distance to the camp, and means of transportation, sometimes all the meat was used, and at other times the Indians butchered the buffalo "lightly," taking tongues and humps only, or obtaining a few and leaving hundreds to rot where they fell.[35] Knowledge about strategies and tactics, weapons, weather conditions, the use of fire as an essential tool in bison drives as well as the necessary rituals and ceremonies that ensured a successful hunt were passed down through generations, as María Zedeño et al. note.[36]

Communal hunts were of great importance not only to the subsistence of the Plains Indians, but also to their safety and their social and cultural life. The kill brought a surplus of meat to families and clans participating in the hunt. They would dry the meat, make pemmican, extract fat from the bones, make tools, and tan hides, and almost every part of the animal was used.[37] Aside from providing essential supplies of food, successful communal hunting served a number of social purposes in Plains culture. It enabled the people to live together in large bands, which rendered them "less vulnerable to their enemies, and also facilitated the maintenance of tribal cultural traditions."[38] Many groups came together to work cooperatively to make these kills possible. The hunt was also an exciting event where families and friends were reunited, marriages arranged, stories and experiences shared, trade goods exchanged, business conducted, ceremonies held, songs sung, prayers offered, and which was preceded by prehunt rituals and concluded with feasting and celebrations that sometimes lasted several days.[39]

The drives were not always successful, though. Often the buffalo broke away through the drive lanes. The Plains people, however, were eager not to let any buffalo escape. They believed that bison possessed many of the same attributes as people, and that they thus "were aware of the world around them, perceived the behaviour of humans, and recognized patterns of actions and their consequences."[40] Animals that escaped the fall had seen that they had been tricked and would help other buffalo avoid the trap.[41] Plains hunters thus "tried to kill all the animals ... because they had to ensure their own future and that of the generations to come, and ensure that bison would continue to be successfully tricked into stampeding to the brink of a cliff. It was not an option, not a decision of conservation or waste; it was the crux of survival," argues Brink.[42] Also, wounded and disoriented animals posed a serious danger to the people at the site, which had to be eliminated.

Sacred Skulls and Killing Cliffs: Story Lines and Narratives at Head-Smashed-In

Depicting and interpreting the ecology, mythology, lifestyle, and technology of buffalo hunting and of the Blackfoot people within the context of archaeological evidence, a state-of-the-art interpretive center was built in 1987. While most visitors explore the exhibitions on their own, a guided facility tour leads through the center, the theater, and the cliff-top trail, introducing Blackfoot culture and history and the mechanics of the buffalo jump. Blackfoot interpreters guide the tour and offer information. In addition to the exhibitions, the ten-minute documentary film *In Search of the Buffalo*, which features a reenactment of a buffalo drive and related activities set one thousand years ago, is shown at the theater. For children and students specific educational programs are provided.

The tour and film frame the interpretation in the past, and the only reference to contemporary Blackfoot culture is presented in the small exhibition *Lost Identities—A Journey of Rediscovery*, picturing Blackfoot people of different communities today, and by the presence of Blackfoot staff, who work as guides and in the gift shop. Furthermore, the exhibits on five levels are for the most part narrated by "an authorized Western scientific voice, reflecting the status of the real-life author of the text panels," i.e., the curator and archaeologist Jack Brink. Blackfoot voice, on the other hand, appears in a transitory and impermanent way as words made of light projected onto rocks. This presentation of knowledge in an authoritative and permanent mode versus a momentary and light mode implies to the readers that archaeologists provide the facts, whereas the Blackfoot deliver the stories.[43]

The signature display in the interpretive center is a replica of the killing cliff with buffalo perched at the top and a model of an archaeological dig at the bottom. The buffalo of the display are leisurely standing at the top and grazing, but not running in a deathly pursuit. No animal actually falls over the cliff, and the tourists don't have to react to a scene at which a whole herd is stacked at the bottom of the cliff, which makes the bison jump "'safe' for popular consumption."[44] This presentation, according to Dorst, "aestheticizes the practice of driving bison over a cliff," as it is not a representation of "real" bison falling, "but a romanticized, visually arresting image of such an event," which "helps to locate the practice in the remote, imagined past of primitive cultures."[45]

The details of this rhetoric reveal a dominating discourse that runs throughout the interpretive program of the center. According to *American History Illustrated*, Head-Smashed-In Buffalo Jump is "representative of the North Americans' ingenuity, of their understanding of ecological balances, and of their economical use of the land and its bounty."[46] This rhetoric of binary standards of buffalo hunting in the plains has been used for decades, as Krech claims: "White people wasted and caused the extermination of the buffalo, whereas Indians were skilful, ecologically aware conservationists."[47] Since the opening of the center 2.75 million visitors have heard this message. Given that buffalo were of significant cultural importance for the Plains people, the animals have become "a symbol of contemporary relations to the environment,"[48] and thus have been selected for "elevation to emblematic status in our collective iconography of traditional Indian lifeways."[49] Being a

World Heritage Site and thus an institution of popular education, Head-Smashed-In participates in the production and dissemination of this icon and the narratives, images, and binary constructions "that constitute the unexamined conventions of a popular discourse."[50]

Other significant displays such as a painted buffalo skull and replicas of medicine bundles as well as murals have been criticized by Blackfoot elders for various reasons. The sacred buffalo skull, painted by Piikani Elder Joe Crow Shoe in 1982 and gifted to the center, has become the symbol of the site, and images of it have been used in marketing material and merchandise, which has caused disagreement among the Blackfoot, as Ian Clarke, former regional director at Alberta Culture and Tourism, explains: "We had some Native people who say that it should never be used in any images, because of spirituality. The one thing that allows us to use it, we think, is Old Joe Crow Shoe's intent in the first place."[51] As for the medicine bundles, the replica status has been questioned by community members. Medicine bundles are powerful and sacred objects and require certain rights and knowledge to be handled, gained through participation in sacred societies. The creator of the medicine bundles at HSIBJ, Joe Crow Shoe, had the right to work with bundles. The bundles shown in the center, therefore, are viewed as real bundles that have no place being on display.[52]

The use of selected knowledge is also reflected in the guided tours and educational programs. Even though the interpreters are expected to talk about traditional culture and lifestyle only, they give tours from a Blackfoot perspective, challenging the information presented by the panels and pointing out historical and current problems of the Blackfoot such as alcohol abuse and residential schools. And although general guidelines exist for the tours and programs, the Blackfoot guides approach the topics differently and present a unique personal insight into Blackfoot culture. They might also present alternative Blackfoot explanations for scientific phenomena and reveal inaccuracies in Western depictions of the buffalo hunt and lifestyle of the Blackfoot people.[53]

Setting the Stage and Using the Props: Blackfoot Involvement

The various and somewhat controversial narratives of the Blackfoot as ecologically sensitive people, stereotypical Indians, people of the past, and contemporary custodians of their cultural heritage are being communicated through interpreting the site. At Head-Smashed-In Buffalo Jump many people have entered the process to learn to read the historical text entailed in the geographical place. When officials developed the story line for the galleries, they worked together with the Piikani, whose reserve is close to the site and who played an important role in the development of the center. The government did not consult the elders of the Siksika and the Kainai, however, and thus the story line was developed without the voice of the Kainai elders, who believed that "their people had built and used the buffalo jump every bit as much as the Piikani" and who did not always agree with the stories of "their fellow traditionalists of the Piikani."[54] This conduct raises questions of who has the right to interpret another culture and hence "gain authenticity for one's case."[55]

Furthermore, the heritage site was preserved as an archaeological site in the 1950s, and the exhibitions and narratives at the site reflect that, as Clarke explains: "the World Heritage Site is because of the buffalo jump and what the buffalo jump means" and "the Native people of this country survived thousands of years by their ingenuity and their knowledge." The Blackfoot staff, however, has got a "tendency to talk about Blackfoot culture instead of going back and being grounded on these core values," which has been a constant source of consternation for the non-Indigenous management.[56]

Archaeology is a Western concept, though, containing both a record of the past and the interpretations and values that people apply to that record today. Many Indigenous people do not view archaeological artifacts or sites as things of the past, but rather as active elements of their contemporary world, and objects, places, and stories are valued as much for their "heritage" values as for "being repositories of beings and powers of importance within their worldview."[57] This has major implications for understanding the critical reactions that some Indigenous communities have to archaeology and the tensions at the site, and it also identifies the need for alternative heritage management strategies.[58]

Today, the Piikani play a major role in the operation of the site, holding the majority of jobs at the center, including those as site interpreters. Explaining and decoding their own history and culture, they often make the connections between facts and stories that are not present in the exhibitions. While the interpretive matrix developed by the historical "experts" as "the official story that goes out here," the Blackfoot guides are reading and interpreting the artifacts with their own personal background and knowledge, as head of interpretation Stan Knowlton explains: "There are reminders, other than text. . . . When I go through the building I can see bits and pieces of the story. I generally go through and fill in the blanks from the way I was taught. . . . It's almost like a stage, there are all the props here, and it's just a matter of going through and explaining what all the props mean, the deeper meaning behind them,"[59] making connections between the artifacts and stories, traditions, colonialism, and contemporary life ways.

Despite government ownership, the Blackfoot people have come to claim the site "as their own" and it has become a place of weddings, funerals, medicine bundle openings, meetings of elders, and other ceremonies that reflect the esteem in which the place is held. Participation, however, is a process that is more than making communities the beneficiaries of a tourism project. Jobs are an important benefit, but they do not replace empowerment. Although the Piikani and to some extent the Kainai have been involved with the heritage site, and their communities have gained certain cultural, spiritual, and economic benefits, there is little sociopolitical empowerment through the site for the Indigenous heirs of the ancient buffalo jump. Moreover, involvement with a government institution is a double-edged sword, as community members sometimes face serious challenges, being accused by their people of selling cultural knowledge or receiving inappropriate payment.[60]

Conclusion

Heritage sites serve as keepers of stories of diverse cultures and peoples. Cultural heritage, including archaeological and historical records, which are "part of the shared record of humanity,"[61] can be expressions of identity and sovereignty. While different groups and stakeholders attempt to gain or regain control over their own heritage, they express their tribal identity, and their narratives influence the amount of information derived from it, and thus the contents of the stories narrated by cultural heritage. While the argument has been made that cultural heritage belongs to the public and "should be used for the greater good of contributing to the knowledge of humankind," many Indigenous peoples assert that increased protection and control of cultural heritage significant to them is fundamental to the continuity, revival, and survival of their cultural identity. As heritage can be considered as an asset of economic, social, cultural, and political capacity-building, heritage sites associated with Indigenous cultures require attention to the relation between the respective Indigenous communities and the site itself.[62] This link that binds heritage and Indigenous communities is related to spiritual values, historical significance, and traditional occupations. Heritage thus holds a strong connection with identity and individual and collective memories.

Empowerment, which can be both a process and an outcome, can be seen as a social action process through which individuals, organizations, and communities gain expertise on their lives, so as to modify their social and political environment in order to improve their quality of life. It also means participation, education, and opportunities to use the acquired knowledge in a way contributive to society, thus linking "the acquisition of knowledge and skills to social needs and mobilization."[63] Indigenous empowerment, i.e., the increasing awareness of spiritual, political, social, racial, educational, gender, and economic strengths of individuals and communities, has gained importance to First Nations, and the value of community-led cultural heritage management is increasingly being explored among First Nations and the government.[64]

Heritage sites are "commonly viewed by the public as expert bodies that hold truths on cultures, heritage and the past."[65] This image, however, is "self-perpetuating" as the site "tells the story it needs to tell about the past in order to place itself as both an outcome of and a means of continuing the ongoing dynamics of self-transformation that the logic of culture promotes."[66] Heritage sites thus not only influence how a community is treated by others, but also how a community views itself. Cultures are conceptual constructs, not physical entities available for collections, and stories told about these cultures need to be polyvocal and told from different angles. These narratives shape people's perception of the heritage and of the people related to it. As powerful places of (self-) representation they play an important role in the healing processes of Indigenous communities.

Gradually, Indigenous interests and values have been taken into consideration by site managers who "progressively have come to consider Indigenous communities as authorities of their own cultural heritage and have started to cooperate with them."[67] This development reveals changing power relations between heritage sites and source communities, in which "both parties are held to be equal and which involves the sharing of skills, knowledge and power to produce something of value to both parties."[68] Sharing power, though, is neither simple nor conclusive, but a complex and unpredictable first step in building new relations between heritage sites and Indigenous communities. For Indigenous people such as the Blackfoot, a close connection with their cultural heritage means building up strength and capacity in a highly challenging and demanding postcolonial world, and their engagement in the storytelling at Head-Smashed-In Buffalo Jump is thus enriching both the community and the heritage site.

Notes

1. James Claude Malin, *The Grassland of North America: Prolegomena to Its History* (Gloucester MA: Peter Smith, 1967).

2. Geoff Cunfer, "Overview: The Decline and Fall of the Bison Empire," in *Bison and People on the North American Great Plains: A Deep Environmental History*, ed. George Cunfer and Bill Waiser (College Station: Texas A&M University Press, 2016),

1–29; Jack W. Brink, *Imagining Head-Smashed-In: Aboriginal Buffalo Hunting on the Northern Plains* (Edmonton: AU Press, 2008), 11.

3. For a discussion of space and place see, for example, Ian Convery, Gerard Corsane, and Peter Davis, eds., *Making Sense of Place: Multidisciplinary Perspectives* (Woodbridge UK: Boydell, 2012); Marcel Hunziker, Matthias Buchecker, and Terry Hartig, "Space and Place: Two Aspects of the Human-Landscape Relationship," in *A Changing World: Challenges for Landscape Research*, ed. Felix Kienast, Otto Wildi, and Sucahrita Ghosh (Dordrecht: Springer, 2007), 47–62.

4. Arnold R. Alanen and Robert Melnick, eds., *Preserving Cultural Landscapes in America* (Baltimore: Johns Hopkins University Press, 2000); Beverly A. Sandalack, "Head-Smashed-In: Some Challenges Where Site Is Museum," in *Museum & Place*, ed. Kerstin Smeds and Ann Davis (Paris: ICOFOM, 2019), 162–70.

5. Hartmut Lutz, "'To Know Where Home Is': An Introduction to Indigeneity and Immigration," in *What Is Your Place? Indigeneity and Immigration in Canada*, ed. Hartmut Lutz and Thomas Rafico Ruiz (Augsburg: Wißner, 2007), 9.

6. Nora Mitchell and Susan Buggey, "Category V Protected Landscapes in Relation to World Heritage Cultural Landscapes: Taking Advantage of Diverse Approaches," in *Landscape Conservation: An International Working Session on the Stewardship of Protected Landscapes; Proceedings of a Special Meeting of the IUCN World Commission on Protected Areas* (Woodstock VT: Conservation Study Institute, IUCN, and the World Conservation Union and QLF/Atlantic Center for the Environment, 1999), 19.

7. Mitchell and Buggey, "Category V Protected Landscapes," 163.

8. UNESCO, "World Heritage," accessed September 20, 2017, http://whc.unesco.org/en/about/.

9. There are many museums and heritage sites throughout the Great Plains that are telling the story of the Plains Nations and buffalo hunting, among them the Glenbow Museum and Blackfoot Crossing in Alberta, Wanuskewin Heritage Park near Saskatoon, the Buffalo Nation Luxton Museum in Banff, the Museum of the Plains Indian in Browning, Montana, and the Plains Indian Museum in Cody, Wyoming; Sandalack, "Head-Smashed-In," 163.

10. In 1981 Head-Smashed-In Buffalo Jump was inscribed under criterion vi, which recognizes its direct association with "the survival of the human race during the pre-historic period." ICOMOS, *World Heritage List No. 158* (Paris: ICOMOS, 1981).

11. The site was used for the slaughter of bison from 3,600 BC to 2,600 BC, then intermittently toward 900 BC, and finally, continuously from 206 AD to 1850.

12. For studies on buffalo jumps see, for example, Douglas B. Bamforth, "Origin Stories, Archaeological Evidence, and Post-Clovis Bison Hunting on the Great Plains," *American Antiquity* 76, no. 1 (2011), 24–40; Shawn Bubel, "The Fincastle Site: A Late Middle Prehistoric Bison Kill on the Northwestern Plains," *Plains Anthropologist* 59, no. 231 (2014), 207–40; Christopher M. Johnston, "Running of the Buffalo: Investigations of the Roberts Ranch Buffalo Jump (5LR100), Northern Colorado" (master's thesis, Colorado State University, 2006); Damian R. Kirkwood, "Butchering Practices at the Vore Buffalo Jump (48CK302): Investigating Organization with

the Nearest Neighbor Test" (master's thesis, University of Wyoming, 2016); Charles A. Reher and George C. Frison, "The Vore Site, 48CK302: A Stratified Buffalo Jump in the Wyoming Black Hills," *Plains Anthropologist* 25, no. 88 (May 1980): 25–88.

13. Brink, *Imagining Head-Smashed-In*, xiv.

14. Brink, *Imagining Head-Smashed-In*, xiv.

15. Brink, *Imagining Head-Smashed-In*, xiv.

16. George Bird Grinnell, *Blackfoot Lodge Tales: The Story of a Prairie People* (Lincoln: University of Nebraska Press, 1962), 230.

17. The term "Blackfoot" refers to the four members of the Blackfoot Nations known as the Blackfoot Confederacy or Niitsitapi (meaning "the people") that consist of three First Nations bands in Canada and one Native American tribe in Montana: the Siksika, the Kainai (or Blood), and the Piikani (also called Northern Peigan or Piegan) in Canada, as well as the Blackfeet (Southern Piegan or Pikuni) in Montana in the United States. For more information see Betty Bastien, *Blackfoot Ways of Knowing: The Worldview of the Siksikaitsitapi* (Calgary: University of Calgary Press, 2004).

18. There are different versions of this story; see for examples Lorraine Goodstriker, quoted in Kate Hassall, *Partnerships to Manage Conservation Areas through Tourism: Some Best Practice Models between Government, Indigenous Communities and the Private Sector in Canada and South Africa* (Canberra: Winston Churchill Memorial Trust, 2006), 30, and Quinton Crow Shoe, quoted in Black Tomato, "A Moment with Quinton Crow Shoe, Head Smashed In Buffalo Jump," *Insight*, accessed May 25, 2020, https://www.blacktomato.com/inspirations/a-moment-with-quinton-crow-shoe-head-smashed-in-buffalo-jump/.

19. Brink, *Imagining-Head-Smashed-In*, 26.

20. Thomas Gasque, *The Power of Naming* (Vermillion: University of South Dakota Press, 2001), 7.

21. Bill Ashcroft, Gareth Griffiths, and Helen Tiffin, "Part Thirteen: Place," in *The Post-Colonial Studies Reader*, ed. Bill Ashcroft, Gareth Griffiths, and Helen Tiffin (London: Routledge, 1995), 345.

22. Ashcroft, Griffiths, and Tiffin, "Part Thirteen," 345; Lutz, "To Know Where Home Is," 12.

23. Colin Calloway, *One Vast Winter Count: The Native American West before Lewis and Clark* (Lincoln: University of Nebraska Press, 2003), 3.

24. Ashcroft, Griffiths, and Tiffin, "Part Thirteen," 345.

25. Robert Bringhurst, quoted in Noah Richler, *This Is My Country. What's Yours? A Literary Atlas of Canada* (Toronto: McClelland & Stewart, 2006) 50–51.

26. In Jeannette Armstrong's Okanaga Nsyilxcen language, the word "Kwtlakin" is a question phrase that exemplifies the connection between land, language, literature, and identity. See Jeannette Armstrong, "Kwatlakin? What Is Your Place?" in *What Is Your Place? Indigeneity and Immigration in Canada*, ed. Hartmut Lutz with Thomas Rafico Ruiz (Augsburg: Wißner, 2007), 31.

27. Armstrong, "Kwatlakin? What Is Your Place?" 31.

28. Melanie K. Smith, *Issues in Cultural Tourism Studies* (London: Routledge, 2003). For concepts of heritage see, among others, David Lowenthal, *The Heritage Crusade and the Spoils of History* (Cambridge: Cambridge University Press, 1998) and Laurajane Smith, *Uses of Heritage* (London: Routledge, 2006).

29. Smith, *Issues in Cultural Tourism Studies*, 81.

30. Gaynor Kavanagh, ed., *Making Histories in Museums* (London: Leicester University Press, 1996), 13; Alan K. Knapp et al., "The Keystone Role of Bison in North American Tallgrass Prairie," *BioScience* 49, no. 1 (January 1999): 30–50; Sylvia Fallon, "The Ecological Importance of Bison in Mixed-Grass Prairie Ecosystems," Buffalo Field Campaign, 2009, https://www.buffalofieldcampaign.org/images/get-involved/students-resource-about-bison/bison-conservation-papers/Fallon-The-ecological-importance-of-bison-in-mixed-grass-prairie-ecosystems-2009.pdf.

31. Russel L. Barsh and Chantelle Marlor, "Driving Bison and Blackfoot Science," *Human Ecology* 31, no. 4 (December 2003): 572.

32. Alberta Community Development, *Buffalo Tracks: Educational and Scientific Studies from Head-Smashed-In Buffalo Jump* (Calgary: Alberta Community Development, 2016), 8.

33. Alberta Community Development, *Buffalo Tracks*, 8.

34. Shepard Krech III, *The Ecological Indian: Myth and History* (New York: W. W. Norton, 1999), 131.

35. Krech, *The Ecological Indian*, 132–34.

36. María Nieves Zedeño, Christopher Roos, Kacy Hollenback, and Mary Hagen Erlick, "Bison Hunters and Prairie Fires: A View from the Northwestern Plains," in *The Greater Plains: Rethinking a Region's Environmental Histories*, ed. Brian Frehner and Kathleen A. Brosnan (Lincoln: University of Nebraska Press, 2021).

37. For more information on pemmican see George Colpitts, *Pemmican Empire: Food, Trade, and the Last Bison Hunts in the Northern American Plains, 1780–1882* (New York: Cambridge University Press, 2015).

38. Eleanor Verbicky-Todd, *Communal Buffalo Hunting among the Plains Indians: An Ethnographic and Historical Review* (Edmonton: Alberta Culture Historical Resource Division, 1984), 11.

39. Brink, *Imagining Head-Smashed-In*, 9.

40. Brink, *Imagining Head-Smashed-In*, 157. As Clint Carroll shows in his article on Cherokee relationships with animals in this volume, animals have been regarded by Indigenous peoples as nonhuman relatives and teachers, who are highly respected for their spiritual abilities and must be treated according to certain protocols; see also Joseph Bruchac, *Native American Animal Stories* (Golden CO: Fulcrum, 1992); Vine Deloria Jr., *God Is Red: A Native View of Religion* (Golden CO: Fulcrum, 2003); Peter Kulchyski, Don McCaskill, and David Newhouse, eds., *In the Word of Elders: Aboriginal Cultures in Transition* (Toronto: University of Toronto Press, 2002).

41. Brink, *Imagining Head-Smashed-In*, 158.

42. Brink, *Imagining Head-Smashed-In*, 157–58.

43. Bryony Onciul, *Museums, Heritage and Indigenous Voice: Decolonizing Engagement* (London: Routledge, 2015), 128, 129.

44. John Dorst, "Watch for Falling Bison: The Buffalo Hunt as Museum Trope and Ecological Allegory," in *Native Americans and the Environment: Perspectives on the Ecological Indian*, ed. Michael E. Harkin and David Rich Lewis (Lincoln: University of Nebraska Press, 2007), 182.

45. Dorst, "Watch for Falling Bison," 188.

46. *American History Illustrated*, as quoted in Krech, *The Ecological Indian*, 123.

47. Krech, *The Ecological Indian*, 123.

48. Sebastian F. Braun, "Ecological and Un-Ecological Indians: The (Non)portrayal of Plains Indians in the Buffalo Commons Literature," in *Native Americans and the Environment: Perspectives on the Ecological Indian*, ed. Michael E. Harkin and David Rich Lewis (Lincoln: University of Nebraska Press, 2007), 192–208, 192.

49. Dorst, "Watch for Falling Bison," 179.

50. Dorst, "Watch for Falling Bison," 174.

51. Ian Clarke, personal communication to author, 2011.

52. Onciul, *Museums, Heritage, and Indigenous Voice*, 92.

53. Stan Knowlton, personal communication to author, 2011.

54. Brink, *Imagining Head-Smashed-In*, 284.

55. Braun, "Ecological and Un-Ecological Indians," 199.

56. Ian Clarke, personal communication to author, 2011.

57. George P. Nicholas, "Policies and Protocols for Archaeological Sites and Associated Cultural and Intellectual Property," in *Protection of First Nations Cultural Heritage: Laws, Policy, and Reform*, ed. Catherine Bell and Robert K. Paterson (Vancouver BC: UBC Press, 2009), 218.

58. Nicholas, "Policies and Protocols," 218.

59. Stan Knowlton, personal communication to author, 2011.

60. Brink, *Imagining Head-Smashed-In*, 290; Trevor Kiitokii, personal communication to author, 2011; Onciul, *Museums, Heritage, and Indigenous Voice*, 236.

61. Nicholas, "Policies and Protocols," 203.

62. Michael Asch, "Concluding Thoughts and Fundamental Questions," in *Protection of First Nations Cultural Heritage: Laws, Policy, and Reform*, ed. Catherine Bell and Robert K. Paterson (Vancouver BC: UBC Press, 2009), 395; Renata N. Biancalana, "The Importance of Heritage in Community Education: The Case of Serra da Capivara National Park, Brazil" (master's thesis, Brandenburgische Technische Universität, 2007), 7.

63. The origins of the theory of empowerment are associated with the Brazilian humanitarian and educator Paolo Freire, who proposed a concept of liberating the oppressed people of the world through education; Paulo Freire, *Pedagogy of the Oppressed* (New York: Seabury Press, 1971); and Paulo Freire, *Education for Critical Consciousness* (New York: Continuum, 1973). See also Biancalana, "The Importance of Heritage"; Mann Hyung Hur, "Empowerment in Terms of Theoretical Perspectives: Exploring a Typology of the Process and Components across Disciplines,"

Journal of Community Psychology 34, no. 5 (September 2006): 523–40; Biancalana, "The Importance of Heritage," 24.

64. Catherine Bell and Robert K. Paterson, eds., *First Nations Cultural Heritage and Law: Case Studies, Voices and Perspectives* (Vancouver: UBC Press, 2008); Catherine Bell and Robert K. Paterson, eds., *Protection of First Nations Cultural Heritage: Laws, Policy, and Reform* (Vancouver: UBC Press, 2009).

65. Onciul, *Museums, Heritage, and Indigenous Voice*, 4.

66. Tony Bennett, "Exhibition, Difference, and the Logic of Culture," in *Museum Frictions: Public Cultures/Global Transformations*, ed. Ivan Karp, Corinne A. Kratz, Lynn Szwaja, and Tomás Ybarra-Frausto (Durham NC: Duke University Press, 2006), 56.

67. Lilla Vonk, *Indigenous Peoples and Ethnographic Museums: A Changing Relationship* (Östersund: Nordic Centre of Heritage Learning and Creativity, 2013), 3.

68. Laura Peers and Alison K. Brown, eds., *Museums and Source Communities: A Routledge Reader* (London: Routledge, 2003), 2.

PART 2

Animals on the Great Plains

5

Kinscapes and the Buffalo Chase
The Genesis of Nineteenth-Century Plains Métis Hunting Brigades

NICOLE ST-ONGE AND BRENDA MACDOUGALL

Introduction

In the spring of 1818, prominent North West Company (NWC) fur trader William McGillivray penned a letter to a board of inquiry tasked with examining the armed disturbances that had occurred near the Hudson's Bay Company's (HBC) fledgling settlement at the confluence of the Red and Assiniboine Rivers.[1] McGillivray mused about the presence in the Northwest of a new population composed principally of descendants of Catholic, French-Canadian fur-trade personnel and their Native wives. He commented that "they one and all look upon themselves as members of an independent tribe of natives, entitled to a property in the soil, to a flag of their own and to protection from the British Government." He continued by noting that this bison-hunting Métis population was by then well-established on the northern plains: "the half-breeds under the denominations of bois-brûlés and métifs have formed a separate and distinct tribe of Indians for a considerable time back."[2]

This chapter examines the processes by which this distinct population that emerged out of the western fur trade coalesced into highly organized, commercial Métis bison-hunting brigades that ranged the length and breadth of the northern Great Plains.[3] The authors seek to explore the nature of Plains Métis hunting brigades' social organization, paying special attention to their use of kinship networks as a means to maintain internal coherence and identity. This focus allows insight into the sense of identity of a mobile people who, because of the very nature of their economy and the possibility of hostile encounters with various hunting rivals, required degrees of internal group cohesion based on extensive social and kinship links. The discussion below analyzes a pattern of familial strategic alliances between three distinct foundational populations of northern plains fur-trade employees and their Métis families. These marital decisions reveal a desire to pool geographic knowledge and tribal connections of the extended families from these three regions to create an environmental *kinscape*. The term kinscape was first used by Shawnee history specialist Sami Lakomäki to describe a terrain of social and geographic space in which overlapping networks of kinship radiated out from each community, connecting it to dozens of others both near and far. In this Shawnee worldview, mobility was understood to be a necessary constituent part of their world, not a disruptive force.[4] We argue that the Plains Métis world was similarly built upon webs of kinship that bound together a highly mobile population specializing in large-scale, commercial bison hunting within a vast but well-delineated ecozone, the northern Great Plains.

Genealogical reconstruction shows that the fathers of the first generation of Métis bison hunters brought with them a closely knit French-Canadian Catholic voyageur culture and formed pivotal marital alliances with several Plains Indian tribes. Subsequent generations tapped into and expanded these Métis-to-Métis and Métis-to-Indian alliances with their own strategic marriages. Like other Plains tribes, the Métis developed a political and social organization based on claims of kinship. But in the case of the Métis, kinship was reinforced by a voyageur-derived common language—Michif French—and a shared Catholic faith.[5] This form of organization was needed as Métis hunting brigades headed deeper into the western plains in search of diminishing bison herds.[6]

Background

This chapter is based on two working premises. First, the emergence of the Plains Métis should be viewed as part and parcel of a wider pattern of eighteenth- and nineteenth-century Native ethnogeneses on the North American Great Plains resulting from the appearance of horses, new technologies, the ever-increasing external pressure from a westward-expanding agrarian frontier, and the dictates of international mercantile economies.[7] Second, Plains Métis were unique within this broader pattern of Plains Native identity formation because they defined their culture and grounded their identity in a purposeful fusion of both Native and largely French-Canadian traits, a fusion made possible by their intrinsic and long-term links with Montreal-centered social and economic fur-trade networks. No other Plains tribe, however mixed and hybrid in their origins and culture, constructed such identities.[8] The Plains Métis were thus both part of a larger trend of Native ethnogenesis in the interior and uniquely separate in that they grounded their nascent identity as the product of *métissage*, a melding of Native and European heritage.[9]

Nineteenth-century observers and participants in the fur trade chronicled the Plains Métis hunting brigades' spread across the northern Great Plains in search of the massive bison herds on which they based their livelihood. Only three factors constrained this rapid expansion. First, there were the northern and western geographic limits to the Great Plains where vast bison herds congregated and where Métis hunters could efficiently hunt them through a combination of horses, guns, and the legendary Red River carts, at least in the summer months.[10] A vast and challenging topography combined with a need for constant mobility at key times to reach the bison herds was linked to the Métis ingenious adaptation of the French peasant two-wheeled carts. These Plains transportation challenges and adaptations echo Leila Monaghan's chapter on Cheyenne and Arapaho women's adaptations to a life also spent in travel by using dog- and horse-drawn travois transport and their preference to inhabit a shortgrass prairie landscape. Second, there was evident pushback from other bison-hunting tribes, such as Dakota Sioux and Blackfeet, who competed with the Plains Métis for access to these same vital herds. Military need thus led to the formation over the course of the nineteenth century of increasingly large well-armed Métis hunting brigades. The sheer efficiency at bison hunting and pemmican production of these "mobile factories" in turn permitted the existence of large groupings of highly mobile families. This reality was comparable to Geneviève Susemihl's description in chapter 4 of earlier Indian control of the famous Head-Smashed-In Buffalo Jump. It not only provided tribes with essential supplies of food for both consumption and trade, but also served a social purpose as it enabled people to live in large bands that were necessary to defend and regulate human access to the jumps. Third, as the Métis conducted their commercial hunts principally in the summer, an environmental constraint existed, namely the need to produce pemmican in a northern-enough latitude to ensure temperatures sufficiently cool to minimize meat spoilage and prevent the rancidification of the fat required in the production process.[11] The Métis brigades' hunting behavior and pattern of travel were not only informed by these environmental constraints, but also by the dictates of their biggest client, the HBC, whose forts dotted British North America's plains' landscape, a subject discussed in George Colpitts's chapter on HBC accounting practices as an influential environmental technology on the northern Great Plains.

The Judith Basin Hunting Brigades

In the hard winter of 1879–80, three Métis hunting brigades were wintering together in the Judith Basin of Montana. Seeking relief and protection for their people from the Sioux and unnamed "whites," four men penned a petition to U.S. Army General Nelson Miles. Three of the four were renowned Métis bison-hunting brigade leaders: Alexandre Wilkie, who was married to Louise Gariepy; Pierre Berger, who was the husband of Judith Wilkie (a sister to Alexandre Wilkie); and Joseph Ouellet, who was married to Magdeleine Paul. The fourth was young Pierre Charbonneau, not a brigade leader but literate and allied to the intertwined Wilkie and Azure clans through his marriage to Rose Azure.[12] The preamble to this petition noted that several families had moved, at the request of American officials, to the Judith Basin in Montana, away from the politically and militarily sensitive Milk River borderlands region where they had been living for five or six years. They settled in the Judith Basin in the autumn of 1879, built houses, and began managing hay fields until white "horse thieves" burned their houses and fields and stole their stock. Desperate, they petitioned the American government for assistance, first to survive the approaching winter and then to rebuild their lives.

Miles forwarded the petition along with a favorable recommendation to Washington DC. He attached to the petition a population roll of the three brigades involved so as to give federal officials a sense of the numbers and identities of these people.[13] The roll named sixty-five heads of household, listed their "tribal" affiliation, and gave the number of people attached to each household—a total of 345 men, women, and children associated with the Berger, Ouellet, and Wilkie brigades. This roll forms the starting point of our analysis on the genesis of Plains Métis bison-hunting society. The formidable challenge involved in reconstructing the history of a highly mobile but largely illiterate society is that it left behind limited physical evidence and practically no directly written sources. While the existence of Métis hunting brigades and the names of their leaders are known through outsiders' written observations, determining exact brigade membership remains a challenge. This petition, with the names of three known Métis leaders and the accompanying population roll, offers a rare physical representation of three well-established brigades in the closing years of the commercial hunts. Not only is it a snapshot of conditions on the plains in 1879, the population roll provides us with a documented starting point for upstream analyses of these brigades' geneses. The kinscapes, or longitudinal and lateral genealogies, of as many of the sixty-five heads of families listed in that 1879 population roll as possible were reconstructed with one aim in mind—to determine the historical ties, factors, and commonalities that connected those assembled in the Judith Basin that winter of 1879–80. In other words, we ask the following questions of the individuals listed on that 1879 document: Who was there? Why were they there? And how did they get there as a group?

Ancestral Generation

The historical kinscapes for the three Métis brigades enumerated in that 1879 Judith Basin census revealed an association between these hunting families starting in the early nineteenth century.[14] Lateral genealogies also document the generational composition of these commercial bison-hunting Métis brigades that sometimes encompassed three generations of interrelated bands of hunters and their families. Examination of the brigades' membership and activities illuminates two general trends: they engaged for decades in the commercial buffalo hunt and, as a result, they became increasingly interrelated communities.

An analysis of the male progenitors to the Judith Basin families' identities overwhelmingly demonstrates a St. Lawrence Valley/Montreal-to-Trois-Rivières origin. The brigades' paternal ancestors were voyageurs hailing from such old fur-trading parishes as Sorel, Yamaska, Louiseville, Vaudreuil, and Laprairie, all French Catholic peasant communities whose men had toiled in the trade for generations. Most voyageurs returned to their home communities, hopefully with enough money to improve the family farm or establish themselves as *habitants* (farmers). However, when many of these brigades' ancestors were hired in the 1790s, conditions in those rural parishes had become increasingly difficult for many of the old peasant families. Although Quebec historians have long debated whether the socioeconomic changes occurring in the St. Lawrence rural parishes were initiated by agrarian modernization or a dire agrarian crisis, all agree that from the 1790s onward the St. Lawrence Valley rural society underwent profound changes that favored some but certainly not all. An important group of owner-operators, a smaller number of tenant farmers, and a growing force of landless rural laborers emerged in the early nineteenth century.[15] Many of the Judith Basin voyageur ancestors came from families where fathers were listed in sacramental records as *laboureur* (plowman) or *journalier* (common day laborer). Often their deceased children were buried in the *cimetière des pauvres* (pauper's field). In other words, these families were mired at the very bottom of Quebec society.[16] Thus, strong incentives existed for men to leave and engage in fur-trade wage labor. Furthermore, these men had little incentive to return home after an initial period of engagement, a fact reflected in their multiyear employment with fur trading.

Jacques Berger, the paternal ancestor to a prominent Plains Métis family present in the Judith Basin, is a strong case in point. Born to a *journalier* family residing in Verchères, a voyageur parish downstream from Montreal, he engaged into the fur trade in December 1803 with the NWC.[17] Berger's three-year contract listed the distant Athabasca District as the stipulated destination.[18] Surviving NWC ledgers indicate he remained in the interior. From 1811 to 1818 Jacques Berger worked in the Fort des Prairies region.[19] A note in his NWC account lists him as "free" from 1818 onward, though he seems to have worked occasionally as an experienced voyageur (as a "bout" or forward in a canoe) in 1817 and 1821.[20] Company books indicate fifteen years (1803–18) of continuous employment in the interior with no indication that he ever returned to the St. Lawrence Valley. No other Montreal contracts have been located for him, and no entries in surviving ledgers indicate a Montreal-bound trip.

This ancestral generation of those Judith Basin brigades was largely composed of such French-Canadian men who spent years as salaried employees principally for the NWC before becoming freemen in the interior.[21] As Carolyn Podruchny convincingly argues, "Voyageurs created distinct identities shaped by their French-Canadian peasant roots, the Aboriginal peoples they met in the Northwest, and the nature of their employment as indentured servants operating in diverse environments. Voyageurs' identities were also shaped by their constant travels and by their masculine ideals that emphasized strength, endurance, and daring." In short, they created a closely knit "voyageur world" influenced by both their St. Lawrence Valley background and their lived experiences in fur-trade country.[22]

Many voyageur men remained in the interior at the end of their contracts, residing in the Great Lakes District, the Illinois coun-

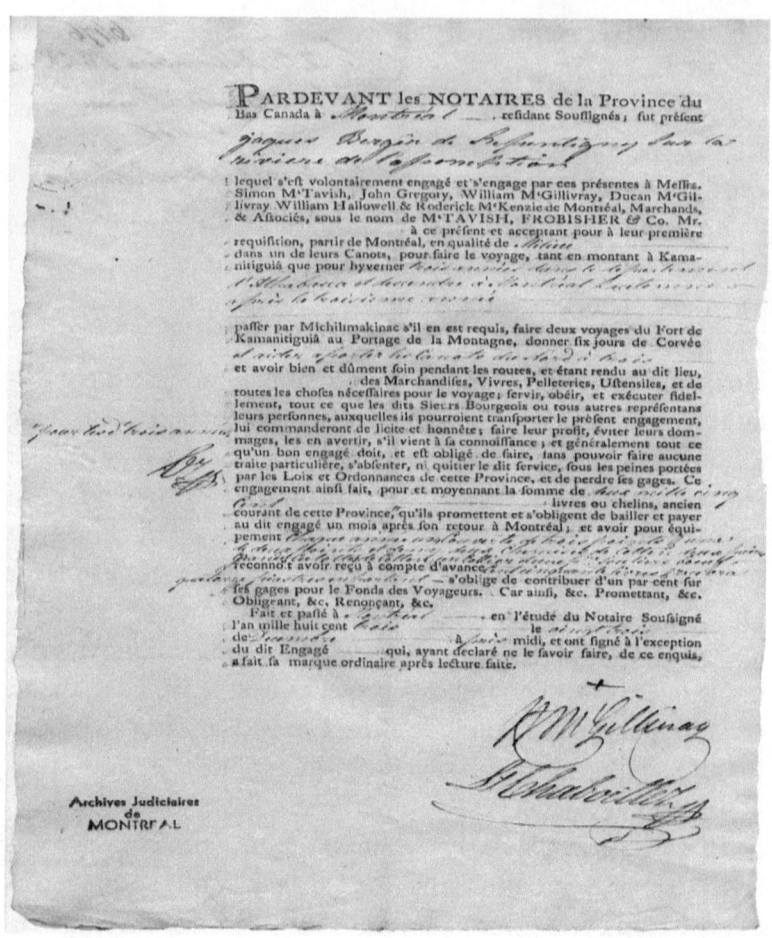

FIG. 7. Archival photo of Jacques Berger contract. Bibliothèque et Archives Nationales du Québec (BANQ), Greffe Louis Chaboillez (notaire), CN601, S74, Jacques Berger 1803-12-23.

try, or the Mississippi valley. However, the male ancestors of Plains Métis hunters followed a distinct pattern of occupation and residence. An analysis of the voyageur forefathers to Plains Métis hunting families listed in 1879 reveals not only employment with the NWC but also a pattern of having worked in one of three districts heavily involved in the production of bison pemmican for the ever-growing fur-trade personnel. Most of these men were dispatched to either the North Saskatchewan River District (Fort

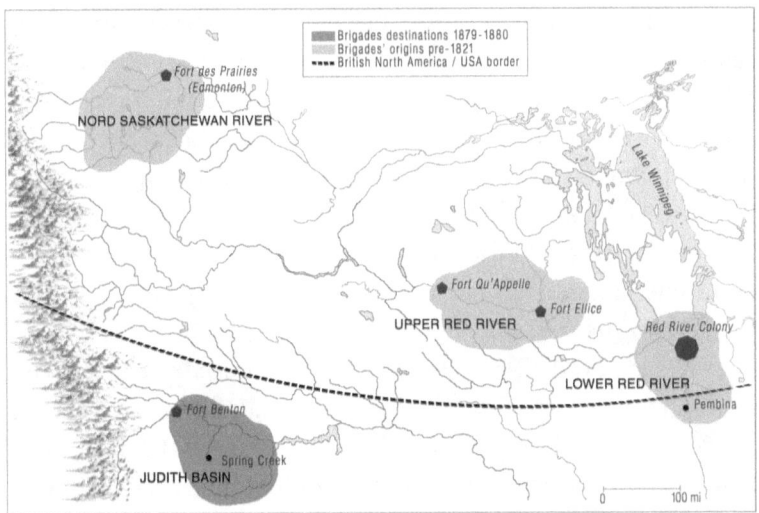

FIG. 8. Map of the Berger kinscape. Map created by Thierry Simonet.

des Prairies) region, or the Red River Valley/Pembina region—the NWC's "Lower Red River" District, or what was historically the NWC's "Upper Red River," the Assiniboine River basin (figure 8).[23] By the early nineteenth century, the provisioning needs existed, useful technologies such as guns and the fabled Red River carts were in place, and increasing numbers of horses and oxen were arriving on the northern plains—all the ingredients for conducting a successful long-term commercial bison hunt. But what factors led to a distinct society emerging from these favorable economic conditions?

The European ancestors to the Plains Métis bison hunters were NWC men sharing a common French-Canadian Catholic voyageur culture and generally employed in pemmican provisioning locales. We argue that this common male cultural heritage and employment in these three posts were the two key catalysts to the creation of a Plains Métis society. Specifically, the link of half the ancestors of the 1879 Judith Basin families to the Fort des Prairies District is a pivotal factor. In 1821, after the NWC and HBC amalgamation, the newly reorganized HBC appointed James Sutherland as chief factor of the Saskatchewan District. During his one-year posting, he was the company's hatchet man, tasked with culling redundant personnel and their families. Upon arriving at Fort Edmonton, Sutherland found sixty-five HBC men and seventy NWC men. Many of these NWC men had wives and children who connected them to surrounding freeman and Indian communities.[24] This was far too many salaried personnel for the size of the trading operations along the Saskatchewan River in the early 1820s, and so he immediately laid off employees, mostly those who had worked for the NWC.[25]

Released Fort des Prairies men were encouraged to either return to Montreal or, especially for those with families, to relocate to the Red River Colony, founded in 1812 at the forks of the Red and Assiniboine Rivers by HBC shareholder the Earl of Selkirk.[26] These Saskatchewan District NWC men and their families were often described as belligerently independent, resistant to taking up farming, and insistent on maintaining close ties with their Indians relatives. In short, their attitudes made them suspect to company and colony officials. Attempts by HBC administrators to resolve their unease produced a set of contradictory policies. For example, although it was HBC policy to encourage former employees, freemen, and their respective families to move to the colony, Red River's administrators made efforts to divert such men and their families away from the colony's heart, at the forks of the Red and Assiniboine Rivers, instead some distance away upstream on the Assiniboine River to an area called White Horse Plains (WHP).[27] There they mingled with Pembina families who had been invited to relocate to WHP in 1824 by HBC officials concerned about potential competition from a growing bison-hunting freeman community on American soil.[28]

This relocation initiative, only partially successful, was not a long-term solution for some. Many freemen and their families remained at or returned to Pembina despite recurrent threats from the powerful Sioux. Like the Métis, the Sioux were transforming their society into one rooted in equestrian commercial bison hunting. Inevitably, throughout the nineteenth century, they clashed violently with Métis hunters for access to receding bison herds.[29]

The Métis hunters were lured to Pembina by its rich fisheries, proximity to large bison herds, growing access to independent traders, and, by the early 1830s, links to well-traveled cart trails to Mississippi valley settlements.[30] Other Métis freemen families remained west of the Red River Settlement as the fur trade's constant need for both pemmican producers and overland freighters dictated that Métis brigades were required along the HBC supply networks in the northwestern interior, irrespective of the company's relocation policies.[31]

Those families from the Fort des Prairies region who did relocate to WHP carried with them physical knowledge of and kin ties to the western plains. Similarly, the families originating from the upper Assiniboine River watershed ("Upper" Red River) and from the Red River Valley's Pembina region ("Lower" Red River), who also settled along the lower Assiniboine River, possessed an equivalent knowledge base and associated kin networks to the eastern and central plains. After 1821 the WHP settlement, later known as the Catholic parish of St. Francois Xavier, contained families originating from three key bison-hunting regions. They shared a common paternal ancestral culture, but were also influenced by, and kin to, several maternal tribes. These families, and the kin ties they built with each other, formed the basis of the three brigades. By the 1840s and 1850s, each brigade had key members with knowledge of and ties to the eastern, central, and western plains' geography and inhabitants.

Genealogical reconstruction of the 1879 Judith Basin families shows deliberate and strategic pooling of knowledge and familial networks between the Saskatchewan District families, the old families from the Red River Valley, and the families who had emerged along the Assiniboine River fur-trade and pemmican-supplying district. The Roman Catholic mission sacramental records from Saint-Boniface (1825–34), the Saint-Joseph mission at Pembina (1848–74), and especially those of the Saint-Francois Xavier mission (1834–89) at White Horse Plains reveal a pattern of commercial-hunting families engaged in strategic marital alliances that linked eastern and central Métis Plains populations with their western counterparts.[32]

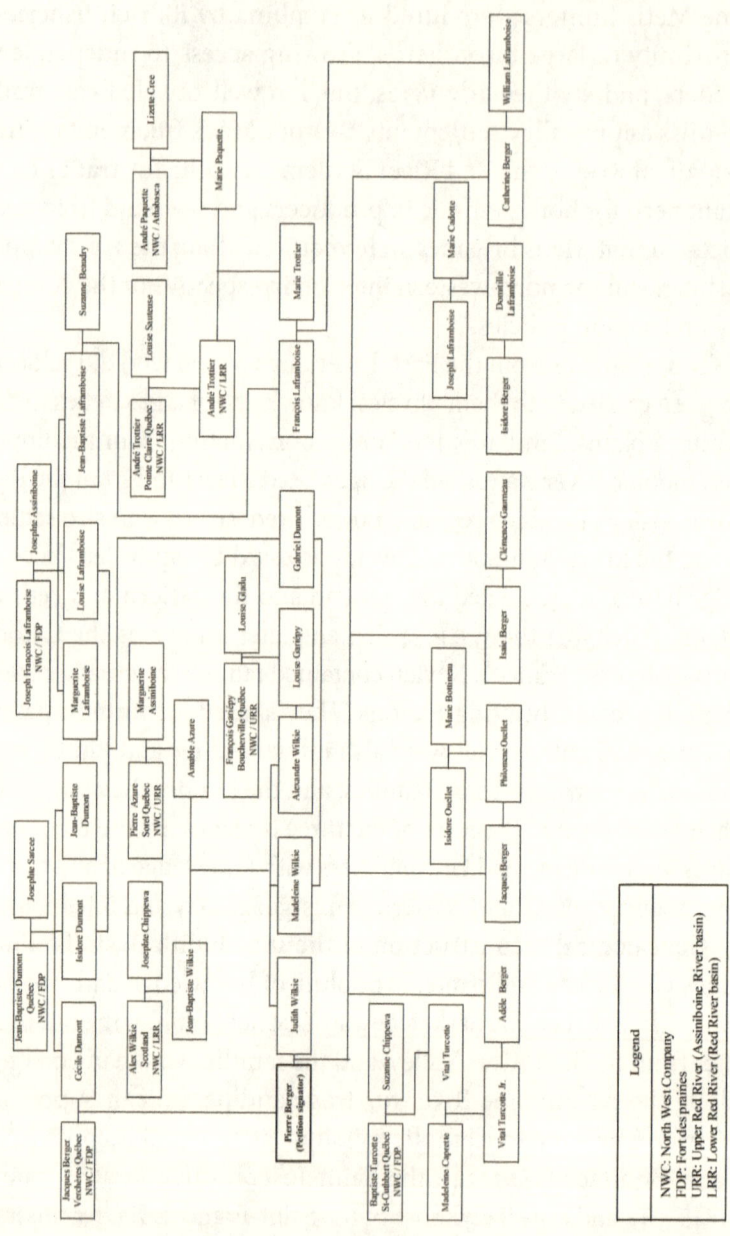

FIG. 9. Pierre Berger graph. Graph created by Thierry Simonet.

Pierre Berger, a brigade leader and signatory of the 1879 Judith Basin petition, was the son of the previously discussed NWC Fort des Prairies (FDP) employee Jacques Berger and his Métis wife, Cecile Dumont. Cecile was the daughter of another NWC FDP employee, Jean Baptiste Dumont, and his Sarcee wife, Josette.³³ Two of Pierre Berger's maternal uncles—Isidore Dumont and 1850 Pembina community leader Jean Baptiste Dumont Jr.—married the daughters (Louise and Marguerite) of Joseph Francois Laframboise, himself also a NWC FDP voyageur, and his Assiniboine wife, Josephte. In 1857 at the Pembina mission, Isidore and Louise (Laframboise) Dumont's son, Gabriel Dumont, wed Madeleine Wilkie. As noted previously, she was the sister of Pierre Berger's wife, Judith Wilkie, and both were the sisters of brigade leader Alexandre Wilkie. Thus, marital alliances across generations and across siblings interwove these plains-focused bison-hunting families. Some, like the Bergers and Dumonts, came from the western plains; others, like the Wilkies, had Red River Valley roots.³⁴

Jacques Berger moved his family to the Red River Colony in the early 1820s.³⁵ In 1846 his son Pierre Berger and Pierre's young family were listed in the Red River Settlement census as having eight horses, two oxen, three carts, and just two acres under cultivation, indicating they primarily practiced a hunting-oriented lifestyle. Pierre was also noted as being "on the Plains" at the time this census was taken. Later, Pierre Berger relocated permanently to the Pembina settlement, possibly to be closer to his wife's (Judith Wilkie) Azure kin, or perhaps because the mid-1840s were extremely challenging for any agriculture pursuits at the forks of the Red and Assiniboine, for the colony faced recurring floods, droughts, early frosts, and locust infestations.³⁶ Judith Wilkie was the daughter of a noted Pembina brigade leader, Jean Baptiste Wilkie, and his wife Amable Azure.³⁷ Amable was the daughter of Pierre Azure and Marguerite Assiniboine and the granddaughter of French-Canadian Joseph Azure, a NWC Upper Red River (Assiniboine basin) employee, and "Lizette," a Chippewa woman.³⁸ Judith Wilkie's marriage to Pierre Berger, plus Madeleine Wilkie's marriage to Gabriel Dumont, linked these deeply Saskatchewan District–

oriented families to a series of interrelated old Red and Assiniboine River basins families, most prominently the Wilkies and the Azures. These strategic marriages were examples of marital alliances that pooled western-originating families with those hailing from either the Red River or Assiniboine River drainage districts. These alliances not only linked individuals whose families hailed from different parts of the northern prairies, they also tied together men and women who had maternal kinship ties with Assiniboine, Sarcee, and Chippewa/Saulteaux peoples.

In the 1850 Minnesota territorial census, Pierre Berger was listed as a Pembina hunter born in British-held Red River and married to a woman from the American side at Pembina.[39] Possibly through his Wilkie wife and their children, he collected American half-breed scrip thanks to both the 1854 Lake Superior and Mississippi Chippewa Treaty and the 1864 Red Lake and Pembina Chippewa Treaty.[40] Berger's association with Pembina continued in the 1860s as he and his family were listed as collecting an annuity at the Turtle Mountain Indian agency. But by the 1870s, he was leading twenty-five bison-hunting families westward to the familiar hunting grounds of Montana, and in 1879 he was signing petitions in the Judith Basin area. In 1880 he signed the Montana petition, requesting a half-breed reservation on American soil, and was listed as a "farmer" in the 1880 Montana census. In 1883, after the demise of the commercial bison hunts, he applied for a homestead in the Spring Creek region of central Montana.[41]

Pierre Berger and Judith Wilkie's large family was one of the key linchpins of the three brigades assembled in the Judith Basin in the winter of 1879. Four sons and two daughters, plus their own families, and accompanied by their spouses' own relatives, formed the Berger brigade and provided links to the other two brigades: the Turcotte family, whose paternal grandparents were NWC FDP voyageurs married to Chippewa women, the above-discussed Laframboise family; and the Trottier family, whose paternal ancestor was a NWC French Canadian working in the Lower Red River and married to a French-Cree woman. All these kin by marriage and descent were hunting families listed on the 1879 Judith Basin census.⁴² These negotiated marital and communal traveling alliances further interwove the families originating from various regions of the interior plains, having ties to a variety of Indian tribes through their maternal ancestors, and were influenced by a predominantly fur-trade voyageur paternal ancestor culture.

Discussion: Plains Métis Kinscapes

The synopsis of the familial background and kinship ties of Pierre Berger, one of the four men who signed the petition, illustrates three key factors in the rise of the professional Métis bison-hunting brigades. First and most paramount was the social and economic dictates of the commercial bison hunts in the highly competitive northern plains environment. Like other groups on the plains, the Métis adapted their culture to meet the logistical, military, and social demands of a plains hunting existence. Within a short time, as the McGillivray letter illustrates, many descendants of mostly French-Canadian voyageurs and their Indian wives adapted to a specialized nomadic lifestyle based on horses, Red River carts, and hunting guns, applied to a steady demand for pemmican and eventually bison robes. Using the traits acquired from French Catholic voyageur culture coupled to those brought in from a range of Indian societies, Plains Métis developed a very clear sense of self and created a unique society molded by the logistics of large-scale commercial hunts and need to maintain a position of strength vis-à-vis other tribes who were also transitioning into a Plains horse culture and bison-hunting lifeway in the early nineteenth century.⁴³

Descended from NWC French-Canadian voyageurs and women from several Indian tribes, the Plains Métis hunting brigades' final form stemmed from a series of deliberate marital alliances between three core foundational populations. Nineteen out of thirty-six traceable paternal ancestors for the 1879 Judith Basin census's families originated from either the Upper or Lower Red River NWC districts. The balance came mostly from NWC men and families arriving from the North Saskatchewan River/Fort des Prairies District. Here, as described for the Berger clan, all married strategically, pooling geographic knowledge of the full breadth of the northern plains and with the intent to better exploit the pemmican and bison-robe trades.

An analysis of familial strategic alliances within the growing Métis bison-hunting population also clearly reveals a desire to forge kinship ties with as many Plains Indian tribes as possible. Genealogical reconstruction shows that the fathers of first-generation Métis bison hunters brought with them pivotal marital alliances with several Plains Indian tribes. The following generation, by then fully committed to commercial bison hunting, tapped into and expanded further these Métis-to-Métis and Métis-to-Indian alliances with their own strategic marriages. Twenty-six women in the traceable foundational generation of the three brigades were first-generation Métis. Of those whose mothers' tribal affiliations were ascertainable, six were Cree, three Chippewa, one Sarcee, one Menominee, one Blackfoot, one Crow, and one Mohawk. From the foundational generation of fur-trade men who married Indian women whose tribal affiliations are clearly listed in fur-trade or sacramental documents, an interesting pattern emerges.

Fourteen "ancestor" women belonging to the families listed in the census accompanying the 1879 Judith Basin petition were described as Chippewa/Saulteaux/Plains Ojibwa, eight were Assiniboine, two were Cree, two were Gros Ventre, two were Dakota Sioux, and two were Blackfoot. Marital alliances with these tribal groups by buffalo hunters reflected, in part, the geographical distribution of those northern Plains tribes and the presence of NWC trade posts within particular tribal territories. But, more importantly, the dominant connection of these commercial buffalo-hunting brigades to the Saulteaux/Plains Ojibwas, Assiniboines, and Crees indicates the emergent association of these particular Métis families with the Iron Alliance or Nehiyaw Pwat Confederacy of the northern plains.[44] This confederacy was a social, economic, political, and military pact comprised initially of Crees, Assiniboines, and Chippewas/Ojibwas, then joined by Métis by the 1820s and Gros Ventres by the 1860s.[45] The marital alliances between these fur-trade employees and Indian women from the Nehiyaw Pwat Confederacy forged a space on the plains for their descendants, the Métis buffalo hunters. These close ties to Plains tribes were what rendered the Pembina and FDP families so suspect in the eyes of HBC and colony officials, for it gave them both power and a measure of independence.[46] The Métis hunting brigades emerging out of White Horse Plains and Pembina after the 1821 merger relied on this Iron Alliance to circulate freely into evermore westerly bison-hunting grounds. The Iron Alliance also helped the brigades push back militarily and diplomatically against Sioux hunters competing to harvest the same herds.

By the opening years of the nineteenth century, Métis hunting families had most of the ingredients necessary for what can be called ethnogenesis, the coalescence of a new tribe. By then, Plains Métis had found a secure exploitable resource in the bison herds whose products, mostly pemmican but also robes, were marketable. By those same years, the technological means to engage in large-scale exploitation of the herds, guns, horses, and Red River carts were present. Certainly, prior to the NWC-HBC merger of 1821, clusters of Métis hunting families had the kin ties and knowledge to safely hunt in specific regions on the northern plains. However, after 1821, with their partial congregation in the Red River Colony, key Métis families purposely allied themselves with each other and thus acquired the knowledge and kin ties necessary to form hunting brigades capable of pursuing the herds throughout the northern plains.

An analysis of available genealogical data shows that these Métis hunting families experienced both a high birth rate and a relatively low infant mortality rate, a significant advantage in a plains environment that experienced both devastating epidemics such as the 1837 Upper Missouri smallpox outbreak and a pattern of increasing violence. With their shared language and religion and a social organization based on claims of kinship, the Métis were able to assemble large hunting brigades that reached ever deeper into the western plains in search of diminishing bison herds.[47] This form of organization and social cohesion was needed as the Métis were aggressive commercial hunters who claimed the length and breadth of the northern Great Plains as their territorial hunting grounds. By the 1850s Métis brigades' clashes with other hunting groups over the ever-contracting herds were inevitable, notably the famed 1851 Métis victory over the Sioux at Grand Coteau.[48]

The highly organized, weaponized, and mounted Plains Métis brigades were a source of wonder to outsiders who encountered them. In July 1853 surveyor Isaac Stevens came across a large hunting brigade led by Alexandre Wilkie's father, Jean Baptiste, near Devil's Lake in present-day North Dakota. Stevens was so struck by their appearance that he devoted several pages of his journal to their description. He estimated the brigade—really, a mobile village accompanied by a Roman Catholic priest—to comprise 1,300 people, of whom 300 were hunters, along with 1,200 animals and 824 carts. He also discussed their defensive military strategies. Such a show of force may have been deemed necessary, as both they and Stevens had scouting reports that a party of bison-hunting Sioux, some 1,000 lodges strong, was nearby.[49]

Conclusion

The families wintering in the Judith Basin in that hard winter of 1879–80 were members of one of the most formidable tribes to roam the northern Great Plains, the self-styled Nouvelle Nation. For several decades the Métis could claim legitimately to have never lost a military confrontation with either Indians or whites.[50] Proud, colorful, and, most importantly, exceptionally efficient commercial bison hunters, they were dominant players on the northern plains. But, by 1879, profound changes were overcoming all the Plains tribes, including the Métis, their Indian kin, and their Sioux rivals. In October 1879 these Judith Basin families sent their first petition to the American army requesting aid in resisting the depredations of roving, horse-stealing bands of Sioux.[51] Prior to this petition, there is little evidence that the Métis required aid from any outsiders to handle the Sioux or other hostile tribes. Beyond requesting protection from "white" horse thieves in the second December 1879 petition, the four Métis leaders asked the American government to furnish them with "teams, plows and seeds." This plea indicates that they realized a whole way of life was ending and their very existence was in a precarious state, going beyond even a difficult winter.

That these professional hunters were seriously contemplating attempting a full-time farming lifestyle was unheard of for families with ties to the White Horse Plains and Pembina communities. These extended kinscapes emerging from three northern plains hunting locales negotiated marital strategic alliances that allowed them to deploy formidable hunting brigades westward from the Red River Colony to hunt the length and breadth of the northern Great Plains. Suddenly, in the late 1870s in the Judith Basin, rather than seeing all the northern prairies as their territory within which to travel and hunt, the three Judith Basin Métis brigades were setting their sights on small, location-specific plots of land—a pattern increasingly replicated by other former bison-hunting Métis brigades elsewhere on the prairies and northern parkland. By the early 1880s the large buffalo herds had all but vanished from the Great Plains. In 1885 the Plains Métis experienced a catastrophic military defeat at their settlement at Batoche on the South Saskatchewan River at the hands of Canadian regular soldiers and militias, leading to the hanging of their leader, Louis Riel, and their general dispersal.[52] For the Berger family and others from those 1879 brigades who chose to remain in Montana, difficult years lay ahead. They became "landless Indians" living on the edges of towns and cities in shanty settlements dismissively called "Moccasin Flats."[53] It took until the middle of the twentieth century before Métis residing on either Canadian or American soil made much collective headway politically, legally, or economically.[54] Perhaps one thing encouraging these collective modern-day efforts are the enduring memories of having once been the most powerful and affluent peoples of the northern plains. In fact, some of their descendants finally gained in early 2020 federal recognition as members of the Little Shell Native American tribe.[55]

Notes

1. The present-day city of Winnipeg in the province of Manitoba, Canada.

2. William Coltman, "Statement of William McGillivray to W. B. Coltman, March 14, 1818," in *Papers Relating to the Red River Settlement*, quoted in Gerhard J. Ens, "The Battle of Seven Oaks and the Articulation of a Metis National Tradition, 1811–1849," in *Contours of a People: Metis Family, Mobility and History*, ed. Nicole St-Onge, Carolyn Podruchny, and Brenda Macdougall (Norman: University of Oklahoma Press, 2012), 102–3. See also Adam Gaudry, "Métis," in *The Canadian Encyclopedia*, https://www.thecanadianencyclopedia.ca/en/article/metis, last edited September 11, 2019.

3. See, for example, Elliott Coues and David Thompson, *New Light on the Early History of the Greater Northwest: The Manuscript Journals of Alexander Henry and of David Thompson, 1799–1814* (New York: Harper: 1897), 1:224–28; W. S. Keating, S. H. Long, and Lewis David von Schweinitz, *Narrative of an Expedition to the Source of St. Peter's River, Lake Winnepeek, Lake of the Woods* [. . .] (London: G. B. Whittaker, 1825), 43–44; Bertha L. Heilbron, *With Pen and Pencil on the Frontier in 1851: The Diaries and Sketches of Frank Blackwell Mayer* (1932; repr., St. Paul: Minnesota Historical Society, 1986), 237–38.

4. Sami Lakomäki, *Gathering Together: The Shawnee People through Diaspora and Nationhood, 1600–1870* (New Haven CT: Yale University Press, 2014), 229–30.

5. The first Roman Catholic missionary priest arrived in the Red River Colony from Montreal in 1818. Luc Dauphinais, *Histoire de Saint-Boniface: À l'ombre des cathédrales* (Saint-Boniface MB: La Société historique de Saint-Boniface / Les Éditions du Blé, Saint-Boniface, 1991). For a sustained discussion of Métis Catholicism, see Émilie Pigeon, "Au nom du Bon Dieu et du Buffalo: Métis Lived Religion on the Northern Plains" (PhD diss., York University, 2017).

6. Brenda Macdougall and Nicole St-Onge, "Rooted in Mobility: Métis Buffalo Hunting Brigades," *Manitoba History* 71, no. 21 (Winter 2013): 16–27.

7. Gary Clayton Anderson, *The Indian Southwest, 1580–1830: Ethnogenesis and Reinvention* (Norman: University of Oklahoma Press, 1999), 3–8. See also Colin G. Calloway, *One Vast Winter Count: The American West before Lewis and Clark* (Lincoln: University of Nebraska Press, 2003), 301–12; and Theodore Binnema, *Common and Contested Grounds: A Human and Environmental History of the Northwestern Plains* (Toronto: University of Toronto Press, 2001).

8. Patricia C. Albers, "Changing Patterns of Ethnicity in the Northeastern Plains, 1780–1870," in *History, Power, and Identity: Ethnogenesis in the Americas, 1492–1992*, ed. Jonathan D. Hill (Iowa City: University of Iowa Press, 1996), 90–118.

9. Nicole St-Onge, "Plains Métis: Contours of an Identity," *Australasian Canadian Studies* 27, nos. 1–2 (2009): 95–115. For a broader context of fluid identities on the plains, see Pekka Hämäläinen, "The Rise and Fall of Plains Indian Horse Cultures," *Journal of American History* 90, no. 3 (2003): 485–513.

10. James D. McKillip, "A Métis Metier: Transportation in Rupert's Land" (master's thesis, University of Ottawa, 2005).

11. George Colpitts, "A Métis View of the Summer Market Hunt on the Northern Plains," in *Bison and People on the North American Great Plains: A Deep Environmental History*, ed. Geoff Cunfer and Bill Waiser (College Station: Texas A&M University Press, 2016), 201–24.

12. Pierre Charbonneau's father was one of the few voyageur forefathers not linked to the NWC. He was hired out of Montreal in 1815 by the HBC and never returned east. He dictated his memoirs in his dotage. Georges Dugas, *Un voyageur des Pays d'en haut* (Montreal: C. O. Beauchemin, 1890).

13. Judith Basin December 1879 petition, U.S. National Archives and Records Administration (NARA) 1 RG393 U.S. Army Commands 1821–1920, entry 1175 PT, Department of Dakota Letters Received, box 64, file 698 DD1880.

14. Three core sources helped to reconstruct the genealogies. The online *(Métis) Digital Archives Database Project* transcription of original western sacramental and census records (http://dadp.ok.ubc.ca/home) is the principal source. This database has been supplemented with Gail Morin, *Métis Families: A Genealogical Compendium*, 3rd ed., 11 vols. (self-pub., CreateSpace, 2016); and the Gabriel Dumont Institute of Native Studies and Applied Research, *Virtual Museum of Métis History and Culture, Biographies and Essay Collection*, http://www.metismuseum.ca/browse/index.php?id=15.

15. Allan Greer, *Peasant, Lord, and Merchant: Rural Society in Three Québec Parishes, 1740–1840* (Toronto: University of Toronto Press, 1985).

16. Christian Dessureault, "L'égalitarisme paysan dans l'ancienne société rurale de la vallée du Saint-Laurent: éléments pour une re-interprétation," *Revue d'histoire de l'Amérique française* 40 (Winter 1987): 373–407; and Robert Englebert and Nicole St-Onge, "Paddling into History: French-Canadian Voyageurs and the Creation of a Fur Trade World, 1730–1804," in *De Pierre-Esprit Radisson a Louis Riel: Voyageurs et Métis / From Pierre-Esprit Radisson to Louis Riel: Voyageurs and Métis*, ed. Denis Combet, Luc Cote, and Gilles Lesage (Winnipeg: Presses Universitaires de Saint-Boniface, 2014), 71–103.

17. *Programme de recherche en démographie historique* (PRDH), Université de Montréal, 1999–2015, https://www.prdh-igd.com/en/home. Jacques Rousseau was born in 1785, the seventh of twelve children, to J. Bte Rougeau Berger and Marie Louise Roussel. On his burial reference, J. Bte Berger was listed as a laborer residing in Laval.

18. Voyageur Contracts Database (VCD). The online version of this database containing thirty-five thousand contracts from mostly the Montreal area is hosted by the Centre du Patrimoine (Saint-Boniface, Manitoba) at http://dadp.ok.ubc.ca/.

19. Hudson's Bay Company Archives (HBCA), Provincial Archives of Manitoba (PAM), North West Company Ledger, F.4/32, "Berger, Jacques." Fort des Prairies was close to present-day Edmonton, Alberta, along the North Saskatchewan River.

20. He is shown in the spring 1821 NWC/HBC merger list as working in the Fort des Prairies area. HBCA, PAM, North West Balances, 1821, F.4.46, "Berger, Jacques."

21. Some of the ancestors of these French Catholic Métis families were Scots with surnames such as Grant and Wilkie. Often upper echelon employees or even partners in the NWC, they allied with local women and had families who normally remained in the interior. The progeny of some of these men merged into the growing French Catholic Métis hunting population. Historian Colin Calloway has asserted that Scots, coming from a clan-based society, apprehended more immediately the Native kinship-based world they entered. Colin G. Calloway, *White People, Indians, and Highlanders: Tribal People and Colonial Encounters in Scotland and America* (Oxford: Oxford University Press, 2008).

22. Carolyn Podruchny, *Making the Voyageur World: Travellers and Traders in the North American Fur Trade* (Toronto: University of Toronto Press, 2006), back cover excerpt.

23. At the turn of the nineteenth century, the Assiniboine River basin was called the Upper Red River, while the actual Red River Valley was coined the Lower Red River. Charles M. Gates, *Five Fur Traders of the Northwest* (St. Paul: Minnesota Historical Society, 1965), 97n63. See also George Woodcock, "Grant, Cuthbert (d. 1854)," in *Dictionary of Canadian Biography*, vol. 8 (University of Toronto/Université Laval, 2003), accessed March 3, 2020, http://www.biographi.ca/en/bio/grant_cuthbert_1854_8E.html.

The histories of men working in the fur trade come from a variety of sources. Montreal-area voyageur contracts can be accessed at http://dadp.ok.ubc.ca/. Post-1804 NWC personnel lists can be found at L. R. Masson, *Les Bourgeois de la Compagnie du Nord-Ouest: écrits de voyage, lettres et rapports inédits relatifs au Nord-Ouest canadien, publiés avec une esquisse historique et des annotations* (Québec: de l'Imprimerie générale A. Coté et cie, 1889–1890), 1:395–413. The 1811–21 account book is available at HBCA F.4/32 NWC, and the 1821 NWC-HBC merger master list is located at HBCA f.4/40 Servants Account 1821.

24. Heather Devine, "Les Desjarlais: The Development and Dispersion of a Proto-Métis Hunting Band, 1785–1870," in *From Rupert's Land to Canada*, ed. Theodore Binnema, Gerhard J. Ens, and Rod Macleod, (Edmonton: University of Alberta, 2001), 131–33.

25. Brock Silversides, *Fort de Prairies: The Story of Fort Edmonton* (Victoria BC: Heritage House, 2005), 10.

26. *Canadian Encyclopedia*, online edition, s.v., accessed March 3, 2020, "Red River Colony," http://www.thecanadianencyclopedia.ca/en/article/red-river-colony.

27. Nelly Laudicina, "Droit et Métissages, Évolution et usage de la loi a la colonie de la Rivière Rouge, 1811–1869," (PhD diss., University of Paris IV–Sorbonne & University of Ottawa, 2012), 92, quoting Beaver House, HBCA, D4/8, pp. 14–18. White Horse Plains is approximately sixteen miles upriver from the fork of the Red and Assiniboine Rivers. Freemen were company employees who had completed their contractual obligations to the company (or had deserted) and chosen to continue to live in the interior, often with their Native wives and children.

28. Laudicina, "Droit et Métissages," 101–2.

29. The transformation of the Teton Sioux into mounted commercial bison hunters is described in Kurt Anderson, "Illusions of Independence: The Teton Sioux and the American Fur Trade" (PhD diss., Oklahoma State University, 2011). See also David G. McCrady, *Living with Strangers: The Nineteenth-Century Sioux and the Canadian-American Borderlands* (Toronto: University of Toronto Press, 2010).

30. Rhoda R. Gilman, Carolyn Gilman, and Deborah L. Miller, *The Red River Trails: Oxcart Routes between St. Paul and the Selkirk Settlement, 1820–1870* (St. Paul: Minnesota Historical Society, 1979). For the genesis of the Pembina Métis community, see Jacqueline Peterson, "Gathering at the River: The Métis Peopling of the Northern Plains," in *The Fur Trade in North Dakota*, ed. Virginia L. Heidenreich (Bismarck: State Historical Society of North Dakota, 1990). Other Métis hunters likely followed disgruntled former NWC traders Joseph Renville and Kenneth MacKenzie when they founded the Columbia Fur Company (CFC; also known as Tilton & Co.). The CFC operated from 1822 to 1829, with its flagship, Fort Tecumseh, located near the mouth of the Bad (Teton) River, not far from its American Fur Company's successor, Fort Pierre. The CFC derived its Upper Missouri profits principally from the buffalo-robe trade.

31. James McKillip, "A Métis Métier: Transportation in Rupert's Land" (master's thesis, University of Ottawa, 2005).

32. Nineteenth-century Métis marriages normally were arranged by the bride's parents. Brides were usually young at the time of first nuptials, between the age of fourteen and twenty. See, for example, Doris Jeanne MacKinnon, *The Identities of Marie Rose Delorme: Portrait of a Métis Woman, 1861–1960* (Regina SK: University of Regina Press, 2012). Roman Catholic sacramental records for the western missions and parishes were accessed at the Centre du Patrimoine, Saint-Boniface, Manitoba. They were transcribed into an online database accessible at the Digital Archives Database Project (http://dadp.ok.ubc.ca/home).

33. The Tsuut'inas (Tsuu T'inas), or Sarcees, are an Athabaskan (Dene) nation whose reserve adjoins the southwestern city limits of Calgary, Alberta, http://www.thecanadianencyclopedia.ca/en/article/sarcee-tsuu-tina.

34. Alexandre Wilkie, of Scottish origin, was hired on as a clerk for seven years in 1800 by a NWC partner firm, Forsyth Richardson & Co. The contract was signed in the Montreal offices of notary public John G. Beek. Wilkie's destination merely mentions "Indian and Interior Countries." In the 1804 NWC roster, he is listed as a clerk in the Lower Red River District. During his time there, he contracted a country marriage with "Josephte Chippewa." Eventually Wilkie returned to Montreal, where he died in 1833 and was buried in the Presbyterian cemetery of Saint-Gabriel Street Church.

35. Jacques Berger apparently did not remain long in the British colony. Charles Larpenteur describes a Blackfoot-speaking old trapper and hunter called "Berger" who was a former HBC employee at Fort des Prairie. Until the early 1840s, Berger resided near Fort Union. This means his brigade-leading son Pierre would have had kin in situ in the Upper Missouri bison-hunting ranges from the very beginning of

the Berger brigade's existence. Charles Larpenteur, *Forty Years a Fur Trapper on the Upper Missouri* (Chicago: Lakeside, 1933), 92–93.

36. W. F. Rannie, "One Damned Thing after Another: The Environmental Challenges of the Red River Settlement," in *Papers of the 2010 Rupert's Land Colloquium*, ed. Anne Lindsay and Jennifer Ching (Winnipeg: Ruperts Land Centre, 2010), 353–74.

37. The son of a Scottish NWC clerk, Alexandre Wilkie worked in the Lower Red River District with Josephte, his Chippewa spouse.

38. In the 1850 Pembina census, the Berger-Wilkie children were listed as being nine, six, four, and one year old. Interestingly, the second marriage of Judith's sister, Madeleine, to Gabriel Dumont meant that the two Wilkie sisters had married a set of cross cousins. Pierre Berger's mother, Cecile Dumont, was the sister of Gabriel Dumont's father, Isidore Dumont. Cross-cousin marriages and alliances were a recurring pattern in Plains Métis brigades' composition.

39. Patricia H. Harpole and Mary D. Nagle, *Minnesota Territorial Census, 1850* (St. Paul: Minnesota Historical Society, 1972), 24.

40. United Sates, Department of the Interior, *Half-Breed Scrip, Chippewas of Lake Superior: The Correspondence and Action Under the 7th Clause of the 2d Article of the Treaty with the Chippewa Indians of Lake Superior and the Mississippi, Concluded at La Pointe in the State of Wisconsin, September 30, 1854* [. . .] (Washington DC: Government Printing Office, 1874); and Charles J. Kappler, *Indian Affairs: Laws and Treaties* (Washington DC: Government Printing Office, 1904), 2:861–62 (article 7).

41. Martha Harroun Foster, *We Know Who We Are: Métis Identity in a Montana Community* (Norman: University of Oklahoma Press, 2006).

42. In both cases the maternal grandparents' generation were Joseph Caplette, who was a NWC Upper Red River (Assiniboine River basin) voyageur for the Turcotte family, and Andre Trottier, a NWC Red River employee involved in the 1816 Seven Oaks battle whose mother was a Saulteaux woman for the Laframboise family. These are, again, examples of strategic alliances uniting families from different geographic foci and different maternal tribal affiliations.

43. An older generation of scholars coined the term "people-class" to describe such societies based on economic hyperspecialization. See Abram Leon, *The Jewish Question: A Marxist Interpretation* (1950; repr., New York: Pathfinder, 1974), 74.

44. Nicholas Vrooman, "Cree, Assiniboine, Ojibwa & Michif: The Nehiyaw Pwat Confederacy/Iron Alliance in Montana" (paper presented at the Montana Historical Society annual meeting, September 2014), https://www.scribd.com/document/340180950/Cree-Assiniboine-Ojibwa-and-Michif-The-Nehiyaw-Pwat-Confederacy-Iron-Alliance-in-Montana.

45. David G. Mandelbaum, "The Plains Cree," *Anthropological Papers of the American Museum of Natural History* 37, no. 2 (1940): 173; and Floyd W. Sharrock and Susan R. Sharrock, "A History of the Cree Indians Territorial Expansion from the Hudson's Bay to the Interior Saskatchewan and Missouri Plains," in *Chippewa Indians VI* (New York: Garland, 1974), 206–8. This work was prepared for the Indian Claims Commission, 1974, Docket 221b-191.

46. Laudicina, "Droit et Métissages," 92.

47. For a discussion of the Michif language, see Peter Baker, *A Language of Our Own: The Genesis of Michif, the Mixed-Cree-French Language of the Canadian Métis* (Oxford: Oxford University Press, 1997).

48. William Morton, "The Battle of Grand Coteau, July 13 and 14," *Manitoba Historical Society Transactions* 3, no. 16 (1960): 37–49.

49. Bertha L. Heilbron, "Minnesota as Seen by Travelers: Isaac I. Stevens and the Pacific Railroad Survey of 1853," *Minnesota History* (June 1926): 127–49.

50. Bob Beal and Rob Macleod, *Prairie Fire: The 1885 North-West Rebellion* (Toronto: McClelland & Stewart, 1994), 260–61.

51. NARA 1, RG393 U.S. Army Commands 1821–1920, entry 1175 PT, Department of Dakota Letters Received, box 64, file October 1879.

52. W. Hildebrandt, *The Battle of Batoche: British Warfare and the Entrenched Métis* (Ottawa: Parks Canada, 1985).

53. Nicholas C. P. Vrooman, *The Whole Country Was . . . "One Robe": The Little Shell Tribe's America* (Billings MT: Drumlummon Institute, 2012), 387–98.

54. Jean Teillet, *Métis Law in Canada* (Vancouver BC: Pape Salter Teillet, 2013); Gabriel Furshong, "Will the Little Shell Tribe Finally Be Recognized?" *High Country News*, December 7, 2015, http://www.hcn.org/issues/47.21/will-the-little-shell-tribe-finally-be-recognized.

55. Jim Robbins, "125 Years Later, Native American Tribe in Montana Gets Federal Recognition," *New York Times*, February 3, 2020, https://www.nytimes.com/2020/02/01/us/little-shell-montana-tribe.html.

6

Fauna and Flux on the Plains' Edge
Animal Kinship, Place Making, and Cherokee Relational Continuity

CLINT CARROLL

Introduction

Throughout Cherokee history, animals have figured prominently as agents of creation, originators of disease, keepers of knowledge, and helpers to human beings.[1] In common with many Indigenous traditions, Cherokee animal stories impart lessons that draw upon distinctive animal traits and behaviors in order to teach humans about their own nature.[2] These stories convey a voiced relationality with nonhuman animals, and this has extended to the structure of Cherokee society through the matrilineal clan system. As elder Benny Smith shows, each of the seven Cherokee clans can be associated with specific animals, even though their common English glosses vary: Deer, Panther (also referred to as Long Hair), Bear (also referred to as Blue), Bird, Hawk (also referred to as Paint), Wolf, and Small Prairie Animal (also referred to as Savannah or Wild Potato).[3] While the matrilineal clan system continues to govern Cherokee ceremonial practices today—for example, at numerous stomp grounds throughout northeastern Oklahoma—matrilineal clans once overtly governed Cherokee life before the political centralization of the Cherokee Nation in the early 1800s. As I and others have described, profound changes in Cherokee society caused by the encroachment of the United States and its citizens into Cherokee lands led to the de-emphasis of the matrilineal clans and the centralization of political authority under a constitutional government.[4]

Such settler colonial pressures and policies punctuated Cherokee life from the eighteenth to the twentieth century, as experienced through the deerskin trade (ca. 1715–60), Removal and Reconstruction eras (ca. 1830–60), the U.S. Civil War (1861–65), the Allotment era (1887–1934), and Oklahoma statehood in 1907. Although scholars have described the social, political, and environmental changes to which each of these historical eras and events contributed,[5] less studied are Cherokee perspectives toward—or, more accurately, *kinship with*—nonhuman animals amid these tumultuous times and into the present. As such, this chapter asks: How have Cherokee relationships to nonhuman animals both changed and exhibited continuity through time? Specifically, how did Cherokees voice or enact this relationality during the post-Removal era in the Indian Territory—an area that occupies the easternmost fringes of the Great Plains? Lastly, what might these dynamic perspectives offer Cherokee environmental policy and governance today?

This topic is an understudied element of Cherokee life in the western lands, considering that Cherokee relationships to plant life have received the most scholarly attention.[6] Yet animals—as integral components of ecosystems, a means of human survival, and nonhuman *teachers*—deserve serious consideration when seeking to understand Indigenous environmental adaptation. I approach the above questions through an analysis of selected ethnohistorical accounts. Although some scholars have focused on the incorporation of domesticated animal species into Cherokee lifeways, and thus how this influenced Cherokee sociocultural change,[7] I focus solely on "wild" animal species—a philosophically loaded category that nonetheless has a Cherokee linguistic corollary: *inage anehi*, or "those that live out there." As such, this chapter explores both sociocultural change *and* continuity in Cherokee society through the lens of human-animal sociality. And while I recognize that attempting to answer the above questions with regard to an Indigenous nation characterized by diverse socioeconomic standings and perspectives since at least the eighteenth century renders my conclusions incomplete, I maintain that this project offers useful insights to the topics of Indigenous animal kinship, place making, and what I term "relational continuity," or the persistence of ethically and culturally grounded relationships with other-than-human animals despite social and spatial change. Due to limitations of space and the historical record, I focus selectively on two animals that are both represented in the Cherokee clan system: deer and panther. First, I turn to a brief contextualization of the topic in the relevant scholarship.

Human-Animal Sociality, Indigenous Perspectives, and Environmental History

In his writings on Indigenous religions and metaphysics, Standing Rock Sioux scholar Vine Deloria Jr. repeatedly stressed how Indigenous perspectives on "the environment" often contradict Western European worldviews.[8] As Onondaga Faithkeeper Oren Lyons asserts, these contradictions stem from the fundamental view that other-than-human beings are construed by Indigenous peoples as "relatives," in contrast to a Western view that treats various life forms as "resources."[9] North American anthropologists have observed and recorded numerous examples of this in their work with Indigenous peoples,[10] but only recently has the conversation turned to the implications of *taking seriously* (i.e., literally) such perspectives for the practice of social science.

Anthropologist Paul Nadasdy offers a thorough discussion of this topic, drawing on his own and others' work with northern Indigenous hunting peoples of North America.[11] Nadasdy's point of departure is the contradiction within social scientific research between what social scientists seek to study and how they present their findings. Adding to Elizabeth Povinelli's critique,[12] Nadasdy asserts that in working with Indigenous peoples, social scientists must acknowledge dynamics of uneven power relations, authority, and legitimacy within the act of research, and therefore actively question the ethics of simultaneously promoting Indigenous knowledge while undermining its foundational premises. In other words, taking Indigenous knowledge seriously requires that social scientists present Indigenous knowledge of—and experiences with—animals as *facts* rather than abstract "beliefs" or "customs." Doing so not only has implications for how anthropologists might lend their expertise to Indigenous land-based struggles, but also for how social scientists carry out their research. Ultimately, Nadasdy argues that the study of Indigenous hunting traditions (and therefore human-animal sociality) calls for expanding the analytic concept of "society" to include animals.[13]

Nadasdy's and others' contributions in this regard have relevance for environmental history and specifically the study of social and environmental change as experienced by Indigenous peoples. If, as in many Indigenous traditional perspectives, animals are regarded as nonhuman persons, then their presence or absence on the land as a result of human or extrahuman activities throughout history can tell us something about Indigenous experiences of change. For example: What embodied teachings of the Wolf clan in Cherokee society persist without contact with (and therefore ongoing relationships to) wolves? Reading "environmental" changes as changes in the *social fabric* of Indigenous societies may thus lend itself to new interpretations of historical circumstances and their contemporary legacies.[14]

That animals are a part of many Indigenous understandings of "society" is expressed in the Cherokee language as *nigada gusdi didadadvhni*—"we are all related." This phrase is understood to extend beyond the human realm to include other-than-human beings, and teaches us to acknowledge the interdependence and sacredness of life in all its forms.[15] As Vine Deloria Jr. has stated, such an understanding cannot be separated from how many Indigenous peoples view their inhabitation of the world as rooted in a set of relational responsibilities.[16] In a similar vein, Dave Aftandilian proposes a Native American "theology of animals," drawing on published Creek and Cherokee perspectives.[17] Although he acknowledges that an overarching Native American theology risks obscuring the cultural diversity among present-day Native nations, he follows recent work by Native scholars and theologians in identifying central precepts that can be related across cultures.[18]

His resulting synthesis identifies four main tenets of a Native theology of animals: (1) animals are older, more powerful, and more knowledgeable than humans; (2) animals have abilities to cross between realms of existence and are therefore highly regarded for their supernatural and spiritual abilities; (3) a spiritually based "natural law" describes how humans should treat other animals with humility and respect and behave according to principles of reciprocity in return for the sustenance that animals provide; and (4) animals are viewed as nonhuman relatives.[19] This set of concepts aligns with my ethnographic observations and conversations with contemporary Cherokees in Oklahoma.[20]

Aftandilian states, "When native peoples stop encountering animals in their daily lives, and stop depending on them for subsistence and spiritual power, the animals become correspondingly less important in their theologies."[21] Others have similarly written about such dynamics to describe the loss of knowledge of and relationships with nonhumans that can result from settler colonial violence and increased participation in market economies.[22] And yet, in line with Potawatomi scholar Kyle Whyte's discussion of contemporary Indigenous species restoration projects,[23] we might view Indigenous adaptations through time as enacting *technologies of relationality*. Whereas "technology" typically connotes material innovations to overcome practical problems (often through the use of Western science), I propose that Indigenous cultural technologies informed by ethical frameworks of relationality lead to innovations that decenter modernist and Western interpretations.[24] In the stories I present below, Cherokees used technologies of relationality to make sense of the social and geographical changes that resulted from dispossession and therefore were able to maintain their place as Cherokees in relation to other beings and lands. One could argue that this relational continuity then informed key elements of life during the decades that followed removal, as I have discussed elsewhere.[25] And yet, although herein I center Cherokee relational continuity, I do not intend to evade the reality of differential social and environmental practices among a quite diverse population of Cherokee citizens in the past and at present. These have included enclosing vast amounts of land to support chattel slavery and tenant farming.[26] However, throughout time, the majority of Cherokees viewed these practices as deviations from ancestral teachings and social ideals, such as respect for life, individual autonomy, and communal ownership of land.[27]

Following a brief discussion of Cherokee experiences of migration/removal, I then discuss ethnohistorical accounts of animals in the Indian Territory (present-day northeastern Oklahoma) juxtaposed with corresponding Cherokee traditional stories. I seek to make sense of how Cherokees experienced social and political change through their actions toward and voicings about nonhuman animals. I draw upon both traditional stories recorded by ethnographers and the oral histories contained in the Indian-Pioneer Papers of the Western Historical Collections at the University of Oklahoma. Although the Indian-Pioneer Papers can provide only selective accounts of Cherokee life, my intent is to highlight narratives of how Cherokees both described and experienced the landscape and its fellow inhabitants.

Migration/Removal and Cherokee Place Making

The lands west of the Mississippi River in present-day Arkansas and Oklahoma were populated by Cherokees well before the forced removal of the Cherokee Nation beginning in 1838 on the Trail of Tears. Cherokee people had inhabited these areas some say as early as 1721.[28] The gradual emigration is often attributed to the increasing depletion of game in the eastern homelands caused by the deerskin trade.[29] However, traditionalist accounts stress that these Cherokees, known as Western Cherokees, and later, Old Settlers, sought to move away from conflict with European-Americans, thus upholding ancient Keetoowah religious precepts against violence.[30] Nevertheless, the peaceful outlook of the Keetoowahs did not hold true for all Western Cherokees—in 1794, after their bloody attack of two stranded boats at the Muscle Shoals massacre, the Chickamauga Band of Cherokees also settled in the western lands. During this early period of settlement, Cherokees mainly inhabited the areas around the St. Francis and White Rivers in what was then considered Spanish Louisiana. Historical work on Cherokees in this region shows that the Old Settlers had established a way of life similar to common Cherokee lifestyles in the eastern lands, employing a mix of subsistence hunting and both small- and large-scale agricultural and animal husbandry practices.[31]

The early Keetoowah Cherokee migration was also informed by prophecy, which foretold "a white ball from way east, who is your enemy, coming and your grand children's [sic] feet are directed west; they shall have great trials on the edge of the prairie.... But if these younger generation [sic] should endeavor to follow God's instruction, there is a chance to turn back east and if not, the next move shall be [further] west."[32] Additional conversation with contemporary Oklahoma Cherokees about this prophecy has indicated that moving beyond the "great prairie" would signal the end of the Keetoowah Cherokees as a people.[33] Such conditions eventually led to many Cherokee communities reestablishing themselves at the very edge of the plains in the westernmost hill-country of the Ozark Highlands and Boston Mountains. Perhaps not coincidentally, the oak-hickory forests of this region afforded Cherokees many of their familiar plants that they had known and used in the east.[34]

The Cherokee inhabitation of the western lands was not without conflict from other Native peoples who called these lands home, namely the Osages and Quapaws, who viewed Cherokees as invaders. Although the U.S. government attempted to regulate relations between the tribes, from 1805 to 1807 Cherokees and Osages fought over the use and occupation of the territory. In October 1818 the Old Settlers and the Osages signed a treaty between themselves on their own accord, but the Osages later abandoned the pact due to the increasing number of Cherokees and other Native peoples (relocated Shawnees, Delawares, and Oneidas) who continued to settle in the area. As a result, warfare between Cherokees and Osages continued until around 1824.[35]

Contemporary Cherokee ethnohistorical accounts tell of the initial exploration of what later became the Cherokee lands of the Indian Territory during the tense period of conflict with the Osages.

Elder and Keetoowah traditionalist Crosslin Smith has recounted to me the journeys of Ugewaleda, a renowned Cherokee leader and half-brother to the well-known intellectual, Sequoyah.[36] Ugewaleda's journeys through present-day Arkansas and Oklahoma resulted in Cherokee place-names that are still used today, which provide insight into past environmental conditions as well as how Cherokees made sense of place away from their familiar homelands. Ugewaleda's story also appears in the Doris Duke Papers of the Western Historical Collections, and I recount this version below (also provided by Crosslin Smith, in 1967):

> One story I'd like to relate is the story of a warrior. He was a leader, and according to the traditional Cherokee's record book, he was a half-brother to Sequoyah, the man who devised a way for the Cherokees to read and write. . . . The story goes, the Osage tribe for some reason or another, had their hunting party in the Cherokee territory. And they come across a Cherokee hunting party and without warning the Osage hunting party fired three arrows at the Cherokee hunting party and killed three Cherokee hunters. . . . They fled without a fight—they escaped [to the] westernly [sic] direction. And when the Cherokee hunting party finally got the dead back to the camp and reported to their chief, the chief decided, "Well, if this is what the Osages wanted to do maybe they should pay it back, or maybe we ought to select a leader and pick out warriors and pursue." After some thinking went into this situation, this man [Ugewaleda]—in Cherokee the meaning of [his] name is "Turn the Page"[37]—was given the responsibility of leading a small war party to pursue the Osage hunting party.
>
> [During his journey he named Fort Smith, Arkansas] as a "place of the old fence" and the Cherokees have always known this place as [*uweti disoya*] since probably before statehood and possibly before territorial days. [It is said that he came across an old fence that was likely built by the Spanish.] And [he named] Sallisaw, [Oklahoma] "place of the swamps" [*amayulv disaluyi*]. [That] land was in swamps—that much water was there. Now, today this land is dry and it stands to reason that this man travelled this land before

any. Maybe the Spanish Exploration took place first, but it's hard to say. But then, Vian, Oklahoma was named as a "place of the garfish" [*dahnugo*] because . . . this man saw a large garfish in that area in the water. . . . But now leaving Vian, he come to a place where there were spotted deer feeding out in the field [likely the characteristic pronghorn antelope of the Great Plains, then unfamiliar to Cherokees]. [It was] an open country at that time and he called this "the place of the spotted deer" [*tsusqua gali*]. The location in English is Ft. Gibson [Oklahoma].

And as he crossed the Arkansas River at the present town of Ft. Gibson, just a few miles to the west, this is where he caught up with the Osage hunting party. [They were] all exhausted and [it] seemed like [there was] no fight left in them. And in exchange for these three Cherokee scalps that the Osages had taken, the leader gave a command to take all the scalps, Osage scalps, and that of the three [Cherokee] scalps too. He retrieved everything and went back to his base camp, back in the east, and reported to his chief [of his] successful . . . encounter with the enemy.[38]

This story recounts early Cherokee experiences in the western lands that, although incited by warfare, inscribed in place-names descriptions of the land's features and its animal inhabitants. These place-names continue to hold these observed landscape features for Cherokee speakers even in their present-day absence, thus encoding environmental knowledge and relationships to place in the language. I have discussed elsewhere that, in coming to know these lands, Cherokees inscribed themselves onto the landscape; conversely, the land made its imprint upon Cherokees as a place of warfare, spiritual experience, removal, and renewal.[39]

Decades after Ugewaleda's journey west, the Trail of Tears in 1838–39 resulted in the loss of over one-fourth of the Cherokee population, and with them many elders and knowledge-keepers, dealing a significant blow to Cherokee cultural transmission.[40] Yet, in the reconstruction period after the Removal, Cherokees began to regain footing in the reestablishment of the tribal government and educational institutions. Following another period of turmoil during the American Civil War, Cherokees again rebuilt their communities and enjoyed a brief era of prosperity.[41] This era has been partially captured in the recollections of Cherokee people who were alive during the U.S. Works Progress Administration's Indian-Pioneer Oral History Project of the 1930s, which comprises the Indian-Pioneer Papers. I now turn to selected accounts by Cherokee people of animals in the Indian Territory included in these papers, juxtaposing them with traditional stories recorded by anthropologists in order to glean meaning regarding Cherokee relationships to animals amid profound social and political change.

Animal Stories and the Continuity of Cherokee Relationality

Many accounts in the Indian-Pioneer Papers speak of environmental change, including the early presence and then absence of once-abundant animals. These accounts are widespread and prove unwieldy for attempts at comprehensive descriptions. Necessarily, I have selectively chosen in-depth accounts that speak to Cherokee relationality with nonhuman animals, specifically ones that I could relate directly to Cherokee oral traditions and cultural frameworks—in this case, the matrilineal clan system. What follows are accounts of two animals—panther (*tlvdatsi*, or *Puma concolor*) and deer (*awi*, or *Odocoileus virginianus*)—both of which have seen times of flourishing and near decimation in eastern Oklahoma.[42]

The following story, titled "A Pit Panther," is recounted in 1937 by John Henry West, a Cherokee from Vian, Oklahoma. I juxtapose the story with an account by anthropologist James Mooney, titled "The Underground Panthers," from his work with Eastern Band Cherokees in North Carolina (published in 1900). The stories provide glimpses into both ancestral perspectives toward panthers and more recent physical encounters and acts of relationality with them.

JOHN HENRY WEST, "A PIT PANTHER"

I remember very distinctly when I was about ten years of age, two neighbors by the name of George Griffin and Bill Toonewee, who were Cherokees, killed a large male panther on the side of the mountain west of Porum. Later, George Griffin was out hunting alone and discovered the female panther crawling on a ledge of rock waiting to leap upon him and he shot it. Fearing he had only wounded the animal and not having another load in his gun, he ran home for assistance. Griffin, Toonewee, and another fellow returned to the place and found the panther dead.

On examination of the animal, they saw that she was suckling her young. They made a search and located her den, pried away some rocks and captured two young kittens. They took them home, let them run around in the house at their will and they soon accustomed themselves to their situation and would play about in the house like a couple of house cats. When Mrs. Toonewee would be knitting by the fireside after the evening meal, the panther kittens would get the balls of yarn out of her work basket and bat them around the room. In their play one evening, the female jumped and fell into the fireplace, and was so severely burned that she died from the effects. The male, after the death of its mate, became greatly attached to Mrs. Toonewee's little daughter Susie, who was about ten years of age. It followed her every step. Tom, as the panther was named, would go with Susie to the spring which was about two hundred yards from the house. Sometimes in their play Susie would hide from Tom, and if he did not immediately find her, he would give the inimitable scream that only the panther is capable of giving, leaping about among the bushes and trees until he located Susie. Then he would leap and play about her in a fit of glee.

This close companionship and play continued until the panther was almost grown. Then the parents of Susie became uneasy for fear that in their play the child would be injured by the animal. As much as they regretted separating this little Indian girl from her companion of the forest they took Tom to Muskogee and sold him to a show for twenty dollars.[43]

JAMES MOONEY, "THE UNDERGROUND PANTHERS"

A hunter was in the woods one day in winter when suddenly he saw a panther coming toward him and at once prepared to defend himself. The panther continued to approach, and the hunter was just about to shoot when the animal spoke, and at once it seemed to the man as if there was no difference between them, and they were both of the same nature. The panther asked him where he was going, and the man said that he was looking for a deer. "Well," said the panther, "we are getting ready for a Green-corn dance,[44] and there are seven of us out after a buck, so we may as well hunt together."

The hunter agreed and they went on together. They started up one deer and another, but the panther made no sign, and said only "Those are too small; we want something better." So the hunter did not shoot, and they went on. They started up another deer, a larger one, and the panther sprang upon it and tore its throat, and finally killed it after a hard struggle. The hunter got out his knife to skin it, but the panther said the skin was too much torn to be used and they must try again. They started up another large deer, and this the panther killed without trouble, and then, wrapping his tail around it, threw it across his back. "Now, come to our townhouse," he said to the hunter.

The panther led the way, carrying the captured deer upon his back, up a little stream branch until they came to the head spring, when it seemed as if a door opened in the side of the hill and they went in. Now the hunter found himself in front of a large townhouse, with the finest *detsänûñ'lï* he had ever seen,[45] and the trees around were green, and the air was warm, as in summer. There was a great company there getting ready for the dance, and they were all panthers, but somehow it all seemed natural to the hunter. After a while the others who had been out came in with the deer they had taken, and the dance began. The hunter danced several rounds, and then said it was growing late and he must be getting home. So the panthers opened the door and he went out, and at once found himself alone in the woods again, and it was winter and very cold, with snow on the ground and on all the trees. When he reached the settlement he found a party just starting out to search for him. They asked him where he had been so long, and he told them the story, and then he found that he had been in the panther townhouse several days instead of only a very short time, as he had thought.

He died within seven days after his return, because he had already begun to take on the panther nature, and so could not live again with men. If he had stayed with the panthers he would have lived.[46]

Perhaps these two stories raise more questions than answers. How did the Toonewees discuss the matter of two panther kittens running around the house? Was the story of "The Underground Panthers" told by the Toonewees around their evening fire? Were panthers mentioned as the animal representatives of the Long Hair Clan, perhaps even in the context of Mr. and Mrs. Toonewee's clan affiliations? In what ways did such cultural contexts inform the adoption of Tom the Panther into the Toonewees' family? These are details about which we can only speculate, and yet, the relationship (West describes this as "companionship") between Tom the Panther and Susie Toonewee is clear—despite its melancholy ending, the story provides a glimpse into how Cherokees enacted relationality with nonhumans and in the process blurred the boundaries (even if temporarily) between "wild" and "domestic," "human" and "animal."

The following story, titled "An Incident with a Deer," is recounted in 1938 by George Whitmire, a Cherokee from Muskogee, Oklahoma. I juxtapose this story with another excerpt from anthropologist James Mooney on Little Deer (Awi Usdi) to illustrate the significance of deer to Cherokee people since ancestral times.

GEORGE WHITMIRE, "AN INCIDENT WITH A DEER"

I recall an incident that occurred when I was about 16 years of age and was working for W. S. Hyatt, a white man who had our ranch leased after the death of my father. I was riding over the range one morning in search of some cattle that were missing from the herd and was riding along through the tall prairie grass, expecting nothing to happen, and like a flash, a fawn about half grown leaped up out of the grass in front of my horse. I was riding a very fast horse, and the instant the fawn leaped up and started I put the spurs to my horse and took after it. Taking my lariat from my saddlehorn, by the time the horse came into position I threw and caught the fawn with his neck and one foreleg in the noose, which made a nice safe throw of the deer. I leaped from my horse and proceeded to tie him up, but believe me it is a much harder job tying a deer than it is a steer for they can handle their feet so fast and their little hoofs are almost like a knife when they strike. I managed to loop and tie his feet without his breaking a leg, got him all tied up good, placed the little fellow on my horse and took him to the ranch. I put a stake rope on him so he could not hurt himself, then unhobbled him.

After a day or so his spell of fright gradually left him and he began to drink warm sweet milk which I would feed him when we milked the cows. He soon became accustomed to his situation and looked forward to feeding time morning and evening; he would watch for me as I came from the milk lot. He would run to the end of his rope and surge against it trying to meet me when he would see me with his bucket of milk.

After keeping him on a stake rope about one month he had become such a pet I put a little sheep bell on him and after he became accustomed to the bell I turned him loose and let him run at liberty about the place. He would follow me every step and was the greatest pet I ever had. He would go away into the nearby woods and would be gone sometimes most of the day but would always come back home in the evening. On one occasion in the evening after one of his days' absence from the place, my mother was on the back porch of the home and saw the deer out back of the corral and called for me to come and see what he had with him. Other members of the family and I went out on the rear porch, and there was Buck, the deer, with three other deer he had brought home with him. As soon as the wild deer saw us they broke into a wild dash back for the hills. My deer stood there with his head high in the air, watching them as they disappeared in the timber as though, he was wondering what they had to fear and why they ran away. After they had vanished from view, he came on to the house, apparently very disgusted.

Finally his trips to the hills became more frequent and his absence from home much longer, first staying away overnight, then later two or three days at a time. Realizing that it was only a matter of time until I would lose him entirely, we killed and butchered him before some hunter had a chance to shoot him.[47]

JAMES MOONEY, "LITTLE DEER (AWI USDI)"

The deer, *ahwi*, which is still common in the mountains, was the principal dependence of the Cherokee hunter, and is consequently prominent in myth, folklore, and ceremonial. One of the seven gentes [clans] of the tribe is named from it (Ani-Kawi, "Deer People").... The powerful chief of the deer tribe is the Awi Usdi, or "Little Deer," who is invisible to all except the greatest masters of the hunting secrets, and can be wounded only by the hunter who has supplemented years of occult study with frequent fasts and lonely vigils. The Little Deer keeps constant protecting watch over his subjects, and sees well to it that not one is ever killed in wantonness. When a deer is shot by the hunter, the Little Deer knows it at once and is instantly at the spot. Bending low his head, he asks of the blood stains upon the ground if they have heard if the hunter has asked pardon for the life that he has taken. If the formulistic prayer has been made, all is well, because the necessary sacrifice has been atoned for; but if otherwise, the Little Deer tracks the hunter to his house by the blood drops along the trail, and, unseen and unsuspected, puts into his body the spirit of rheumatism that shall rack him with aches and pains from that time henceforth. As seen at rare intervals—perhaps once in a long lifetime—the Little Deer is pure white and about the size of a small dog, has branching antlers, and is always in company with a large herd of deer. Even though shot by the master hunter, he comes to life again, being immortal, but the fortunate huntsman who can thus make prize of his antlers has in them an unfailing talisman that brings him success in the chase forever after.[48]

George Whitmire's account notably ascribes agency to his friend and "pet" through the validation of Buck's intelligence and the recognition of his relationality with the Whitmires. This is evident in how Whitmire describes Buck's apparent communication with other "wild" deer to bring them to the homestead and show them his human family. Again, questions arise out of this juxtaposition between the ethnographic and the ethnohistorical: Were there dinner-table conversations about Awi Usdi at the Whitmire's house during their acquaintance with Buck the Deer? In what way did such ancestral knowledge of "the powerful chief of the deer tribe" factor into George Whitmire's initial decision to pursue and capture Buck? And although the account similarly concludes on a melancholy note—in this case, the killing of his adopted relative by his own hands—Whitmire voices his regret when faced with the risk of losing Buck to an opportunistic (and unfamiliar) hunter.

The cases of panther and deer above illustrate Cherokee enactments and voicings in the western lands that, although they differ in substance from the ethnographic material obtained from Cherokees in the eastern homelands by Mooney, still exhibit relationality with nonhuman animals, and thus perspectives that honor their agency as "other-than-human persons."[49] As Cherokees made their way west—some led by religious precepts, others by gunpoint—how they made sense of themselves as a people was shaped in relation to their surroundings, including their nonhuman coinhabitants of the land. The Keetoowah prophecy that warns of cultural demise after crossing over the edge of the "great prairie" can be seen as a practical reality when one considers the network of Cherokee relationships that would be compromised in the absence of familiar nonhuman plant and animal relatives (which, to a large extent, are still present in the Ozarks of northeastern Oklahoma). And yet, Cherokees like the Whitmires, who did venture onto the plains (peripheral though these places may be), maintained relational continuity with nonhuman animals and thus their connection as Cherokees to the natural world.

Such an emphasis on continuity should not be taken as an argument for cultural stasis nor antiquated theories from cultural ecology.⁵⁰ Vine Deloria's work on the contrast between viewing history *spatially* versus *temporally* emphasizes the centrality of place to many American Indian philosophies and religions. He writes, "it must be spaces and places that distinguish us from one another, not time nor [Western] history."⁵¹ Therefore, "reading" Indigenous migrations and forced removals through relationality with land and nonhuman beings centers Indigenous adaptability *and* continuity. In moving west as displaced Indigenous people, Cherokees and the plains had to get to know one another. In seeing the old (animals) in the new (place), Cherokee mobility forged novel attachments and voicings of animal kinship particular to that place.

In sum, these selected accounts of Cherokee people's relationships to animals, despite the changing social and environmental conditions that resulted from Cherokee migration/removal to the Indian Territory, exhibit continuity when viewed in the context of Cherokee technologies of relationality. Such stories—however nuanced and subjective these encounters may have been—suggest that as Cherokees adapted to changing environmental conditions, they did so through a lens of relationality to animals that maintained their worldview as Cherokees. Viewing Indigenous agency through this lens invites us to approach persistence and innovation as a matter of cultural continuity—maintaining an Indigenous outlook on the world in the face of drastic changes in circumstances and place. This approach also shows how Indigenous change is not always reactive to outside pressures or impositions. We see this in the experiences of mobility and place making that preceded the Trail of Tears, specifically in the story of Ugewaleda. Further, this approach pushes us to reconsider not only how we view the role of technology on the Great Plains, but how we understand that which constitutes technology itself. Indeed, perhaps what our societies need today more than ever is an understanding of how cultural technologies can work to counteract dominant technocratic narratives of control over and management of the earth, and instead to reinforce our roles and responsibilities as kin.⁵²

Conclusion

What insights might this historical outlook hold for contemporary times? Elsewhere I have argued that in North America, Indigenous environmental governance operates within a continuum of *resource-based* and *relationship-based* practices, wherein constitutionally and bureaucratically organized tribes like the Cherokee Nation have the ability to articulate environmental policies that necessarily employ both Western and Indigenous perspectives.[53] My ethnographic work with a collective body of Cherokee elders shows how the assertion of Indigenous relationship-based perspectives on land and governance alters Western processes like natural resource management by presenting alternative ways of interacting with and "governing" nonhuman nature. Given the recent inclination to incorporate such perspectives into tribal governance, this opens the discussion for how we might enact relational continuity as a guiding principle for tribal environmental policy.

In the many conversations I have had with Oklahoma Cherokee elders and knowledge-keepers during the course of my ethnographic field work since 2004, animals have maintained their significance in Cherokee relational systems as nonhuman teachers, messengers, and mediators. The Cherokee Nation currently touts numerous wildlife conservation measures, such as a culturally protected species list (which includes the bald eagle, black bear, and mountain lion), a bison herd, and a recent bald eagle reintroduction program. And yet, as Onondaga elder Oren Lyons once remarked to the United Nations, "Where is the seat for the buffalo or the eagle? Who is representing them here in this forum?"[54] Strategically engaging the arena of environmental governance to give voice to other-than-human beings would mirror numerous other efforts that have been spearheaded by Indigenous peoples around the world.

Political representation for—and the acknowledgement of corresponding rights to—the natural world and nonhuman persons (plants, animals, landforms, and bodies of water, among others) would demonstrate Cherokee relational continuity within tribal environmental policy and governance, and show how Cherokees can articulate and assert alternatives to Western approaches in local, regional, national, and global arenas. As Steve Pavlik writes, "The fact is that if countries like Switzerland, Germany, and Ecuador can rewrite their constitutions to recognize the rights of nature, why not the Indigenous tribes for whom it is a far more inherent part of their culture? . . . It is quite obvious that tribes can do so if they possess the desire and political courage."[55] Indeed, our era of profound climate change calls for such bold strategies for maintaining and preserving our knowledge and land-based practices as Indigenous peoples. Perhaps, as I have attempted to show in this piece, in understanding the adaptive capacity *and* cultural continuity of Cherokee people, we can all draw important conclusions for our approaches to the pressing environmental issues of our time. In this light, rather than what we might fix with machines and inventions, we might refocus on how—as humans—we can maintain (or, in many cases, reestablish) our relationships to the other beings of the earth that position us as good relatives rather than adversaries.

Notes

I thank Cherokee/Creek scholar and my respected mentor Dr. Tom Holm for inspiring me to take up this topic, my friend and elder Crosslin Smith for sharing his knowledge with me, Drs. Kathleen Brosnan and Brian Frehner for creating the time and space to flesh out the ideas herein, and the Center for Native American and Indigenous Studies writing group at CU Boulder for all the helpful feedback. I also thank the Osage and Kiowa Nations on whose lands we gathered to discuss and think through this volume.

1. For published versions of many Cherokee animal stories, see James Mooney, *Cherokee History, Myths, and Sacred Formulas: 7th and 19th Annual Reports of the Bureau of American Ethnology* (Cherokee NC: Museum of the Cherokee Indian, 2006). For more contemporary accounts of Eastern Band Cherokees in North Carolina, see Barbara R. Duncan and Davey Arch, *Living Stories of the Cherokee* (Chapel Hill: University of North Carolina Press, 1998). For stories specific to Oklahoma Cherokees, see the work of Anna and Jack Kilpatrick, e.g., Jack Kilpatrick and Anna Kilpatrick, *Friends of Thunder: Folktales of the Oklahoma Cherokees* (Norman: University of Oklahoma Press, 1964).

2. See, e.g., Irving A. Hallowell, "Ojibwa Ontology, Behavior, and World View," in *Teachings from the American Earth: Indian Religion and Philosophy*, ed. Dennis

Tedlock and Barbara Tedlock (New York: Liveright, 1975), 141–78; Howard L. Harrod, *The Animals Came Dancing: Native American Sacred Ecology and Animal Kinship* (Tucson: University of Arizona Press, 2000).

3. Benny Smith, "A Perspective of the Clans" (unpublished manuscript, n.d.).

4. See, e.g., Rennard Strickland, *Fire and the Spirits: Cherokee Law from Clan to Court* (Norman: University of Oklahoma Press, 1975); William G. McLoughlin, *Cherokee Renascence in the New Republic* (Princeton NJ: Princeton University Press, 1986); Duane Champagne, *Social Order and Political Change: Constitutional Governments among the Cherokee, the Choctaw, the Chickasaw, and the Creek* (Palo Alto CA: Stanford University Press, 1992); W. Dunaway, "Rethinking Cherokee Acculturation: Agrarian Capitalism and Women's Resistance to the Cult of Domesticity, 1800–1838," *American Indian Culture and Research Journal* 12, no. 1 (1997): 155–92; Laura E. Donaldson, "'But We Are Your Mothers, You Are Our Sons': Gender, Sovereignty, and the Nation in Early Cherokee Women's Writing," in *Indigenous Women and Feminism: Politics, Activism, Culture*, ed. Cheryl Suzack, Shari M. Huhndorf, Jeanne Perreault, and Jean Barman (Vancouver: University of British Columbia Press, 2010), 43–55; Theda Perdue, *Cherokee Women* (Lincoln: University of Nebraska Press, 1998); Clint Carroll, *Roots of Our Renewal: Ethnobotany and Cherokee Environmental Governance* (Minneapolis: University of Minnesota Press, 2015).

5. Gary C. Goodwin, *Cherokees in Transition: A Study of Changing Culture and Environment Prior to 1775*, University of Chicago Department of Geography Research Paper No. 181 (Chicago: Committee on Geographical Studies, 1977); Duane H. King, ed., *The Cherokee Indian Nation: A Troubled History* (Knoxville: University of Tennessee Press, 1979); McLoughlin, *Cherokee Renascence in the New Republic*; William G. McLoughlin, *After the Trail of Tears: The Cherokees' Struggle for Sovereignty 1839–1880* (Chapel Hill: University of North Carolina Press, 1993).

6. See, e.g., Paul B. Hamel and Mary M. U. Chiltoskey, *Cherokee Plants and Their Uses: A 400 Year History* (Sylva NC: Herald, 1975); Sarah H. Hill, *Weaving New Worlds: Southeastern Cherokee Women and Their Basketry* (Chapel Hill: University of North Carolina Press, 1997); J. T. Garrett, *The Cherokee Herbal: Native Plant Medicine from the Four Directions* (Rochester VT: Bear and Company, 2003); William H. Banks Jr. *Plants of the Cherokee* (Gatlinburg TN: Great Smoky Mountains Association, 2004); David N. Cozzo, "Ethnobotanical Classification System and Medical Ethnobotany of the Eastern Band of the Cherokee Indians" (PhD diss., University of Georgia, 2004); Karen C. Hall, "Ethnobotany of the Eastern Band of Cherokee Indians: A Path to Sustaining Traditional Identity with an Emphasis on Medicinal Plant Use," (PhD diss., Clemson University, 2006); R. Alfred Vick, "Cherokee Adaptation to the Landscape of the West and Overcoming the Loss of Culturally Significant Plants," *American Indian Quarterly* 35, no. 3 (March 2011): 394–417.

7. Arlene Fradkin, *Cherokee Folk Zoology* (New York: Garland, 1990); Ethan Moore, "From Sikwa to Swine: The Hog in Cherokee Culture and Society, 1750–1840," *Native South* 4, no. 1 (2011): 106–20.

8. See Vine Deloria Jr., *God Is Red: A Native View of Religion* (Golden CO: Fulcrum, 2003); Vine Deloria Jr. and Daniel R. Wildcat, *Power and Place: Indian Education in America* (Golden CO: Fulcrum, 2001); Vine Deloria Jr., *Spirit & Reason: The Vine Deloria, Jr. Reader* (Golden CO: Fulcrum, 1999); Vine Deloria Jr., *Metaphysics of Modern Existence* (Golden CO: Fulcrum, 2012).

9. Oren Lyons, "Commencement Address," College of Natural Resources, University of California, Berkeley, May 22, 2005, accessed November 24, 2017, https://nature.berkeley.edu/news/2005/05/fall-2005-commencement-address-chief-oren-lyons.

10. See, e.g., A. Irving Hallowell, "Ojibwa Ontology, Behavior, and World View," in *Keepers of the Game: Indian-Animal Relationships and the Fur Trade*, ed. Calvin Martin (Berkeley: University of California Press, 1982); Robert Alain Brightman, *Grateful Prey: Rock Cree Human-Animal Relationships* (Berkeley: University of California Press, 1993); Howard L. Harrod, *The Animals Came Dancing: Native American Sacred Ecology and Animal Kinship* (Tucson: University of Arizona Press, 2000).

11. Paul Nadasdy, "The Gift in the Animal: The Ontology of Hunting and Human-Animal Sociality," *American Ethnologist* 34, no. 1 (2007): 25–43.

12. Elizabeth A. Povinelli, "Do Rocks Listen? The Cultural Politics of Apprehending Australian Aboriginal Labor," *American Anthropologist* 97, no. 3 (September 1995): 505–18.

13. See also Richard W. Stoffle, Richard Arnold, and Angelita Bulletts, "Talking with Nature: Southern Paiute Epistemology and the Double Hermeneutic with a Living Planet," in *Collaborative Heritage Management*, ed. Gemma Tully and Mal Ridges (Piscataway NJ: Gorgias, 2016), 75–99.

14. For a recent review of the field that raises similar questions around the construction of "the environment" in environmental history, see Paul S. Sutter, "The World with Us: The State of American Environmental History," *Journal of American History* 100, no. 1 (June 2013): 94–119.

15. This phrase was taught to me by Cherokee National Treasure, Medicine Keeper, and first-language Cherokee speaker, Mr. John Ross.

16. Deloria writes, "The relationships that serve to form the unity of nature are of vastly more importance to most tribal religions. The Indian is confronted with a bountiful earth in which all things and experiences have a role to play. The task of the tribal religion, if such a religion can be said to have a task, is to determine the proper relationship that the people of the tribe must have with other living things and to develop the self-discipline within the tribal community so that man acts harmoniously with other creatures." Deloria, *God Is Red*, 87. See also pp. 151–53.

17. Dave Aftandilian, "Toward a Native American Theology of Animals: Creek and Cherokee Perspectives," *CrossCurrents* 61, no. 2 (June 2011): 191–207.

18. Clara Sue Kidwell, Homer Noley, and George E. Tinker, *A Native American Theology* (Maryknoll NY: Orbis Books, 2001)

19. Aftandilian, "Toward a Native American Theology of Animals," 196–99.

20. See also Albert L. Wahrhaftig and Jane Lukens-Wahrhaftig, "New Militants or Resurrected State? The Five County Northeastern Oklahoma Cherokee Organi-

zation," in *The Cherokee Indian Nation: A Troubled History*, ed. Duane King (Knoxville: University of Tennessee Press, 1979), 223–46.

21. Wahrhaftig and Lukens-Wahrhaftig, "New Militants or Resurrected State?" 202.

22. Kyle Powys Whyte, "Our Ancestor's Dystopia Now: Indigenous Conservation in the Anthropocene," in *The Routledge Companion to the Environmental Humanities*, ed. Ursula K. Heise, Jon Christensen, and Michelle Niemann (London: Routledge, 2017), 206–15; Luisa E. Maffi, "Introduction: On the Interdependence of Biological and Cultural Diversity," in *On Biocultural Diversity: Linking Language, Knowledge and the Environment*, ed. Luisa E Maffi (Washington DC: Smithsonian Institution Press, 2001), 1–50.

23. Whyte, "Our Ancestor's Dystopia Now."

24. Here, I draw from numerous other Indigenous scholars who have discussed at length land-based ethical frameworks (Coulthard and Simpson, as "grounded normativity") and relationality (Yazzie and Baldy, as "radical relationality") in their work. See, e.g., Glen Sean Coulthard, *Red Skin, White Masks: Rejecting the Colonial Politics of Recognition* (Minneapolis: University of Minnesota Press, 2014); Leanne Betasamosake Simpson, *As We Have Always Done: Indigenous Freedom through Radical Resistance* (Minneapolis: University of Minnesota Press, 2017); Melanie K. Yazzie and Cutcha Risling Baldy, "Introduction: Indigenous Peoples and the Politics of Water," *Decolonization: Indigeneity, Education & Society* 7, no. 1 (2018): 1–18.

25. Clint Carroll, "Shaping New Homelands: Environmental Production, Natural Resource Management, and the Dynamics of Indigenous State Practice in the Cherokee Nation," *Ethnohistory* 61, no. 1 (2014): 123–47.

26. Carroll, "Shaping New Homelands," 123–47.

27. Carroll, "Shaping New Homelands," 123–47; Albert L. Wahrhaftig, "Making Do with the Dark Meat: A Report on the Cherokee Indians of Oklahoma," in *American Indian Economic Development*, ed. Sam Stanley (The Hague: Mouton Press, 1978).

28. Russell Thornton, *The Cherokees: A Population History* (Lincoln: University of Nebraska Press, 1990), 43.

29. Goodwin, *Cherokees in Transition*.

30. The Cherokee Keetoowah Society (historically referred to as "Nighthawk Keetoowahs" and not to be confused with the Keetoowah Society, Inc.—a political arm that later broke away from the Keetoowah religious foundations) is a traditionalist group that maintains non-Christian forms of Cherokee religious practice in Oklahoma. Some say that Keetoowah is the original name given to Cherokees by the Creator in their genesis as a people. Kituwa Mound in present-day North Carolina is often referred to as the Cherokees' "mother town." For a synopsis of the Nighthawk Keetoowahs in Indian Territory / Oklahoma and their leader, Redbird Smith, see Robert K. Thomas, "The Redbird Smith Movement," in *Bureau of American Ethnology Bulletin 180: Symposium on Cherokee and Iroquois Culture* (Washington DC: Smithsonian Institution, 1961).

31. Robert A. Myers, "Cherokee Pioneers in Arkansas: The St. Francis Years, 1785–1813," *Arkansas Historical Quarterly* 56, no. 2 (1997): 127–57.

32. Levi Gritts, "Night Hawks Religion," in *Oklahoma Historical Society Papers* (Muskogee: Oklahoma Historical Society, 1930), 2.

33. Crosslin Smith, personal communication, September 2, 2017. See also Albert L. Wahrhaftig, "In the Aftermath of Civilization: The Persistence of Cherokee Indians in Oklahoma" (PhD diss., University of Chicago, 1975).

34. Vick, "Cherokee Adaptation."

35. McLoughlin, *Cherokee Renascence in the New Republic*, 263.

36. Crosslin Smith, personal communication, January 5, 2017. See also Crosslin F. Smith, *Stand as One: Spiritual Teachings of Keetoowah* (Taos NM: Dog Soldier Press, 2018).

37. In the original interview, Smith interprets the meaning of "Ugewaleda" as "Log Splitter"; however, by personal communication (November 4, 2017), he has related to me this alternate meaning. Mr. Smith recounted that his interviewer for the Doris Duke Oral History Project had misinterpreted his explanation of the name.

38. Crosslin F. Smith (Cherokee), interview date: April 15, 1967, interviewed by B. D. Timmons, transcribed by Mary Hair, general subject: Old Cherokee Ways (T-45), Doris Duke Collection of the Western History Collections, University of Oklahoma Libraries, Norman OK. Note: I edited this interview transcript for clarity, and also added supplemental information from personal communication with Mr. Smith.

39. Carroll, *Roots of Our Renewal*, 57–82.

40. Russell Thornton, *The Cherokees: A Population History* (Lincoln: University of Nebraska Press, 1990).

41. See Rennard Strickland and William M. Strickland, "Beyond the Trail of Tears: One Hundred Fifty Years of Cherokee Survival," in *Essays on Cherokee Removal*, ed. William Anderson (Athens: University of Georgia Press, 1991), 112–38.

42. See Jason R. Pike, James H. Shaw, and David M. Leslie Jr., "The Mountain Lion in Oklahoma and Surrounding States," *Proceedings of the Oklahoma Academy of Science* 77 (1997): 39–42; "The History of a Heritage: Celebrating 75 Years of Oklahoma Deer Seasons," *Outdoor Oklahoma*, November/December 2008, 9–15.

43. Interview with John Henry West (Cherokee), Vian OK, interview date: September 15, 1937, interviewed by James S. Buchanan, S-149, Western History Collections, University of Oklahoma Libraries, Norman OK.

44. The Green-Corn dance is an annual ceremony conducted by Cherokees to celebrate the ripe corn crop.

45. *Detsänûñ'lï* is the Cherokee word for a ceremonial dancing ground.

46. Mooney, *Cherokee History, Myths, and Sacred Formulas*, 324.

47. Interview with George Whitmire (Cherokee), Muskogee OK, interview date: January 29, 1938, interviewed by James S. Buchanan, Western History Collections, University of Oklahoma Libraries, Norman OK.

48. Mooney, *Cherokee History, Myths, and Sacred Formulas*, 264.

49. Hallowell, "Ojibwa Ontology, Behavior, and World View."

50. See, e.g., Julian Haynes Steward, *Theory of Culture Change: The Methodology of Multilinear Evolution* (Urbana: University of Illinois Press, 1972).

51. Deloria, *God Is Red*, 62.

52. On "thinking through the lens of kin in our understanding of relations between peoples, and between peoples and place," see Kim TallBear, "Annual Meeting: The US-Dakota War and Failed Settler Kinship," *Anthropology News* 57, no. 9 (September 2016): e92–e95. See also Nick Estes, *Our History Is the Future: Standing Rock Versus the Dakota Access Pipeline, and the Long Tradition of Indigenous Resistance* (New York: Verso, 2019).

53. Carroll, *Roots of Our Renewal*, 7–9.

54. Oren Lyons, "Our Mother Earth," *Parabola* 7, no. 1 (1984): 91–93.

55. Steve Pavlik, "Should Trees Have Legal Standing in Indian Country?" *Wicazo Sa Review* 30, no. 1 (2015): 23.

7

Bison and Bookkeeping

Accounting for an Environmental Imagination in Great Plains Trading Posts

GEORGE COLPITTS

Edward Ermatinger scribbled the following in the first page of his account book at Fort Ellice in present-day southwestern Manitoba in 1823: "A fool striving to come up to his own conception of greatness is thus more a fool than ever while content to follow Nature[.] He is just what Nature made him but the moment he presumes to improve his he becomes what he would make himself." These lines appear just above the trading post's final tally of fur and bison exports that year, suggesting some of the ways that accounting books could powerfully join human work, imagination, and nature in the northern Great Plains. As if providing proof of his own improvement, Ermatinger's tally reduced bison and animal life to units of account: the six hundred packs of fur, twenty kegs of bison grease, eighty kegs of pounded meat, ten casks of salted meat, ten bags of dried bison tongues, and seven hundred bags of pemmican created at Fort Ellice that year.[1]

As a category of useful knowledge, one that could manipulate nature for human material gain, accounting figures importantly in Great Plains environmental history.[2] Not only did this technique help facilitate the transformation of nature; accounting shaped the region's very imagination. As some of the first European and American newcomers on the Great Plains, traders grounded their very thinking and way of knowing nature in accounting. Their business success depended on it. Only through their careful adherence to double-entry bookkeeping could the fur trade, as a transformative event in nature, be sustained from distant metropolitan centers, whether St. Louis, Montreal, or London.³ In the case of the Hudson's Bay Company (HBC), year in, year out, individuals like Ermatinger maintained accounts to support the company's vast North American operations.⁴ Moreover, in the early nineteenth century, when the HBC adopted managerial accounting techniques by then supporting large-capital textile works and, soon, American transcontinental railways, it entered, without coincidence, a phase in its business history remarkable for environmental transformation.⁵

Technological adaptations mark the environmental history of the Great Plains, as contributions to this anthology make clear. New technologies and their use have remarkably reshaped the region's water, grass, animal, and energy systems. They have also deeply reconfigured the Great Plains' very imagination. As a technology in its own right, accounting helped business, but it also shaped the mindsets of traders themselves. As historian Douglas Francis has suggested, technology was not simply something "'out there,' external objects or processes that humans can react to and possibly control"; rather, it was also "'in here,' a force within the human mind that controls our ways of thinking."⁶ Bookkeeping, as a technology, similarly acted on the human imagination. As Anke te Heesen has argued, double-entry bookkeeping was so pervasive in the nineteenth century that it was not only used by early colonial naturalists, but it likely shaped the very way they studied nature.⁷ As a way to think, double entry prompted traders to draw particular observations of the complex interplay of people and nature on the Great Plains. As Mary Poovey has suggested, this bookkeeping practice provided the very foundations for empirical natural history, science, and mathematical studies that, by the nineteenth century, relied upon "facts" to gain a particular understanding of nature.⁸ By the time Ermatinger was keeping books at Fort Ellice, the HBC accounting system privileged what business historians have distinguished as "explicit," or *knowing how*, information that could move up and down its various levels of organization and lend itself to numbering, quantification, and statistical comparison.⁹ Dominating the earliest records of Great Plains nature, this form of knowledge framed traders' observations of Native people and, of interest here, a key animal species of the region, the North American bison. How a trader's useful knowledge of bison allowed for the animal's transformation and use can offer important insights into the broader environmental history of the Great Plains so notable for its accelerated change in the nineteenth and twentieth centuries.

The Post Diary in Double-Entry Accounting

Great Plains historians draw extensively on letters, newspaper reports, travel journals, and, in the case of the fur trade, post diaries, to explore the environmental history of the Great Plains.[10] However, in the case of the fur trade, most of the documents written by traders, even their post diaries, were not meant to record all their insights into post life, plains people, or wildlife. They were business documents serving a post's accounting responsibilities. This holds true for the vast and arguably unique archival record of the HBC and the many hundreds of diaries surviving from its plains posts in the eighteenth through nineteenth centuries. The HBC adopted double-entry accounting when it began its operations in the late seventeenth century, at a time when other overseas trading companies used this tool to expand their global reach.[11] A means of ascertaining a firm's real standing, double entry was critically important in spatially dispersed business empires. But this form of accounting had an imaginative dimension as well, especially since it derived rhetorical force by persuasively convincing stockholders, potential investors, state overseers, and its own managers that a firm's business affairs were balanced, honestly reported, and transparent.[12]

Most fundamentally, a firm adopted double entry to make sense of the otherwise bewildering interrelationships connecting credited individuals in merchant enterprise. Through this bookkeeping protocol, a firm created categories of knowledge to make sense of their business transactions with individuals, factors, agents, overseas suppliers, and home sellers. By maintaining a series of accounting books, a merchant's observations were progressively transformed into useful knowledge by end-of-year, when a final ledger was reckoned. Most firms relying on commissioned agents, factors, or traders working at a distance demanded that they write a narrative diary to help make sense of their accounts. The Montreal companies crediting the fur trade on the Red, Assiniboine, and Missouri Rivers in the eighteenth century, for instance, insisted that all traders write diaries—to the point that some even scrawled entries on birchbark when they ran out of paper.[13] Alongside the diary, a trader also maintained a series of accounts. He began with an *inventory* of goods on hand, the "neat stock" at the beginning of a season. Then the trader rigorously kept a *daybook* to list chronologically all transactions occurring each day as credits, debits, "straight barter," or gifts. A trader then used the daybook to write a *journal account* describing all transactions under separate generalized headings. At this point, too, a trader translated all values (in the fur trade, commonly first appearing as the "made beaver" unit) into a common currency "money of account," in the HBC's case, the British pound sterling. The penultimate record was the end-of-year *ledger*, which reassembled charges, end-of-year remainders, and accounts into a balanced debit and credit ledger.[14] In essence, double entry transformed knowledge. A trader translated his business observations into accounting units that could be reassembled into a useable form. John Mair suggested as much in his 1768 English textbook on double entry. The daybook, he said, was only meaningful to merchants when "they took the materials or things contained in it, and, by digesting them into another form," wrote the journal accounts and finally the ledger.[15]

Following the company's establishment in 1670, the HBC's London committee used double-entry bookkeeping to estimate profits or losses from its posts at James and Hudson Bays. Once traders moved inland to expand business at the doorway of the Great Plains in 1774 at Cumberland House, they continued writing accounts and post diaries. The company then expanded this record keeping as operations extended in the 1780s to posts on the North Saskatchewan River, and by 1793, those deep in bison territory on the Red, Assiniboine, and Qu'Appelle Rivers.

Now within tallgrass prairie, often in the shelter of river valley complexes, plains traders were tasked with trading furs that offered the greatest sterling returns. However, the Canadian fur trade needed food energy to support northern subarctic posts. Much of a trader's actual work on the plains was trading bison products from Crees and Assiniboines, and sometimes Plains Ojibwas. Traders then coordinated labor at their posts to transform these raw products into pemmican that could feed the company's northern subarctic transport and post system.[16]

Traders left many documents, but accounting responsibilities significantly influenced their written observations. The plains bison, as a valued trading commodity, constituted the largest mammal in North America. Newcomers could only effectively harness bison biomass energy if they transformed the animal, through accounting, into something not in its very nature. Even traders who came to appreciate the bison's power and behavior often used diaries to provide useful knowledge for the animal's real exploitation. Montreal trader Alexander Henry the Younger, for instance, wrote diary entries on the character and sheer destructive force of bison, especially the "superherds" so impressing him in present-day North Dakota on the Red River in 1801–2.[17] But Henry also used his diary, along with his daybooks, to help explain to his crediting merchants and partners transactions and costs reflected in his ledger by end-of-year. Typically, he appended to his annual narrative diary an end-of-year balance sheet revealing the degree to which his post had transformed bison into credits of bagged pemmican, kegs of grease and salt meat, and skins.[18] Most striking was Henry's end-of-year tabulations of pound weight provisions supporting his trade, counting the total numbers of cows and bulls by their average dressed weight, and, strikingly, his anatomical weighing of a butchered traded bull that listed its pound weight of consumable meat alongside the weights of its discarded head, hide, legs, entrails, and dung.[19]

Post Diaries and Daybooks

The moment when servants arrived in spring to build stockades and flooring, reinforce chimneys, gather firewood where it could be found, and seek out Indigenous people to supply food, a post's trader began work as an accountant. He first completed a careful inventory of "stock on hand." Already on the journey inland, he had begun and continued to maintain the post diary that recorded any occurrence of note, including the arrival and departure of Indigenous people and the work of a post. Since a trader was to capture in his diary all "occurrences" (itself a term related to the Latin *factum*, "a datum of experience"), diaries offered daily weather observations, usually the date when river and lake systems froze or their ice broke up, and records of stochastic events such as spring floods, summer drought, mild winters or sudden dumps of snow, or interruptions in Indigenous hunting, all of these matters affecting bison and the trade for its flesh and fat.[20]

Although some traders did write reflective nature observations in their diaries, they tended to record occurrences that gave meaning to the information they were sending home in accounts. The post diary and accounts, in this respect, used two systems of language to record the same phenomenon, a point made clear in a comparison of Edward Ermatinger's Fort Ellice diary and his daybook. Located in the valley complex of the Assiniboine River, where Plains people often seasonally organized pounds to kill large numbers of bison, Ermatinger filled his diary with references to bison, bands of Plains tribes, and the work at post. On November 5, 1822, in narrative form, Ermatinger's diary recorded the arrival of six Crees from Rattle Snake's party. They had camped close to the fort the night before "but bring nothing. Indeed they are so miserably poor that they beg a little meat from us to eat." He then noted post employees bringing in logs and firewood before he described the return of a hunting party led by a servant, Jack Anderson, with the meat of "three bulls." Ermatinger then noted late in the day the arrival of White Buffalo and four other Assiniboines, who brought news that four Native hunters hired by the fort in their camp had killed "a few bulls."[21]

In narrative form, the diary entry recorded occurrences transpiring over a discernible period of time, but it offered critical qualitative assessments: one group's plenty, another's poverty, the apparent success or failure in the hunt, and descriptions of work transforming nature. In his daybook entry for the same day, November 5, Ermatinger wrote the same information but in a different form. He transformed the diary "occurrences" into a bare list of post transactions with numerical values. For November 5, then, the six Crees from Rattle Snake's band (those noted in the diary as having been "miserably poor") are transformed into a "gratis" transaction: they receive eighteen inches of tobacco as gifts. Jack Anderson receives a credit to his account "by 3 bulls and 3 tongues," both "bulls" and "tongues" now firmly counted as discrete units of account. Ermatinger listed White Buffalo and his followers receiving fifteen inches of tobacco as gifts and, separately, their straight barter transaction: for trade goods they exchanged skins as well as bison commodities: twenty-one "bladders of grease" (bison bladders carrying standard quantities of marrow fats) and two "bags" of pounded meat (skin bags containing standard quantities of dried and pounded bison meat). Gratis transactions completed the entries that day: the gifts sent via White Buffalo's followers to the post's hired Assiniboine hunters and to White Buffalo, as a camp leader, receiving a large, special, gift.[22]

The daybook, then, captured in a different form the diary's narrative information. Both the trader and his employer were likely using the diary to double-check daybook transactions. Indeed, the challenge for traders adhering to double entry was to correctly identify which exchange was a "gift," "credit," "debit," or "straight barter" transaction. The daybook later helped the trader to write accounts that brought all transactions under common headings, such as "provisions," "country produce," or "skins," converted to their sterling value. A section of the daybook was specifically helpful to traders in that respect. The trading room account, prefacing the transactional record, kept a running tally of the post's entire stores. On November 5, following the trader's gifting and barter trade with White Buffalo's Assiniboines, the trading room account counted the entirety of skins now in inventory (334 muskrat, for instance), as well as the total bison meats now on hand: 420 pounds of pounded meat, 649 pounds of grease, and 1,082 pounds of dried meat.

Seeing Bison through Accounting

But what of the bison that historically captivated the attention and imagination of many newcomers to the Great Plains? While visitors to the West might have drawn on romantic or natural history conventions to write extensively about bison, post diarists more often wrote about bison in ways that supported accounting. Peter Fidler's diaries stand as an example. An individual otherwise alert to science, empirically minded, and trained in cartography and surveying, Fidler adhered to bookkeeping conventions to write his post records after the company sent him into the very heart of bison country. He arrived to establish Chesterfield House on the lower Saskatchewan River in present-day Saskatchewan in 1800. Here, he had every opportunity to observe the xeric grasslands trammeled seasonally by massive bison herds. However, Fidler actually framed his diary descriptions of bison around his immediate needs as a trader. Near the end of August that year, on his journey up the South Saskatchewan River's strong current to build the post, he mapped markers where he found "the buffalo are plentiful." It was on the north side of the Saskatchewan, having traveled "SSW1, ESE½, EbN1, ESE¾," that his crew killed three buffalo: "they are very plentiful here." The south side of the river on September 4 was "full of buffalo." At another point, he recorded precisely the location where there were "vast numbers of buffalo, and in general they are all crossing from the south to the north side the river." In his second season, in 1801–2, Fidler noted in his diary "great numbers of buffalo about the house" on October 29. He recorded "thousands on thousands of buffalo in sight from the house" on December 29. On January 11 he recorded "millions of buffalo all round the house not ¼ mile off, and from a high eminence the ground is black quite round to a great distance."[23]

Whatever his personal interests and scientific curiosity, Fidler as a diarist followed a cardinal directive in double-entry accounting: making "his stock or capital personate himself."[24] His diary, then, becomes detached from himself and his private interests. His observations are brief and factual. On his journey to establish his post, Fidler's diary identifies where the bison are as neat stock on hand. Fidler continued to inventory the animals in their aggregate, resorting to the factual numbers ("thousands upon thousands" or "millions") to estimate the extent of sundries available to his post hunters or through trade with Plains Native people nearby.

Instead of describing the bison's behavior, individuality, power, and unique adaptation to prairie environment, Fidler's diary provides useful knowledge. It is fortunate that an early draft and a later revision of Fidler's Chesterfield diaries survive to suggest the discipline he imposed on himself in that respect. For the final journal sent to London, he removed information not necessary for business purposes. From his draft, for instance, Fidler removed on September 9 his observation that some herds of buffalo came down the bank and very nearly ran over the campsite. He also removed his reference altogether of the thousands of buffalo, taking their seasonal cue to migrate, on both sides of the river on September 21. His final diary removed a comment he had previously made about bison coming from the plains and closer to the river now that the season had changed (October 3). And Fidler removed from his draft his comment that there were many buffalo "across at the rivers [sic] edge" on January 22 but kept his remark that the post had by then converted from traded bison flesh some sixteen bags of pemmican of seventy-six pounds each.

Fidler made the more remarkable edit to his entry of September 12, 1800, where he completely removed a full description of bison in the rut: "A little above our tent an old Bull came down the Bank in to a puddle near the river about 6 inches deep & he kept walking round & round in a small circle as if he had been light headed & kept so till we passed him above ½ mile before he left off when he went away, although we passed within 100 yards of him, this is the first sight of anything of the kind."[25]

From his rough to final diary sent to London, then, Fidler seems to have crafted his written observations into a form best supporting his accounts and final ledger reckoning. The bison itself as an animal, its herd behavior, response to seasonality, watering habits, and wallowing were not information needed by the post or factoring into its accounting system.

Diaries more often assessed the cost of work at a post transforming the natural world and bison as a trade commodity. At Fort Carlton on the Saskatchewan, James Bird, for instance, journaled the visits of Crees and Assiniboines from their bison pounds throughout winter months. He recorded the numbers of animals they offered in trade, specifying the butchered flesh arriving in various forms—shoulders, thighs, sometimes staged and dried meat in bales. Often, he simply counted these component parts together to arrive at an equivalent to a single animal, these numbers transforming bison (the animal) into a meaningful accounting unit.[26] He could equate these numbers to the post's actual work transforming bison into pemmican. The diary, for instance, noted men making "kegs" for fat and beat meat (February 15); Indigenous women preparing bull skins (*taureaux*) for pemmican bags (May 17), fats then being rendered (May 24), and the first of many bags of pemmican being completed and dispatched to Cumberland House (May 28). All of this narrative information supported what would appear in post accounts as credits in pemmican transfers to other posts and their movement in the larger system of the fur trade.

The ways traders transformed bison in credit and debit transactions is also seen in John Pruden's diary kept at Carlton House on the Saskatchewan River. He used his 1815–16 diary to record with precision his servants "digging the garden and transplanting 355 cabbage plants," the barley first growing by July 4, the first berries ripening for picking in the season (July 7), the cabbages stunting in size due to a caterpillar plague, and by August 11, the twenty-four ten-gallon kegs of lady finger potatoes, and sixty-one kegs of baker potatoes harvested. He also estimated that the post's harvest was one-third the previous year's due to the dryness of the summer months.[27]

As bison moved off plains grazing areas into parkland shelter in fall, bison then dominated Pruden's diary entries as numbered entities. Their close proximity to the post was communicated in an entry noting that bison had destroyed a good portion of the post's horse hay, requiring men to build fences around its stacks (October

30); by December 19, Pruden estimated that these animals ate a full third of the post's horse fodder. Wolves were noted according to the proportion of meat lost to these scavengers (typically one bison in four or five, killed by hunters, was consumed by wolves). With herds and wolves so near, Pruden's diary reduced them to numbers: the numbers of animals taken by the hired hunting camps, those killed by independent Indigenous parties, and those taken by the house's own servants (the animals in each of these categories having a different cost to the post). And he recorded the animals by their arrival in dressed weight as the 3, 9, 5, 9, 7, and 20 bison killed by the post's Native hunters, and the 2, 22, and 3 killed by the post's servants from November 10 to 20. By November 21 Pruden's diary noted 180 animals killed "large and small" by hunters. The animal, already reduced into a numerical form, was then further reduced into more precise discrete numbers: by January 16 the men had begun stocking the ice house and "putting and stowing 120 thighs of buffalo meat" weighing 3,640 pounds. The bison as an animal had been moved from a state of nature to one able, now, to move into the company's accounting system.

Traders undoubtedly disciplined themselves to write diaries in such a way. Perhaps not surprisingly, when they moved outside the strictures of their post accounting responsibilities, diarists wrote differently. Such is apparent in the diary of W. H. Cook, posted to Fort Hibernia, later named Fort Pelly, in 1818–19.[28] Cook had joined HBC service in 1785 first at York Factory and then rose in rank to become an inland trader by 1797. Torn between a career in the fur trade and his preference to become a settler, he quit the service in 1813 to try his hand at farming on the unlikely northern agricultural frontier of the Nelson River. With that a failure, he returned to trading in 1816, soon to be appointed to Fort Pelly to oversee the district trade. Following his service in 1818–19, Cook took his retirement to farm at Red River.[29]

While in post during his last year of company service, Cook closely followed his directives as an accountant. His diary recorded the cost of engaging nearby Ojibwas as hunters (October 28), the cost of tobacco sent to camps to encourage hunting for the post, and the fifty cords of wood servants built up by December 21. He calculated the time it took men to reach bison by foot (December 24) and the comparative costs of procuring meat by horse and sleds. Once numbering the hunted animals returning to the post in butchered form, Cook weighed the product by the pound going finally into the ice house: 700 pounds of meat on February 19, 1,100 pounds on February 27, and so on.

While he served as the post's trader, Cook remained faithful to his accounting responsibilities in his diary entries. However, they changed significantly when he left the post, soon to retire permanently and begin a settler's life. Maintaining the diary while accompanying the boat brigade to Norway House, Cook now recorded the spring buds coming into leaf on trees. He noted the different tree species and changing forest composition along the Assiniboine as his party moved downstream. For the first time, Cook used his diary to describe in detail wildlife: the snowshoe rabbits still in white robe standing out on their runs across brown mud, and the crowded hoof prints of bison and moose along river edges: the "amazing number of buffalo paths this day and some skeletons of buffalo lying along the paths which seemed to mark this part of the country as an established presence" (May 7, 1819). When his boat brigade chanced upon a buffalo crossing the river, he described its sheer muscular power, his men killing the animal "as it was attempting to ascend the bank, which happened to be about twelve feet high and almost perpendicular" (May 8, 1819).

Abstracting Bison into a Thing Not of Its Nature

While in his posting, Cook needed to write a diary that helped him transform bison into a thing not of its nature. In his diaries Cook began converting the bison into a unit of account that could then help him explain his overall transactional costs. When the HBC adopted cost and management accounting in the early nineteenth century, a trader had to account for all charges arising in his locale: the salaries of his men, the cost of labor and provisions within post, and the real costs of Native products procured through trade or in labor arrangements. An overriding concern for traders was to adhere to trading standards (essentially, set prices to buy and sell goods), these factoring into the transaction costs a trader calculated in his journals of account and final ledger reckoning. Their diaries, then, carefully described Indigenous work for posts since a trader had to purchase all of it with trade goods: the berries collected by women in season, the firewood that Native bands gathered, the fish they netted, or the labor women and children provided in gardens. Above all, a trader was conscious of current and often changing exchange values attached to the fleshy and fatty parts of the bison's anatomy. Each had a corresponding sterling value. In diaries bison appear as humps, thighs, shoulders, grease (marrow), fat (tallow traded by the bag), robes, skins, and bales or bags of dried, half-dried, green, and pounded meat, sinew, and tongues. The values attached to these butchered elements were, in turn, volatile, reflecting periods of competition between traders, climatic factors, or, from the 1840s onward, the growing regional collapse of bison populations that started to raise their price. Not surprisingly, traders noted in their post diaries environmental cues that signaled potential changes in price for traded commodities—a "killing" winter affecting bison hunts, regional herds being thinned from overhunting, or, by the 1850s, the unmistakable east-west recession of the bison frontier as herds started to enter an extinction gradient.

The very technique of moving animals into a new abstract unit of account became both the means by which the HBC contended with the progressive disappearance of bison and, ironically, the very motive force for overhunting on the British portion of the Great Plains. By the 1820s the HBC organized the entirety of the British portion of the Great Plains as separate accounting "districts" (Saskatchewan, Red River, and Swan River). Within each, the company could use summative district accounts to strategize its bison purchases. By the late 1820s the company turned to independent Métis buffalo brigades for bison purchases to ensure supply, but it also traded across the three plains districts from all Indigenous people to maintain competition between hunters and keep prices low, even when bison herds thinned and in many places started to disappear altogether. Each post's accounts flowed to district managers to provide information for district accounting, which provided critical information to strategize in the changed circumstances that the company itself had helped initiate. For instance, the Saskatchewan District maintained five-year comparisons of bison products traded at each of its posts (fats, pemmican, greases, dried meat, tongues, and bosses). These identified regions where bison populations were in decline and where purchases would be expensive. The company could then redirect purchases to regions of plenty.[30] Indeed, to the very end of the bison era in the 1870s, accounting helped the HBC purchase selectively from Plains hunters still accessing bison through horse power or intensively hunting remnants of what constituted the last of the great herds in British territory.[31]

Conclusion

In many respects, information flowing from a post's diary and accounts, and from them to regional accounting districts, functioned because of the ways traders in their diaries transformed bison from its very nature. Final ledgers so abstracted bison that the animal itself was lost in balanced post debits and credits. Such abstraction is evident in the accounts of Fort Pelly in 1831–32. Its last page provides an end-of-year balance sheet listing the post's debits on the left page, its credits on the right. The post's debited charges (ranging from servant wages to gifts given to Indigenous people) now balanced its credits. Of the latter, the largest was the "fur &etc." (including bison tongues) valued at £3,654. Notably, the balance sheet does not even list pemmican, representing the post's greatest labor output and the larger number of transactions with Plains people. Rather, the bison and the transformational work associated in pemmican production are represented in the sterling credit transfers from Fort Pelly to various other posts. Fort Pelly had sent tons of pemmican to support the northern fur trade at Norway House, Island Lake, York Factory, Red River, the Saskatchewan, and Ile-a-la-Crosse throughout the year, valued at a mere £288. The balancing line of "apparent gain" of £2,594 certified a good season of trade. It also provides a numerical sense of nature's transformation in this section of the Great Plains.[32]

It would be easy to frame this history in a declensionist perspective, a theme so often dominating any discussion of bison on the Great Plains. However, by examining how accounting practices transformed bison as an animal into units of account, historians are in a better position to understand the region's environmental history as one of ongoing transformation, both in terms of its physical world as well as in its imagination. The company's accounting system continued to support key transformations in the region's natural systems and imagination. Even as the great herds declined in number in the early 1870s, the HBC relied on double entry to support its switch from bison biofuel to steam power. In the 1870s the company launched its first steamboats on Lake Winnipeg and the North and South Saskatchewan Rivers. Their increased cargoes accelerated mercantile activities and commerce; steam power, however, required vast wood supplies procured in the parkland and prairie forest fringe. Bookkeeping remained critical for traders to make sense of otherwise bewildering new transactions entered with Indigenous and non-Indigenous wood suppliers, wage-earning crews, and settlement merchants using this transportation. Certainly, accounting was necessary for the HBC's business when it became one of the largest landowners in the region after the British government transferred its territories to the Canadian government in 1869–70. Double-entry bookkeeping now accounted for the company's homestead land sale transactions with legions of homesteaders and the newcomers purchasing subdivided lots in towns, many growing around its trading posts. As members of an increasingly vibrant and diverse mercantile community, HBC traders continued to abstract the region's natural wealth in double entry. They could imagine Canadian's new farming Eden as accountants.

Whether they did so in post diaries, journals of account, or balanced ledgers, company traders used accounting to exploit the Great Plains environment. The useful knowledge offered in double entry undoubtedly helped expand the HBC's operations in the eighteenth and nineteenth centuries. As part of his bookkeeping protocol, a trader wrote diaries to support accounting. In that respect, their entries began the bison's transformation, in narrative form, as a unit of account. The trader fully transformed bison as he moved its units of account further through a post's accounting system. A trader rarely committed to post diaries what he had seen of the animal—its behavior and power, or its sheer dominant presence on the Great Plains. His diary, after all, supported a trader's accounting. As a technology, accounting helped introduce significant physical change to this region. But it also shaped the very imagination of traders who became actors in the rapid environmental transformation of the Great Plains in the nineteenth century.

Notes

1. Edward Ermatinger's "Day Book" trading account, Fort Ellice Accounts, 1822–23, B.63/d/1, Hudson's Bay Company Archives (hereafter HBCA).

2. Joel Mokyr, *The Gifts of Athena: Historical Origins of the Knowledge Economy* (Princeton NJ: Princeton University Press, 2002), 3.

3. Double-entry bookkeeping organized Pierre Chouteau Jr. and Company, the Upper Missouri Outfit, and the American Fur Company. See the inventories, daybooks, accounts, and ledgers in the Missouri Historical Society's microfilm collection, *Papers of the St. Louis Fur Trade, Part 2: Fur Company Ledgers and Account Books, 1802–1871*; Montreal merchants used double entry in their independent businesses associated with the North West Company (NWC). Some of their accounting books have survived in the McGill Library's Rare Books and Special Collections. A good example of NWC double entry is offered in Harry Duckworth, ed., *The English River Book: A NWC Journal and Account Book of 1786* (Montreal: McGill-Queen's University Press, 1990).

4. Arthur J. Ray and Donald Freeman, *"Give Us Good Measure": An Economic Analysis of Relations between the Indians and the Hudson's Bay Company before 1763* (Toronto: University of Toronto Press, 1978); Gary Spraakman and Alison Wilkie, "The Development of Management Accounting at the Hudson's Bay Company, 1670–1820," *Accounting History* 5, no. 1 (2000): 59–84.

5. Gary Spraakman, "The Impact of Institutions on Management Accounting Changes at the Hudson's Bay Company, 1670–2005," *Journal of Accounting & Organizational Change* 2, no. 2 (2006): 101–22; Gary Spraakman and Robert Davidson, "Transaction Cost Economics as a Predictor of Management Accounting Practices at the Hudson's Bay Company, 1860 to 1914," *Accounting History* 3, no. 2 (1998): 69–101; and Gary Spraakman and Julie Margret, "Sir George Simpson: 19th Century Fur

Trade Governor and Precursor of Systematic Management," *Management Decision* 43, no. 2 (2005): 278–92. Richard White, *Railroaded: The Transcontinentals and the Making of Modern America* (New York: W. W. Norton, 2011); Thomas Johnson and Robert S. Kaplan, *Relevance Lost: The Rise and Fall of Management Accounting* (Boston: Harvard Business School Press, 1987), 19–21.

6. R. Douglas Francis, *The Technological Imperative in Canada: An Intellectual History* (Vancouver BC: UBC Press, 2009), 7.

7. Anke te Heesen, "Accounting for the Natural World: Double-Entry Bookkeeping in the Field," in *Colonial Botany: Science, Commerce, and Politics in the Early Modern World*, ed. Onda Schiebinger and Claudia Swan (Philadelphia: University of Pennsylvania Press, 2005), 237–51.

8. Mary Poovey, *A History of the Modern Fact: Problems of Knowledge in the Sciences of Wealth and Society* (Chicago: University of Chicago Press, 1998), 42–43.

9. R. M. Grant, "Toward a Knowledge-Based Theory of the Firm," *Strategic Management Journal* 17 (December 1996): 109–22; George Colpitts, "Knowing Nature in the Business Records of the Hudson's Bay Company," *Business History* 59, no. 7 (2017): 1–29.

10. Classic fur-trade diary sources include George R. Brooks, ed., "The Private Journal of Robert Campbell," *Bulletin (Missouri Historical Society)* 20 (January 1964): 6–24, 107–18; Charles Larpenteur, *Forty Years a Fur Trader on the Upper Missouri: The Personal Narrative of Charles Larpenteur, 1833–1872*, edited, with many critical notes, by Elliott Coues (Minneapolis: Ross & Haines, 1962); Annie Heloise Abel, ed., *Chardon's Journal at Fort Clark, 1834–1839* (Lincoln: University of Nebraska Press, 1997); "The Fort Benton Journal 1854–1865, and The Fort Sarpy Journal, 1855–1856," *Contributions to the Historical Society of Montana* 10 (1940).

11. Ray and Freeman, *Give Us Good Measure*, 83–118; Vahé Baladouni, "The Accounting Records of the East India Company," *Accounting Historians Journal* 8, no. 1 (Spring 1981): 67–69; Rafael Donoso Anes, "The Double-Entry Bookkeeping Method Applied in Spain to Account for Transactions Related to the Minting Process of Gold and Silver in the Sixteenth Century," *Accounting Historians Journal* 21, no. 11 (June 1994): 97; Cheryl S. McWatters and Yannick Lemarchand, "Accounting Representation and the Slave Trade: The *Guide du commerce* of Gaignat de L'Aulnais," *Accounting Historians Journals* 33, no. 2 (December 2006): 1–37. Bruce G. Carruthers and Wendy Nelson Espeland, "Accounting for Rationality: Double-Entry Bookkeeping and the Rhetoric of Economic Rationality," *American Journal of Sociology* 97, no. 1 (July 1991), 32; John Ryan, "Historical Note: Did Double-Entry Bookkeeping Contribute to Economic Development, Specifically the Introduction of Capitalism?," *Australasian Accounting, Business and Finance Journal* 8, no. 3 (September 2014): 86–98.

12. Poovey, *A History of the Modern Fact*, 54. James A. Aho, "Rhetoric and the Invention of Double Entry Bookkeeping," *Rhetorica: A Journal of the History of Rhetoric* 3, no. 1 (Winter 1985): 21–43.

13. L. R. Masson, "Extracts from Mr. John McDonnell's Journal," in *Les bourgeois de la Compagnie du Nord-Ouest*, vol. 1 (New York: Antiquarian Press, 1960), 283n1.

14. For a description and examples of inventories and waste books, see John Mair, *Book-keeping Modernized: or, Merchant-Accounts by Double Entry, According to the Italian Form*, 8th ed. (Edinburgh: Bell and Bradfute, and William Creech, 1800), 5–6.

15. Mair, *Book-keeping Modernized*, 3.

16. George Colpitts, "Energizing the Fur Trade," in *Powering Up Canada: The History of Power, Fuel, and Energy from 1600*, ed. Ruth Sandwell (Montreal: McGill-Queen's University Press, 2016), 39–59.

17. Barry Gough, *Journal of Alexander Henry the Younger, 1799–1814*, vol. 1 (Toronto: Champlain Society, 1988), 54–55, 106–7.

18. Gough, *Journal of Alexander Henry the Younger*, 131.

19. Gough, *Journal of Alexander Henry the Younger*, 317.

20. Poovey, *A History of the Modern Fact*, 96.

21. November 5, 1822, Fort Ellice Journal, 1822–23, B.63/a/3, fol. 10d, HBCA.

22. November 5, 1822, Fort Ellice Account Book, 1822–23, B.63/d/1, fols. 7 and 8, HBCA.

23. Peter Fidler, "Chesterfield House Journal," in *Saskatchewan Journals and Correspondence: Edmonton House, 1795–1800, Chesterfield House 1800–1802*, ed. Alice M. Johnson (London: Hudson's Bay Record Society, 1967), 256, 259, 264, 298, 306.

24. Mair, *Book-keeping Modernized*, 16.

25. Peter Fidler, "Chesterfield House Journal," 261n, 270, 263, 306.

26. February 2, 6, 15, 17, 29, 1796, Fort Carlton Journals, b.27/a/1, HBCA.

27. John Pruden, Carlton House Post Journal, 1815–16, B.27/a/5.

28. Fort Pelly Journal, 1818–19 by William Hemmings Cook, B.159/a/7, HBCA.

29. Sylvie Van Kirk, "William Hemmings Cook," in *Dictionary of Canadian Biography*, vol. 7 (1836–1850), http://www.biographi.ca/en/bio.php?id_nbr=3329.

30. See the running comparisons of all posts in the Saskatchewan District over a five-year period listed in Fort Edmonton's Recapitulation Account Book, 1859–64, B.60/d/150, HBCA.

31. For instance, when climatic conditions reduced pemmican production on the upper North Saskatchewan River, the company increased purchases from other districts to keep its purchasing price low. The diversion of production from Fort Edmonton to Red River's district in 1935 is recounted in John Rowand to George Simpson, January 7, 1835, fol. 99; John Pruden to Committee, January 31, 1835, fol. 101; Alexander Christie to Committee, December 14, 1835, fol. 137; all from Governor George Simpson Correspondence Inward, 1828–37, D.5/4, HBCA.

32. Pembina River Accounts, 1812, Pembina Account Book, 1811–12, B.160/d/1, fol. 10, HBCA.

8

An Uncommon Nuisance

Cattle Feeding, Nuisance Complaints, and Legal Remedies on the Southern Plains

JACOB A. BLACKWELL

In July 1966 Neuhoff Brothers Packers, Inc., of Hill County came before the Tenth District Court of Civil Appeals of Texas to contest a temporary nuisance action against their cattle-feeding operation. A neighboring farmer, Rudolf T. Janek, complained of offensive odors emanating from the feedlot, which fattened twenty-five thousand head on 150 acres. A chemist hired by the plaintiffs found elevated levels of contamination and algal blooms in a nearby creek. Janek and other plaintiff's witnesses testified that the odors were particularly noxious when the wind came from the north, the direction of the Neuhoff feedlot. Although the feedlot manager maintained that the smell was not noticeable beyond one hundred feet, Mrs. Janek observed that the smell of manure "came into the house, got into the clothes, and that she could not hang out a washing." Not persuaded by the testimony of Neuhoff Brothers' own chemist regarding the source and degree of contamination in the creek, the appellate court upheld the lower court ruling and forced the feedlot to take measures to abate the nuisance.[1]

The Janeks were not alone in sensing a change in the wind. Beginning in the early 1950s, cattle feeding increasingly became an industrial-scaled operation that brought employment and wealth to the southern and central plains. Although the practice of fattening cattle on concentrated feed grains in the months prior to slaughter had a long history, these new feedlots housed tens of thousands of animals rather than the mere hundreds that had fed in earlier installations in the midwestern Corn Belt and elsewhere.

Like other innovations over the previous millennia, the new feedlots represented an adaptation to the Great Plains environment. These operations—great machines that consumed vast inputs of feed, water, pharmaceuticals, and energy and transformed them into beef—didn't just get by in the warm, arid climate of the southern and central plains. They depended on it to allow cattle to flourish and to keep neighbors' complaints to a minimum as their operations grew ever larger. This increased intensity of cattle feeding created economies of scale that made the operations more efficient, but it also magnified the environmental consequences, as foul odors and effluent troubled neighbors downwind and downstream. Moving into the 1960s, these new operations challenged existing traditions of common law solutions to nuisances, eliciting action from legislatures and courts. Environmental regulations and nuisance lawsuits threatened the cattle-feeding industry, prompting responses from cattle raisers' organizations in southern and central plains states, including Kansas, Oklahoma, and Texas. Neuhoff Brothers, located midway between Dallas and Waco, Texas, frequently incurred nuisance complaints from their neighbors, as did other large-scale cattle feeders in more thickly populated areas. While they frequently exercised their ability to influence state legislation to their advantage, feedlot operators discovered that the best defense against legal action was to locate in sparsely settled regions—a criterion the Great Plains suited perfectly.

Large-scale cattle feeding in the southern and central plains benefited from a number of changes to agriculture in the region over the course of the twentieth century. Farmers busted the sod to plant wheat during the early decades of the century, resulting in the environmental catastrophe of the Dust Bowl in the 1930s.[2] When drought returned in the 1950s, potential disaster prompted adaptation as farmers turned to the Ogallala Aquifer, a layer of gravel and sediments underlain by impermeable strata. This formation had accumulated water for millions of years, and plains farmers used technological innovations in the form of new gas-powered wells and center-pivot irrigation equipment—often fueled by natural gas drawn from their own land—to tap this water and spread it

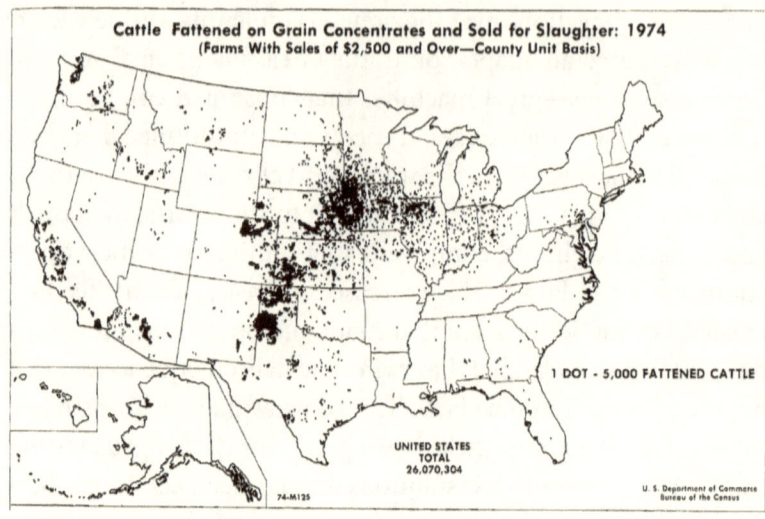

FIG. 10. Map showing cattle-feeding concentrations with industrial feedlots on the southern and central plains near the peak of U.S. per capita beef consumption. From *1974 Census of Agriculture*.

over their parched fields.[3] The expense of this equipment prompted farmers to replace much of their wheat with more valuable—and thirstier—crops such as sorghum and corn. Feeding these grains to cattle produced huge quantities of beef to fill the supermarket shelves that served the booming and newly prosperous American population. Annual U.S. beef consumption increased from 71.3 pounds per capita in 1945 to a peak of 129.8 pounds in 1976. Grass-fed beef no longer satisfied consumers' desires for tender, marbled cuts; while a mere 2.2 million cattle, or 5.1 percent of the nation's herd, were on feed in 1935, that figure reached 28 million head by 1978.[4]

During the nineteenth century, the packing industry centered on Chicago, where railroads brought cattle from across the Great Plains for slaughter and packing. The major meatpacking firms, including Armour, Swift, Wilson, and Cudahy, established satellite operations in major rail terminals across the region, such as Omaha, Nebraska; Kansas City, Missouri; and Fort Worth, Texas. These terminal markets and their stockyards dominated the industry through World War II.[5] From that point on, the increasing ease of shipping by truck rather than rail decentralized the beef indus-

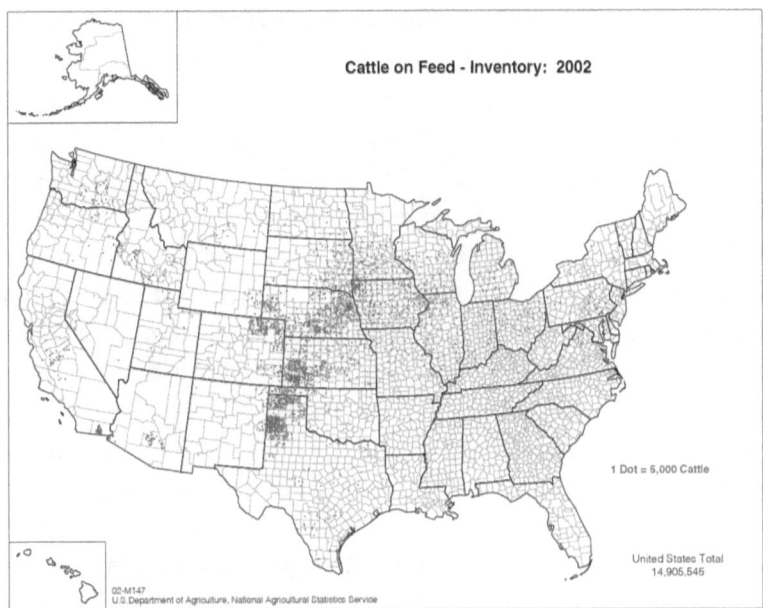

FIG. 11. Map showing cattle feeding has diminished in the Corn Belt but continues in the Great Plains Beef Belt. From *2002 Census of Agriculture*.

try. Feedlots could now locate further from major hubs, and the packing plants followed them. This confluence of factors, including a new source of water and new crops, an increased supply and demand for beef, a decentralized method of transportation, combined with the sparse population and warm, arid climate of the southern and central plains, brought this new industry into being.[6] Unlike the old midwestern feedlots, where farmers turned over a portion of their corn fields to fatten a few hundred head of cattle at a time and spread the resulting manure on neighboring fields, these industrial feedlots in the new Beef Belt of the southern and central plains were full-time cattle fattening operations where tens of thousands of animals dined on specialized diets. The increased scale of these new operations gave them greater efficiency than their midwestern predecessors, but the concentration of cattle created concentrations of manure and other nuisances.

Prior to the mid-twentieth century, nuisances from cattle-feeding operations escaped the attention of legislatures and were largely governed by common law solutions. Inherited from English traditions, common law relied on the rulings of judges rather than the dictates of legislatures. Along with judicial precedent, it placed great emphasis on local customs and practices, developing in diverse forms across the North Atlantic colonies and eventually coalescing into a unified American common law.[7] This legal tradition protected and encouraged users that developed resources in the most dynamic manner, which were also the users that created the most profound environmental changes.[8] Much of the reasoning of this law failed to adequately protect the new feedlots from neighbors who complained of the nuisances they created. Such concepts as priority and prescription, or the notion that an unexercised right could be forfeited, could not overcome the right of residents, including newcomers, to abate a nuisance. To defend themselves from legal action, feedlot operators located in areas with few neighbors and sought action from their state legislatures.[9]

Kansas led the way in developing industrial cattle feedlots in the Great Plains. Earl Brookover observed feedlots near Bakersfield, California, in the 1940s, and opened his lot near Garden City in 1951.[10] Fittingly, the Sunflower State also led the way in regulating feedlots. In 1963 Kansas passed an act establishing a licensing procedure for its burgeoning cattle feedlots. Codifying the distinction between the new industrial feedlots and their part-time predecessors, Kansas defined a feedlot as a place regularly devoid of crops or other vegetation. All lots accommodating more than one thousand head were required to pay an annual licensing fee; the license was optional for smaller lots. The money collected contributed to the state's fund for controlling animal disease. While the act gave broad power to the livestock commissioner, it presented little in the way of mandatory penalties. The law showed as much concern for the control of cattle disease and pests as it did for the nuisance created by feedlot odors or the pollution of lakes and streams. In addition, feedlot operators had only to adhere to "established practices in the feedlot industry" to remain in compliance. The agriculture commissioner could revoke the license of an offending feedlot, but not before receiving a complaint; in addition, the operator had the right to appeal any penalty to the agriculture board and convene a hearing in their home county.[11]

The legislation also promised assistance to Kansas feedlot operators. It required the agriculture commissioner to conduct research on feedlot operations and methods for abating pollution, and it obliged the state's universities to render assistance in this undertaking. The commissioner had to make all such information available to feedlot operators and offer guidance as they set up their facilities. Perhaps most crucially, the first section of the law defined feedlots as agricultural enterprises; although they were still subject to applicable zoning regulations, this definition would have critical implications for future feedlot litigation in Kansas.[12]

Oklahoma soon followed the example of its neighbor to the north. The Oklahoma Feed Yards Act (OFYA), passed in 1969 with sponsorship from three western Oklahoma legislators, read much like the Kansas legislation.[13] It similarly required fees and licenses for feedlots, and it gave smaller operators, in this case those feeding fewer than 250 head, the option not to be licensed. Rather than a single commissioner, the power to enforce the act rested with the board of agriculture, as advised by a five-member panel of feedlot operators. In other aspects of its regulations Oklahoma's act mirrored the earlier legislation more closely. The board could investigate complaints against feedlots. The section covering Duties of Owners and Operators listed the same seven items, and it spelled out the required duties in identical language. These included removal of excrement, chemical control of pests, providing for drainage of the feedlots so as to avoid contaminating waterways, providing veterinary services, providing means for scraping the feedlots, maintaining weather-resistant facilities, and adhering to the aforementioned "established practices" of the industry. Both Kansas and Oklahoma accepted compliance with the regulations as "prima facie evidence that a nuisance does not exist."[14]

Passage of the OFYA received vocal support and cooperation from the Oklahoma Cattlemen's Association (OCA). The *Oklahoma Cowman*, the OCA's official mouthpiece, concluded that the growth of Oklahoma's cities necessitated some action to avoid conflicts between cattle feeders and their neighbors; the *Cowman* and other publications noted the OFYA's requirement that feedlots comply with the zoning laws of these expanding cities. The journal reassured readers that all regulations drawn up under the OFYA were based on the advice of the panel of cattle feeders, and it emphasized the point that no feedlot licensed under the OFYA could be construed as a nuisance. One OCA chairman observed that, "if we hadn't begun this work, someone not familiar with our problems would have done it for us and would have made a law much more difficult to live with."[15] The OCA also sought to use the OFYA to police its own ranks, as compliance would mostly burden the "fringe operators" who failed to adhere to industry norms.[16]

Other states integrated feedlot regulations into broader environmental regulations. The Nebraska Environmental Protection Act, passed in 1971, created the state's Department of Environmental Quality and set standards for air and water protection. The act did not, however, make licensing or inspection of feedlots, or any other livestock operations, mandatory, but instead relied on voluntary requests or complaints from neighbors. Through the 1990s Nebraska did not maintain records of how many feedlots operated in the state or how many animals they accommodated, and enforcement of pollution standards for feedlots remained lax.[17] Like Nebraska, Texas—the largest of the cattle-feeding states—responded to the times by revising much of its existing environmental legislation during the 1960s and 1970s. The Texas Air Control Board, created in 1965, and the Texas Water Quality Board, which followed in 1967, advanced the state's administration of polluters.[18] Although feedlot operators faced little interference from the former, the Texas Water Quality Board and its successors implemented the standards of the federal Environmental Protection Agency. The Clean Water Act of 1972 gave the EPA authority to regulate potential water pollution, but it proved reticent to exercise its power in relation to feedlots. Prompted by a lawsuit from the National Resources Defense Council, a 1973 court order forced the young agency to take a more aggressive stance. While 98 percent of Texas feedlot capacity was without pollution controls in 1968, only 2 percent of capacity lacked such controls by 1975.[19]

Such legislation concerning feedlots in many cases responded to a bevy of lawsuits that appeared during the 1950s and 1960s. Several court cases throughout the southern and central plains states questioned whether or not these new industrial feedlots constituted agricultural enterprises and were thus eligible for the numerous privileges afforded to such operations. In the 1964 case of *Fields v. Anderson Cattle Company*, a home-owning couple from the vicinity of Emporia, Kansas, sued the operators of three nearby feedlots for creating a nuisance. After a trial court ruled in favor of the homeowners, the feedlots appealed to the state's supreme court. Their appeal rested on the argument that, as agricultural enterprises, the county's zoning regulations regarding nuisances did not apply. As the state's feedlot act had not been passed when the case first went to trial, no mention of it was made in the decision; nevertheless, a majority of the court's justices agreed, and they maintained that the feedlots had taken sufficient action to abate the nuisance. In a dissenting opinion, Justice Fatzer concluded that, unlike the precedents cited in the case, the feedlots did not constitute agricultural enterprises, and as they were a mere seven hundred feet from the city limits of Emporia, or well within the city's three-mile zoning area, they should be enjoined from pursuing feeding operations. He noted, however, that, "what may be a nuisance in one location ... may not be a nuisance ... in another location."[20] Bruce Wingerd, a Kansas lawyer who weighed in on the feedlot nuisance issue, found this lesson of location to be the key takeaway from the case, noting that the penalties initially levied against the feedlots decreased in proportion to their distance from the plaintiff.[21]

A decade later the Brookover Feed Yard of Garden City, Kansas, sued the state's commissioner of labor, contending that the facility's workers performed agricultural labor, exempting the feedlot from making contributions for them under the state's employment security law. The labor commissioner, Darrell D. Carlton, had judged that while the employees who engaged in raising crops on the feedlot company's land were agricultural laborers, the majority of the employees, including the mill and clerical workers at the feedlot and offices, were not. The Kansas Supreme Court, this time citing the feedlot statute, accepted a broad definition of agricultural labor and ruled that all of the feedlot's employees, including those engaged in clerical work, were connected to the raising of livestock.[22]

In states where statutes did not explicitly define feedlots as agricultural enterprises, courts proved less accommodating. In Colorado the ton mile tax assessed fees to any commercial carriers moving heavy cargo over the state's highways. Such fees were then used to pay for road maintenance. Agricultural enterprises were exempt from this tax. In 1965 the massive Monfort Feed Lot near Greeley, along with other feedlot operators, sued Hugh Weed, the state's director of revenue, for exemption from the tax and a return of all monies previously paid under it. After hearing from Kenneth Monfort, the Colorado Supreme Court found that his own description of his operation did not match that of a farm or ranch but was instead "something new and different therefrom." No crops were grown on the feedlot itself, but were instead hauled in, over the state's highways, from various farms in the vicinity; additionally, the feedlot did not own the cattle, but instead fed livestock belonging to others. On this basis, the supreme court reversed the decision of the trial court that had found in favor of Monfort.[23]

In Oklahoma, where the legislature had neglected to define feedlots as agricultural enterprises while aping Kansas's statute, the supreme court combined three cases—one each from Beaver, Texas, and Cimarron Counties in the Panhandle—as it rendered a 1973 decision that, much like the contemporary case in Kansas, concerned the payment of unemployment taxes. The feedlots contended that they were agricultural enterprises and therefore exempt, as they were essentially farmers or ranchers. In seeking a precedent, the Oklahoma Supreme Court compared the feedlot case to that of a chicken hatchery, where the operation purchased chicken eggs, incubated them, and then sold the resulting chickens. Another precedent involved a hay baler who served as an independent contractor to a number of farmers. In neither case had the courts found the plaintiff to be engaged in an agricultural enterprise. To rule in favor of the feedlots would not only contradict these earlier cases, but also open all manner of enterprises, including livery stables and veterinarians, to the agricultural exemption, a move that went well beyond the intention of the legislature as the court saw it. The decision of the friendlier trial courts overturned, the feedlots were ordered to pay their unemployment taxes.[24]

The disparity between the decisions of the county trial courts and the Oklahoma Supreme Court in that case again reveals the importance of location in deciding matters of nuisance in agricultural enterprises. Bruce Wingerd noted this on the local scale, as differences of less than a mile in the case of *Fields v. Anderson* resulted in penalties varying by thousands of dollars. Location mattered on a larger scale as well. Feedlots in more rural areas of scarce population, particularly those in the newly established Beef Belt of the southern and central plains, generally faced fewer legal obstacles than those in more populous locales. Beef Belt counties such as Deaf Smith County, Texas (8.8 inhabitants per square mile, per the 1960 census); Finney County, Kansas (12.3); and Texas County, Oklahoma (6.9) presented few neighbors to offer objections. Hill County, Texas, home of Neuhoff Brothers, had twenty-four residents per square mile, while Lyon County, Kansas, home of Anderson Cattle Company, had over thirty. Feedlots in such areas in eastern Kansas, Oklahoma, and Texas often found their more numerous neighbors lacked enthusiasm for their ventures.

One of those feedlots, the Garland Grain Company of Dallas County, Texas, learned first-hand that local courts could be less than accommodating to alleged nuisances. Opened in 1960, the Garland Grain Company's feedlot became the subject of a nuisance suit in 1964 after several dozen neighboring homeowners complained of the resulting smell, flies, birds, as well as the pollution of a nearby creek. The county trial court agreed and issued a permanent injunction against the feedlot. Upon appeal the following year, the Twelfth District Court of Appeals found a number of problems with the jury's decision. First, they noted that the experts hired by the plaintiffs to measure the pollution levels in the creek could not confirm that the feedlot led to any contamination; their measurements revealed that it was polluted both upstream and downstream from the feedlot. In addition, the court noted that the plaintiffs themselves reported, despite the proximity to several towns, that it was a largely agricultural region composed of farms and ranches. Many of the plaintiffs themselves kept cattle that often drank from and befouled the creek. Further, the court found that, as the feedlot was certified by the County Board of Health and provided an economic benefit to the community, the injunction of the trial court was an excessive penalty. The court of appeals lifted the injunction and urged the plaintiffs to seek monetary damages instead. In this, the court of appeals followed a long tradition in American law of favoring the most dynamic users of property: with halting a productive business out of the question, cash payments rather than real relief would have to suffice for the homeowners. Although the feedlot prevailed in its appeal, the trial court's decision expressed the area's hostility to such enterprises in the future.[25]

Not all feedlots fared so well. In 1972 the Fifth District Court of Civil Appeals, in Dallas, heard another case concerning a feedlot nuisance. Robert McFarland, a farmer in what was then largely rural Collin County, sued nearby Meat Producers, Inc., whose feedlot accommodated over fourteen thousand cattle. McFarland sought a permanent injunction against Meat Producers, Inc., calling the feedlot a permanent nuisance that had reduced the value of his land substantially, producing odors that "would seriously disturb and annoy persons of ordinary sensibilities." Meat Producers, Inc. responded that McFarland only grew crops on his land and did not live on it, and that as the cattle-feeding operation had ceased at the time of the trial, no injunction was necessary. In addition, Meat Producers, Inc. found that the alleged damages were much too high for farmland. The court disagreed, noting that cattle feeding had only ceased due to falling prices and might resume at any time. Also, although the land was currently only used for farming, the nuisance caused by the feedlot precluded other possible uses, thus justifying the estimated devaluation. In order for McFarland's land to regain its value, the feedlot must be dismantled completely to hinder resumption of operations. Mere damages would not suffice for the Fifth District as they had for the Twelfth.[26]

A key case in the history of Kansas feedlot jurisprudence also involved plaintiffs who sought a complete injunction. A group of landowners from the area near Wichita, led by Earl W. Dill, sued the Excel Packing Company for allegedly creating a nuisance through the operation of a feedlot that devalued neighboring land. Two of the plaintiffs claimed that their land was suitable for subdivision and sale as home sites. Dill and company also sought a halt to the drilling of wells to supply water to the feedlot, as that practice was seriously impairing their water supply. The trial court granted the injunction, and Excel appealed to the Kansas Supreme Court. The court considered a number of facts in the case as it delivered its verdict. It found the claims of the homeowners that their land was suitable for subdivision to be spurious, as the area lacked sufficient water, sewers, and roads for such development. And as in many cases concerning feedlot nuisances, the court found that "the prime factor which gives us pause in resolving this case is the location at which the operation of the feed lot is conducted." Being in a thoroughly agricultural region, the feedlot was a normal and reasonable use of land, and the flies and odors associated with it would be impossible to eliminate. The court, in overturning the trial court's injunction, offered a stern rebuke to Dill and the other landowners for choosing to build their homes in an agricultural area, lacking in zoning regulations, where cattle and hog raising, among other pursuits, had been conducted for some time. The court observed the landowners "desire to get away from the congestion of traffic, smoke, noise, foul air and the many other annoyances of city life. But with all these advantages in going beyond the area which is zoned and restricted to protect them in their homes, they must be prepared to take the disadvantages."[27] The decision in *Dill v. Excel* served as a precedent in many other Kansas nuisance suits.[28]

Nebraska has a longer and more complex history with cattle feeding than the southern plains states; it is part of the midwestern Corn Belt and hosted many small feedlots that served the packing houses of Chicago and Omaha. Later, it developed industrial feedlots similar to those of the Beef Belt. The center of the state's cattle-feeding industry shifted from the eastern, corn-growing region toward the more sparsely inhabited western stretches. One case illustrates the reception industrial feedlots received in the former location. In the 1975 case of *Botsch v. Leigh Land Company*, the plaintiff claimed that the construction of a feedlot, with its attendant manure lagoons, had created a nuisance that impaired use of their farm property. After a trial court dismissed the petition for an injunction, the plaintiffs appealed to the state's supreme court. The court agreed that the odor generated by the feedlot made the plaintiff's property "well-nigh uninhabitable." While the court conceded that rural residents should expect to deal with the aggravations of agricultural enterprises, those enterprises could still be operated in a fashion that could mitigate the nuisance. Even in a region where nearly every farm sported a small-scale feedlot, the Leigh Land Company's operation proved particularly noxious. The supreme court remanded the case to the trial court and eventually ordered a permanent injunction against the feedlot, along with $4,800 in damages for the plaintiff. Five years later Leigh Land Company appealed the injunction, pointing out that it had drained lagoons and introduced a plan for regularly scraping the feedlot pens. This time the court sided with the feedlot and allowed operations to resume.[29]

By demonstrating how even an agricultural enterprise could constitute a nuisance in an agricultural area, the case of *Botsch v. Leigh Land Co.* set a precedent for feedlot cases in Nebraska. The supreme court reiterated its position in the 1980 decision of *Gee v. Dinsdale Brothers*. In that case the defendant opened a large cattle-feeding operation across the road from the plaintiff's farm in eastern Nebraska. After operation commenced, the plaintiffs complained that it brought foul odors, flies, and rodents to their property. At the trial court, a sympathetic jury awarded them $50,000 in damages, a verdict the feedlot owners judged to be excessive. On appeal, the supreme court found ample evidence suggesting the feedlot might be operated so as to present a nuisance. Its lagoons were drained but once a year, manure was packed into mounds and only rarely removed, and dead cattle were often left to decompose in the pens. The court heard of swarms of flies coating the Gee family's farmhouse. Darlene Gee described them as "thick, thick, thick. Thick on the sides of the house, thick on the sides of the shed, just thick everywhere. On the cars, inside the cars, inside the house." The court noted a similar situation concerning rodents. In addition, the dust from the dried manure became "heavy enough so that when you breathe your nostrils get to burning and you hurt if you breathe heavy." The supreme court again found that a feedlot "materially prejudiced" its neighbor and did constitute a nuisance; the jury's substantial award was affirmed.[30]

While feedlots in the more densely populated eastern sections of the southern and central plains states encountered legal obstacles, their counterparts further west rarely faced this problem. A search of the courthouse records in Texas County, Oklahoma, the heart of that state's industrial feedlot belt, revealed no nuisance suits against the major feedlot owners. Such a case in neighboring Beaver County raised little concern from the cattle industry.[31] Despite the tens of thousands of cattle they fed at any one time, these industrial feedlots could appease both regulators and their few neighbors by adhering to standard pollution controls. One case in western Oklahoma did attract the industry's notice, though. Near the town of Alva, a homeowners' association sued the Sternberger and Baker feedlot, which had opened uncomfortably close to their rural neighborhood, resulting in odor and fly problems. The Oklahoma Supreme Court agreed with the homeowners and the decision of the trial court, issuing a permanent abatement to the nuisance.[32]

This final decision hit a bit too close to home for feedlot operators throughout the state. In 1993, the year after the Alva decision, an amendment to the Oklahoma Feed Yards Act (OFYA) clarified feedlots' responsibilities regarding offensive smells. Authored by a representative and state senator from the feedlot-heavy Panhandle region, the amendment stipulated that no feedlot could be deemed a nuisance unless it "endangers the health or safety of others"—provided it was located three miles outside of the nearest town and lay within a mile of no more than ten residences. Mere foul odors would never again suffice to shut down a cattle-feeding operation in the Sooner State. Although the amendment also enacted higher penalties than the 1969 act—a $10,000 maximum fine rather than $100, with possible imprisonment—it substantially weakened the regulations themselves.[33]

Much of the state legislation in recent decades, particularly in Oklahoma, responded to the growth of pork production, which presented both opportunities and challenges to cattlemen. In 1991 Oklahoma eased its statutes limiting corporate ownership of agricultural enterprises and related industries. Shortly thereafter, Seaboard Farms moved into the Oklahoma Panhandle and began constructing huge, shiny barns where thousands of pigs were born, raised, and fattened for slaughter at a local plant. The industry brought hundreds of new jobs to an otherwise stagnant local economy, but neighbors who had tolerated the cattle feedlots for decades found the new odors overpowering, and Seaboard and its partners, who included such cattle feedlot operators as the Hitch family of Texas County, Oklahoma, found themselves subjected to criticism and litigation. Wanda Smith, a neighboring farmer, complained of the odors, noting "I'd rather smell my own sweat than the hogs."[34] While foul odors could no longer constitute a nuisance, the spraying of hog waste on fields raised concerns over contamination of the Ogallala Aquifer. Both supporters and opponents of the hog industry formed advocacy groups, and the battle lines were drawn.[35]

This conflict eventually prompted vigorous responses from the state's legislature as well. In 1997 the Confined Animal Feeding Operation Act largely supplanted the OFYA. Its advisory board included three operators, as had the OFYA before it, but it also required a hydrogeologist, a soil scientist, an ecologist, an engineer, a water quality scientist, a member named by the state's secretary of the environment (secretary of energy and the environment, since 2013), an ecologist, and two members of the public. This time "best practices" of the industry received detailed explication, including the requirement that animal waste not come into contact with any state waters. Operators had to report all spills over one hundred gallons and perform tests for various contaminants. A mandated pollution prevention plan had to include detailed studies of surface and groundwater, employee training methods, and a log of all training and maintenance on the facilities. Crucially, however, the act maintained the language from the OFYA accepting compliance with the licensing process as "prima facie evidence that a nuisance does not exist," so long as it posed no health threat to others.[36] Finding this legislation insufficient to deal with the burgeoning hog industry, in 2005 the Oklahoma legislature passed the Oklahoma Swine Feeding Operations Act, which set more rigorous standards for the controversial industry while sparing cattle feedlots.[37]

Other states in the region concurrently dealt with similar issues. In 1998 Nebraska passed its Livestock Waste Management Act, which placed strict regulations on operations that fed cattle, swine, and other animals in large numbers.[38] In Colorado, where the state's hog numbers swelled from 190,000 to 790,000 during the 1990s, a proposal known as Amendment 14 sought to regulate the location and operation of the giant pig farms, particularly their handling of manure and odors.[39] After it passed in 1998, observers expected that the demanding legislation would force consolidation of the industry, as only the largest swine feeders, the ones that raised the greatest concern for Amendment 14's supporters, would possess the means to make the required improvements.[40]

While courts occasionally presented challenges to the cattle-feeding industry by ruling in favor of aggrieved neighbors in nuisance suits, feedlot operators prevailed more often than not, generally protecting their status as agricultural enterprises and avoiding or winning nuisance suits in more sparsely settled regions, particularly the southern and central plains of the Oklahoma and Texas Panhandles, western Kansas, and eastern Colorado. These lawsuits confirmed the decision of the industrial feedlots to locate in this Beef Belt, where the climate encouraged cattle growth while keeping human populations sparse. At the same time, lawsuits punished those that operated elsewhere in more humid—and more populous—parts. The cattle feeders held even greater sway in the state legislatures, which passed lax or vague regulations when they acted to control the industry at all. These statutes dictated responses to alleged nuisances that overrode the common law approaches of earlier decades. When more stringent legislation appeared around the turn of the twenty-first century, it largely targeted the more noisome swine operations.

Maintaining this political control in the future may prove problematic. In the 1980s, noting the outmigration from much of the Great Plains, Deborah and Frank Popper proposed ridding the region of agriculture and setting much of it aside as a "Buffalo Commons."[41] Although the population decline in much of the plains is real, it does not necessarily signal agricultural decline. Increasing efficiency in farming and cattle feeding brought about by continuing innovation means fewer people can produce more food. The decline of rural populations means fewer neighbors to complain about the smell, making the Beef Belt even more hospitable to feedlots, but it also saps the political strength of cattle-raising regions. Competing water demands—whether from growing cities or oil and gas production—combined with the depletion of the Ogallala Aquifer pose a looming threat to cattle feeding on the Great Plains. Farmers can conserve water more carefully with innovative irrigation equipment, and feedlot operators can ship in more grain from outside the region, but the economic advantages of cattle feeding in the region erode as a result. As rural populations dwindle in many parts of the United States, other regions of the country might hold more appeal for cattle feeders. The Beef Belt has played a key role in the U.S. cattle industry for decades, but continued relevance is never guaranteed. As Joshua Specht recently argued, the cattle industry has depended on certain locations throughout its development, but it has never hesitated to abandon them when prodded by economic, political, or environmental circumstances. Ohio Valley drovers, Texas cattle drives, and Chicago meatpackers have all fallen by the wayside.[42] Keeping the plains at the center of the beef industry in the future will require continuing innovation.

Notes

1. Neuhoff Bros. Packers, Inc. v. Janek, 405 S.W.2d 233, 1966 Tex. App. LEXIS 2607 (Tex. Civ. App. Waco 1966).

2. Donald Worster, *Dust Bowl: The Southern Plains in the 1930s* (New York: Oxford University Press, 1979).

3. John Opie, *Ogallala: Water for a Dry Land*, 2nd ed. (Lincoln: University of Nebraska Press, 2000); Daniel Macewan Balkwill, "Oklahoma's Forgotten Drought: Regional and Federal Responses to the Climate Crisis of the 1950s" (PhD diss., University of Oklahoma, 2012).

4. U.S. Department of Commerce, Bureau of the Census, *Census of Population and Housing, 1940–1980* (Washington DC: Government Printing Office); Jimmy M. Skaggs, *Prime Cut: Livestock Raising and Meatpacking in the United States, 1607–1983* (College Station: Texas A&M University Press, 1986), 166–67, 179.

5. William Cronon, *Nature's Metropolis: Chicago and the Great West* (New York: W. W. Norton, 1991), 207–59; J'Nell Pate, *Livestock Legacy: The Fort Worth Stockyards, 1887–1987* (College Station: Texas A&M University Press, 1988), 43–44.

6. Jacob Blackwell, "Feeding Cattle: Origins and Consequences of Commercial Beef Production on the Southern Plains" (master's thesis, University of Oklahoma, 2013), 55.

7. William E. Nelson, *The Common Law in Colonial America, Volume I: The Chesapeake and New England, 1607–1660* (New York: Oxford University Press, 2008), 5–6.

8. Morton J. Horwitz, *The Transformation of American Law, 1780–1860* (New York: Oxford University Press, 1992); Theodore Steinberg, *Nature Incorporated: Industrialization and the Waters of New England* (New York: Cambridge University Press, 1991), 16.

9. Bruce E. Wingerd, "The Feed Lot—Nuisance or Not?" *Journal of the Bar Association of the State of Kansas* 36, no. 1 (Spring 1967): 10.

10. John Fraser Hart, *The Changing Scale of American Agriculture* (Charlottesville: University of Virginia Press, 2003), 42–48.

11. *Kansas Statutes Annotated*, 2000, Title 47, Section 15.

12. *Kansas Statutes Annotated*, 2000, Title 47, Section 15.

13. *Oklahoma Session Laws 1969*, Ch. 116, pp. 138–41.

14. *Oklahoma Statutes 1971*, Title 9, Section 9-201 through 9-215.

15. "Commission Picked to Regulate Feeding," *Oklahoma Cowman*, January 1968, 36; "Licenses Required of Oklahoma Feedlots," *Oklahoma Cowman*, September 1969, 36; "Feedlot Licensing Law Rules Being Drawn Up," *Oklahoma Farmer-Stockman*, January 1968, 15; Joseph A. Stout Jr., *Oklahoma Cattlemen: An Association History* (Stillwater: Oklahoma State University Press, 1981), 68.

16. "Feedlots: New Industry Standards," *Daily Oklahoman*, August 15, 1969.

17. J. David Aiken, Annette M. Higby, and Nancy L. Thompson, *A Farmer's Handbook on Livestock Regulation in Nebraska* (Lincoln: Nebraska Pork Producers Association, 1994).

18. "History of the TCEQ and Its Predecessor Agencies," Texas Commission on Environmental Quality, accessed May 2, 2015, https://www.tceq.texas.gov/agency/organization/tceqhistory.html.

19. John M. Sweeten, *Cattle Feedlot Management Practices for Water and Air Pollution Control* (College Station: Texas Agricultural Experiment Station, 1990), 2.

20. Fields v. Anderson Cattle Co., 193 Kan. 558, 396 P.2d 276, 1964 Kan. LEXIS 407 (1964).

21. Wingerd, "Feed Lot—Nuisance or Not?," 11.

22. Brookover Feed Yards, Inc. v. Carlton, 213 Kan. 684, 518 P.2d 470, 1974 Kan. LEXIS 432 (1974).

23. Weed v. Monfort Feed Lots, Inc., 156 Colo. 577, 402 P.2d 177, 1965 Colo. LEXIS 789 (1965).

24. State ex rel. Oklahoma Employment Security Administration, 1973 OK 147, 517 P.2d 425, 1973 Okla. LEXIS 479 (Okla. 1973).

25. Garland Grain Co. v. d-c Home Owners Association, 393 S.W.2d 635, 1965 Tex. App. LEXIS 2141 (Tex. Civ. App. Tyler 1965); Steinberg, *Nature Incorporated*. For a similar case, see Livestock Feeder Co. v. Few, 397 S.W. 2d 297, 1965 Tex. App. LEXIS 2977 (Tex. Civ. App. Waco 1965).

26. Meat Producers, Inc. v. McFarland, 476 S.W.2d 406, 1972 Tex. App. LEXIS 2658 (Tex. Civ. App. Dallas 1972).

27. Dill v. Excel Packing Co., 183 Kan. 513, 331 P.2d 539, 1958 Kan. LEXIS 394 (1958).

28. Wingerd, "Feed Lot—Nuisance or Not?," 10-11.

29. Botsch v. Leigh Land Co., 195 Neb. 54, 236 N.W.2d 815, 1975 Neb. LEXIS 733 (1975); Botsch v. Leigh Land Co., 205 Neb. 401, 288 N.W.2d 31, 1980 Neb. LEXIS 734 (1980); Botsch v. Leigh Land Co., 210 Neb. 290, 313 N.W.2d 696, 1981 Neb. LEXIS 1051 (1981).

30. Gee v. Dinsdale Bros., Inc., 207 Neb. 224, 298 N.W.2d 147, 1980 Neb. LEXIS 954 (1980).

31. Blackwell, "Feeding Cattle," 86–87; "Feedlots Are Here to Stay," *Oklahoma Farmer-Stockman*, May 1970, 8.

32. Woodlake Estates, Inc. v. Sternberger, 2007 OK CIV APP 115, 173 P.3d 98, 2006 Okla. Civ. App. LEXIS 169 (Okla. Ct. App. 2006).

33. *1993 Oklahoma Supplement Statutes*, Title 2, Section 9-210; "Feedlot Near Alva Ordered to Close," *Daily Oklahoman*, February 8, 1992.

34. "Odors 'Nauseating,' Farmers Complain," *Daily Oklahoman*, May 4, 1997; "Sierra Club Lawsuit Informed Litigation," *Daily Oklahoman*, July 2, 2000.

35. Blackwell, "Feeding Cattle," 85–87; Opie, *Ogallala*, 155–77; Richard Lowitt, *American Outback: The Oklahoma Panhandle in the Twentieth Century* (Lubbock: Texas Tech University Press, 2006), 99–102.

36. *Oklahoma Statutes 2011*, Title 2, Sections 20-40 through 20-53.

37. *Oklahoma Statutes 2011*, Title 2, Sections 20-1 through 20-26.

38. *Revised Statutes of Nebraska, Reissue of Volume 3B, 2010*, Article 24, Sections 54-2401 through 54-2438.

39. Scott H. Reisch, "Colorado's Not-So-Little Pig Farms Meet the Big Bad Wolf," *Colorado Lawyer* 28, no. 6 (June 1999): 85.

40. Reisch, "Colorado's Not-So-Little Pig Farms," 88.

41. Deborah Epstein Popper and Frank J. Popper, "The Great Plains: From Dust to Dust," *Planning* 53, no. 12 (1987): 12.

42. Joshua Specht, *Red Meat Republic: A Hoof-to-Table History of How Beef Changed America* (Princeton NJ: Princeton University Press, 2019), 122.

PART 3

Modern Agriculture and the Transformation of the Plains

9

Measuring Expertise

Ralph Parshall and Watershed Management, 1920–1940

MICHAEL WEEKS

The presence of the federal government in the development of water resources in the American West during the first half of the twentieth century is unmistakable. While historians have highlighted the role played by the Bureau of Reclamation in that process, a diverse collection of researchers from agencies outside of Reclamation manipulated the region's waters.[1] These scientists and engineers were employed within various bureaus and divisions of the USDA or as collaborative researchers at land-grant colleges. They designed irrigation infrastructure, shored up leaky reservoirs, developed inventions for efficient measurement and distribution of water, and acted as consultants for farmers and agribusiness. Their work impacted the amount of water available to farmers, affected the quantity and economic value of individual water rights, and enabled farmers to correlate crop selection with predicted runoff from snowpack. Since these scientists and engineers aimed to squeeze every drop of economic value from existing watersheds, their work usually occurred inside labs or at the site of canals, ditches, and modest reservoirs. Their labors did not inspire the sort of visceral response effected by a massive Reclamation dam. Yet, evidence of their collective impact on the plumbing of Western agriculture abounds.

Presence, however, cannot be confused with power. For, when it came to questions about how to employ the research of federal water engineers, mutual irrigation companies made most of the decisions. They were generally concerned only with the total amount of water available to the farmers who had vested their water rights in the company. Consequently, they embraced irrigation innovations such as improved flumes and canals selectively and only when farmers—a conservative group when it came to gambling with their water—could be convinced that new technology would reliably deliver more water. As a result, state-sponsored hydrologists and engineers targeted their research toward projects that could provide measurable and secure benefits to irrigators, promoted their work directly to farmers, and even contributed some of the labor necessary for implementation. As this chapter illustrates, the presence of state-sponsored scientists and engineers was palpable in part because they adapted their efforts to the needs of local irrigators.

No area of the West illustrates that dynamic better than the region historical geographer William Wyckoff calls the Northern Colorado Piedmont.[2] The physical geography of this region includes the South Platte River, its Rocky Mountain tributaries, and the irrigated lands adjacent to these waters. Defined by its cash crops and proximity to rail transportation, the Piedmont was one of the most agriculturally productive regions of the West by the 1920s.[3] However, its success hinged on a precarious and unpredictable water supply. The Piedmont's primary source of surface water, the South Platte, carried a paltry 1.6 million acre-feet of widely varying annual flow. From an anthropocentric view, farmers' water needs, combined with water's sparse availability, elevated the role of those capable of manipulating the resource.

The Piedmont is essential to any understanding of water and agricultural development in the American West. The miners and farmers who descended on the region beginning in the late 1850s codified the Doctrine of Prior Appropriation, which formed the legal framework for most water diversion in the West. It apportioned water ownership to users based on the seniority of their settlement and their ability to divert and use the resource. That method of water diversion was quickly appropriated throughout the arid West.[4] In addition, Piedmont farmers were notable by the quantity of water they diverted. While much literature regarding agriculture in the West emphasizes California's irrigated farmland, the Piedmont consistently ranked first or second in the nation for greatest number of irrigated acres through the first thirty years of the twentieth century. Moreover, despite the lack of available water, Piedmont farmers prioritized thirsty crops such as sugar beets and alfalfa, propelling a domestic sugar industry that led the nation in sugar production throughout the period under study.[5]

By 1920 Colorado Piedmont farmers received their water from one of the most complex systems of water delivery in the world, supporting a lucrative agriculture. The overwhelming majority of farmers prioritized cash crops such as sugar beets, potatoes, beans, and a variety of grains. They owned stock in dozens of irrigation companies that allocated water each year based on the size and seniority of individual water rights and the volume of water that ran off from each year's snowpack. Irrigation companies maintained hundreds of small reservoirs to corral the spring runoff before it raced downstream. And, every ditch and canal was interconnected—enabling well-supplied users in a given year to sell water out of their full ditches to farmers who risked coming up high and dry.[6] In 1930 the Piedmont boasted 1.4 million irrigated acres, 40 percent of Colorado's total. Where water flowed, so did money. The value of water rights for irrigation from the Cache la Poudre—a tributary of the South Platte—averaged $400 apiece in 1880 and $4,500 in 1917. Lands with excellent water rights had escalated in value as well. By 1922 land near Greeley was selling for more than $300 per acre. Fifty years earlier, $300 could fetch eighty acres and drought-proof water rights.[7] But make no mistake. This was not a land of plentiful water. The Piedmont's sophisticated network of diversions, ditches, and reservoirs masked water's scarcity while precariously propping up productivity and land values.

Moving water to a growing agricultural region such as the Piedmont in the early twentieth century required ongoing research and expertise beyond the resources of water managers. It required engineering. In the twentieth century, irrigation engineers from Colorado Agricultural College (CAC) and the USDA's Bureau of Agricultural Engineering developed techniques for measuring water more effectively, shoring up leaky infrastructure, predicting annual water flow through measuring snowpack, and moving water from the wetter side of the Continental Divide to the arid plains. No irrigation engineer played a more crucial role during the 1920s and 1930s than Ralph Parshall.

On the surface it seems that the work of irrigation engineers such as Parshall and the aims of mutual irrigation companies, who managed water for irrigators, would be synonymous. After all, both understood that more water use resulted in greater agricultural productivity. At that point, however, interests diverged. While water engineers argued that efficient water use increased supply, farmers, and the irrigation companies they formed, simply wanted more water, and they were not so interested in how efficiently it flowed. Consequently, no category of diversion fired their imagination more than transmountain diversion projects, which promised to fill their canals and ditches with water from west of the Continental Divide, where more water and fewer users suggested untapped abundance. While Parshall supported such projects on the principle that resources should be appropriated for human use in perpetuity, they also grated against his sense of technocratic efficiency. For Parshall, the most commonsensical approach to water needs involved shoring up leaky infrastructure and replacing inefficient technologies with new ones. He feared that large reclamation projects would distract attention from those solutions, sacrificing efficient use of local resources for the sake of providing water with an exorbitant price tag. Eventually however, Parshall lined up behind Reclamation's massive Colorado-Big Thompson Transmountain Diversion Project in the mid-1930s, writing the primary economic document supporting it. His actions demonstrate the presence and limits of federal water power during the period.

During the 1920s and 1930s, Ralph Parshall, a USDA irrigation engineer, developed measurement techniques that vastly increased the efficiency of water distribution in the South Platte Watershed and, as a consequence, gave him a platform to influence some of the most important water decisions of his time. Parshall was born

FIG. 12. Ralph Parshall kneeling next to a Parshall Flume. It was common for Parshall to calibrate flumes for the specific needs of users. Irrigation Research Papers, CSU Morgan Library Archives and Special Collections. Used by permission.

in 1881 and grew up on a Piedmont farm. He entered CAC in 1899, majoring in civil engineering. His passion for hydraulics led him into the new field of irrigation engineering. After spending several years working on irrigation at the Colorado State Engineer's Office and completing graduate work at the University of Chicago, Parshall was hired by CAC as an assistant professor of civil engineering in 1907. His formal employment with the university ended in 1913 when he took a position as assistant irrigation engineer with the Bureau of Agricultural Engineering of the USDA. In 1918 the bureau promoted Parshall to the rank of senior irrigation engineer, a post he held for thirty years. Parshall planned and built hydraulics laboratories on the CAC campus, where dams and irrigation structures on the Piedmont and throughout the irrigated West were tested and modeled. These included Hoover and Grand Coulee Dams, as well as impoundments within the Tennessee Valley and the Panama Canal Zone.[8] With his background in farming and irrigation engineering and connections to engineers at the state and federal levels, Parshall was equipped to diagnose the weaknesses within the Piedmont's irrigated agriculture and trained to develop technical solutions.

Ralph Parshall possessed a faith in technocratic expertise that helps to explain his particularly instrumental view of rivers. As a water engineer, Parshall's work drew fairly clean lines between conservation and preservation. When evaluating a river, he was concerned with its ability to supply water for people in perpetuity. Water unappropriated for human use was water wasted. It also explains his disdain for the management practices of mutual irrigation companies. By allowing so much water to be lost to seepage, poorly measured allocations, and ditch-side vegetation that gulped the passing flow, Parshall believed that these water managers were not just incompetent but also poor conservationists. Parshall did not value river water for its mere existence in the stream, for its support of flora and fauna, or for its ability to create esthetic beauty. Those were desirable only insofar as they supported a resource that could be renewed and reused in perpetuity.[9] Moreover, as an engineer, his primary interaction with water occurred after it had been drawn from streams, when it flowed through engineered channels and into constructed lakes. The preeminent value of a watershed was in its ability to deliver water efficiently and in sufficient quantities. As an irrigation engineer, his primary purpose was to make a watershed yield the greatest quantity of usable water. And the highest praise Parshall could give to water managers was that they wasted not a single drop of the resource with which they were entrusted.

Ralph Parshall's greatest contribution to efficient water management came from a device he invented in 1923. Eventually named after him in 1929, it was called the Parshall Flume, and it revolutionized the measuring of water in canals and ditches and, as a consequence, made water diversion more equitable. As Parshall saw it, the single greatest barrier to efficient water management was measurement. He argued that at least 25–30 percent of water was unavailable to junior appropriators due to measurement inaccuracies that enabled senior appropriators to take far more than their legally allotted share of water.[10] The Parshall Flume capitalized on the previous work of hydrologists who had determined that there was a unique relationship between the depth of water and its flow. They identified what they called "critical flow," the point where water transitioned from slow and deep to fast and shallow, and a depth at which that flow could be measured. According to tests made by Parshall and his students, this new innovation had an error factor of less than 3 percent. If Parshall's estimates were correct, this breakthrough could make 20 percent more water available to junior irrigators on the Piedmont by preventing senior appropriators from taking more than their allotted share. By 1927 the Parshall Flume was already being used in Hawaii, Canada, Central and South America, and Africa. Yet most irrigation companies on the Piedmont were not rushing to upgrade their aging systems.[11]

Why not? The answer is found more in the practical politics of water than in its engineering. Stockholders in irrigation companies received their water allocation based on measurements in ditches and canals. Since older technology often registered flows that were lower than the reality, irrigators actually received more water than these outdated gauges registered. Installing new Parshall Flumes would require ditch companies to collect money from their stockholders for the installation of devices that would likely reduce their allocation of water. Further, when it came to their most important resource, farmers and their irrigation companies did not wish to invest money in new technology, especially when it might curb their water allocations. As Colorado State University irrigation engineer Chris Thornton pointed out, "there is something inherently conservative in ditch companies; they don't want to spend money and they don't want to mess with (their water)." As long as they received their water, farmers had little interest in altering the system that delivered it to them.[12]

The failure to quickly integrate these new flumes into Piedmont agriculture figured heavily into Parshall's crusade for efficiency and in the specifics of his message. From the late 1920s through the 1930s, Parshall was a regular guest on the radio station KOA, which broadcast throughout the Piedmont. Since Parshall grew up farming irrigated lands in northern Colorado, he understood quite well how to appeal to this target audience. During several interviews, Parshall argued that accurate water measurement would result in better farmers. Pointing out that too much irrigation could often be just as detrimental to a crop as too little, he stated that Parshall Flumes would enable farmers to know exactly how much water they were applying to their crops, facilitating better harvests and more wealth. Speaking to the junior appropriators in the region, he called attention to their stresses over water scarcity, stating that better measurement would result in more water security since senior appropriators could not take more than they were allotted. He also appealed to the time and money saved through technical improvements, arguing that the flows generated by the Parshall Flume made it effectively self-cleaning, saving the time and money usually needed to remove debris from ditches. Parshall tugged at notions of fairness and logic, arguing "it is just as reasonable to have one's water measured as measuring one's crop for sale." Throughout all of his broadcasts, Parshall played the role of educator, explaining how his flume operated, hoping for converts among those who doubted its engineering or were repelled by their own lack of installation know-how. Parshall had long been a champion of technocratic efficiency. The radio offered him the platform to broadcast his ideas.[13]

To ensure broader usage of the flume, Parshall went beyond the airwaves rhetoric by designing flumes calibrated to meet the needs of individual irrigators and even participating in some of the installation work. From the time that Parshall developed his namesake flume until the 1950s, he worked to improve the device. Motivated by the various needs of farmers as well as the demands of industry and municipalities for accurate measurement, Parshall developed flumes with throat widths ranging from 3 inches to 50 feet that could measure water flowing at rates up to 3,000 cubic feet per second. Due to variances in flow, depth, and site conditions, Parshall calibrated flumes to meet a panoply of needs. He even played the role of consultant on occasion, visiting an installation site and working with irrigators to determine the Parshall

Flume most suited to the need. In 1950 Parshall published his final article on the installation and use of small Parshall Flumes. In 1953 he did the same for large flumes. The articles, though published in routine and rigorous scientific fashion, represented more than four decades of dedication to water measurement.[14]

Ralph Parshall's work and promotion of the flume were not indicative of an overbearing federal bureaucracy, nor do they reflect the triumph of state-sponsored science over water management in the West. Parshall had to convince farmers and their irrigation companies that efficient water measurement was in their best interests. Even Parshall's laboratory research reflected this dynamic. In order to develop his original flume, Parshall entered into a nonbinding agreement with the Jackson Ditch Company to build an experimental hydrology lab adjacent to the Cache la Poudre River, in the town of Bellvue, that could accommodate a much wider variance of flows than the facilities at Colorado Agricultural College. Once the Parshall Flume was developed, Parshall, along with fellow USDA researchers and graduate students at CAC, employed the Bellvue lab to calibrate individual flumes so that they met the requirements of irrigation companies and individual farmers. When looking back at Parshall's career, retired Colorado State hydrologist Tom Trout argues that Parshall often conducted himself more like an agricultural extension agent than a USDA scientist since he logged so many hours adapting technology to farmers' needs.[15] Regardless of his job title or employer, Ralph Parshall's influence on the Piedmont was tethered to his willingness to promote his flume and then tailor it to meet farmers' demands.

Evaluating the success of Parshall and his flume requires differing metrics. As an engineer, Parshall's impact is unquestionable. In the long term, the Parshall Flume was a resounding success. Worldwide, variations on it remain the standard for measuring water in a ditch or canal. Further, Parshall's reputation as a steward of the public good has grown exponentially. Since neither he nor CAC ever attempted to patent the design (though Parshall did patent the measuring gauge inside the flume), it could be reproduced cheaply. However, during his own time and on his own turf,

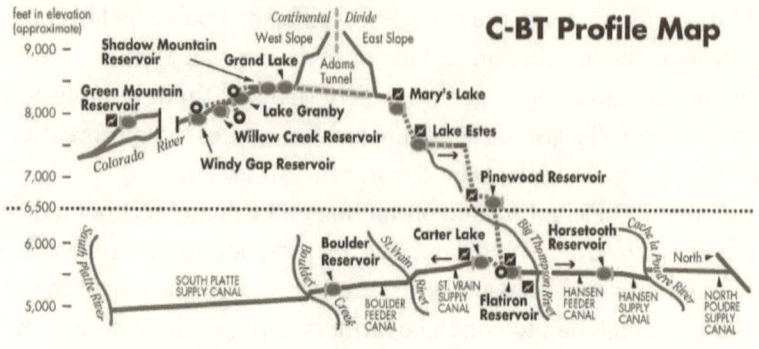

FIG. 13. Elevation profile map of the Colorado-Big Thompson Project. This Bureau of Reclamation transmountain water-diversion project, approved by Congress in 1937, provides over three hundred thousand acre-feet of water annually to Northern Colorado farmers and municipal users from the headwaters of the Colorado River. It is also a significant supplier of hydroelectricity to the region. Northern Colorado Water Conservancy District. Used by permission.

the Parshall Flume was only slowly adopted on the Piedmont, and often not as a result of either his logical and impassioned crusades or his willingness to adapt the flume to meet local needs. In fact, many irrigation companies did not install Parshall Flumes until the 1950s when crumbling infrastructure and attractive federal loans conspired to push them toward an efficiency that Parshall argued should have been achieved decades earlier.[16]

While Parshall struggled to gain converts for his gospel of efficiency on the Piedmont, he had little trouble finding those who simply wanted more water. In the tension between technocratic efficiency and decentralized irrigation companies, all sides agreed that irrigating the arid landscape demanded more water. Nature, politics, and economics conspired in the mid-1930s to resurrect a transmountain diversion project that transcended all previous efforts in scale and scope. Called the Colorado-Big Thompson Project (C-BT), it tapped into the Colorado River's headwaters and reengineered some of its flow through a tunnel that ran underneath Rocky Mountain National Park and into a host of rivers, canals, and reservoirs, until water flowed into irrigation ditches. Farmers, local boosters, and Great Western Sugar, the region's largest economic driver, revived the project in 1933 as crop prices plummeted on the Piedmont and drought constricted the region's water supply. Based on preliminary estimates, early advocates projected that 285,000 acre-feet of water could be added annually to Piedmont water supplies through such a transmountain diversion.

Five separate Piedmont counties and several cities lined up behind the idea. In 1934 the federal Bureau of Reclamation agreed to conduct engineering studies in advance of a project proposal. The Public Works Administration then provided $150,000 to complete it. Over the next three years support for the project emerged from a variety of sources, including all but one member of Colorado's Congressional delegation, editors of all of the newspapers on the Piedmont, a majority of local elected officials, mutual irrigation companies and their farmers/stockholders, and academics such as Ralph Parshall.[17]

As Colorado's resident expert on irrigation engineering and a well-respected public figure, Parshall was enlisted by the USDA's Bureau of Agricultural Economics and CAC to research and write a report on the economic benefits of the C-BT. It was published in January 1937. In it Parshall, aware that a massive reclamation project might be viewed as a government handout to wealthy farmers in the midst of the Depression, characterized the farmers on the Piedmont as "hardy, self-reliant American farmers and townspeople" who needed additional water to "stabilize the present economic achievement and make secure the possibilities of future progress." In a nod to popular New Deal programs, Parshall stated that the guarantee of sufficient water would be like "social security" for existing farmers, giving them access to the same safety net that working-class Americans were entitled to. Seeking to demonstrate that the C-BT was a difference maker, Parshall argued that its greatest value was that its flows would be available late in the growing season, when junior water users often ran out of water and when an additional application of water to high-value crops such as sugar beets and potatoes might make the difference between a modest profit and debt. In stark financial terms, Parshall stated that irrigation added $64 million worth of property value to the

Piedmont, a region valued at $200 million. This additional property value resulted in local, state, and federal taxes that could be invested in schools, infrastructure, and economic development. By harnessing and redirecting the energy of the Colorado River, Piedmont farmers could adapt to the fiscal and climactic impacts of the 1930s.[18]

Knowing that C-BT detractors might argue that the nation was suffering from too much agricultural production, Parshall turned that caution on its head by claiming that more water would shift agricultural production away from crops grown in surplus and toward crops not grown in sufficient quantities. For example, he argued that wheat, whose national supply had far outstripped its demand, was a crop of choice on the Piedmont only when water was in short supply. By contrast, domestic sugar beets, which demanded more water than wheat, supplied less than 50 percent of the nation's sugar demand. Consequently, according to Parshall, increasing Piedmont water supplies would push farmers to grow more beets and less wheat, thus aligning the nation's agriculture more closely with consumer demand. This was a tendentious argument in 1937, since sugar beet acreage was based on an acreage quota system, adjusted annually by the Secretary of Agriculture.[19] However, there was some accuracy to Parshall's conviction that more water would supply more beets since studies in the 1930s revealed that slightly more water yielded more beets.[20] Parshall concluded that increased water on the Piedmont resulted in self-reliant, productive Americans who created real economic value in their region and beyond. In other words, the C-BT was an overwhelmingly good investment.[21]

To garner support for the project and sympathy for Piedmont farmers, Parshall employed some misleading water logic. To demonstrate the value of C-BT water, Parshall compiled a dizzying array of statistics that compared the availability of water in a given year to crop yields, broken down by regions and irrigation companies. Despite available data sets extending back to the early 1900s, Parshall always chose the ten-year period from 1925 to 1934. This enabled him to contrast the year of highest water availability and

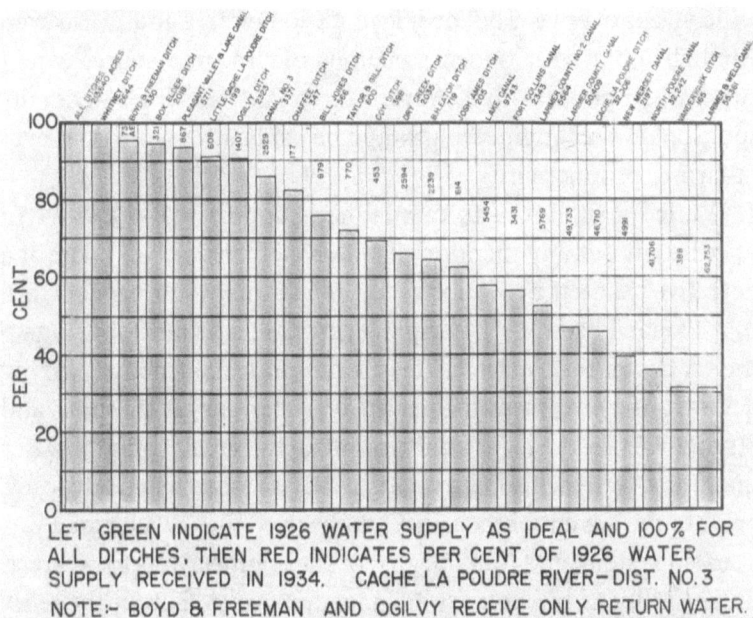

FIG. 14. Chart taken from Ralph Parshall's *Agricultural Economic Summary Relating to the Colorado-Big Thompson Project*, written in 1937. In an attempt to promote the passage of the massive water project, Parshall compared the high water year of 1926 (represented by the bar farthest to the left) to the drought year of 1934 (represented by the other bars and broken down by the allotments received by each irrigation company). Suggesting that the full ditches of 1926 should be viewed as ideal, Parshall argued that the additional water from the Big Thompson Project would result in ideal conditions into the foreseeable future. Irrigation Research Papers, CSU Morgan Library Archives and Special Collections. Used by permission.

greatest yield, 1926, to 1934, the least productive, lowest water year. Further, when referring to 1926, Parshall consistently called it a year of either optimal or even normal production when, in fact, 1926 represented an abnormally high water year. Then, when calculating money lost due to lack of water, Parshall presented 1926 as a "break even" year, while all others represented losses. From there, Parshall went on to display how the extra water brought by the C-BT would make the difference between disaster and solvency for farmers. He argued that, previously, when farmers lacked sufficient water in a given year, they could buy it for prices that varied widely year over year but averaged $4.30 per acre-foot. However, Parshall and C-BT supporters claimed that the new source would run only $2 per acre-foot. According to Parshall's logic, federally sponsored water engineering would be paid back many times over in farmer productivity.[22]

While Parshall was an unqualified supporter of the C-BT in 1937, he left out any mention of water inefficiencies in favor of a narrative that left no doubt as to the region's water needs. Until 1937 Parshall had built his engineering career around shoring up the cracks in the South Platte's irrigation infrastructure. Fixing dams, controlling seepage, measuring water, surveying snow, and removing silt were all attempts to make the greatest use of water that was already within the watershed. His research and advocacy, prior to the advent of the C-BT, emphasized that a watershed was a sealed system, and that the goal of the engineer was to create as much utility as possible within that system. In fact, in the early 1930s, he generally tried to redirect conversations about transmountain diversion.[23] In his mind, reversing water's flow during the Depression would result in costly water that farmers could not afford. The best answer was found in efficient use of the watershed. However, by the time the idea of the C-BT entered broad Piedmont consciousness, Parshall had witnessed the slow progress of his flume alongside the resistance of mutual irrigation companies to shoring up their creaky systems. The C-BT promised more water without requiring local districts to pay much for the works that would deliver it, since the region was only required to repay $25 million of the overall cost of a project that was budgeted to cost $50 million.[24] Whether Parshall foresaw that the C-BT would run far over budget or not, he understood that it was a good financial deal for Piedmont farmers. So, for a time, Parshall stopped beating the drum of efficiency and instead preached the gospel of water abundance.

Understanding why the C-BT was a good deal for farmers goes a long way toward explaining why engineers such as Parshall, farmers, and local water managers should occupy an important space in our understanding of water in the West. Parshall's initial skepticism about large water projects and transmountain diversion revolved around the ratio of benefit to expense, and $2 per acre-foot was a bargain when compared to what users might pay for water on demand otherwise. In addition, the $25 million price paid over forty years was palatable. Yet, the total costs of the C-BT when it was finally built out in 1959 were approximately $150 million. The same farmers, irrigation companies, local boosters, and sugar company who were primarily responsible for crafting the C-BT and gaining Reclamation support obtained an overwhelming bargain. But their success was not just in the price tag. In the process of obtaining more water, Piedmont water users gave up none of their autonomy to the federal government. Since its formation in 1902, the Bureau of Reclamation emphasized that its projects were aimed at opening up new lands to farming and that—owing to its ideological emphasis on small farms—individual farmers could only water a maximum of 160 acres. Piedmont C-BT supporters succeeded in eliminating both of these restrictions. Local irrigation companies intended to use C-BT water for an already well-developed farming region. Further, even though the average Piedmont farm was less than 100 acres at the time the project was approved, C-BT legislation opened the door for successful farmers and agribusiness to consolidate smaller farms into larger ones without concerning themselves with access to sufficient Reclamation water.

Distribution of C-BT water also points to a delimited federal power. The Bureau of Reclamation managed all of the water coming from the initial point of diversion until it flowed into irrigation company canals. From that point forward, the bureau relinquished control over the distribution of C-BT water to the Northern Colorado Water Conservation District. Formed in 1937, the district functioned to disperse C-BT water to irrigation companies on demand. Once irrigation companies ordered a specified amount of water, Reclamation's only task was to deliver it. Decisions on how to disburse it were entirely in the hands of irrigation companies and the conservation district they had created.[25] Ralph Parshall was fully aware of these facts when the Bureau of Agricultural Economics hired him to write the economic rationale for the C-BT. Though an employee of the federal government, he viewed the project through much the same lens as he viewed his namesake flume. Whether through efficient measurement or increased quantity, both the flume and the C-BT aimed to make water more available and secure to a broader swath of farmers. He was effective to the degree that he adapted to their needs.

The C-BT reminds us of the critical yet boundaried power of engineers such as Ralph Parshall. While Parshall's work on irrigation with the Bureau of Agricultural Engineering and his deep roots on the Piedmont made him the ideal choice to craft the C-BT's economic rationale, his influence rarely penetrated the politics or culture of water management. To a large extent, the same leaky and inefficient infrastructure that diverted the region's water remained in place. What held true for C-BT water also held true for the Parshall Flume. Despite the clear advantages in water distribution made possible by the flume, its adoption on the Piedmont proceeded in fits and starts. Parshall's greatest influence came when he employed technocratic expertise to provide scaffolding for irrigation systems developed around local needs and on a timetable that he rarely influenced.

Beyond the Parshall Flume and the C-BT, much of Parshall's work for the USDA reflected the same ethos. As the Piedmont endured a drought in 1934, Parshall joined a growing list of federal and state scientists throughout the West intent on predicting how mountain snowpack could be measured and then employed to help farmers and municipalities predict the volume of water available in a given season. In the winter of 1934–35, Ralph Parshall assumed responsibility for coordinating federal snow surveys in Wyoming and Colorado, establishing sixty-eight snow courses in Colorado and at least fifty in Wyoming. Since snow surveys involved lands managed by various government agencies and some private landholders and required expertise housed in various governmental agencies, Parshall's work required coordination with the U.S. Forest Service, National Park Service, Army Corps of Engineers, U.S. Geological Survey, Bureau of Reclamation,

National Weather Bureau, Colorado Agricultural College (CAC), and local municipalities.[26] Ever conscious of communicating his research findings to the public, Parshall regularly contributed to a series of articles published through CAC titled "Irrigation Water Prospects." In each article interviewers queried Parshall about the progress of statewide snow surveys and asked him to provide an outlook for farmers regarding how much water would be available from runoff in that year. When Parshall retired in 1948, he had become northern Colorado's recognized expert on how snowfall translated to available water.[27]

Agricultural needs also inspired Parshall's work on devices designed to remove debris from ditches, called sand traps. Water diverted from streams carries with it sand, silt, rocks, and a host of debris. Those materials accumulated over time in ditches and canals, reducing the carrying capacity of waterways and occasionally clogging delivery mechanisms. To address this, Parshall developed experiments at the Bellvue Lab using experimental sand traps installed at the point of diversion from the river. The most successful sand trap, called a vortex tube, contained a large opening that stretched diagonally across an irrigation canal at a point immediately after stream diversion. Debris passing over the vortex tube was trapped and eventually expelled into a sluiceway that forced the offending matter back into the stream. In this way "cobblestones as large as 7.5 pounds" were removed from the irrigation channel. Vortex tubes initially installed in 1933 were reported to efficiently remove 90 percent of all sand, silt, and debris before they found their way into irrigation systems.[28]

Ralph Parshall's labors display paradoxes and ironies that reveal how federal power operated in the irrigated landscape of the American West. Whether working on flumes, sand traps, snow measurement, or transmountain diversion, Parshall's influence required pinpointing weaknesses in water management and then engineering solutions aimed at delivering water efficiently and in greater quantity. However, broad application of Parshall's work often ensued only to the degree that Parshall himself was willing to promote it and adapt its implementation to local needs.

FIG. 15. Ralph Parshall designed and built this vortex tube in 1939 for the Jackson Lake Irrigation District. Vortex tubes, or sand traps as they were sometimes called, trapped and expelled over 90 percent of the sand, silt, and debris that might otherwise clog farmers' ditches. Irrigation Research Papers, CSU Morgan Library Archives and Special Collections. Used by permission.

Parshall was conscious that devices such as flumes and sand traps would be installed on privately owned property or within rights of way controlled by farmers and irrigation companies. He could not dictate; he had to convince. And serving farmers' needs often required compromise. This was most clearly seen when Parshall signed on to write the economic rationale for the Colorado–Big Thompson Project. Though Parshall supported additional water supplies for Piedmont farmers, he had long complained that such a goal was within the reach of irrigation companies if only they managed their infrastructure more efficiently, including the use of measuring devices such as the Parshall Flume. Essentially, the C-BT diverted more water without requiring greater responsibility in managing the resource. This not only violated Parshall's conservationism, but also enlisted federal power—through the Bureau of Reclamation—to do so. While there is little doubt that Parshall wielded measurable influ-

FIG. 16. Bellvue Irrigation Lab. This is the site where Ralph Parshall, along with colleagues and students, performed countless water experiments from the 1920s through the 1960s. After being supplanted by a modern hydrology lab at Horsetooth Reservoir, Bellvue fell into disuse and disrepair. As with the work of Parshall and so many of his colleagues, it remains hidden in plain sight. Photo by author.

ence on water development in the West, it was a negotiated influence that he could rarely direct.

Understanding federal influence over water development in the West requires examination of the seemingly hidden work of people like Ralph Parshall, whose namesake flume is ubiquitous in canals and ditches throughout the region, yet hidden in plain sight for the casual observer. In search of Parshall's influence during the summer of 2017, I visited the sight of the now defunct Bellvue Hydraulic Laboratory. It was here that Parshall spent countless hours channeling water flows, measuring water under varying conditions, and calibrating flumes and other devices to meet agricultural needs. When I visited, the outdoor lab was overgrown with vegetation. The branches of cottonwood, maple, and ash trees hung low over the concrete channel once used to manipulate the flow of water. Heavy deposits of sand, silt, and other debris accumulated on the outer edges of the flume and at the downstream end of the structure. Weeds and tubers abounded in the channel, aided by water that flowed through its length. Ironically, Parshall himself accelerated the demise of the Bellvue Lab. During the 1950s the Bureau of Reclamation built Horsetooth Reservoir, upstream from Bellvue, to store water from the Colorado-Big Thompson Project. The water flows that could be generated by releasing water impounded by Horsetooth were far greater than those possible at Bellvue, and so Colorado A&M (formerly CAC) contracted with the Bureau of Reclamation to build a modern hydraulics lab at the base of the reservoir. A few years after Parshall's death in 1959, the lab where he spent countless hours had become obsolete, displaced by a project he helped to make possible.

If we wish to understand Horsetooth we must peel back the layers that hide Bellvue. Reclamation reservoirs such as Horsetooth evince the power of the federal government to engineer the water landscape of the West, dwarfing all previous efforts to harness nature for human consumption. The technologies invented and calibrated at Bellvue by Ralph Parshall shrink by comparison. Their presence and function within the irrigated landscape appear both mundane and pedestrian. Yet, submerged beneath their commonplace appearance and hidden by the decay at Bellvue are essential insights that explain how federal water power operated in the American West.

Notes

1. Examples include Norris Hundley, *Water and the West: The Colorado River Compact and the Politics of Water in the American West*, 2nd ed. (Berkeley: University of California Press, 2009); Donald Worster, *Rivers of Empire: Water, Aridity, and the Growth of the American West*, 1st ed. (New York: Pantheon Books, 1986); Donald J. Pisani, *Water and American Government: The Reclamation Bureau, National Water Policy, and the West, 1902–1935* (Berkeley: University of California Press, 2002).

2. In describing the geography of the region as "West," I self-consciously include the Great Plains as a subregion of the American West. This is especially true of the Northern Colorado Piedmont as its climate and topography provide an essential transition between mountain and plain. While the vast majority of Piedmont water tumbling down from the Rocky Mountains conjures images of the American West, the flat and mildly rolling agricultural landscape where that water was employed suggests traditional definitions of the Great Plains. This essay places the Great Plains within a landscape where mountain and plain were integral pieces of each other.

3. For a more detailed description of what defines the Northern Colorado Piedmont, see William Wyckoff, *Creating Colorado: The Making of a Western American Landscape, 1860–1940* (New Haven CT: Yale University Press, 1999), 101–3; Kenneth Christian Jessen, *Railroads of Northern Colorado*, 1st ed. (Boulder CO: Pruett, 1982).

4. On Colorado water law and its impact, see David Schorr, *The Colorado Doctrine: Water Rights, Corporations, and Distributive Justice on the American Frontier*, Yale Law Library Series in Legal History and Reference (New Haven CT: Yale University Press, 2012); Greg Hobbs, *The Public's Water Resource: Articles on Water Law, History, and Culture*, 2nd ed. (Denver CO: CLE in Colorado, 2010).

5. Studies of agriculture in California include Steven Stoll, *The Fruits of Natural Advantage: Making the Industrial Countryside in California* (Berkeley: University of California Press, 1998); Richard Walker, *The Conquest of Bread: 150 Years of Agribusiness in California* (New York: New Press, 2004); Donald J. Pisani, *From the Family Farm to Agribusiness: The Irrigation Crusade in California, 1850–1931* (Berkeley: University of California Press, 1984); Worster, *Rivers of Empire*.

6. On the extent to which irrigation had been developed on the Piedmont by the early twentieth century, see Elwood Mead, *Irrigation Institutions: A Discussion of the Economic and Legal Questions Created by the Growth of Irrigated Agriculture in the West* (New York: Macmillan, 1903), 143–79. For a study on irrigation along the Cache la Poudre River, the largest tributary of the South Platte River, see Rose Laflin, *Irrigation, Settlement, and Change on the Cache La Poudre River* (Fort Collins: Colorado Water Resources Research Institute, Colorado State University, 2005). On the development of mutual irrigation companies and water law in the West, see

Donald J. Pisani, *To Reclaim a Divided West: Water, Law, and Public Policy, 1848–1902* (Albuquerque: University of New Mexico Press, 1992).

7. Robert G. Hemphill and USDA, eds., *Irrigation in Northern Colorado*, Agric. Dept. Bull. No. 1026 (Washington DC: Government Printing Office, 1922); "Colorado Uses Less Than Half Its Available Irrigation Water" (Third Conference on Irrigation, Fort Collins CO, 1930), Irrigation Research Papers, Water Archives, Morgan Library, Colorado State University, Fort Collins CO (hereafter Irrigation Papers), box 5; A. H. Outler, "Jackson Lake," unpublished typescript, n.d., Fort Morgan Museum, Fort Morgan CO.

8. G. H. Palmes, "Ralph Parshall—The Man" (speech on October 12, 1949), "Professional Bibliography: R. L. Parshall," August 6, 1958, Ralph Parshall Papers, Water Archives, Morgan Library, Colorado State University, Fort Collins CO (hereafter Parshall Papers), box 1; "Memorandum Concerning the Request for a Grant of Public Works Administration Funds for the Construction of an Addition to the Irrigation Hydraulic Laboratory of the Colorado Agricultural College at Fort Collins," May 21, 1935, Irrigation Papers, box 16.

9. The literature on the conservation/preservation divide is extensive. For a historical explanation see Thomas Wellock, *Preserving the Nation: The Conservation and Environmental Movements, 1870–2000* (Wheeling IL: Harland Davidson, 2007), 13–73.

10. Ralph Parshall, "The Improved Venturi Flume," Agricultural Radio Program, KOA, March 18, 1927, Irrigation Papers, box 7; Parshall, "Importance of Measuring Irrigation Water," Parshall Papers, box 1, KOA Radio Talks, 1931–35.

11. Parshall, "Improved Venturi Flume"; Chris Thornton, Director, Hydraulics Lab, Colorado State University, interview by author, Fort Collins CO, December 22, 2015; "Parshall," March 14, 1932, Parshall Papers, box 1, KOA Radio Talks.

12. Thornton interview.

13. Parshall, "Suggestions for Increasing Our Irrigation Supply," September 14, 1931, March 14, 1932, April 1, 1932, May 1, 1933, Parshall Papers, box 1, KOA Radio Talks, 1931–35.

14. Ralph Parshall, *Measuring Water in Irrigation Channels with Parshall Flumes and Small Weirs* (Washington DC: U.S. Dept. of Agriculture, 1950); Ralph Parshall, *Parshall Flumes of Large Sizes* (Fort Collins: Colorado A&M College, 1953).

15. Thomas Trout, retired supervisory engineer, USDA, interview by author, Fort Collins CO, July 25, 2017.

16. For an example, see W. R. Keirnes, *Water: Colorado's Most Precious Asset: The Consolidated Home Supply Ditch & Reservoir Company Contributed to Its Development, 1881–1986* (Loveland CO: Mile-High, 1986), 6–7; Thornton interview.

17. Daniel Tyler, *The Last Water Hole in the West: The Colorado-Big Thompson Project and the Northern Colorado Water Conservancy District* (Niwot: University Press of Colorado, 1992), 26–36; Christine Pfaff, Robert Autobee, and Joe Simonds, *The Colorado-Big Thompson Project: Historic Context and Description of Property Types* (Denver CO: publisher not identified, 1999), 76–87.

18. Parshall, *Agricultural Economic Summary Relating to the Colorado-Big Thompson Project* (Fort Collins CO: publisher not identified, 1937).

19. Sugar beet acreage was regulated beginning in 1934 by the Jones-Costigan Amendment to the Agricultural Adjustment Act. The amendment classified sugar as a basic crop commodity and gave the secretary of agriculture the power to determine annual production quotas and benefit payments to growers who took sugar beet acreage out of production.

20. N. R. McCreery, "What More Water Means to You," *Through the Leaves* 24 (July 1936): 110.

21. Parshall, *Agricultural Economic Summary*.

22. Parshall, *Agricultural Economic Summary*.

23. For one example of Parshall's misgivings about transmountain diversion, see Parshall to M. R. Lewis, September 21, 1930, Irrigation Research Papers, box 5.

24. In 1938, when the C-BT passed Congress, water users on the Piedmont paid $1.50 per acre-foot of water on demand. Parshall points out that, from 1925 to 1934 in the Cache la Poudre Valley, the average cost of water on demand was $4 per acre-foot. See Tyler, *The Last Water Hole*, 102; Parshall, *Agricultural Economic Summary*, 32–33.

25. Tyler, *The Last Water Hole*, 58–98.

26. Parshall, "Snow Surveys as a Means of Forecasting Streamflow," Irrigation Papers, box 30, folder 340; Parshall, "Snow Course Markers," Parshall Papers, box 9, American Geophysical Union Snow Reports; Parshall to W. W. McGlaughlin, Chief of the Division of Irrigation, U.S. Bureau of Agricultural Engineering, December 28, 1937, Irrigation Research Papers, box 26, Colorado Big Thompson; Douglas Helms, "Snow Surveying Comes of Age," in *The History of Snow Survey and Water Supply Forecasting: Interviews with U.S. Department of Agriculture Pioneers*, ed. Douglas Helms, Steven E. Phillips, and Paul F. Reich (Washington DC: USDA, Natural Resources Conservation Service), 32–44, accessed September 6, 2017, https://www.nrcs.usda.gov/Internet/FSE_DOCUMENTS/stelprdb1043910.pdf.

27. "News Notes: 1944–1947," Records of the Colorado State University Faculty, Morgan Library, Colorado State University, box 2, Parshall, Ralph L., n.d.

28. "Vortex Sand Trap Gage," August 1933, Irrigation Papers, box 2, folder 11.

10

A "Plow to Save the Plains"

Conservation Tillage on the North American Grasslands, 1938–1973

JOSHUA NYGREN

On February 27, 1940, a South Dakota newspaper touted a "Revolutionary 'Plow to Save the Plains.'" After the Great Plains had endured almost a decade of drought punctuated by catastrophic dust storms, the suitability of the plow to the semiarid, windswept grasslands had come under question.[1] Pare Lorentz's landmark 1936 film, *The Plow That Broke the Plains*, fueled such skepticism and inspired the article's headline. The headline itself (probably an editor's doing) was misleading; Frank L. Duley and J. C. Russel, researchers employed by the U.S. Department of Agriculture's Soil Conservation Service (SCS) and the University of Nebraska, wrote the piece to describe how their methods actually rendered plowing unnecessary. Nevertheless, the catchy turn of phrase did embody the hope Duley, Russel, and many other agricultural scientists invested in this technology over the next three decades: "stubble mulching" promised to save and sustain Great Plains agriculture, not break it.[2]

Stubble mulching represented the first form of "conservation tillage," a suite of technologies that grew to include practices such as "minimum tillage" and "no-till." Conservation tillage eventually became the most widely used agricultural conservation measure throughout the United States and over much of the globe, an expansion that depended on countless scientists and farmers working in various environmental and climatological conditions.[3] Stubble mulching (originally called "subsurface tillage") promised to conserve both soil and soil moisture. By leaving crop residues as a mulch atop the ground instead of plowing them under, the practice prevented soil from drying out and blowing away, helped water soak into the ground, and kept soil moisture from evaporating. While conservation tillage ultimately spread worldwide, it was conceived in a time and place of dust and drought.

Stubble mulching emerged as a technological adaptation to Great Plains aridity. Despite claims that conservation tillage originated in other climatological contexts, its deepest roots lie in the drought of the 1930s and in decades-old dryland farming practices. For the next three and a half decades, public researchers worked with private manufacturers to overcome the challenges farmers faced in stubble mulching. Technological optimism guided their thoughts and actions. They considered technology—both physical equipment and associated practices—the key to conserving soil and soil moisture (and therefore agriculture) on the Great Plains. As stubble mulching grew more effective and efficient, it also grew more expensive—often prohibitively so. Between 1938 and 1973, Duley, Russel, and other researchers developed stubble-mulching technology as a way to sustain farming on the North American grasslands. In the process, they naturalized the role of industrial agriculture in transforming the Great Plains.

The public-private partnerships at the heart of stubble-mulching research illustrate a core element of what I call the *conservation-industrial complex*. In soil conservation, the same type of relationships between state and industry (farm-equipment manufacturers and, later, chemical companies) prevailed as those that guided the broader regime of industrial agriculture.[4] These relationships constituted a network of public and private parties whose interests aligned in conservation.[5] Duley and Russel helped create this network by forging mutually beneficial relationships with manufacturers: private firms lent scientists the equipment needed for research and, in exchange, received publicly subsidized product testing while creating new markets for their wares.[6] By promising to conserve soil, soil moisture, and private economic gain through stubble mulching, the conservation-industrial complex slowly created a logic wherein industrial agriculture made not only economic, but also environmental sense.[7]

Duley and Russel's experiments into stubble mulching present a different environmental historical narrative of the Great Plains. As the introduction to this volume makes clear, the Dust Bowl looms large in the traditional narrative.[8] Many popular accounts suggest the dust storms jolted farmers on the plains—and elsewhere—into practicing conservation and thereafter served as an enduring parable against land abuse.[9] *Remember the moment of conversion*, this rendering seems to warn, *lest you slide back into perdition.*

Such an accounting reduces the region's environmental history to a singular story that discounts several historical realities. First, Duley and Russel rarely invoked the legacy of the Dust Bowl to promote their methods or justify their research.[10] Instead, they appealed to the mindsets of those plains residents who rejected dour interpretations of a region where "the earth ran amok."[11] Even the term "dust bowl," wrote one Nebraskan in 1937, "makes my blood boil."[12] For these people, technological adaptation offered promise and hope—in the words of historian Donald Worster, "salvation through technique."[13] Second, history and human choice did not end when the rains returned. Farmers' decisions whether or not to practice soil conservation after the "dirty thirties" did not hinge on their relationship to the past; they were also conditioned by various factors unique to their present circumstances—including the growing appeal of conservation tillage.[14] Third, the eventual spread of stubble mulching into humid climates shows that the Great Plains offered more to broader soil conservation efforts than a cautionary tale of what could go wrong.

Finally, the rise of conservation tillage on the plains explains how farmers after the Dust Bowl were able to reconcile their older commitment to the "industrial ideal" with the newer imperatives of soil conservation.[15] Researchers created a technological system that gradually presented industrial-scale farmers as the land's best stewards. They noticed early on that stubble mulching appealed most to a specific subset of farmers: those who operated large acreages and had access to capital. As their research proceeded, scientists' deepening partnerships with capitalist enterprises, together with their own technological optimism, set stubble mulching on a path toward increasingly sophisticated and expensive techno-fixes to environmental challenges. By the 1970s conservation tillage allowed various members of the conservation-industrial complex to defend large-scale, input-intensive agriculture as necessary to caring for the land.

. . .

When Duley conceived of the stubble-mulching idea in the mid-1930s, he based it off core concepts in "dryland farming," which by then was a widespread practice on the North American grasslands.[16] Dryland farming refers to a host of methods designed to farm semiarid lands without irrigation. It first emerged in Canada during the 1880s. The superintendent of Saskatchewan's Indian Head Experimental Farm, Angus McKay, was promoting "the dry farming technique" by 1889 and began experiments the following year.[17] Whereas dryland farming in Canada enjoyed federal support around the turn of the twentieth century, in the United States it hinged on private efforts, most notably those of Hardy Webster Campbell.[18] Campbell's proselytizing began in 1895 and broadened in 1902, when he started promoting dryland farming in his *Soil Culture Manual*. Although the specific methods of executing dryland farming remained contested, its defining feature came to be a system of summer fallow. Promoted consistently by Canadians since the 1890s and gaining popularity among Americans around the First World War, summer fallow—or "black fallow," describing its bare soil surface—involved farmers resting their fields (often for twelve to fifteen months) after harvest in order to recharge soil moisture.[19]

Underground soil dynamics performed a key function in Campbell's system of dryland farming. In moist soils, water typically moves upward (like lamp oil up a wick) between soil particles through a process called "capillary action"; the closer compressed the soil particles, the higher water will move toward the surface.[20] Campbell encouraged farmers to control capillary action during fallow by using a "subsurface packer." The packer would compress soil beneath the surface, thereby allowing water to move via capillary action closer to crops' root zone. However, if the soil compression extended all the way to the surface, water would simply evaporate. Consequently, farmers loosened the very top of the soil profile into a "dust mulch," ranging in texture from fine and powdery to somewhat cloddy. Farmers had to cultivate this dust mulch after rains to restore the tilth and lock in soil moisture and several times throughout the year to kill thirsty weeds.[21] This was an expansive system. At any given time half of a dryland farmer's land would be fallowed and out of production.

A chief handicap of this dryland system was the soil it left vulnerable to erosion. By 1920 farmers on the northern grasslands of the United States started to realize dry conditions triggered accelerated blowing on dust-mulched lands.[22] Over the following decade, plains people adopted several different implements and techniques intended to roughen up the soil surface, increasing its resistance to wind. One such technology, the "duckfoot" cultivator, killed weeds from beneath by cutting their roots, leaving behind clods of soil and some crop residue to prevent erosion. By the early 1930s a number of farmers on the American plains wielded this implement in pursuit of a "plowless" summer fallow that would control erosion and conserve soil moisture.[23]

Folks living to the north took similar measures.[24] In the 1920s and 1930s, agricultural experiment stations in Swift Current and Regina, Saskatchewan, began research to conserve moisture and reduce soil blowing.[25] When E. H. Aicher, an SCS official from Montana, visited Lethbridge, Alberta, in 1935, he was impressed to discover "something new in land preparation, particularly summer fallow." For seven years farmers near the village of Monarch had used duckfoot cultivators to leave stubble on the surface, sometimes even spreading straw "by hand" for added protection against wind erosion. Aicher claimed this system resulted in higher yields, fields "entirely free from weeds," and, despite drought conditions, "ample" soil moisture five inches deep.[26]

In 1935 Charles S. Noble, a wealthy landowner near Lethbridge, invented an alternative to duckfoot cultivators. After the three or four cultivations required during a fallow, the implements still covered too much stubble for many Alberta farmers' liking. This was particularly problematic given the intense Chinook wind that during the 1930s, Noble's son recalled, "foretold a two or three-day period of dusk at noon."[27] Together with a former employee, Noble Sr. built a crude prototype for what became the Noble Blade. This implement consisted of a straight blade running perpendicular to the direction of travel.[28] It performed the same function as the device Duley and Russel would soon develop: it cultivated fields without disturbing surface residues. Within a few years, Noble was marketing his namesake blade. He also kept in regular contact with Duley, Russel, and others in the USDA. They offered mutual encouragement, monitored each other's developments, and traded information on specs and modifications. As early as 1938, the SCS became a core customer for Noble.[29]

Thus, when Frank Duley and J. C. Russel began their experiments in 1938, they did not start from scratch. As a Nebraska newspaper described it in 1939, stubble mulching was a "new dry land farming system."[30] It sought the same ends as the incumbent dryland agriculture, but through different means. Stubble would replace dust as mulch, and Duley and Russel's device would improve on the duckfoot cultivator. Further, the close relationship Noble maintained with Duley, Russel, and others in the SCS reveals how the cozy public-private partnerships that became a hallmark of the conservation-industrial complex were present in the earliest research into conservation tillage.

Frank Duley was the main driver behind the experiments he and Russel began at the University of Nebraska. Duley was born in 1888 and raised on a farm near Grant City, Missouri. Educated at the University of Missouri (BS and MA) and the University of Wisconsin (PhD), he started his career in 1915 as a soils professor at Missouri.[31] In 1923 he coauthored a landmark research bulletin in the study of sheet erosion in humid regions.[32] Duley worked as a professor at Kansas State College from 1925 to 1933, at which point he joined the newly created Soil Erosion Service (precursor to the SCS) to manage an erosion-control demonstration project headquartered in Mankato, Kansas. In 1936 Duley became director of research for the northern Great Plains region of the SCS, based out of Kansas State.[33]

Apparently, it was in this capacity that the stubble-mulching idea began to germinate. In a May 1936 research program, Duley prioritized the absorption of rainfall into the ground as his staff's "major line of research," and he suggested crop residues could have some bearing on the matter.[34] The plan also called for research into controlling erosion while cultivating summer-fallowed fields.[35] Perhaps, as a newspaper article later posited, the idea dawned on Duley while touring western Kansas, where he noticed how the "dust swirls" blowing over black-fallowed fields seemed denser than those whirling over fields whose stubble hadn't been adequately buried.[36] Whatever the case, Duley seems to have settled the basic features of his research program by 1936 or 1937. At the invitation of the chair of the University of Nebraska Agronomy Department, he transferred his headquarters to Lincoln in September 1937. The following May, Duley sat across a table from Russel, planning the experiments that would occupy much of his research energies until he retired in 1959.[37]

Duley placed tremendous faith in research and technology to solve problems and sustain agriculture on the grasslands. As early as 1935, he confessed he found "no solution" in land-retirement plans rooted in the idea that some lands were unfit for plow agriculture and "should never have been broken out." As he saw it, "The people who broke it out thought it would pay"; he believed restoring profitability ought to be the government's goal.[38] According to Duley, research formed the foundation for all other conservation efforts, especially in the context of the Dust Bowl.[39] Wind erosion attracted national attention, and "the whole country . . . [is] eagerly watching us to see if we can stop the dust storms." To a great extent, "the future popularity of the Soil Conservation Service" hung in the balance.[40]

Duley applied his technophilia to his research. Since drought was responsible for the dust storms, he reasoned, the SCS should help farmers adapt to aridity. "We cannot increase the amount of rainfall," he and Russel admitted, but they could make "more

FIG. 17. Two of Duley and Russel's early V-sweeps attached to a carrier, ca. 1940. Courtesy of Archives & Special Collections, University of Nebraska, Lincoln.

effective use" of that which fell. Indeed, their research began in 1938 with moisture conservation as its "principal objective."[41] Yet, to abandon the plow was to lose the traditional means of weed control, cultivation, and seedbed preparation.

Their preferred solution was a V-shaped implement whose blades swept beneath the soil surface, killing weeds by slicing their roots. This device shared much in common with duckfoot cultivators—their prototype was even welded onto a duckfoot apparatus—but the researchers stressed a critical advantage: it killed weeds and loosened topsoil "without covering the mulch."[42] For years Duley and Russel would continue to study other implements that would achieve similar results as, or work in conjunction with, their V-sweeps.[43] Throughout their studies, technological adaptation remained the key to sustaining Great Plains agriculture.

Early results were promising. Their experiments showed that stubble left on the surface increased absorption of water into the soil.[44] The mulch also shielded soil from evaporation, which Duley and Russel labeled the region's "greatest single source of [soil moisture] loss."⁴⁵ These methods resulted in water storage and wheat yields that more than doubled those under plowing.⁴⁶ Even without this boosted production, Duley and Russel stressed that erosion control (which they observed but did not initially measure) alone justified the practice.⁴⁷ By the eve of U.S. entry into World War II, stubble mulching seemed poised to revolutionize dryland agriculture. While Duley and Russel cautioned against premature enthusiasm, they concluded "without equivocation" that surface residues would help conserve both water and soil on the Great Plains.⁴⁸

The centrality of Great Plains aridity and erosion to the rise of stubble mulching might come as a surprise to some. Most accounts of the origins of conservation tillage begin with or feature the Ohio iconoclast Edward Faulkner.⁴⁹ In 1943 Faulkner published his classic *Plowman's Folly*, a diatribe against the moldboard plow. "Plowing," he insisted, "is wrong."⁵⁰ He claimed to have invented a superior, plowless style of farming in his backyard. Faulkner's condemnation of agricultural orthodoxy elicited an immediate firestorm and, together with his self-serving narrative, won him heroic status within countercultural farming circles.⁵¹ Once conservation tillage became more common in the 1970s, some of its loudest, most enthusiastic proponents were the machinery and herbicide manufacturers seeking to capitalize on it. Some historians, having generally accepted Faulkner's claims of discovery, view these later developments as a classic case of industry co-opting countercultural energies and stripping them of their critiques.⁵²

Frank Duley's research challenges key foundations of this interpretation. It challenges the chronological foundation, as Duley's idea preceded Faulkner's own eureka moment.⁵³ It challenges the geographic foundation, as stubble mulching emerged first as an adaptation to specific conditions on the Great Plains, not in Faulkner's Ohio. (Indeed, Duley and Russel held little hope it would spread elsewhere. They associated the practice so closely with the particular climatic context of the plains that they believed it "would never become practical in regions of high rainfall." Wetter conditions, they reasoned, led to more aggressive weed growth that the V-sweeps could not control.)[54] Finally, it challenges the narrative arc itself, which relies on a fall from grace into capitalist exploitation. Yet, industrial interests did not swoop in decades later to co-opt the momentum of countercultural farming; they were enmeshed in conservation tillage from the beginning.

Private manufacturers' commitment to stubble mulching depended on consumer demand, which was initially slow. Canadian scientist Asael Palmer described how Albertans' cultural attitudes, which also prevailed in the United States, predisposed them against stubble mulching: "If a fellow didn't have a black fallow, he wasn't a good farmer. He was a sloppy farmer."[55] Americans also needed convincing. Upon observing Duley and Russel's plots at the University of Nebraska in 1939, after just one year of tests, a number of farmers "appeared skeptical," the *Lincoln Star* reported, "with the prevailing attitude that 'it's a swell idea *if* it will work.'"[56]

Public institutions on both sides of the border worked to overcome grassroots skepticism of this promising technology. One strategy involved rebranding. Farmers found Duley and Russel's preferred term, "subsurface tillage," confusing. The Nebraska Agricultural Extension Service launched a publicity blitz that described the practice as "trash farming" and "Right-Side-Up Farming"— terms that were too colloquial for Duley and Russel's liking.[57] Canadian researchers, however, embraced the term "trash cover" because it conveyed to farmers that, amid the urgency to end soil blowing, any plant residues (not just crop stubble) would do the job.[58] By 1943, at the urging of SCS director Hugh Hammond Bennett, Duley and Russel agreed to rechristen the method "stubble mulching," a name that better communicated the essence of the practice and leveraged the lexicon of dryland farming.[59]

In both the United States and Canada, key pillars of the state agricultural apparatus put their weight behind stubble mulching in the early 1940s. In addition to Nebraska Extension's myriad news stories, county extension agents joined with local Farm Bureau chapters to establish demonstration plots. Most soil conservation districts in Nebraska offered their members a try-without-buying arrangement through loans of stubble-mulching equipment.[60] In

Canada, agricultural scientists partnered with farmers, who demonstrated to visitors stubble mulching and other conservation methods and, in return, received up to $600 annually.[61] Through demonstrations, loans, and direct payments, various arms of the state worked to normalize this new technology.

By the mid-1940s more farmers were taking up stubble mulching. Sheer desperation may have driven some decisions. In 1940 Duley speculated the ongoing drought left farmers with "not much to lose even if the idea does not work."[62] Whatever their reasons for trying the practice, many farmers reported improved production and efficiency—heightened imperatives during World War II. Ed Larson of Buffalo County credited it with boosting his wheat crop by several bushels per acre and taking only 40 percent the time of plowing. "Any way you look at it," another farmer beamed in 1943, "subsurface tillage is cheaper. You can get so much more done."[63]

Saved time and labor were particularly attractive in larger-scale operations. In 1940 the median Nebraska farm encompassed between 180 and 219 acres.[64] Duley cited examples of two farmers who summer-fallowed 480 acres and 1,600 acres, respectively, under stubble-mulch management.[65] Wartime labor shortages revealed another advantage of this efficiency: it required fewer workers. A. H. Sibbernsen, who operated 800 acres near Bennington, Nebraska, described his farm as "a 7-man place," but with two sons fighting in the war, five workers still "get the work done on time."[66] The benefits of increased efficiency through stubble mulching would only accrue after the war, as agriculture became defined by larger farms and fewer people. In the meantime, demand for this technology was clearly on the rise.

And that meant a hungry market. Private manufacturers proved eager to capitalize on Duley and Russel's publicly funded experiments. Duley estimated that between 1939 and 1941, plains farmers bought or made an estimated 1,500 subsurface-tillage implements.[67] By then, he noted the "distinct progress" made by private industry in the development of stubble-mulching equipment, "almost entirely" because of his research. He acknowledged that some zealous firms made unsubstantiated claims about what stubble mulching could achieve, but he dared not suppress their enthusiasm. Resigned that there was "no way of constraining it," Duley instead hoped to monitor industry's product development and "point out directly to the designing engineers" how to improve.[68] The best way to beat those who might overcommercialize his technology, he believed, was to join them.

Public-private collaborations ramped up during World War II. Duley and Russel field tested several machine and implement designs introduced by various companies (including International Harvester, John Deere, and the Noble Company) during the war years.[69] Manufacturers "have always been agreeable and even anxious" to loan equipment for testing, Duley reported in 1945, which he considered "very fortunate." He and Russel reciprocated by reporting on equipment performance, identifying design flaws, and recommending modifications.[70] As the United States emerged from the war, the mutually beneficial relationships at the heart of the conservation-industrial complex had taken root.

Throughout the late 1940s and early 1950s, these interests became further entwined. While acknowledging implement research was not the purpose of their experiments, Duley and Russel counted their relationships with industry as a completely positive, even natural byproduct. They enjoyed "implements and improvements ... freely put at our disposal." In turn, their research "unquestionably" stimulated new markets for equipment throughout the plains.[71] Duley took pride in helping create what the *Daily Nebraskan* suggested in 1951 was a "multi-million dollar [industry]" around stubble mulching.[72]

During this period public researchers and private firms focused on overcoming lingering resistance to the practice. They defined such resistance as technical problems requiring technical solutions. Most notably, operating in stubble-covered soil proved difficult. Plant residues obstructed seeding and tended to clog equipment, at which point they would drag across the surface.[73] Throughout the 1940s Duley and Russel modified V-sweeps, discs, seed drills, and other implements to solve these challenges, and they passed their solutions to manufacturers.[74] Stubble-mulching implements soon performed better. By the early 1950s the market swelled with implements tailor-made for specific conditions. As a result, the SCS argued, "many problems which formerly perplexed farmers have disappeared."[75] The agency credited the "improved equipment and the interest shown by the farm-equipment people" for the technology's growing acceptance among farmers.[76]

Indeed, stubble mulching continued to spread throughout the Great Plains. Earl Bondy joked that when he became the SCS conservationist in Haskell County, Kansas, in 1948, "I knew every stubble mulch farmer in Western Kansas—and both of them were good conservation farmers."[77] Humor aside, the practice was actually gaining popularity. Between 1947 and 1950, the SCS helped Nebraska farmers apply stubble-mulching methods to an additional 1.3 million acres, more than double the previous acreage. Nationwide, meanwhile, that number jumped from barely 15 million acres to over 35 million acres—the vast majority of which were in the ten Great Plains states.[78] This rapid spread led the *Nebraska State Journal* to opine in 1948 that "the big era of the plowman" was coming to a close.[79] By 1951 SCS chief Hugh Bennett declared stubble mulching "the basic conservation measure" for dryland wheat farming.[80]

Conservation tillage emerged on the Great Plains not separate from industrial agriculture, but integrated within it. Its expansion owed to a system of mutually beneficial relationships that linked public researchers, private firms, and at least some dryland farmers. These relationships continued to guide the development of the technology throughout the 1950s and 1960s, as researchers worked to increase the efficiency and expand the geographic range of stubble mulching. In the process, these scientists developed technological systems that sent a clear message: the same values and tools that helped define industrial agriculture would also help farmers protect the land.

In the 1950s public and private researchers turned their attention to making stubble mulching more efficient. Russell R. Poynor, an engineer with International Harvester (IH) and a former SCS employee, singled out stubble mulching in 1951 as a practice that could reduce "the number of trips over the field," particularly by "combining or eliminating some operations."[81] Within a few years, agricultural engineers at the University of Nebraska answered his call. In 1957 L. W. Hurlbut and Howard D. Wittmuss launched studies to do for seedbed preparation and planting what the combine-harvester had done for harvesting: integrate several steps into one.[82] During planting, Nebraska farmers typically made six to twelve passes across each field, including trips to cut and shred crop residue, apply fertilizer, cultivate up to seven times, plant, and apply insecticides. Hurlbut and Wittmuss hoped to reduce that total to just a few trips.[83] Cooperating with companies such as IH and John Deere, they developed an integrated "Till-Plant" system specifically suited for Nebraska conditions.[84] By the early 1960s several manufacturers were testing and marketing till-planters, and the research team boasted that this system reduced production costs as much as eight dollars per acre, an annual savings of up to fifteen million dollars in Nebraska alone.[85] Measured in terms of individual economic efficiency, this more elaborate stubble-mulching technology seemed to be paying off.

Hurlbut and Wittmuss also predicted their system would generate a number of environmental benefits. It integrated Duley and Russel's system of stubble mulching, thereby increasing soil moisture and reducing erosion and runoff. Further, at a time when farm machinery was growing larger and heavier, fewer trips across the field would reduce soil compaction and improve soil structure.[86] In the minds of these researchers, however, those were ancillary benefits. As a 1968 report explained, "Increased efficiency in crop production is the goal of this project."[87] In an agricultural regime obsessed with maximized efficiency and profits, this iteration of stubble mulching promised harmony between economic production and environmental protection.

In the 1950s researchers worked to spread stubble mulching beyond the semiarid plains, and to do so they enlisted new allies in the conservation mission: agrochemical companies. One obstacle in humid regions was lower yields compared to plowing.[88] T. M. McCalla, a microbiologist who joined Duley's team in 1941, had determined by the early 1950s that surface residues created an ideal habitat for microorganisms, including "denitrifiers" that reduced the amount of nitrates in the soil by 5–10 percent.[89] The result, IH's Russell Poynor told Canadian engineers in 1955, was "short and spindly, and sometimes yellow" corn plants, owing to nitrogen deficiencies. Poynor proposed a solution: fertilization "at much higher rates than ever previously . . . thought practical," which he claimed made stubble mulching competitive with conventional farming. "Heavy fertilization" seemed to unlock the potential of stubble mulching in humid corn country.[90]

Agrochemicals held even greater promise in the control of weeds, which had thwarted would-be stubble mulchers ever since Duley and Russel began their experiments in 1938. Weeds "sapped" the ground of moisture, the researchers advised in 1939, undercutting "the prime objective" of the practice.[91] In normal plains weather, farmers could control weeds by using V-sweeps early in the growing season, but in wetter weather (or in humid environments) many unwanted plants survived the sweeps by quickly shooting down new roots.[92] This is precisely what Duley and Russel observed in 1943, when weeds resprouted "so luxuriantly that the soil was soon dried beyond all possibility of effective penetration."[93] Into the 1950s the Soil Conservation Service acknowledged stubble mulching failed to gain adherents "in the eastern part of the country where summer rains make weed control a greater problem."[94]

From the late 1950s through the 1960s, several Nebraska researchers worked to overcome these difficulties with synthetic herbicides. In 1956 J. G. Geiger, the Swiss company that created DDT, introduced the preemergent, broadleaf herbicide Simazine.[95] The following year, Hurlbut and Wittmuss tested Simazine with promising results.[96] By the late 1960s, when researchers combined herbicides with till-planting, they proclaimed weed control "practically 100 percent effective."[97] The combination of herbicides and tillage during summer fallow (known as "chemical fallow") eliminated many thirsty weeds and dramatically increased soil moisture. Whereas stubble mulching and black fallowing might retain up to 35 and 20 percent of annual precipitation, respectively, chemical fallow could yield a storage rate of nearly 50 percent.[98] In the semi-arid plains, chemical inputs enabled wiser use of a scarce resource.

Herbicides also proved instrumental to conservation tillage beyond the Great Plains. Most notably, these chemicals made possible "no-till" technology, the most advanced form of conservation tillage. No-till farmers keep the ground permanently covered with crop residues, injecting seeds directly into the ground. Herbicides alone kill unwanted plants, completely replacing plows as well as V-sweeps and other tillage implements.[99] Harry Young Jr., a farmer in humid Kentucky, developed the first successful no-till operation in 1962, largely by participating in a sprawling public-private network that included the machinery and chemical industry.[100] Conservation tillage, whose roots were deepest in the North American West, was moving eastward.[101]

In the 1960s the centrality of herbicides to a conservation practice offered an enticing carrot to agrochemical producers. Conservation tillage not only offered chemical manufacturers a chance to expand the market for their products, but also greenwash a reputation that had been bruised since the publication of Rachel Carson's *Silent Spring* in 1962.[102] By the early 1970s, for instance, Dow Chemical Company had launched a campaign in its official magazine, *Down to Earth*, to delegitimize environmentalists' critiques of agricultural pollution and present chemical-wielding farmers as environmental stewards.[103] In 1973 *Down to Earth* cited no-till as one of "a number of new uses for herbicides which could have profound ecological benefit."[104] On the Great Plains, researchers even rechristened chemical fallow as "ecofallow" during the 1970s, presenting similar opportunities for brand resuscitation.[105] In the eyes of the conservation-industrial complex, input-intensive agriculture made environmental as well as economic sense.

Although conservation researchers won over the farm-equipment and agrochemical industries, they remained frustrated by the limited popularity of conservation tillage. In March 1972 the University of Nebraska assembled scientists and field personnel from across the Midwest to brainstorm solutions to farmers' reluctance. Their primary challenge, Harold Wittmuss explained in his opening remarks, was no longer research or technical modifications. Rather, it was how to translate the "knowledge in our libraries" into "technology... on the farm."[106] Conferees identified a number of factors hindering wider embrace of conservation tillage, including traditionalism and "fear of criticism or ridicule by neighbors" (due to the continued association of residue-strewn fields with poor farming).[107] Unlike in the 1940s, technological innovation alone no longer seemed capable of overcoming cultural resistance.

Among the various suggestions for converting farmers were calls to better leverage public-private partnerships. "Farmers accept mulch tillage systems," one person argued, "when the SCS technicians, the County Extension Director, and the farm machinery dealer tell the same story about tillage."[108] Others agreed, urging their peers to "enlist [the] help of dealers of machinery, seed, fertilizer, herbicides, and insecticides with participation in meetings and demonstrations."[109] Nothing short of the participation of the entire conservation-industrial complex, it seemed, would secure the potential of conservation tillage.

The conference deliberations also revealed the degree to which conservation tillage was suited to large-scale, well-capitalized agriculture. The chemicals and elaborate machines inherent to modern stubble mulching entailed hefty upfront costs. Given these investments, many farmers demurred on the grounds they "cannot afford to miss."[110] One conferee argued, "Small farmers can afford to remain conventional," but noted "large farmers are taking it on" to get bigger.[111] Others echoed findings from the 1940s that large-scale farmers were typically the first to adopt conservation tillage because it helped them save time.[112] Into the 1980s soil conservation districts tried to increase access to the practice by renting out equipment, but even its staunchest advocates acknowledged some of the equipment "costs so dearly that only the very largest farmers can afford it."[113]

By the 1970s conservation researchers had designed technological systems to conserve resources and improve productivity. They saw the tools, methods, and alliances of industrial agriculture as vital to environmental protection. Their efforts were beginning to transform the Great Plains. Yet, they could not escape the reality that conservation tillage was leaving many farmers in the dust.

...

Scarcely a year and a half after the 1972 conference, events on the world stage so revolutionized the economics of agriculture that conservation tillage suddenly offered new incentives to farmers. The energy crises triggered by the OPEC oil embargo of October 1973 sent production costs skyrocketing. Almost overnight, research such as Hurlbut and Wittmuss's studies into reducing the number of trips across the field seemed like a godsend, for conservation tillage promised to save up to 80 percent the cost of fuel.[114] Even as the crises receded, Americans remained conscious of fuel efficiency. "Today," Earl Bondy argued in 1980, "the rising cost of petroleum makes conservation tillage even more urgent."[115] From the perspective of many farmers—those with the means and inclination to compete in industrial agriculture—fuel savings offered by tillage technology helped offset the initial capital investments.

Increased efficiency continues to shape Great Plains farmers' decision-making. No-till saves Justin Knopf, who farms five thousand acres near Salina, Kansas, up to ten or twenty times the time and fuel compared to the plow agriculture his family practiced when he was younger. Yet, these efficiencies come at a cost. "Change is . . . expensive," he explained to writer Miriam Horn around 2014. Knopf's expenses include a seeder that cost $175,000 and a sprayer that ran $225,000—investments that compel him to rent land from others. "If I only farmed my own ground I wouldn't be able to afford [the technology]."[116]

Knopf considers these outcomes the necessary price of environmental protection. "Many of the larger-scale farms are the ones on the cutting edge of environmentalism," he insists. Despite criticisms of its reliance on synthetic herbicides, no-till prevents erosion, conserves water, stores soil carbon, and reduces fossil fuel usage. But according to Knopf, in order for the environmental benefits of no-till technology to outweigh their financial costs, "you need to be at a certain scale."¹¹⁷ Between the 1930s and 1970s, stubble-mulch researchers had helped create that logic. Decades later, it remains strong.

In the middle of the twentieth century, Frank Duley, J. C. Russel, and other agricultural scientists strove to adapt farming to the semiarid grasslands through stubble mulching. Their faith in technology to solve agricultural challenges of the Great Plains—particularly aridity—saturated their writings. It motivated their efforts to work with farm-equipment and agrochemical companies to overcome lingering technical obstacles to the spread of stubble mulching. The rise of synthetic fertilizers and herbicides in the 1950s and 1960s seemed to unlock the potential of conservation tillage, both on the Great Plains and beyond. Researchers noted on several occasions that the technology tended to appeal most to the larger-scale farmers who could afford it.

At the 1972 conference in Lincoln, a scientist shared a poem that captured the salvation he and his peers found in the technology. In "That Cornfield in the Sky," William Moldenhauer framed their crusade in nirvanic terms. Once in heaven, he wrote, "you'll find no weeds or insects" and "you can only use mulch tillage." In the meantime, however, farmers and researchers could taste heaven on earth, thanks to technology: "New advances could well make / The present surge succeed / With a pesticide for every bug / And one for every weed."¹¹⁸ Neither Moldenhauer nor his peers ever fully addressed, however, that their technological salvation was not for everyone. Narrow was the path to that cornfield in the sky, and few had the means to enter.

Notes

Several people deserve thanks for offering comments and rendering assistance with this essay, including Kathleen Brosnan, Sterling Evans, Brian Frehner, Brandon Luedtke, and all the participants at the workshop from which this volume emerged.

1. Although the lands I examine were largely stripped of grasses by the 1930s, I periodically describe them as "grasslands" to reflect the environmental conditions (chiefly aridity) to which native grasses had adapted. On settlers' conceptualization of the region as the "Great Plains" in response to the 1930s drought, see Molly P. Rozum's essay in this volume.

2. F. L. Duley and J. C. Russel, "Revolutionary 'Plow to Save the Plains' Is Developed by SCS," *Evening Huronite*, February 27, 1940; Pare Lorentz, *The Plow That Broke the Plains* (Washington DC: Resettlement Administration, 1936). Russel dismissed some alternative names for the practice as "purely colloquial," explaining "we do not like them." J. C. Russel to W. V. Lambert, November 30, 1948, 2, box 101, folder 1, William V. Lambert Papers, 1923–60 (hereafter "Lambert Papers"), record group 08-01-03, University of Nebraska–Lincoln Archives & Special Collections (hereafter "UNLASC"). Duley and Russel's technological optimism aligns far more closely to the spirit of the Canadian film *Heritage*. See Blaine Allan, "Canada's *Heritage* (1939) and America's *The Plow That Broke the Plains* (1936)," *Historical Journal of Film, Radio and Television* 19, no. 4 (October 1999): 439–72.

3. On this expansion in Kentucky and Australia after 1960, see C. Milton Coughenour and Shankariah Chamala, *Conservation Tillage and Cropping Innovation: Constructing the New Culture of Agriculture* (Ames: Iowa State University Press, 2000). In recent years conservation tillage has come into wide usage in Canada (60 percent of cropland in 2001), in the United States (51 percent of cropland in 2017), and on the Brazilian and Argentine grasslands (approximately 80 percent of farmers as of 2016). See David R. Montgomery, *Dirt: The Erosion of Civilizations* (Berkeley: University of California Press, 2007), 211; National Association of Conservation Districts, "USDA Releases 2017 Ag Census Data," April 11, 2019, https://www.nacdnet.org/2019/04/11/usda-releases-2017-ag-census-data/; Miriam Horn, *Rancher, Farmer, Fisherman: Conservation Heroes of the American Heartland* (New York: W. W. Norton, 2016), 140.

4. Recent studies of the interconnections between public and private institutions in industrial agriculture include Shane Hamilton, *Supermarket USA: Food and Power in the Cold War Farms Race* (New Haven CT: Yale University Press, 2018); Gabriel N. Rosenberg, *The 4-H Harvest: Sexuality and the State in Rural America* (Philadelphia: University of Pennsylvania Press, 2016); Margaret Weber, "The American Way of Farming: Pioneer Hi-Bred and Power in Postwar America," *Agricultural History* 92, no. 3 (Summer 2018): 380–403.

5. I explore another iteration of the conservation-industrial complex in "The Bulldozer in the Watershed: Conservation, Water, and Technological Optimism in the Post–World War II United States," *Environmental History* 21 (January 2016): 126–36.

6. The conservation-industrial complex also included a tangled web of alliances between public institutions, as reflected in Duley's and Russel's joint employment by federal and state agencies. Duley was paid by the SCS (and, in the 1950s, the USDA's Agricultural Research Service) but was hosted by Nebraska's Agronomy Department. Russel's primary affiliation was with the university, but he was paid by both institutions. Other stubble-mulch scientists were employed by the University of Nebraska but received research grants from the federal government under the Hatch Act of 1887. Russel to Lambert, November 30, 1948, 1; L. W. Hurlbut and H. D. Wittmuss, "Annual Progress Report, 1958: Hatch 572, The Integration of Machine Operations Required in Crop Culture," 1958, box 4, folder 22, RG 10-01-03, UNLASC.

7. In places like Montana and Kansas, many plains residents needed no convincing of the economic benefits of the "industrial ideal." See Deborah Fitzgerald, *Every Farm a Factory: The Industrial Ideal in American Agriculture* (New Haven CT: Yale University Press, 2003), especially 10–32 and 129–56; Donald Worster, *Dust Bowl: The Southern Plains in the 1930s* (New York: Oxford University Press, 1979), 80–97.

8. The historiography surrounding the Dust Bowl is among the most extensive and contested in American environmental and agricultural history. The primary disputes revolve around the causes of and responses to the disaster—and therefore its meaning. It is not the purpose of this study to engage in this ongoing debate, but rather, to move beyond it. See Worster, *Dust Bowl*; Paul Bonnifield, *The Dust Bowl: Men, Dirt and Depression* (Albuquerque: University of New Mexico Press, 1980); R. Douglas Hurt, *The Dust Bowl: An Agricultural and Social History* (Chicago: Nelson-Hall, 1984); Pamela Riney-Kehrberg, *Rooted in Dust: Surviving Drought and Depression in Southwestern Kansas* (Lawrence: University Press of Kansas, 1994); Geoff Cunfer, *On the Great Plains: Agriculture and Environment* (College Station: Texas A&M Univ. Press, 2005); William Cronon, "A Place for Stories: Nature, History, and Narrative," *Journal of American History* 78 (March 1992): 1347–76; Pamela Riney-Kehrberg, Geoff Cunfer, R. Douglas Hurt, and Julie Courtwright, "Historians' Reaction to the Documentary, The Dust Bowl," *Agricultural History* 88, no. 2 (Spring 2014): 262–88; Hannah Holleman, *Dust Bowls of Empire: Imperialism, Environmental Politics, and the Injustice of "Green" Capitalism* (New Haven CT: Yale University Press, 2018); Douglas Sheflin, *Legacies of Dust: Land Use and Labor on the Colorado Plains* (Lincoln: University of Nebraska Press, 2019).

9. For example, see Robert W. Rice, *Fundamentals of No-Till Farming* (Athens GA: American Association for Vocational Instructional Materials, 1983), 22; Horn, *Rancher, Farmer, Fisherman*, 88, 93–94, 97–98.

10. One exception is F. L. Duley, "Keeping the Dust under Cover," *Journal of Soil and Water Conservation* 6, no. 1 (1951): 34–37.

11. Worster, *Dust Bowl*, 13.

12. E. C. Hole to R. M. Loper, September 22, 1937, box 59, folder A2, RG 10-01-02, UNLASC. Great Plains residents were not alone in rejecting their region's reputation for soil erosion. See Paul Sutter, *Let Us Now Praise Famous Gullies: Providence Canyon and the Soils of the South* (Athens: University of Georgia Press, 2015), 67–68.

13. Worster, *Dust Bowl*, 211.

14. On the sheer variety of factors shaping farmers' decisions during this period, see J. L. Anderson, *Industrializing the Corn Belt: Agriculture, Technology, and Environment, 1945–1972* (DeKalb: Northern Illinois University Press, 2009).

15. Deborah Fitzgerald describes the "industrial ideal" as an aspiration to make "every farm a factory" by embracing large-scale production, mechanization, standardization, managerial expertise, and imperatives of efficiency. See *Every Farm a Factory*, especially 21–29.

16. Philip Nelson notes these roots in "To Hold the Land: Soil Erosion, Agricultural Scientists, and the Development of Conservation Tillage Techniques," *Agricul-*

tural History 71, no. 1 (Winter 1997): 74–75. For more on the connections between the American and Canadian plains, see Sterling Evans, *Bound in Twine: The History and Ecology of the Henequen-Wheat Complex for Mexico and the American and Canadian Plains, 1880–1950* (College Station: Texas A&M University Press, 2007).

17. Peter A. Russell, "The Far-from-Dry Debates: Dry Farming on the Canadian Prairies and the American Great Plains," *Agricultural History* 81, no. 4 (September 2007): 498, quoted on 495.

18. Russell, "The Far-from-Dry Debates," 501.

19. Russell, "The Far-from-Dry Debates," 501, especially 500–515; Mary W. M. Hargreaves, *Dry Farming in the Northern Great Plains, 1900–1925* (Cambridge MA: Harvard University Press, 1957), 86–92.

20. Nyle C. Brady and Ray R. Weil, *Elements of the Nature and Properties of Soils*, 3rd ed. (Boston: Prentice Hall, 2010), 135–36.

21. Hargreaves, *Dry Farming in the Northern Great Plains, 1900–1925*, 86–92; Russell, "The Far-from-Dry Debates," 503.

22. Mary W. M. Hargreaves, *Dry Farming in the Northern Great Plains: Years of Readjustment, 1920–1990* (Lawrence: University Press of Kansas, 1993), 28, 196.

23. Hargreaves, *Dry Farming in the Northern Great Plains, 1920–1990*, 50–52; O. A. Fitzgerald and Cecil Hagen, "The School Teacher and the Rod Weeder," *Crops and Soils* 72, no. 3 (September 1951): 16–17.

24. James H. Gray, *Men against the Desert* (Saskatoon: Modern Press, 1967), 70–80.

25. Dominion Experimental Farms, *Fifty Years of Progress on Dominion Experimental Farms, 1886–1936* (Ottawa: J. O. Patenaude, 1939), 76–77, 129.

26. E. H. Aicher to H. J. Clemmer, October 3, 1935, 1–2, box 386, folder "Dominion Experimental," RG 114, NARA-Kansas City. One Canadian scientist recalled the scattering of straw was a common practice in certain localities in Canada. Asael Palmer, interview by James H. Gray, June 10, 1966, part 1, 14:50–15:40, Provincial Archives of Saskatchewan, http://climateandchange.usask.ca/audio.html. Special thanks to George Colpitts for alerting me to this collection of interviews.

27. S. F. Noble, "Noble Blade Meets West's Farm Needs," *Lethbridge Herald*, February 23, 1952. Many Canadians welcomed and anticipated the warm Chinook wind for the midwinter thaw it delivered. While this writer might have taken liberties in connecting the Chinook with dust storms, the 1930s drought may in fact have resulted in a desiccated, snowless plains fully exposed to the gusting wind. On anticipation of the Chinook, see Curtis McManus, *Happyland: A History of the "Dirty Thirties" in Saskatchewan, 1914–1937* (Calgary: University of Calgary Press, 2014), 234. On connections between the Chinook and erosion, see Gray, *Men against the Desert*, 74–76.

28. A photo of an original Noble Blade is viewable online through the University of Lethbridge Digital Collections at http://digitallibrary.uleth.ca/cdm/singleitem/collection/crs/id/746/rec/7.

29. In 1938 the SCS ordered nineteen of the fifty blades Noble manufactured. Noble, "Noble Blade Meets West's Farm Needs"; Noble Farms Limited to Steve Kortan, September 5, 1940, box 80, folder 2, RG 114, NARA-Kansas City. Throughout the

1940s Duley and Russel "closely coordinated" their work with research in other states and Canadian provinces. See University of Nebraska Agronomy Department, "Soils Research, 1949," 1949, 1, box 5, folder 3, RG 10-01-02, UNLASC. For more on Noble, see Gray, *Men against the Desert* 78, 229–32. Farmers in other arid contexts, such as the Palouse region of the Pacific Northwest, also developed technological solutions around this time. See Andrew P. Duffin, *Plowed Under: Agriculture & Environment in the Palouse* (Seattle: University of Washington Press, 2007), 92.

30. "Radical Type of Farming: Land Would Always Remain Right Side Up, Says Russel," *Lincoln Star*, June 22, 1939, 20.

31. T. M. McCalla, "In Memorium: Frank L. Duley," *Soil Science* 126, no. 6 (December 1978): 321–22.

32. These experiments established the standard methods for measuring erosion and runoff under controlled conditions and demonstrated quantitatively the role of vegetation in reducing sheet erosion. F. L. Duley and M. F. Miller, *Erosion and Surface Runoff under Different Soil Conditions*, Research Bulletin no. 63 (Columbia: University of Missouri, College of Agriculture, Agricultural Experiment Station, 1923); C. M. Woodruff, "Pioneering Erosion Research That Paid," *Journal of Soil and Water Conservation* 42, no. 2 (1987): 91–92.

33. F. L. Duley, interview by George S. Round, October 10, 1974, 7–8, 10, box 15, folder 18, G. Round Oral Histories, RG 08-16-05, UNLASC. On the Limestone Creek demonstration project, see Neil M. Maher, "'Crazy-Quilt Farming on Round Land': The Great Depression, the Soil Conservation Service, and the Politics of Landscape Change on the Great Plains during the New Deal Era," *Western Historical Quarterly* 31, no. 3 (Autumn 2000): 319–39.

34. F. L. Duley, "Soil Erosion Research: Suggested Program," May 1936, 3, 4, box 58, folder 15, RG 10-01-02, UNLASC.

35. Duley, "Soil Erosion Research," 4, 11–12.

36. "Stubble-Mulch Farming Saves Soil," *Nebraska State Journal*, September 26, 1948.

37. Duley, interview, 10; Russel to Lambert, November 30, 1948. Upon retirement from the USDA and UNL, Duley spent five years working for Colorado State University in Pakistan under a contract with the U.S. Agency for International Development. Russel stopped working with Duley in 1953, when he began a six-year tenure as a soil scientist in Iraq through the University of Arizona's partnership with Abu Ghraib College. Thus, their careers parallel those of other New Dealers who sought to internationalize conservation as part of fighting the Cold War. See McCalla, "In Memorium," 321; F. L. Duley and T. M. McCalla, "Annual Report, 1954: Soil and Moisture Conservation and Related Microbiological Studies," 1954, 2, box 7, folder 2, Agronomy Annual Reports, RG 10-11-02, UNLASC; "Russell [sic], Ruthanna Louise," *Lincoln Journal Star*, September 29, 2013, https://journalstar.com/lifestyles/announcements/obituaries/russell-ruthanna-louise/article_47d1dd85-19b8-593f-ba90-63f3b0103832.html; Sarah T. Phillips, *This Land, This Nation: Conservation, Rural America, and the New Deal* (New York: Cambridge University Press, 2007), 242–83.

38. As quoted in "Emporians See Erosion Work," *Emporia Gazette*, May 29, 1935, 2. On the land-use planning movement that brought about land retirement efforts, see Worster, *Dust Bowl*, 182–97; Phillips, *This Land, This Nation*; Sara M. Gregg, *Managing the Mountains: Land Use Planning, the New Deal, and the Creation of a Federal Landscape in Appalachia* (New Haven CT: Yale University Press, 2010).

39. Duley, "Soil Erosion Research," 8. Duley and other researchers repeated this argument over the years. For instance, see F. L. Duley, "Annual Report, 1945: Soil and Moisture Conservation and Related Microbiological Studies," 1946, 61, box 4, folder 1, RG 10-11-02, UNLASC; D. E. Smika, "Annual Progress Report, 1962: The Relation of Cropping and Tillage Practices to Crop Production and Maintenance of Soil Fertility under Dryland Conditions," February 26, 1962, box 8, folder 1, RG 10-01-03, UNLASC.

40. Duley, "Soil Erosion Research," 11. More broadly, conservation was central to New Deal politics in rural America. See Phillips, *This Land, This Nation*; Neil M. Maher, *Nature's New Deal: The Civilian Conservation Corps and the Roots of the American Environmental Movement* (New York: Oxford University Press, 2008).

41. Duley and Russel, "Revolutionary."

42. F. L. Duley, "Annual Report, 1938: Development of Soil and Water Conservation Practices for Regions of Limited Rainfall," 1939, 8–9, box 1, folder 7, RG 10-11-02, UNLASC; F. L. Duley and J. C. Russel, "New Methods of Rainfall and Soil Moisture Conservation," *31st Annual Report: Nebraska Crop Growers Association*, 1939, 53–54. Other devices, such as the rod weeder, achieved similar results, but apparently the V-sweeps operated better in heavy residue. F. L. Duley and J. C. Russel, "Illustrated Report—Soil and Moisture Conservation Project," December 1940, 13–17, box 2, folder 3, RG 10-11-02, UNLASC.

43. For instance, see F. L. Duley, "Annual Report, 1946: Soil and Moisture Conservation and Related Microbiological Studies," 1947, 15–20, box 4, folder 2, RG 10-11-02, UNLASC.

44. Stubble protected the soil surface from pounding raindrops, which could dislodge particles that upon drying formed an impervious crust. Duley, "Annual Report, 1938," 1939, 15, 21, 23; F. L. Duley, "Surface Factors Affecting the Rate of Intake of Water by Soils," *Soil Science Society of America Proceedings, 1939* 4, no. 1 (1940): 60–64.

45. Duley and Russel, "Illustrated Report," 10.

46. George S. Round, "Right-Side-Up Farming," *Country Gentleman* 109 (November 1939): 78; F. L. Duley, "Annual Report, 1940: Development of Soil and Water Conservation Practices for Regions of Limited Rainfall," 1941, 4, 6, box 2, folder 2, RG 10-11-02, UNLASC.

47. Duley and Russel, "Illustrated Report," 25; Duley, "Annual Report, 1940," 8–12, 17; "Stubble-Mulch Farming Saves Soil."

48. Duley and Russel, "New Methods," 60–61. These were the results of experiments at the experimental farm outside Lincoln, Nebraska, in the humid part of the state. Experiments at the stations in North Platte and Alliance were inconclusive due to drought conditions. Duley, "Annual Report, 1940," 30–31.

49. See Charles E. Little, *Green Fields Forever: The Conservation Tillage Revolution in America* (Washington DC: Island Press, 1987), 30–40; Randal S. Beeman and James A. Pritchard, *A Green and Permanent Land: Ecology and Agriculture in the Twentieth Century* (Lawrence: University Press of Kansas, 2001), 53–56; Randal Beeman, "The Trash Farmer: Edward Faulkner and the Origins of Sustainable Agriculture in the United States, 1942–1952," *Journal of Sustainable Agriculture* 4, no. 1 (Winter 1993): 91–102; Jared Margulies, "No-Till Agriculture in the USA," in *Organic Fertilisation, Soil Quality and Human Health*, ed. Eric Lichtfouse, Sustainable Agriculture Reviews 9 (Dordrecht, The Netherlands: Springer, 2012), 11–15. A notable exception is Nelson, "To Hold the Land."

50. Edward H. Faulkner, *Plowman's Folly* (Norman: University of Oklahoma Press, 1943), 3–4.

51. Beeman and Pritchard, *Green and Permanent Land*, 70–72; Nelson, "To Hold the Land," 76–78. Examples of the self-serving origins story include Faulkner, *Plowman's Folly*, 66–67; Louis Bromfield, *Pleasant Valley* (New York: Harper & Brothers, 1943), 167–68.

52. Beeman and Pritchard, *Green and Permanent Land*, 72–74, 149–51.

53. Faulkner claimed his "nudging" the USDA (around 1937) to look into mulching preceded Duley's experiments, but the idea was on Duley's mind by 1936. See Faulkner, *Plowman's Folly*, 67–68.

54. "Radical Type of Farming," 20.

55. Palmer, interview, part 2, 13:00–14:10. These aesthetic markers of "good" farming continue to this day. For instance, see Horn, *Rancher, Farmer, Fisherman*, 131.

56. "Radical Type of Farming," 20, emphasis added.

57. Russel to Lambert, November 30, 1948, 2; Round, "Right-Side-Up Farming."

58. Palmer, interview, part 2.

59. Bennett coined the term "stubble mulching," according to Russel, in response to farmers confusing "subsurface tillage" with subsoiling or with "some special sort of tillage" of the subsoil. Russel to Lambert, November 30, 1948, 2. See also H. H. Bennett, "The Abolition of the Plow," *New Republic* 109 (October 4, 1943): 454; F. L. Duley, "Stubble Mulch Farming for Soil Defense—In a Food-for-Freedom Program," 1943, box 3, folder 2, RG 10-11-02, UNLASC.

60. Duley, "Annual Report, 1940," 38–39; E. H. Doll, "State Farmers Adapt Available Machines and Keep Pace with Subsurface Findings," *Nebraska State Journal*, December 26, 1943, 3.

61. Palmer, interview, part 2.

62. Duley, "Annual Report, 1940," 43–44.

63. Doll, "State Farmers Adapt," 3.

64. The average farm was 391 acres. U.S. Census Bureau, *Sixteenth Census of the United States: 1940: Agriculture*, vol. 2, pt. 2 (Washington DC: Government Printing Office, 1942), 564.

65. Duley, "Annual Report, 1940," 37–39. Large-scale farmers elsewhere, such as an Idaho farmer working 6,000 acres, also enjoyed significant time and cost savings.

Hugh H. Bennett, *Report of the Chief of the Soil Conservation Service, 1945* (Washington DC: Government Printing Office, 1945), 19.

66. A. E. McClymonds, "Subsurface Tillage Wins for Sibbernsen," *Soil Conservation* 11 (September 1945): 68.

67. "Subsurface Tillage Rapidly Taking Hold," *Lincoln Star*, January 12, 1941.

68. Duley, "Annual Report, 1940," 32–33.

69. F. L. Duley, "Annual Report, 1942: Development of Soil and Water Conservation Practices for Regions of Limited Rainfall," 1943, 29–31, box 3, folder 1, RG 10-11-02, UNLASC.

70. Duley, "Annual Report, 1945," 18–20, 56–57, quoted on p. 18.

71. Duley, "Annual Report, 1946," 16–18.

72. "Dr. F. L. Duley Will Address Student Soil Conservationists," *Daily Nebraskan*, April 25, 1951, 4.

73. For instance, see Torlief S. Aasheim, "Summary of Cooperative Tillage Field Trials—1949," in *Diverted Acres*, Extension Service Publication, Ag.-36 (Bozeman: Montana State College Extension Service, 1950), 13.

74. For instance, see Duley and Russel, "Illustrated Report," 11–20; Duley, "Annual Report, 1946," 15–18, 83; F. L. Duley, "Annual Report, 1948: Soil and Moisture Conservation and Related Microbiological Studies," 1949, 33–45, box 5, folder 2, RG 10-11-02, UNLASC.

75. Robert M. Salter, *Report of the Chief of the Soil Conservation Service, 1952* (Washington DC: GPO, 1952), 39–40. See also Hugh H. Bennett, *Report of the Chief of the Soil Conservation Service, 1951* (Washington DC: Government Printing Office, 1951), 52.

76. Hugh H. Bennett, *Report of the Chief of the Soil Conservation Service, 1949* (Washington DC: Government Printing Office, 1949), 32.

77. "'Mr. Stubble Mulch' Completes Long SCS Career," *Salina Journal*, May 15, 1980.

78. Approximately 75 and 70 percent of the stubble-mulch acreage was in plains states in 1947 and 1950, respectively. In 1950 stubble-mulched acreage totaled approximately 18 percent of all cropland in the ten plains states (according to total cropland acreage in Census of Agriculture state reports), including 12 percent of Nebraska cropland. For figures on stubble mulching, see Hugh H. Bennett, *Report of the Chief of the Soil Conservation Service, 1947* (Washington DC: Government Printing Office, 1947), 22; Hugh H. Bennett, *Report of the Chief of the Soil Conservation Service, 1950* (Washington DC: Government Printing Office, 1950), 19–21. These figures may have included all forms of "crop residue management," not solely Duley and Russel's subsurface tillage. W. V. Lambert, "Nebraska's Conservation Job," 1948, 5, box 101, folder 1, Lambert Papers.

79. "Stubble-Mulch Farming Saves Soil."

80. Bennett, *Report of the Chief, 1951*, 52.

81. R. R. Poynor, "New Developments in Tillage Equipment and Methods," August 28, 1951, 10, box 776, folder 09139, International Harvester Company Corporate Archives Central File, McCormick Mss 6Z, Wisconsin Historical Society (hereafter "Harvester Archives"). On Poynor's background with SCS, see IHC, "News Release," March 5, 1947,

1, M2008-017, reel 45, International Harvester News Releases: 1947, Wisconsin Historical Society, https://content.wisconsinhistory.org/digital/collection/ihc/id/49227.

82. L. W. Hurlbut and Howard Wittmuss, "The Integration of Machine Operations Required in Crop Culture," 1957, 1, box 4, folder 22, RG 10-01-03, UNLASC.

83. Hurlbut and Wittmuss, "Annual Progress Report, 1958."

84. L. W. Hurlbut and Howard Wittmuss, "The Integration of Machine Operations Required in Crop Culture," 1958, box 4, folder 22, RG 10-01-03, UNLASC.

85. L. W. Hurlbut, H. D. Wittmuss, and Kermit Wilke, "Annual Progress Report, 1961: Hatch 572, The Integration of Machine Operations Required in Crop Culture," 1961, box 4, folder 22, RG 10-01-03, UNLASC; L. W. Hurlbut and Kermit Wilke, "Annual Progress Report, 1962: Hatch 572, The Integration of Machine Operations Required in Crop Culture," 1962, box 4, folder 22, RG 10-01-03, UNLASC; L. W. Hurlbut and K. W. Wilke, "Annual Progress Report, 1963: Hatch 11-7, The Integration of Machine Operations Required in Crop Culture," 1963, box 4, folder 22, RG 10-01-03, UNLASC.

86. For example, see Hurlbut and Wilke, "Annual Progress Report, 1962"; Poynor, "New Developments," 10.

87. B. R. Somerhalder, "Research Resume: The Integration of Machine Operations and Cultural Practices in Irrigated Agriculture," April 15, 1968, box 4, folder 22, RG 10-01-03, UNLASC.

88. Other difficulties included colder soil temperatures. For instance, see G. R. Free, "Stubble-Mulch Tillage in New York," *Soil Science Society of America Proceedings* 17, no. 2 (1953): 165–70.

89. Duley and McCalla, "Annual Report, 1954," 52; T. M. McCalla et al., "Agronomic Research," 1952, [20], box 1, folder 1, RG 10-01-03, UNLASC.

90. Poynor did not indicate whether stubble mulching remained competitive when plowed plots were also fertilized. "A Mechanical Solution to Stubble Mulch Tillage in Row Crop Production," June 22, 1955, 3–4, box 775, folder 07285, Harvester Archives. See also Poynor, "New Developments," 9.

91. Duley and Russel, "New Methods," 54–55. See also Aasheim, "Summary," 13.

92. Duley, "Annual Report, 1940," 25.

93. University of Nebraska Agronomy Department, "Soils Research, 1943," 1943, 2, box 5, folder 3, RG 10-01-02, UNLASC.

94. Robert M. Salter, *Report of the Chief of the Soil Conservation Service, 1953* (Washington DC: Government Printing Office, 1953), 38. For an example of a humid-lands farmer for whom stubble mulching worked, see Doll, "State Farmers Adapt."

95. Amrith S. Gunasekara, *Environmental Fate of Simazine* (Sacramento: California Department of Pesticide Regulation, April 2004), 3, http://citeseerx.ist.psu.edu/viewdoc/download?doi=10.1.1.444.9905&rep=rep1&type=pdf; Edmund Russell, *War and Nature: Fighting Humans and Insects with Chemicals from World War I to Silent Spring* (New York: Cambridge University Press, 2001), 86.

96. Hurlbut and Wittmuss, "Integration of Machine Operations, 1957," 7.

97. B. R. Somerhalder and S. A. Weeks, "Machine Operations and Cultural Practices in Irrigated Agriculture," n.d., box 4, folder 22, RG 10-01-03, UNLASC.

98. D. E. Smika, "Progress Report, 1969: Cropping and Tillage Practices under Dryland Conditions in the Central Great Plains," September 10, 1969, box 8, folder 1, RG 10-01-03, UNLASC. Nebraska researchers also discovered that the wrong chemicals (such as atrazine) in the wrong amounts could lead to crop kills. See R. W. Bovey and C. R. Fenster, "Aerial Application of Herbicides on Fallow Land," *Weeds* 12, no. 2 (April 1, 1964): 117–19.

99. An accessible and favorable overview of no-till farming is Montgomery, *Dirt*, 211–13.

100. Coughenour and Chamala, *Conservation Tillage and Cropping Innovation*.

101. See the introduction to this volume for this theme.

102. Rachel Carson, *Silent Spring* (New York: Houghton Mifflin, 1962).

103. For example, see Dow Chemical, "It's Our Environment, Too," *Down to Earth: A Review of Agricultural Chemical Progress* 27 (Fall 1971): back cover.

104. Keith C. Barrons, "Some Environmental Benefits of Herbicides," *Down to Earth: A Review of Agricultural Chemical Progress* 29 (Summer 1973): 32.

105. For example, see G. A. Wicks, "Ecofallow: A Reduced Tillage System for the Great Plains," *Weeds Today* 7, no. 2 (Spring 1976): 20–23; Syngenta, "Ecofallow: More Crop per Drop with Paraquat," Paraquat Information Center, May 26, 2014, https://web.archive.org/web/20170402204532/http://paraquat.com/news-and-features/archives/ecofallow-more-crop-per-drop-with-paraquat.

106. Howard Wittmuss and Wesley F. Buchele, "Preface," in *Tillage Practices for Improving Runoff Water Quality [Papers]: March 22–23, 1972* (Lincoln: University of Nebraska, 1972), 2.

107. Douglas Lowe and C. M. Woodruff, "Why Farmers Don't Accept Mulch Tillage," in *Tillage Practices*, U1; Mervin G. Danielson and Earl J. Bondy, "Problems in Changing to 'Mulch Tillage,'" in *Tillage Practices*, V1.

108. William C. Moldenhauer and John K. Maddy, "Why Farmers Accept Mulch Tillage," in *Tillage Practices*, T4.

109. Ernest Behn and D. E. Lane, "'Mulch Tillage' Promotion Methods," in *Tillage Practices*, X1. See also Danielson and Bondy, "Problems in Changing to 'Mulch Tillage,'" V2.

110. Lowe and Woodruff, "Why Farmers Don't Accept Mulch Tillage," U1.

111. Lowe and Woodruff, "Why Farmers Don't Accept Mulch Tillage," U1.

112. Moldenhauer and Maddy, "Why Farmers Accept Mulch Tillage," T1.

113. Tim McCabe, "Tillage" (SCS photo, 1984), 114-H-6-WA-90,550, NARA-II (College Park MD); Little, *Green Fields Forever*, 22.

114. Soil Conservation Service, *Save Fuel . . . Use Conservation Tillage*, SCS Program Aid 1263 (Washington DC: USDA, 1980).

115. "'Mr. Stubble Mulch' Completes Long SCS Career."

116. Horn, *Rancher, Farmer, Fisherman*, 131.

117. Horn, *Rancher, Farmer, Fisherman*, 111–18, 122, 129–31; Montgomery, *Dirt*, 211–13; Little, *Green Fields Forever*, 101–22.

118. William C. Moldenhauer, "That Cornfield in the Sky," in *Tillage Practices*, Z3.

11

From Wheat to Wheaties

Minneapolis, the Great Plains, and the Transformation of American Food

MICHAEL J. LANSING

On December 24, 1926, a barbershop quartet stepped up to a radio microphone in Minneapolis. The live Christmas Eve spot for the local radio station capitalized on the ongoing singing craze.[1] Recently purchased and renamed by the Washburn-Crosby Company, the largest maker of white flour in the world, the station hired them to sing forty seconds of catchy advertising for a new product:

> Have you tried Wheaties
> They're whole wheat with all of the bran
> Won't you try Wheaties
> For wheat is the best food of man
> They're crispy and crunchy the whole year through
> The kiddies never tire of them and neither will you
> So just buy Wheaties, the best breakfast food in the land.[2]

The first radio jingle in world history worked. Wheaties sales picked up across the listening area. Soon the nascent National Broadcasting Company (NBC) began broadcasting the quartet nationally. For the next three years, the four men earned fifteen dollars a week to sing the jingle live on the air.[3]

The product they hawked represented a new direction for a flour industry facing hard times. Since the 1870s Minneapolis-based Washburn-Crosby (alongside other milling companies) harnessed the energy produced by falling water at the Mississippi River's largest waterfall to make high-quality white flour sold the world over. Driven by the Mill City's demand, a wheat monoculture replaced the diverse grasslands of the northern plains. High-protein hard spring wheat grown there made it possible for Minneapolis to make flour for the world. The industry not only made flour but also transformed the northern plains and turned Minneapolis into one of America's largest cities.[4]

Yet by the 1920s cultivating wheat in the city's northern plains hinterland became less tenable. Climatic shifts and plant diseases combined with collapsing crop prices to force thousands of farmers off their land. Meanwhile, the production and transmission of electricity made it possible to power flour mills nearly anywhere, ending the Minneapolis millers' energy monopoly. Furthermore, winter wheat from the southern plains became an alternative source for upstart flour millers in that region. Finally, the white flour the Minneapolis millers sold, stripped of bran and sold as an especially pure source of nutrition, troubled the interior of human bodies. A decades-long epidemic of dyspepsia that afflicted hundreds of thousands with indigestion, acid reflux, constipation, and even ulcers led to vociferous calls to improve the nation's digestion through the addition of fiber to daily diets.[5]

Washburn-Crosby's Wheaties, introduced in 1924 as the company's first nonflour food product, emerged as the company's response to these intersecting environmental crises. Its eventual success made it a prime example of a new strategy premised on diversification, spatial integration, and value-added processing that fueled the transformation of Washburn-Crosby into General Mills—now one of the largest makers of packaged foods in the world. In the process, the eventual success of Wheaties transformed agriculture on the Great Plains and altered intestinal landscapes even as it solved problems facing the Minneapolis milling industry.

The early years of the late-coming but successful breakfast cereal offer a new window into the environmental history of the Great Plains.[6] The rise of Wheaties as a prominent player in American breakfasts encompassed intertwined and mutually constitutive processes of cultivation, production, distribution, and consumption.[7] While most histories examine the cultural, social, and economic aspects of emerging food systems, ecological aspects also stand out. Spatial relations proved especially important. Wheaties encompassed dynamics that tied together a city and its hinterlands as well as the human innards of thousands of consumers far from the Great Plains.[8]

Flaked cereal represented a novel industrial manipulation of the grain grown across the region. Transforming kernels of hard wheat into a packaged breakfast product entangled farmers, soil, plants, machinery, millers, scientists, politicians, marketers, consumers, and human intestines into a new food system. The rise of Wheaties brought together these diverse actors. Indeed, the cereal created novel patterns of ecological circulation, reconfiguring Great Plains wheat agriculture, "good for you" foods, and human guts alike.[9]

The rise of a wheat monoculture on the Great Plains lay at the center of the story. Minneapolis's emergence as the world's flour milling center grew from the late nineteenth-century transformation of an ecologically complex grassland into a monoculture landscape. After whites confined the Native peoples of the region to reservations, railroads began connecting the Midwest to the Pacific. Their success depended on the government-subsidized sale of land to settlers. Construction inefficiencies multiplied by corruption and mismanagement could not undercut the successful marketing of wheat-focused agriculture as the future for many families.[10] Thousands flooded into the region. Experimentation with wheat seeds led to the eventual creation and adaptation of Marquis hard spring wheat. By 1918 farmers planted over twenty million acres of this seed from Nebraska to Saskatchewan and from Minnesota to Alberta.[11]

Railroads shipped those wheat kernels from flatland farms to the shores of the upper Mississippi River. At St. Anthony Falls, migrants from New England used their connections to Boston-centered capital, industrial knowledge, and savvy marketing to create a new, highly desirable bread flour and build a city. Emphasizing the technological processes that allowed them to separate the bran and germ from the wheat kernel's endosperm, they also changed American and European diets.

The emergence of processed food in the United States during the 1870s and 1880s counted bread flour as a primary product. Just as the rise of a meatpacking industry in Chicago introduced industrial proteins to the world, Minneapolis's flour industry offered the first truly industrial grain-based carbohydrates in world history. It also made up a significant portion of a burgeoning food industry that itself counted for 20 percent of all industrial manufacture. Americans, in turn, began to eat differently. Touted as innovative, nutritious, and vital to health, foods made via industrial processes appealed to those who could afford them. The nutritive limits of these foods only became clear later.[12]

Minneapolis-made bread flour embodied not only the reach of capital and technological innovation but also visions of industrial progress tied to race. Campaigns touting the purity and quality of their proprietary high-protein wheat flour argued that it made for better, whiter bread. The longstanding association between wheat and civilization swept up Great Plains farmers and Minneapolis food makers alike. Deployed by the latter to make sweeping claims about the product cultivated by the former, Minneapolis-patent white flour seemed to represent the apex of human achievement through its color. The careful separation of bran and germ from endosperm in the wheat kernel itself not only produced the whitest flour but also defined the former as impure waste. Advertising emphasized this via depictions of racial hierarchies tied tightly to the ascendant ideology of social Darwinism. Flour millers' claims to the simultaneous whiteness of flour and those behind its cultivation and manufacture conflated purity of product with racial purity. This confirmed the product's quality and increased sales.[13]

Consumers across North America and Europe agreed with the heady claims made by the Minneapolis milling companies. Transforming the energy of falling water and prairie loam into caloric and economic power, Minneapolis millers and wheat traders made money and accrued the ability to connect diverse places into a burgeoning food system. They not only created subsidiary businesses in Buffalo and took over half of the Canadian wheat-trading market by 1915, but also cultivated a global market for their product. A slow process of corporate consolidation among Minneapolis millers followed. By 1920 the Washburn-Crosby Company stood above all the other flour millers as the city's most successful flour maker.[14]

Even so, the foundation of the flour-maker's power—the embodied energy of farmer-cultivated hard spring wheat from the northern plains—faced serious challenges. In the wake of World War I's inflated grain prices, the combined effects of uneven rainfall, depressed commodity prices, a fungus known as wheat rust, and reduced exports rippled across the region. Recurring droughts left already depleted soils dry. The end of the Great War reintroduced European and South American wheat to global markets. The intensity of wheat monoculture left farmers' fields more susceptible to disease, especially wheat rust. It also extracted nutrients from the soil without replenishment. Commodity prices plummeted as international demand for wheat and wheat products weakened. Plains farmers began looking for a way out.[15]

As early as 1920, growing production costs and shrinking yields convinced some in South Dakota to abandon wheat cultivation.[16] In 1921 the dean of Montana's agricultural college argued that a lack of consistent rainfall made dryland wheat farming impossible without extensive irrigation across much of the state.[17] By 1922 most northern plains farmers knew something had to give. Rex Willard, economist at North Dakota Agricultural College, noted that wheat farming across the region was, at best, a "risky business." Indeed, farmers needed to embrace "radical changes" to continue to survive in agriculture. His careful study of over one hundred farmers over five years made it clear that wheat farming—a monoculture—was untenable: it concentrated risk in a single commodity, drained the soil of nutrients, and increased susceptibility to pests. Thousands of farmers fleeing the region agreed. In 1923 prairie and plains politicians even held a "wheat conference" in Chicago to identify solutions for "the dissatisfied condition of a large portion of our agricultural population." Unfortunately, it offered little succor.[18]

Problems in the city's northern plains hinterland further complicated already pressing issues facing Minneapolis millers in the early 1920s. Wheat rust ruined crops and limited millers' options for ensuring the uniformity of their flour—one of its central selling points. Wartime flour rationing—organized at the federal level by Washburn-Crosby's own leader, James Ford Bell—and the resulting decline in home baking during World War I reduced consumer demand for white bread flour. Special federal freight rules that favored Minneapolis ended. Meanwhile, special rules continued to apply to Buffalo, making the milling concerns there especially competitive.[19]

Yet the biggest challenge to the Minneapolis millers came from new ways to power milling machinery. Between 1880 and 1920, a broader shift from organic energy to mineral energy made new power regimes possible. By the early 1920s networked grids providing electricity to places far removed from easy sources of water power transformed the milling industry in the United States. The emerging power grid ensured widespread access to energy that could power industrial flour mills nearly anywhere. New technologies meant that local power production no longer determined industrial futures.[20]

Loosed from localized hydromechanical power, flour millers everywhere seized on the opportunity to power machinery in novel ways. Whether fueled by hydropower, coal, or internal combustion engines, these mills could easily compete with the Minneapolis-based companies. Again, Buffalo benefited most from the emerging electricity infrastructure. Drawing on the massive hydropower grid emanating from Niagara Falls, it cost one-third less to mill flour in the Queen City than in Minneapolis. In fact, flour mills in other locations became equally important challengers to Minneapolis-based flour makers. On the Great Plains, for instance, local flour mills in Oklahoma and Texas began expanding into an industrial concern. Competitors began locating mills closer to both wheat production and to seaports with more direct connections to consumers, eliminating the advantage of locating flour production in Minneapolis. As James Ford Bell told Washburn-Crosby's directors in 1920, "small units well diversified may enjoy decidedly enhanced benefits."[21]

The geography of flour milling began shifting as the industry drew on more diverse forms of power. One way to respond to this crisis was to band together. Banding together could take on many forms. Minneapolis millers began coordinating prices for their flour in 1923. But quiet price fixing could not solve underlying problems. Furthermore, it attracted unwanted attention. Subpoenaed by a U.S. Senate–sponsored investigation in 1925, the millers refused to cooperate and stalled the challenge in the courts until the early 1930s. By then, diversified product lines and shrinking flour sales rendered the illegalities moot.[22]

Corporate mergers offered a more direct response to the growing environmental challenges to the mutually dependent Minneapolis flour-making and the northern plains wheat monoculture. In the mid-1920s John Pillsbury—owner of the Pillsbury Flour Mills, second-largest in the nation—reached out to his childhood friend James Ford Bell, president of Washburn-Crosby Company, the largest. Proposing that the two companies merge, Pillsbury hoped that such consolidation would protect the Minneapolis-based millers' prosperity. Bell rejected the offer, though he was offered a job as head of the proposed concern. Later, he remembered that "the Pillsbury company were in the same position we were, with too much of our production facilities concentrated in an area that was declining in wheat production." Because energy constraints no longer dictated the location of production, Bell saw that such a merger would intensify their common problems rather than solve them.[23]

Even though Washburn-Crosby rejected the notion of a local merger, they were already rethinking their business. A flaked breakfast cereal featuring wheat bran—the very part of the wheat kernel the entire city's milling industry worked to efficiently eliminate—offered a potential way forward. Bran-based fiber offered a clear solution to a national epidemic situated in people's abdomens. As an overarching condition that included nearly everything that might go wrong in an intestinal tract or stomach, dyspepsia afflicted hundreds of thousands. And many pointed to a lack of fiber in the American diet as the primary cause.

Reformers believed a new vegetable- and fiber-rich diet they called "biologic living" could cure most dyspepsia. John Harvey Kellogg's *The Stomach: Its Disorders, and How to Cure Them* (1896) and *Constipation: How to Fight It* (1915) brought these new ideas about diet to a broad audience. He and others harangued Americans for their diets of heavy proteins and overrefined carbohydrates. Indeed, he considered "fine flour bread" one of many notable "constipating foods." In general, a diet with "insufficient bulk" caused most digestive problems. Fiber, in turn, could be counted on to "furnish to the intestines the necessary stimulus to cause them to move the food and food residues along at a proper rate." The stakes were high. One reformer associated with Kellogg argued that "constipation is man's deadliest enemy. It kills more people than war, famine, or pestilence." Another indicted "that great human destroyer—the white bread of America." Kellogg himself believed that the "civilized colon" found in urbanizing industrial nations ruined human health. Answering nature's call more often and changing what one ate seemed to be the only solutions.[24]

Emanating from Kellogg's Battle Creek, Michigan, sanatorium, the calls for more fiber centered on breakfast. They claimed that ready-to-eat cold cereals, doused in milk, offered a healthier alternative than eggs and meat. One of Kellogg's patients—Charles William Post—introduced both Postum and Grape Nuts to a welcome reception. After years of research, Kellogg's brother introduced Corn Flakes in 1906. Furthermore, in the 1910s, new research by scientists allied with the dairy industry argued for the significant nutritional value of pasteurized cow's milk. Picked up by nutritional scientists, the call for a new American diet became a central public health concern. Cereals flooded the market as entrepreneurs tried to cash in on changing consumer desires. Driven by the assurance that cold cereal drenched in milk might eliminate dyspepsia, these reformers began reinventing the American breakfast.[25]

An entrepreneur in Buffalo tried to cash in on the trend by offering the first commercially available wheat flake cereal—Force—in 1901. It never found consumers beyond the Northeast. By the early 1920s, however, Kellogg's insistence on bulk drove a dietary fiber craze. The American Medical Association's popular magazine, *Hygeia*, noted a "national mania" around bran. Bran offered the most efficient way to rearrange one's diet around what seemed to be the ultimate solution for dyspepsia. Combined with new studies that suggested fresh milk's healthy stimulation of intestinal bacteria (especially acidophilus) improved digestion, the emerging consumer demand for cold, bran-centric cereal proved too powerful for the Washburn-Crosby Company to ignore.[26]

Furthermore, cold cereal made from Great Plains wheat offered the best way to deal with what James Ford Bell called white bread flour's "falling ceiling of consumption." He recognized that "the future growth of the company would lie in diversification." The creation of a cold cereal would also help protect Washburn-Crosby against the charge that they proffered unhealthy products.[27]

In 1921 Bell ordered the creation of an experimental "packaged goods" division. It focused its research on "cereal byproducts." That research emerged from an idea brought to the company by a private sanatorium owner in North Dakota. The reformer's wheat gruel mix, cooked on a hot surface, made "little wafers" perfect for breakfast cereal. He patented the process. Then his lawyer approached Washburn-Crosby as a potential partner. Bell directed miller George Cormack and the inventor to take up the challenge of mass producing the cereal. Research suggested the resulting flat flakes proved satisfactory until packaged. There, they "settled to the bottom" and left the box mostly empty. After "the expenditure of $25,000 or $30,000," Bell decided to "abandon the venture."[28]

But Walter M. Ringer, a grocery wholesale executive, convinced Bell in early 1922 that the future of the Minneapolis flour industry lay in "cold packaged cereal." Freeing the company from any legal entanglements related to its first efforts, Bell then told Cormack to keep working on a suitable wheat flake product. Then Bell hired Ringer to create and run Washburn-Crosby's new packaged foods division. While Cormack designed a factory for making the wheat bran-based breakfast cereal, Ringer focused on packaging, marketing, and distribution.[29]

In September 1923 Washburn-Crosby completed the construction of its first-ever "cereal plant" in Chicago to focus on "the packaged cereal field on a large scale." As a railroad colossus, that city offered a better location for national distribution than Minneapolis. In conjunction with Cormack, working in Minneapolis, employees at the new plant drew from the process used by corn-flake manufacturers and tried thirty-six different varieties of wheat in various combinations. Eventually, after "a lot of experimenting," they created a physically uneven flake that combined cracked wheat kernels with malt syrup, sugar, and salt. The fourteenth cereal sample finally held up in taste testing and in the package. The product itself finally rolled out in late 1924. Soon thereafter, an employee's wife won a contest to rename the cereal "Wheaties." Touting the "right amount of bran" for "proper digestion" as well as the "full food value of the wheat berry" retained in the "whole wheat flake," salesmen immediately began selling the new product.[30]

Privately, James Ford Bell—now president of Washburn-Crosby—described the cereal division as "a trial" by the company "to ascertain consumer acceptance and distribution" of a food product with lower production and marketing costs than flour. But as the first nonflour product made by Minneapolis's largest miller, the new breakfast product quickly drew attention. Bell soon learned that the company's chief Minneapolis-based rival, Pillsbury, immediately began examining cold cereal options of their own. Luckily for Washburn-Crosby, their rival's efforts regarding the "development of a wheat flake" were not "very satisfactory."[31]

Though Washburn-Crosby came late to the cold breakfast cereal market, Wheaties represented a value-added product. Furthermore, it introduced new efficiencies in production. Where bread flour required the careful separation of the bran and germ from wheat kernels, breakfast cereal simply required cracking open kernels and exposing the insides to heat and pressure. The profit margin for cereal proved much higher than for flour. Breakfast cereals of every sort were cheap to produce (after initial investments in machinery), and their sales mostly depended on marketing. "Strategic naming and careful coloring" of packaging made it easy to both target and cultivate a consumer audience. The national bran craze—fueled by many consumers' hope that fiber would soothe their indigestion-riddled digestive tracts—made the cereal's potential profitability obvious.[32]

In order to encourage sales, Washburn-Crosby turned its back on its Minneapolis-based ad agency and gave the Wheaties account to a Chicago advertising firm with more experience in "the packaged food business." After "a long study of grocery store display values," the admen rolled out an advertising campaign in October 1925. It touted Wheaties as "body building" and "Nature's Most Perfect Food." Despite a ready audience, sales grew slowly. The product rolled out, Bell later remembered, without "preliminary household or selected market commercial tests." This meant that sales lagged for the first two years.[33]

Washburn-Crosby's breakfast cereal initiative grew from an impulse for experimentation demanded by the crisis at hand. The impulse also fueled related efforts. Its October 1924 purchase of Minneapolis's first radio station—WLAG—represented an attempt to reach consumers for all of the company's products in a new way. It expanded its broadcast reach and then rebranded the station as WCCO (Washburn-Crosby Company) in March 1925. The advertising possibilities proved endless. Invented in 1921 to answer consumer mail, the fictive homemaker Betty Crocker soon went on the air in twelve different cities with menus, recipes, and dietary tips that highlighted Washburn-Crosby products.[34]

Crocker's success gave Washburn-Crosby executives the notion that radio could also be used to sell Wheaties. The cold cereal offered an opportunity, as one put it, to "find out what that radio station of ours is good for." After broadcasting a jingle that emphasized the bran in Wheaties, local sales went up sharply. The future of marketing at Washburn-Crosby started to become clear.[35]

Radio advertisements beamed across the country—including, thanks to rapid improvements in broadcasting technology, distant rural locations across the Great Plains—only worked if merchandizing and distribution matched their reach. This meant that, more than ever, producers also became potential consumers. Great

Plains farmers became an important market for the new products invented by food makers in Minneapolis. To that end, Washburn-Crosby executives started up a new, separate but associated company to ensure that their products could be purchased by rural people in Minneapolis's wheat hinterland.

The Red Owl chain of grocery stores backed by Bell and other Washburn-Crosby shareholders ensured ready retail outlets for the company's existing and new food products across the northern plains. Established in rural towns in western Minnesota, South Dakota, and North Dakota, they offered a multiplicity of processed foods alongside other grocery items. Washburn-Crosby products held a special place on their store shelves, especially after James Ford Bell's oldest son joined the company's management. Growing the distribution and sales infrastructure to match their rapidly expanding radio advertising, the Minneapolis food maker expanded the possibilities for selling new and healthier wheat-based products back to the plains people that cultivated their foundational ingredient.[36]

As wheat farmers' daily diets changed, so did plains wheat economies. As early as 1920, James Ford Bell noted the spread of wheat rust on northern plains agriculture. His observations convinced him that the "constant presence of this menace . . . is going to have very marked bearing upon the future production of wheat in the Northwest. The suggestion that the government take action to destroy the rust and to develop rust resisting wheats does not meet the situation." He privately told Washburn-Crosby's leadership that "in the natural order of events Northwestern farmers would turn their attention to the development of farm products free from this danger and leave the wheat growing to sections where the rust does not constitute a menace." Notably, the southern plains looked much more promising for future wheat growing. "The Southwest has shown a marked improvement in the qualities of wheat produced from year to year," argued Bell, "and it would seem perfectly natural that that section of the country should take up the burden of the lessening production in the Northwest."[37]

Northern plains spring wheat no longer offered clear advantages to the Minneapolis millers. The rise of winter hard wheat on the southern plains in the early 1900s made it possible to produce high-quality white flour from an entirely different source. By the late 1910s only experts could tell the difference between hard spring wheat from the northern plains and hard winter wheat from the southern plains.[38] The gradual decline of wheat monoculture in western Minnesota, North and South Dakota, and eastern Montana transformed the city's longstanding hinterland from a boon into a drag. It needed to be supplemented if the city's flour millers were to survive. New sources of wheat from other parts of the Great Plains would provide them with more and better varieties in its wheat supply. Given the vagaries of wheat cultivation, diverse sources of the grain also proved crucial for creating uniformity in an ever-widening variety of wheat-based food products.

The emergent hard wheat monoculture on the southern plains offered the Minneapolis millers a lifeline—if only they could control it. Control of that area's wheat agriculture remained well beyond the easy reach of Minneapolis traders and millers in the mid-1920s. Washburn-Crosby established a new flour mill in Kansas City in 1922, but only at great expense. Pillsbury simultaneously looked to the southern plains, purchasing a mill in Atchison, Kansas, in 1922 and building a mill in Enid, Oklahoma, in 1928. The effort strained the resources of the struggling company.[39]

Minneapolis millers soon recognized that they needed to use their power—accrued from decades of using water energy to transform the stored solar energy of northern plains wheat into caloric power for people to eat—more efficiently. Expansion was necessary. But without large amounts of capital, they lacked the ability to expand south. Integration of smaller, existing flour-milling companies into their own offered a much easier way to integrate the southern plains wheat economies into the Minneapolis flour companies' hinterlands.

With exactly this in mind, in 1928 Washburn-Crosby's James Ford Bell moved to address the issue. After a failed buyout by eastern milling interests, Bell successfully pursued financing to merge Washburn-Crosby with smaller flour-milling companies. More than simple corporate consolidation, however, this effort took on a distinctly spatial cast. Ignoring fellow Minneapolis millers, Bell looked to the southern plains. By the 1920s Texas entrepreneur Frank Kell had built a small flour-milling empire with large industrial mills in Wichita Falls, Amarillo, Waco, and Oklahoma City. With the promise of money and stock and new efficiencies, Bell enticed Kell into a merger. The dominant miller in Kansas—Red Star Milling, based in Wichita—also joined in. Within a year the Sperry Milling Company, which stood at the head of the wheat economy in California and the Pacific Northwest, became yet another partner. The merger produced an entirely new company with the old Washburn-Crosby Company and James Ford Bell at the center—General Mills.[40]

Geography mattered. Wheat farmers across the entirety of the Great Plains now sold their grain to millers who, despite lingering differences in brand names, all worked for the same shareholders. Minneapolis-based flour milling would not only survive but prosper. The merger that spawned General Mills represented a spatial fix for the Minneapolis flour millers' economic troubles as well as a new ecological rearrangement. As one company historian put it years later, "the idea that became General Mills was to organize an overall campaign in buying, manufacturing, and distributing processes that will make a still closer and more reliable ally of nature." Distributing environmental risk in wheat cultivation across the entirety of the plains, and even into the Pacific Northwest, provided a new stability in wheat supplies for food products—a stability that weathered the crisis that struck the Great Plains in the 1930s. Bell tried to ensure the company "a position of some flexibility to accommodate the wide swings of the different crops wherein we find ample proteins or a lack of them." Finally, producing flour far away from the falling water at Minneapolis's St. Anthony Falls took advantage of cheap, fossil-fuel-based energy sources and collapsed distances between maker and consumer. This enhanced product distribution efficiencies.[41]

Paired with an insistence on developing new food products, the novel spatial distribution of flour milling and regional wheat economies ensured a bright future for General Mills even as its leading

Minneapolis-based competitor, Pillsbury, continued to struggle. Learning from the eventual success of Wheaties, James Ford Bell, who graduated from the University of Minnesota in 1901 with a degree in chemistry, poured money into further product research. Expanding a small wheat testing room into a burgeoning relationship with noted wheat scientists at his alma mater, Bell slowly built up the company's research arm and staffed it with young scientists holding advanced degrees in cereal chemistry. To foster that connection, he hired University of Minnesota (and award-winning biochemist) Professor Clyde Bailey to not only lead the research division, but also design and build a new research laboratory in Minneapolis in 1930. That laboratory would invent new packaged foods in the years to come.[42]

Bell understood that General Mills' deep roots in the Minneapolis flour-milling industry provided an "avenue to the home," a path having more to do with becoming "essentially advertisers and merchandisers" than milling products from wheat.[43] The combination of new sources for wheat, intensive research, and aggressive marketing proved potent. Bell expanded the company's packaged foods division. Bisquick (1930), Kix (1937), and Cheerios (originally Cheerioats, 1941) eventually joined Wheaties on grocery store shelves. These developments ensured that General Mills became the only "important food company" (according to the *Wall Street Journal*) to reward shareholders with profit through every quarter of the Great Depression. Much of that success stemmed from "aggressive merchandising and advertising" and "packaged products." Longstanding competitors copied the innovations of General Mills as best they could. After World War II, the emergent food systems they pioneered transformed global eating and ecologies.[44]

Growing sales of Wheaties and other nonflour food products not only showed the way forward for Minneapolis's largest milling company, but also cemented its position as a primary player in America's burgeoning food industry. This gave it important political power. General Mills—like all the other Minneapolis millers and grain traders—needed Great Plains farmers to stay on the land and produce wheat cheaply. As James Ford Bell expanded General Mills' geography of production to other regions in the late 1920s and early 1930s, his company's expansion of control over the wheat monoculture of the southern plains catapulted millers into national debates regarding federal agricultural policy.

During the mid-1920s Great Plains farmers pushed for passage of the McNary-Haugen Act. The legislation proposed federal price supports for farm commodities, including wheat. James Ford Bell led other millers in initially supporting the idea, but Sydney Anderson (R-MN), member of the U.S. House of Representatives and that body's agriculture committee, convinced him of the plan's "socialistic implications." The industry followed Bell's lead. In 1927 Bell met with secretary of commerce, friend, and future president Herbert Hoover to discuss their shared opposition to the McNary-Haugen Act. Backed by businessmen such as Bell and advisors such as Hoover, President Calvin Coolidge vetoed the act twice. Farmers began diversifying their operations to protect themselves and their soil from failure.[45]

When the simultaneous crises of drought and depression struck the Great Plains in the 1930s, General Mills again entered debates regarding federal agriculture policy. Deeply vested in the entire region's wheat monoculture, the Minneapolis company backed a revised version of McNary-Haugen rather than a more radical plan that used domestic allotments and a processing tax on food products to provide farmers with economic relief. General Mills executives vociferously opposed the latter plan. Shuttling back and forth from Minneapolis to Washington DC, James Ford Bell represented the nation's millers in the policy discussions. They lost out. For their part, Great Plains farmers widely agreed on the need for direct aid, though they disagreed on the best approach. The Agricultural Adjustment Act, passed in 1933, provided mixed relief for struggling farmers but cost General Mills $110,000 a day.[46]

By 1933 struggling farmers—like other Americans—still struggled with their digestive systems. Barraged by bran in the 1920s, America's intestines nonetheless found little succor. The ongoing dyspepsia problem sparked further exploration of the effects of dietary fiber on digestive tracts. Experts agreed that roughage remained crucial for intestinal health. Researchers began breaking down dyspepsia into its constituent illnesses—ulcers, indigestion, acid reflux, and constipation. The range of treatments available for post–World War II patients broadened through the adoption of pharmaceutical solutions.[47]

Most important, however, the bran craze of the 1920s gave way to a vitamin craze in the 1930s. The discovery of vitamins in the 1910s led to extensive research and increased consumer concern regarding nutrition's relation to health. Food could no longer be categorized so simply as calories derived from protein, carbohydrate, or fat. Instead, sustenance and health depended on little-understood aspects of the newly identified elements of foodstuffs. Nature's complications, according to the chemists and home economists coming together in the newly christened nutrition sciences, demanded that malnutrition be redefined. Concerns about getting enough calories every day faded into anxieties about access to necessary micronutrients. These micronutrients made for more healthy bodies and addressed a range of issues—including poor digestion.[48]

Concerns about vitamins even led to the creation of a new supplements industry. Sold in tablet form, with little regulation, these vitamins cut into processed food sales. General Mills led the food industry's effort to address this issue. It began isolating vitamins in its research lab in 1933. By 1939 medical authorities called for fortification of wheat products. One year later, General Mills began selling Wheaties fortified with vitamins. The breakfast cereal, boosted by a nearly decade-long advertising campaign touting it as "the breakfast of champions" that birthed modern sports broadcasting and earned a reputation as the "most effectively merchandised" product in America, accounted for 12 percent of the nation's cold cereal sales in 1941. Given anxieties about the ill effects of missing vitamins—especially acute as a nervous nation began to prepare for entry into World War II—enrichment at the breakfast table addressed the challenge posed by vitamin supplements, assured plains farmers a continued market for their wheat, positioned General Mills as patriotic, and ensured continued profits.[49]

The range of locations and actors swept up in the relationships that created and sustained Wheaties breakfast cereal reminds us that food systems not only embody particular political economies but also represent attempts to reorganize material relationships over a wide range of spaces with ecological and social effects. Wheaties' gradual success signaled a new way forward for the threatened Minneapolis flour industry. The bran-centric wheat cereal sustained wheat cultivation on the Great Plains by ensuring that wheat products continued to serve consumers despite changing tastes, changes in power regimes, and shifting understandings of bodily health.

Understanding these entanglements matters now more than ever. As other essays in this volume suggest, the nature of agriculture on the Great Plains continues to drive debates and sustain our current food systems. Questions regarding the ecological and biological healthiness of industrially produced foods loom larger every year. Minneapolis-based General Mills remains one of the leading makers of packaged foods in the world. In a moment where humans must make intentional decisions about how to live in a world they have so profoundly transformed, this story shows that eating breakfast has a deep and complex history rooted on the Great Plains.[50]

Notes

1. Gage Averill, *Four Parts, No Waiting: A Social History of American Barbershop Quartet* (New York: Oxford University Press, 2010).

2. "Have You Tried Wheaties," WCCO radio broadcast recording, undated, accessed March 20, 2017, https://soundcloud.com/user-290254341/the-wheaties-jingle.

3. Charles F. Sarjeant, ed., *The First Forty: The Story of WCCO Radio* (Minneapolis: WCCO Radio, 1964), 76.

4. Lucille M. Kane, *The Waterfall That Built a City: The Falls of St. Anthony in Minneapolis* (St. Paul: Minnesota Historical Society Press, 1966); Jocelyn Wills, *Boosters, Hustlers, and Speculators: Entrepreneurial Culture and the Rise of Minneapolis and St. Paul, 1849–1883* (St. Paul: Minnesota Historical Society Press, 2005); William Cronon, *Nature's Metropolis: Chicago and the Great West* (New York: W. W. Norton, 1991), 376–77.

5. James C. Whorton, *Inner Hygiene: Constipation and the Pursuit of Health in Modern Society* (New York: Oxford University Press, 2000); Ana Carden-Coyne,

"American Guts and Military Manhood," in *Cultures of the Abdomen: Diet, Digestion, and Fat in the Modern World*, ed. Christopher E. Forth and Ana Carden-Coyne (New York: Palgrave Macmillan, 2005), 71–85; Jeremy Hugh Baron and Amnon Sonnenberg, "Early History of Dyspepsia and Gastric Ulcer in the United States: A Matter of Opinion," *American Journal of Gastroenterology* 104, no. 12 (December 2009): 2893–96.

6. Donald Worster, "Transformations of the Earth: Toward an Agroecological Perspective in History," *Journal of American History* 76, no. 4 (March 1990): 1087–106. This essay extends Worster's call for an agroecological history into the study of food, society, and economies. For examples of other attempts to do the same, see especially Nicolaas Mink, "It Begins in the Belly," *Environmental History* 14, no. 2 (April 2009): 312–22 and Nancy Shoemaker, "Food and the Intimate Environment," *Environmental History* 14, no. 2 (April 2009): 339–44.

7. Separating these into distinct categories obscures their relation and mutual constitution. See Benjamin Coles, "The Shocking Materialities and Temporalities of Agri-Capitalism," *Gastronomica: The Journal of Critical Food Studies* 16, no. 3 (Fall 2016): 5–12.

8. Nicholas Bauch, *A Geography of Digestion: Biotechnology and the Kellogg Enterprise* (Berkeley: University of California Press, 2016) and Jeffrey Pilcher, "The Embodied Imagination in Recent Writings on Food History," *American Historical Review* 121, no. 3 (June 2016): 861–87.

9. The emerging literature in material geographies goes beyond so-called "commodity" histories to instead center on the hybrid entanglements at the heart of human-nonhuman relations as well as the systems and structures that result. See, for example, Karen Bakker and Gavin Bridge, "Material Worlds? Resource Geographies and the 'Matter of Nature,'" *Progress in Human Geography* 30, no. 1 (February 2006): 5–27. For an example of this approach in Great Plains history, see John F. Varty, "On Protein, Prairie Wheat, and Good Bread: Rationalizing Technologies and the Canadian State, 1912–1935," *Canadian Historical Review* 85, no. 4 (December 2004): 721–53. When considering agroecological histories, we must reject what some scholars call "capitalist realism"—the notion that capitalism is the only viable imaginary—and instead insist on contingency. See Bruce Braun, "New Materialisms and Neoliberal Natures," *Antipode* 47, no. 1 (January 2015): 1–14.

10. Richard White, *Railroaded: The Transcontinentals and the Making of Modern America* (New York: W. W. Norton, 2012).

11. Theodore Saloutos, "The Spring Wheat Farmer in a Maturing Economy, 1870–1920," *Journal of Economic History* 6, no. 2 (November 1946): 173–90; Alan L. Olmstead and Paul W. Rhode, "The Red Queen and the Hard Reds: Productivity Growth in American Wheat, 1800–1940," *Journal of Economic History* 62, no. 4 (December 2002): 929–66.

12. William Cronon, *Nature's Metropolis: Chicago and the Great West* (New York: W. W. Norton, 1991); Harvey Levenstein, *Revolution at the Table: The Transformation of the American Diet* (1988; repr., Berkeley: University of California Press, 2003), 37–

38; Anthony Winson, *The Industrial Diet: The Degradation of Food and the Struggle for Healthy Eating* (New York: New York University Press, 2014), 99–110.

13. Carl A. Zimring, *Clean and White: A History of Environmental Racism in the United States* (New York: New York University Press, 2016); Lisa Mullikin Parcell and Margot Opdycke Lamme, "Not 'Merely an Advertisement': Purity, Trust, and Flour, 1880-1930," *American Journalism* 29, no. 4 (Autumn 2012): 94–127; Kate Roberts and Barbara Caron, "'To the Markets of the World': Advertising in the Mill City, 1880–1930," *Minnesota History* 58, nos. 5–6 (Spring/Summer 2003): 308–19.

14. For the complexities of manipulated water and the expression of power, see Erik Swyngedouw, *Liquid Power: Contested Hydro-Modernities in Twentieth-Century Spain* (Cambridge MA: MIT Press, 2015). See also Alison Watts, "The Technology That Launched a City: Scientific and Technological Innovations in Flour Milling during the 1870s in Minneapolis," *Minnesota History* 57 (Summer 2000), 86–97; John C. Everitt and Donna Shimanura Everitt, "American Influences in the Canadian Grain Trade: An Overview," *Bulletin of the Association of North Dakota Geographers* 34 (1984): 1–9; William E. Lass, *Minnesota: A History* (1977; repr., New York: W. W. Norton, 1998), 238.

15. Mary Hargreaves, *Dry Farming in the Northern Great Plains: Years of Adjustment, 1920-1990* (Lawrence: University Press of Kansas, 1993); James H. Shideler, *Farm Crisis, 1919-1923* (Berkeley: University of California Press, 1957); Theodore Saloutos, *The American Farmer and the New Deal* (Ames: Iowa State University Press, 1982), 3–14.

16. "State College Agricultural Extension Report," *Citizen-Republican* (Scotland SD), December 2, 1920.

17. "Bankers Group Four Have Very Busy Session," *Glasgow Courier* (MT), May 27, 1921.

18. "Wheat Farming a Big Gamble," *Weekly Times Record* (Valley City ND), August 17, 1922; "Call Wheat Conference," *New York Times*, May 27, 1923, S5.

19. Victor G. Pickett and Roland S. Vaile, *The Decline of Northwestern Flour Milling*, University of Minnesota Studies in Economics and Business, 5 (Minneapolis: University of Minnesota Press, 1933), 1–46.

20. Christopher F. Jones, *Routes of Power: Energy and Modern America* (Cambridge MA: Harvard University Press, 2014); David E. Nye, *Consuming Power: A Social History of American Energies* (Cambridge MA: MIT Press, 1997); Jeremiah D. Lambert, *The Power Brokers: The Struggle to Shape and Control the Electric Power Industry* (Cambridge MA: MIT Press, 2015).

21. Pickett and Vaile, *The Decline of Northwestern Flour Milling*, 47; "Companies Invade East," *Wall Street Journal*, December 10, 1923, 3; James Ford Bell to John Crosby, July 24, 1920, copy in diary, November 1, 1918–1920, box 9, James Ford Bell (hereafter JFB) Papers, Minnesota Historical Society, St. Paul MN (hereafter MNHS).

22. *Competitive Conditions in Flour Milling*, Preliminary Report of the Federal Trade Commission, May 23, 1926 (Washington DC: Government Printing Office, 1926), vi-viii; "Flour Millers Refuse to Open Their Books," *New York Times*, May 11, 1926, 28.

23. James Ford Bell diary, October 1, 1925, October 27, 1925; James Ford Bell, "Corrections for 'Formation of General Mills,'" August 10, 1959, JFB Reminiscences—General Mills file, both in box 9, JFB Papers.

24. J. H. Kellogg, *Colon Hygiene* (Battle Creek MI: Good Health, 1917), 61, 90; "Constipation: How to Fight It," *The Independent* 81, no. 3457 (March 18, 1915): 365; Alfred Watterson McCann, *The Science of Eating* (New York: George H. Doran, 1919), 103; Whorton, *Inner Hygiene*, 183–84; Helen Zoe Veit, *Modern Food, Moral Food: Self-Control, Science, and the Rise of Modern American Eating in the Early Twentieth Century* (Chapel Hill: University of North Carolina Press, 2013); James C. Whorton, *Crusaders for Fitness: The History of American Health Reformers* (Princeton NJ: Princeton University Press, 1982), 221–22.

25. Scott Bruce and Bill Crawford, *Cerealizing America: The Unsweetened Story of American Breakfast Cereal* (Boston: Faber and Faber, 1995), 10–35; Kendra Smith-Howard, *Pure and Modern Milk: An Environmental History since 1900* (New York: Oxford University Press, 2013), 12–35; E. Melanie DuPuis, *Dangerous Digestion: The Politics of American Dietary Advice* (Berkeley: University of California Press, 2015), 89–92; Abigail Carroll, *Three Squares: The Invention of the American Meal* (New York: Basic Books, 2013), 133–58.

26. Bruce and Crawford, *Cerealizing America*, 40–41; Whorton, *Inner Hygiene*, 178–83.

27. Bell, "Corrections for 'Formation of General Mills.'"

28. James Ford Bell, "Story of Origin and Development of Wheaties," June 2, 1943, JFB Reminiscences, topical folder, box 9, JFB Papers, MNHS.

29. Bell, "Story of Origin and Development of Wheaties"; James Gray, *Business without Boundary: The Story of General Mills* (Minneapolis: University of Minnesota Press, 1954), 155–57; James Ford Bell, "Red Owl Stores," May 1960, JFB Reminiscences, topical folder, box 9, JFB Papers, MNHS.

30. "That's When Wheaties Were Born," *Modern Millwheel* 4, no. 4 (May 1940): 5; Mary Mitchell, "The Birth of the Wheatie and of General Mills," *Minneapolis Tribune*, November 19, 1950; William C. Edgar, *The Medal of Gold: A Story of Industrial Achievement* (Minneapolis: Bellman, 1925), 334–35, 345–46, 359–60; "Company Building New Cereal Plant," *Eventually News* 3, no. 3 (March 1923): 1; "What, Why, and Wherefore of Wheaties, Latest Addition to Gold Medal Foods," *Eventually News* 4, no. 21 (June 1925): 10.

31. James Ford Bell, diary, November 24, 1925 and December 30, 1925, box 9, JFB Papers, MNHS.

32. Gary S. Cross and Robert N. Proctor, *Packaged Pleasures: How Technology and Marketing Revolutionized Desire* (Chicago: University of Chicago Press, 2014), 48–51.

33. "Chicago Agency to Handle Advertising," *Eventually News* 4, no. 16 (January 1925): 2; *Eventually News* 4, no. 25 (October 1925): 10; Bell, "Story of the Origin and Development of Wheaties."

34. "Gold Medal Radio Station Now On Air," *Eventually News* 4, no. 13 (October 1924): 12; "The New Gold Medal Station Opens," *Eventually News* 4, no. 19 (April

1925): 13; Susan Marks, *Finding Betty Crocker: The Secret Life of America's First Lady of Food* (Minneapolis: University of Minnesota Press, 2007); "Betty Crocker Goes on Air Nationally," *Eventually News* 4, no. 24 (September 1925): 6.

35. Gray, *Business without Boundary*, 160–69 and William L. Bird Jr., *"Better Living": Advertising, Media, and the New Vocabulary of Business Leadership, 1935–1955* (Evanston IL: Northwestern University Press, 1999), 52–54.

36. Bell, "Red Owl Stores"; Harvey Levenstein, *Paradox of Plenty: A Social History of Eating in Modern America* (1993; repr., Berkeley: University of California Press, 2003), 27.

37. James Ford Bell to John Crosby, July 24, 1920, copy in diary, November 1, 1918–20, box 9, JFB Papers, MNHS.

38. James C. Malin, *Winter Wheat in the Golden Belt of Kansas: A Study in Adaption to Subhumid Geographical Environment* (Lawrence: University Press of Kansas, 1944) and Donald Worster, *Dust Bowl: The Southern Plains in the 1930s* (New York: Oxford University Press, 1979).

39. William J. Powell, *Pillsbury's Best: A Company History from 1869* (Minneapolis: Pillsbury, 1985), 116–17.

40. Gray, *Business without Boundary*, 106–42.

41. James Gray, untitled 25th anniversary history of General Mills manuscript, n.d., JFB Reminiscences, General Mills file, box 9, JFB Papers, MNHS; James Ford Bell, diary, March 23, 1927, box 9, JFB Papers, MNHS; David Harvey, "Globalization and the 'Spatial Fix,'" *Geographische Revue* 2 (January 2001): 23–30. Importantly, this spatial fix came with consequences not only for capitalism, but also for ecology. Thus it counts as what Noel Castree describes as an "environmental fix" in his "Neoliberalising Nature: The Logics of Deregulation and Reregulation," *Environment and Planning A: Economy and Space* 40, no. 1 (2008): 131–52.

42. Gray, *Business without Boundary*, 200–201.

43. James Ford Bell quoted in James Gray, untitled 25th anniversary history of General Mills manuscript.

44. *Five Years of General Mills, Inc., 1928–1933* (Minneapolis: General Mills, 1933); Gray, *Business without Boundary*, 184–89; "General Mills' Gain is Unique," *Wall Street Journal*, July 28, 1932, 1; "General Mills, Inc., Nets $20,606,407," *Washington Post*, August 17, 1933, 11; Bryan L. McDonald, *Food Power: The Rise and Fall of the Postwar American Food System* (New York: Oxford University Press, 2017).

45. James Ford Bell, "The McNary-Haugen Act," September 20, 1954, JFB Reminiscences, topical file, box 9, JFB Papers, MNHS; James Ford Bell, diary, March 3, 1927, box 9, JFB Papers, MNHS; John Philip Gleason, "The Attitude of the Business Community toward Agriculture during the McNary-Haugen Period," *Agricultural History* 32, no. 2 (April 1958): 127–38.

46. Gray, *Business without Boundary*, 193–95; James Ford Bell, draft of letter to Bernard Baruch, n.d., never sent, JFB Reminiscences, individual file, box 9, JFB Papers, MNHS; Janet Poppendieck, *Breadlines Knee Deep in Wheat: Food Assistance in the Great Depression* (1986; repr., Berkeley: University of California Press, 2014),

88–96; Gilbert C. Fite, "Farmer Opinion and the Agricultural Adjustment Act, 1933," *Mississippi Valley Historical Review* 48, no. 4 (March 1962): 656–73.

47. Whorton, *Inner Hygiene*, 217–62.

48. Levenstein, *Revolution at the Table*, 147–60; Charlotte Biltekoff, *Eating Right in America: The Cultural Politics of Food and Health* (Durham NC: Duke University Press, 2013), 45–79.

49. Rima D. Apple, *Vitamania: Vitamins in American Culture* (New Brunswick NJ: Rutgers University Press, 1996); Levenstein, *Paradox of Plenty*, 9–23; "American Research Products, An Important Arm of General Mills," *Modern Millwheel* 3, no. 9 (September 1939): 1; George R. Cowgill, "The Need for the Addition of Vitamin B1 to Staple American Foods," *Journal of the American Medical Association* 113, no. 24 (December 9, 1939): 2146–51; "'Nutr-A-Sured' Spells Progress in Breakfast Foods," *Modern Millwheel* 4, no. 5 (June 1940): 6; "Radio Experts Vote on Best Programs," *Modern Millwheel* 4, no. 8 (September 1940): 1; Gray, *Business without Boundary*, 160–69; Biltekoff, *Eating Right in America*, 45–79.

50. Marion Nestle, *Food Politics: How the Food Industry Influences Nutrition and Health* (Berkeley: University of California Press, 2002), 309–10; James Peltz, "Why Americans Are Eating Less Cold Cereal for Breakfast," *Los Angeles Times*, October 10, 2016, http://www.latimes.com/business/la-fi-agenda-breakfast-cereals-20161010-snap-story.html.

12

"Nature Rarely Establishes Sharp Boundaries"
Settler Society Agricultural Adaptation in the Great Plains Northwest

MOLLY P. ROZUM

Two young Mandan women work with red, blue, and yellow braids of husk-twisted corncobs drawn down from scaffolding perched above their earth lodge. A willow basket of dark red corn sits nearby, and another woman carries a full basket on her back. Pale blue and yellow-green sky conveys distance with buttes and river bluffs winding to the horizon. Clell Gannon, a poet and artist raised in Dakota settler society, painted this scene respectful of Indigenous women who guarded tribal methods of agricultural production.[1] The deep purple cover radiated the richness suggested by the plump ears of corn, some to be dried and saved in reserve for food during drought years, others bearing the best seed to be carefully protected for next year's crop. The image suggests the agricultural diversity, prosperity, abundance, and community of the Village Tribes—Hidatsas and Arikaras as well as Mandans—who lived along the banks of the Missouri River long before the settler colonial Oscar H. Will arrived in 1881 at Bismarck.[2]

The lay archaeologist and business owner George F. Will, Oscar Will's son, commissioned the Gannon painting of a Mandan village at harvest for the 1951 cover of the family seed and nursery company catalog.[3] The agricultural seeds and trees the Will Co. distributed aimed to transform the open grasslands into commercial market agricultural fields. The Will Co. trademark logo, a small circular inset on the cover, depicted a woman in pale blue, cradling a baby, haloed by the canvas of an oxen-pulled wagon, as her husband rides horseback. The scene projected the hopes of

FIG. 18. Oscar H. Will & Co. 1951 annual catalog cover. Oscar Will Papers, North Dakota Institute for Regional Studies, North Dakota State University Archives, Fargo ND.

settler colonials on the northern grasslands. The logo also serves as a pictorial metaphor for U.S. official land policy that promoted family farms to secure territorial claims made through war, treaty, and presidential executive order confiscation.[4]

By 1951 such an agricultural region already had taken root. Two photo insets on the cover, a scientist holding "NoDak Hybrid 301" and a close up of "Will's Pioneer Hybrid K," suggest scientific advances then intensifying the reach and transformative scale of settler society agriculture. The Great Plains environment had challenged the original agricultural settler colonial vision for the space, forcing more adaptation than settlers had planned. In the first half of the twentieth century, the northern grasslands pushed back with multiyear droughts and hot winds, in the 1920s and particularly in the 1930s, contesting settler society's agriculture. The catalog cover suggests resiliency in traditional Indigenous farming and even hints at Indigenous women's success at influencing a few individuals within settler society, such as George Will and Clell Gannon, toward the adoption of Indigenous environmental values and appreciation for Indigenous cultural practices. Such influence, however, did not disrupt the general trajectory of settler society colonization.

Indeed, the long-time Will family business helped settler society grow roots into the soil of the northern grasslands and to create cultural regions that announced settler stability in the area to the rest of the United States. The public knew the Will Co. by the tagline "Pioneer Seedhouse Nursery and Greenhouses of the Northwest."[5] Over the decades, however, as landscapes changed with railroad towns, grain fields, and animal pastures, and after repeated encounters with drought, the regional resonance of the Will Co.'s "Northwest" business territory grew increasingly anachronistic. George Will was born in 1884 into settler society's Northwest, the place his father arrived, but he died in 1955 on the Northern Great Plains. By the 1960s his son, George Will Jr., lived on the Northern Great Plains, but understood a complex relationship between that area and a growing northern Middle West. The Will Co. catalog under third-generation management identified little with a regional Northwest. All three Wills—Oscar, George Sr., and George Jr.—lived in Bismarck. Agricultural science and engineering and environmental experience, however, led each to perceive the space of the place uniquely for the business of seed development and distribution.[6]

Each shift in the Will family company's business model suggests settler society's struggle for agricultural adaptation on the Northern Great Plains. At each stage the company focused on seeds, plants, and trees appropriate for the northern grasslands climate based on changing understandings of both environmental and business constraints on commercial agriculture. The company generally operated under environmental limitations posed by temperature (growing season) and precipitation (semiaridity), or put another way, the need for a normative "hardiness" in tame and wild grasses that survived despite repeated drought, frost, wind, and general climatic variability. These examples of individual regional conception based on changing perceptions of the grasslands environment suggest larger shifting patterns of cultural geography that attached Northwest, Northern Great Plains, and Upper Middle West to the U.S. northern grasslands. A close reading of George F. Will's changing regional lexicon, in the context also of the terminology used by his father and his son, suggests how accruing environmental experience and changed agricultural methods helped shape regional identity.

Oscar Will, founder of the Will seed company, arrived in 1881 to a continental northern grasslands already identified with the Northwest. The "New Northwest" region—Dakota Territory and Minnesota—emerged as a way of helping immigrants place themselves specifically in North America's huge Grasslands West. The massive grasslands biome constituted one West of the post–Civil War's many Wests. The "New Northwest" referred to the northern section of the grasslands, north of the what people of the time thought of as the "central" grasslands states of Kansas and Nebraska, which in turn lay north of "Indian Territory" and Texas or the grasslands "Southwest." The "New" in the Dakota "Northwest" label awkwardly distinguished this U.S. space from three other Northwests: the North-West Territory of British Canada's share of the continent's grasslands; the U.S. "Old" Northwest Territory out of which states such as Ohio, Indiana, and Illinois organized; and an emergent Pacific Northwest centered on Oregon and Washington and actively promoted as a regional label.[7]

From its earliest days, the *northern* location of would-be agricultural fields and settler colonial towns concerned the Will Co. most. Presumably the company's advertising reflected the needs of its larger clientele in what copy referred to as "the cold northwest." Oscar H. Will & Co. assisted homesteaders and land claimants on the northern grasslands. The company advertised "the Earliest, Hardiest and Best" seeds; for example, the "Great Northern Field Bean" purportedly could be harvested "ten days or more earlier than any other known variety." The company raised market quantities of native grasslands plants such as the Bull or Buffalo Berry, listed under "Hardy Ornamental Shrubs." The Will Co. catalog touted "perfectly hardy" forest trees, which "will not partially or totally winter kill like cheap Southern grown stock, sold by smooth-mouthed tree agents and slippery dealers, without responsibility." The company provided trees to settlers who desired to acquire additional land under the U.S. Timber Culture Act, designed to transform the grasslands with trees. The Will Co. took pleasure in what it called "Improved Pride of Dakota White Flint Corn," selected from Arikara corn, known to stand "frost, heat and poor cultivation." When Oscar Will's son George Will wrote about growing corn as late as 1930, he stressed "the much greater length of days in the north" which resulted in packing "a much longer growing season into the same number of days."[8] The company saw the northern cold climate and the short growing season to be distinct agricultural problems on the northern grasslands.

After Oscar Will passed away in 1917, his son George Will became president of the company and claimed, "no seed house can serve the Northwest better or more faithfully than can we."[9] George Will identified regularly, if unconsciously, with the Northwest. References to the "Northwest" in the company catalog continued until 1922, when for the first time an annual letter to customers referred to the "breeding of seeds, grains and nursery stock especially adapted to the severe requirements of the Northern Great Plains." For the next ten years, however, the Will Co. catalog letter referred only to the Northwest, using phrases such as "this great Northwest," "Northwestern Agriculture," the "wealth of the Northwest farmer," and "growers of the Northwest."[10] George Will's clearest statement of the Northwest's regional boundaries appeared in his 1930 book *Corn for the Northwest*. In this practical handbook for farmers of settler society, Will addressed "the growing and almost compulsory interest in diversified farming in both the American and Canadian Northwest . . . yearly turning toward the thought of corn growing over a larger and larger number of people in that territory." Defining the area of focus further Will noted, "Within the past decade or two most of southern Minnesota and most of eastern South Dakota have come to be just about as much a part of the Corn-Belt territory as Iowa or Nebraska. There the altitude is low, rainfall is fairly heavy, and the season is much longer than in *most of the rest of the Northwest*." His phrasing suggests southern Minnesota and eastern South Dakota, though "just about" part of agricultural areas further east and south—the Corn Belt—remained within the Northwest, at least for him in 1930.[11] Will's subtle subdivision of the region suggests his years of experience with the northern grasslands and his conclusions about the boundaries of dent variety corn, which required a humid climate with twenty or more inches of annual precipitation to grow well.

Will became convinced Indigenous corn varieties held the answer to successful settler society farming on the northern grasslands, importantly, based on flint and flour varieties, not dent variety corn. While Indigenous women had developed seed "suited to the climate," Will thought the contribution of settler society to a regional agricultural system should be "to adapt this corn to large-scale farming and cultivation in larger areas."[12] A Corn Belt core, from southern Ohio to eastern Iowa, its history traced by geographer John C. Hudson, based on "the practice of fattening hogs and beef cattle on corn," existed by 1850 and had been identified by agricultural scientists by the late 1920s. However, Will did not so much want northern grasslands agriculture to join the Corn Belt region. That system relied on soft dent corn that had trouble growing in northern climes and in dry years. Rather, Will advocated agricultural diversification in which corn, specifically Indigenous-sourced northern and western adapted varieties, played an important role.[13]

In 1930 Will noted the "more intelligent and determined" farmers had adopted the dry farming system then proposed by agricultural scientists based on crop rotation, "summer fallow" (land unseeded), and livestock. Will thought "properly acclimated" corn could replace the summer fallow rotation. Noting the "Argentine market" for "small flint type of corn," Will argued such corn at its "best" would be "a cash crop surer and often more valuable than small grains." At its worst, an unmarketable crop could contribute to farm success as "green feed or silage." He found the two climate concerns for farming on the northern grasslands, temperature and precipitation, could be solved by incorporating Indigenous "flint" and "flour" corn varieties or possibly a hybrid mixture of the two. Flint seed was "resistant to cool weather" and grew at "lower temperatures," while flour seed had "rather more drouth resistance." Profitability overall meant every year a chance to profit; adding corn meant no more summer fallow. Actually, in 1930, Will had to admit the then-declining interest in corn caused by an agricultural system organizing around power—tractor—wheat farming. The agricultural scientist O. E. Baker had then recently noted the "level surface" of the Great Plains in combination with "modern machinery" had actually increased the profitability of raising grain "in the semi-arid sections" previously not thought possible. But that system, Will predicted, would collapse with overproduction resulting in low commodity prices.[14]

Will's flint-flour diversified dry-farming system had two primary hurdles. The emergent monocrop large-machine farming eliminated cultivated crops "deemed too much trouble and too complicated to work in with power farming." Monocrop meant leaving land fallow and out of production. Will knew the expansiveness of tractor farming attracted farmers. Nevertheless, he thought the "one-crop proposition" misguided. Additionally, Will also felt "white settlers" held "a prejudice" against flour corn precisely because of its association with "Indians." He found it difficult to overcome the local folklore that flour corn did not make good "feeding," despite his publicizing of modern "chemical analysis" that showed it equal to other varieties. He understood "prejudice" worked against the adoption of his flint-flour corn and wheat diversified dry-farming system, saying, "because the idea that corn which was a favorite with the Indians would not suit the white people," settler society turned away from the crop.[15]

George Will grew up in a family business that from its start used the regional label Northwest; that he continued long-used regional company language does not surprise. The gradual introduction and dominance of the label "Great Plains," however, suggests his generation's changing conception of the region. The role of aridity or adequate precipitation for settler society's commercial agriculture grew in his thinking as settler society struggled to adapt a commercial agricultural system to the Great Plains environment.

In the 1930s Will began to use the "Great Plains" or "Northern Plains" more regularly in the company catalog and his other academic writings on Indigenous culture and Village Tribe archaeology sites along the Missouri River—an interest that dated back to his college days at Harvard University.[16] He often intermixed his use of labels, sometimes suggesting a synonymous relationship between the Northwest and the Great Plains and at other times an overlapping, but not identical association. Indeed, Will also used "the northern Great Plains" or some version of "great plains" throughout his 1930 *Corn for the Northwest*. He made a case for Indigenous corn varieties by explaining how the crop could add profitability to "the great wheat farms now developing in the semi-arid sections of the Great Plains."[17] Here Will suggested semiaridity characterized only sections of the Great Plains. In a 1930 column he wrote on "Drought Resistant Shrubs and Plants," Will noted the last two dry years had renewed interest in hardy plants by "horticulturalists in the Northwest," but also that the problem was not new "in the Great Plains region."[18] In 1935 the company urged perseverance claiming, "we have faith in the Northern Great Plains and the whole Northwest," suggesting Will conceived of the plains as *part* of a larger Northwest. The 1937 catalog noted the previous year had been the "worst drouth in the history of the Northwest." But Will still advocated the countryside, writing, "in spite of the damage, it has made us wonder at the ability of Northern Great Plains soil combined with Northern Great Plains climate to produce something under even the most adverse conditions."[19]

Will even projected the Great Plains label back some fifty years when writing of a time when few if any residents used that regional label. A turning point in his perception of where he lived seems to have been reached. In 1940 he referred to "Northern Plains customers" and noted the previous year had been the fiftieth anniversary of North Dakota statehood. He honored the "Pioneers who helped build these Great Plains states" and noted that "Oscar H. Will & Co. has been a factor in Great Plains agriculture for 58 years." As if Will had gained new insight he wished to announce, this annual letter contained the words "Great Plains" at least five times with no mention of the Northwest. From this point, 1940, the company literature, without changing its name, used the regional label "Great Plains," often "Northern Great Plains" more frequently.[20]

Droughts hitting grasslands relentlessly in the 1930s seem to have shifted Will's thinking. Instead of foregrounding temperature and a short growing season, the company now began to discuss annual and seasonal precipitation totals more. Aridity moved ahead of frost in his list of potential northern grasslands agricultural problems. Water, long a question, became an overriding concern. Will's catalog letters to customers not surprisingly showed an increasing emphasis on regional drought. Will now looked south for environmental connections and solutions to low rainfall, rather than north to Canada for temperature hardiness as in earlier years. In 1936 he reported on sunflowers and trees with reference to "the Great Plains from North Dakota well into Mexico," and in 1939 he considered an area from North Dakota and Montana "to Texas." Will began to emphasize heat and rates of general evaporation and plant transpiration, instead of cold temperatures and short growing seasons.[21] By 1946 he wrote, "In this region of the Northern Plains where agriculture is the basic industry the presence or absence of moisture mean success or failure for the population."[22] In the 1930s the Northern Great Plains entered the regional lexicon through its association with drought.

The U.S. population at large knew a general location for the elongated Great Plains environment or region at the continent's center. Exact boundaries remained uncertain. Will had used the label first around 1922, the year he presented a paper in Argentina on "Indian agriculture . . . in the great plains region." Perhaps he came away from the conference with a strong association of plains Indigenous spaces. Since gaining practical experience in archaeology at college, Will had maintained friendships and scholarly collaboration with anthropologists and archaeologists.[23] Company catalogs also showed evidence of his continual contact with agricultural, soil, and plant scientists throughout the area. Undoubtedly these professionals influenced Will.

A delineation of plains boundaries Will might have seen came by way in 1923 of a special issue on the Great Plains in a well-known geography journal. None of the experts agreed. "Since," as the soil expert phrased it, "nature rarely establishes sharp boundaries" and "man must usually do so," each author defined the parameters of the Great Plains according to the feature explored. All agreed the Rocky Mountains marked the western boundary of the Great Plains. Each scientist, however, varied the position of the eastern boundary. Both the soil and agricultural scientists placed the eastern boundary "a few miles *east* of the northwestern corner of Minnesota" (around the 96th meridian). A climate specialist included *most* of the Dakotas and explained the entire area (to a western boundary between the 103rd and the 104th meridians) received enough "annual precipitation" to practice "successful farming by ordinary methods." A botanist drew the eastern boundary of the Great Plains at the 97th meridian, and noted the region included "only the western portion" of the "Tall Grass" formation. These essays suggest imprecision in regionalization. Even though scientists and trained observers early understood aridity to be a general problem associated with the plains, the boundaries of a "Great Plains" remained inexact.[24]

Will never mentioned reading historian Walter Prescott Webb's 1931 *The Great Plains*, though surely, eventually, he must have known the book. Webb made popular John Wesley Powell's 1878 report on the continent's "Arid Region." Powell had argued then that on or about the 100th meridian there existed a water line. West of this line precipitation fell below twenty inches annually, and unaided agriculture would struggle to succeed. However, even Walter Prescott Webb argued, "the history of the Plains is the history of the grasslands" and popularized an expansive "Prairie Plains" concept to encompass ambiguity, especially on the northern grasslands. Webb also acknowledged the *plane* or slope inherent in the way he conceived of the Great Plains. Using an unusually expansive definition of the "plains environment," Webb connected what he called the "High Plains" to the "Prairie Plains" *across* an arid line he located at the 98th meridian. On the Northern Great Plains, the same "Prairie Plains" habitat boasting tallgrasses in Illinois and Iowa spilled west of his arid line.[25] These ideas formed the cultural context in which George Will thought of the transforming grasslands space and perhaps help explain his varied regional terminology and delineations.

Eventually, in the 1940s, Will conducted tree ring studies from downed massive-trunked burr oaks along the Missouri River to help him understand the region's climate over hundreds of years. The results caused Will to wonder, could a dry period be "merely a recurrence of conditions which have occurred before, may occur again, and may be nothing in the long time climactic record?" He soon argued tree-rings-suggested moisture levels since 1405 showed "no gradual longtime deterioration."[26] The cyclical nature of drought was an important environmental insight that incorporated drought securely into the region's identity. This conception of a normative climate cycle meant periods of drought might follow average and even high precipitation years, suggesting in turn that settler society's agriculture could adapt to Northern Great Plains constraints. If drought recurred on the northern grass-

FIG. 19. Walter Prescott Webb's map of land regions of the United States, 1931. Reproduced from *The Great Plains*, by Walter Prescott Webb, by permission of the University of Nebraska Press. Copyright 1931, 1959 by Walter Prescott Webb.

lands in a routine but uncertain cycle, however, Will's diversification and long-term planning for times of crop failure would need to become part of a new general regional agriculture.[27]

By the mid-1950s the Will Co. had introduced a new comical mascot, "Mr. Hardy Pioneer Hybrid," a personified corncob standing on a map of Montana, North Dakota, and South Dakota. Mr. Hybrid wore a cowboy hat and boasted a gun holster. The logo printed on a special tag signaled the Will Co. "guarantee of early, heavy yielding, hardy hybrids adapted to northern conditions." Speaking to an agricultural world in which industrial corn hybrids already held much sway, Will explained the company policy of going "slowly." He experimented with his own hybrids in test gardens and sold a few corn hybrids identified as "safe" for the region. But Will noted most hybrids originating elsewhere had been "disappointing" due to days required for maturity and susceptibility to drought. Instead, Will urged growers "to plant the old reliable native varieties which have been tested in this climate for many years." The catalog still advertised "a very early, very hardy, heavy

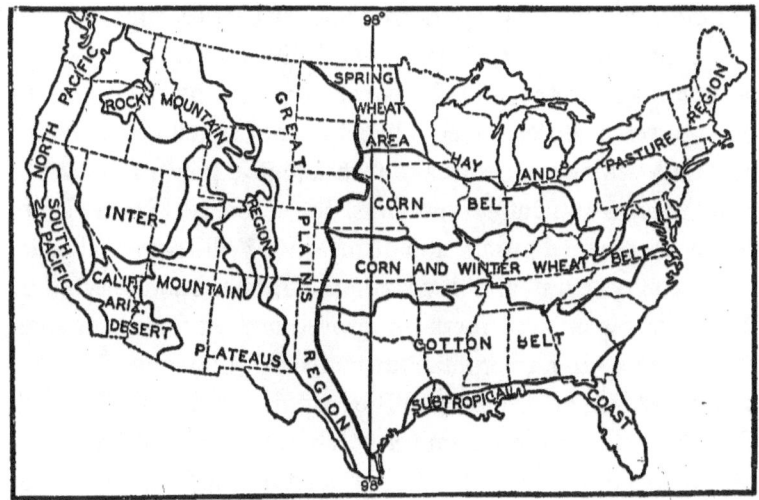

FIG. 20. Walter Prescott Webb's map of agricultural regions of the United States, 1931. Reproduced from *The Great Plains*, by Walter Prescott Webb, by permission of the University of Nebraska Press. Copyright 1931, 1959 by Walter Prescott Webb.

yielding field flint corn with multicolored kernels" as a good field corn for "hogging-off." He also warned growers to "go easy on the Wheat."[28] Hybrid corn experimentation began in the 1920s, developed commercially in the 1930s, and was widely adopted by 1940, but hybridization, generally across the Corn Belt and new power farming, resulted in an increasing standardization. Standardization worked against seed diversity. Will advocated for maintenance of "extensive" seed varieties to suit the "diversity of conditions" within the overall mercurial environment. Already in 1930 Will had noted with trepidation the decline of seed variety in the "central states" Corn Belt. The few standard seeds produced by the big companies failed to meet the intricacies of the northern and western land as well as they did in the eastern and southerly well-established Corn Belt areas.[29]

Will's vision of a patchwork of corn fields, each planted to the variety best suited to local conditions within the larger climatically temperamental northern grasslands, would pass unadopted by local settler populations suspicious of Indigenous corn varieties.

Agricultural science, corporatized intensively over time, eventually surpassed Will's small-farm vision. Even the cowboy hat and holstered gun of the Will Co. corncob mascot played on myths that bolstered settler society's belief in the capacity of its members to develop the science and technological power required to adapt to environmental constraints. The corporate hybrid plan of efficient mass seed production disregarded Will's principal belief in the ability of flint and flour corn seeds, raised and selected by Indigenous women farmers—improved by him for settler society's farmers—to find profitability in diverse attunements to complex grasslands environments. The corporate vision aligned with Corn Belt farming relied on select laboratory-adapted seeds for use across a broad and expanding agricultural landscape scaled for large power machinery. George Will Sr. always worked with cornfields that constituted "little more than the ultimate, rectilinear-grid version of the hill-culture maize practiced by aboriginal North Americans," to use geographer John Hudson's description of corn production in the United States *until* the 1950s. Hybrids, mechanization, synthetic nitrogen, herbicides, and pesticides, along with industrial irrigation, nearly eliminated this pre-1950 world of corn growing and with it, the senior George Will's Indigenously rooted corn agriculture for the Great Plains Northwest.[30]

Despite steadfast promotion of his Indigenous-sourced, corn-enhanced, dry-farming system for the Great Plains Northwest, some evidence suggests George Will Sr.'s sense of inregion divisions based on growing characteristics had sharpened by 1955, the year he died. Aside from the "Northwest" in the company's name, most internal references still referred to seeds and plants adapted to the Northern Great Plains. The 1955 catalog, however, also newly suggested an understanding of a division based on aridity. The catalog's "Field Seed Department" directed customers to choose either "Great Plains Pasture Mixture" or "Midland Pasture Mixture." The Great Plains Pasture Mixture included crested wheat grass, what the catalog claimed as "our hardiest, most drought resistant pasture grass." The "Midland" mixture had an extra explanation, noting it should be used in "eastern North Dakota."[31] That west-

Will's Hardy Pioneer Brand Hybrid Seed Corn
Hardy—Heavy Yielding—Early

We were the first to breed hardy hybrids for the northern plains. Our hybrids are grown especially for the rugged climatic conditions of the cold Northwest.

NODAK HYBRID 301. The standard yellow dent hybrid for North Dakota and the northern plains. Large and medium flats. F.O.B. Bismarck per bushel $11.00.

FIG. 21. Mr. Hardy Pioneer Hybrid, Will Co. logo, Oscar H. Will & Co. catalog, 1955. Oscar Will Papers, North Dakota Institute for Regional Studies, North Dakota State University Archives, Fargo ND.

ern "Great Plains" North Dakota required drought hardiness in seeds was axiomatic. The new awareness came in the suggestion that eastern North Dakota might now be characterized as part of a "Midland" region. The shift suggests Will's Great Plains region had narrowed to "proper" modern boundaries based on aridity. By 1930 Will already had a conception that "the central states," the center of the Corn Belt, had a different "environment there," and he thought parts of South Dakota and Minnesota might align better there than with the Northwest by some factors.[32] By 1955 his perception that eastern North Dakota might lean toward middle America had been strengthened.

The uniformity of industrialized agricultural landscapes inscribed new regional perception pressure points across the grasslands. Any grasslands located in a reliably humid, well-watered area hosted the cultural capacity to join the Middle West, a region emergent in 1902, increasingly visible by 1912, and by the 1940s expanding westward.[33] As Will worked to develop a diversified farming for the semiarid Great Plains Northwest, other professionals in the Midwest Corn Belt area worked to drain water-logged tall grasslands. From the 1880s through the 1920s, draining reached "to the edge of the prairies," into the Red River valley, and reshaped the

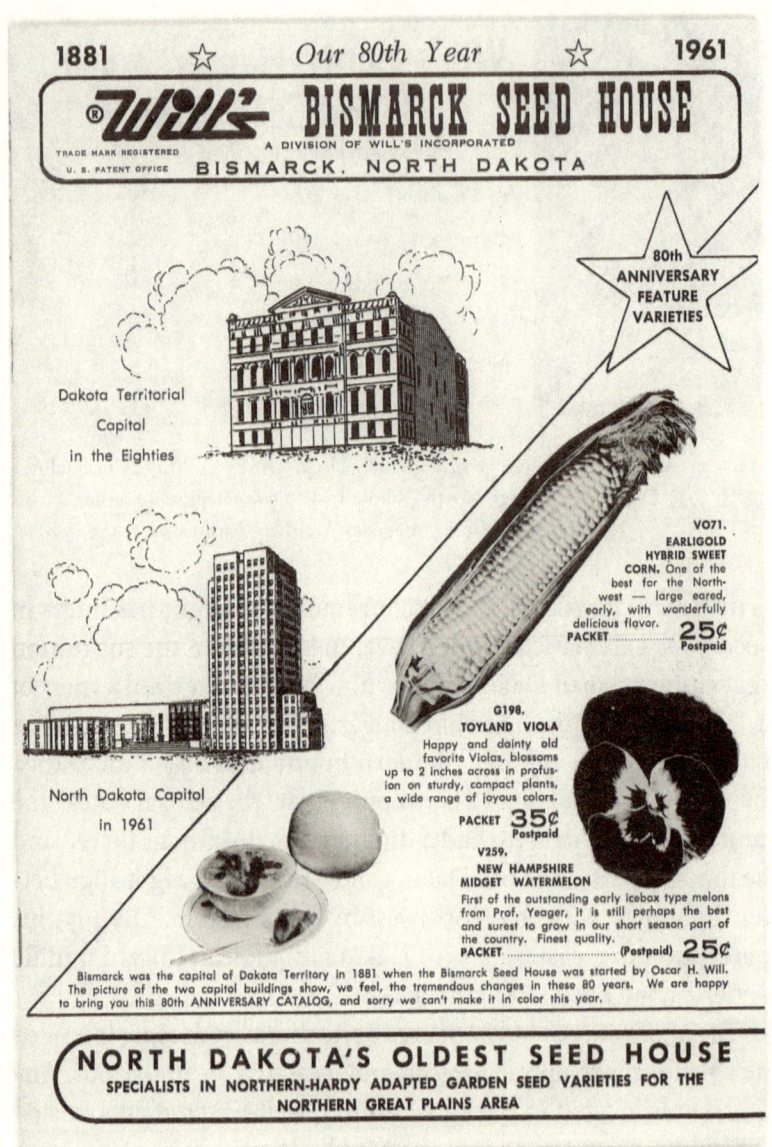

FIG. 22. Will's Bismarck Seed House 1961 annual catalog cover. Oscar Will Papers, North Dakota Institute for Regional Studies, North Dakota State University Archives, Fargo ND.

landscape, making it uniform.³⁴ As commercial Corn Belt agriculture replaced native tallgrasses, even in the eastern Dakotas, many northern grasslands settler societies began to identify more easily, if not always, with the Middle West region built on former tallgrass lands.³⁵

In 1955 George F. Will's son, George Will Jr., assumed the presidency of the family seed company, and his business model shifted the company's service region. In 1960 Oscar H. Will & Co. did not issue a catalog for the first time since the 1880s, while the younger Will reorganized under a new name. In 1961 customers received "Will's Bismarck Seed House" catalog in their mailboxes with two new taglines: "North Dakota's Oldest Seed House" and "Specialists in Northern-Hardy Adapted Garden Seed Varieties for the Northern Great Plains Area." Gone from the cover were Clell Gannon's depictions of Indigenous women's agricultural practices. Gone was the Northwest regional association. The new cover boasted symbols of settler society dominance: line-drawn images of the Dakota Territorial capitol as it looked in the mid-1880s and the North Dakota capitol as it looked in 1961.

Inside, Will Jr.'s letter to customers expressed his hope "to keep alive the Will reputation for quality and hardiness in garden seeds." The key word was "garden." The new company headed by Will Jr. focused on flower, vegetable, and lawn seeds, along with garden supplies. The new catalog did not speak to agricultural pasture and crop field seeds or corn fields good for hogging-off. Will Jr.'s 1961 catalog text referred to gardening as a "hobby." The message touted the benefits of "fresh, full flavored," simply "wonderful home grown vegetables" to counter "this mechanized, machine processed, deep frozen super market age."³⁶ Modern industrial farming had edged out small agricultural seed houses. Local gardening had a different customer base. The growth of corporate agribusiness weakened the profitability of local small agricultural seed supply businesses such as the original Oscar H. Will Co. in the same way chemical and technological innovation increasingly made it difficult for farmers the old company served to continue farming at a small scale. George Will Jr. possibly might have chosen to contract with a larger seed corporation or, as he did do, change his business model.

The new Will Bismarck Seed (Garden) House, suddenly freed from the constraints of aridity through the garden hose, reached out further east for customers. The new trade area map included Montana and both Dakotas, the prime territory of the original Oscar H. Will Co. The map also included Wyoming, Nebraska, and Minnesota, states where the old company had many regular customers. The addition of Iowa and Wisconsin suggests the new Will seed house aimed to reach into the northern or Upper Middle West.[37] The trade map combined state boundaries and environmental features into what the catalog referred to as the "4th zone," most likely the U.S. Department of Agriculture's "Fourth Hardiness Zone." Hardiness maps depicted the reach of "winter minimum temperatures" and areas of likely "winter injury," environmental knowledge necessary to garden success. Reorganization seems to have returned the Will Co. to an emphasis on its *northern* location. With the easy potential to irrigate small garden patches—as one catalog instructed, "Let your garden hose do the work"—precipitation remained less important in calculations of success than length of growing season.[38]

Aridity, raised in the cultural consciousness of settler society from the 1880s through the 1930s, formed a pressure point for regional conceptions. Lines of aridity illuminated the limits to (unaided) commercial agriculture as envisioned by settler society, not Indigenous agriculture and uses of grasslands resources.[39] Indigenous peoples, to suggest an alternate way of thinking about the northern grasslands, exploited grasslands by seasonal growth rhythms using mobility to access diverse resources and also raised riparian corn acreages. They did not "compartmentalize" or "draw borders" using rectangular boxes that evoke the homestead grid undergirding settler society's agricultural landscapes.[40] The intricately adapted small fields planted by Indigenous women farmers provided subsistence and enough surplus crops for small-scale trade and storage; these agricultural spaces also left traditional Indigenous narrative sites in place to perpetuate Indigenous values, history, and culture. The emergence of new contours and features on grasslands landscapes reflecting settler society agriculture, whether plowed by Will's small family farmer or the massive machinery of the industrial corporate farm, placed stress on Indigenous populations and their conceptions of regional space and place. Persistent place-centered Indigenous storytelling, however, resisted settler society's pressure to eliminate their traditional cultural geography.[41]

George Will Sr. had held suspect the effects of the expanding industrial agriculture that eventually caused his son to reorganize the family business. Will Sr. welcomed seed breeding, technological advances that saved labor, and an expansion of production that took his settler society agriculture to a level far removed from the Missouri River system developed by Mandans, Arikaras, and Hidatsas in which they found agricultural success. Will did not envision Arikara and Mandan peoples adapting their own agricultural practices to benefit themselves in the modern commercial situation with which settler society surrounded them. With the confidence of his race and its scientific advances, George Will Sr. envisioned settler society building on—exploiting—Indigenous knowledge to adapt settler society to the Great Plains environment. He sought to *improve* Indigenous women's agricultural products through commercialized innovations to benefit settler society. George Will, however, appreciated deeply the agricultural knowledge of Indigenous women. He argued Indigenous women farmed by scientific principles, though many members of settler society rejected Will's plan because of its association with Indigenous peoples. Further, the rise of new technologies, including power farming, and agricultural sciences that expanded the Corn Belt westward and northward, outpaced the small-scale family farm adapted locally to environmental conditions of Will's vison. North Dakota–born George F. Will embraced Indigenous corn because *his* deepest hope was to stay living in a prosperous settler society on the northern grasslands, whether he (or his son or father) thought of the space as Northwest, Middle West, West, or Northern Great Plains.

Notes

1. "'I Shall Love the Land': The Art of Clell Gannon," *North Dakota History* 76, nos. 1 and 2 (2010): 26–33.

2. Lorenzo Veracini, *Settler Colonialism: A Theoretical Overview* (New York: Palgrave Macmillan, 2010), 96–98.

3. Oscar H. Will & Co. catalog, 1951, Oscar Will Papers, Institute for Regional Studies Archives, North Dakota State University Libraries, Fargo (hereafter OWP, NDIRS).

4. Roy W. Meyer, *The Village Indians of the Upper Missouri* (Lincoln: University of Nebraska Press, 1977), 110–15.

5. Oscar H. Will & Co. catalog, 1951, OWP, NDIRS.

6. Keith H. Basso, *Wisdom Sits in Places* (Albuquerque: University of New Mexico Press, 1996), xiii, 6; Yi-Fu Tuan, *Space and Place* (Minneapolis: University of Minnesota Press, 1977), 8–10; and Tuan, *Topophilia* (Englewood Cliffs NJ: Prentice-Hall, 1974).

7. James Shortridge, *The Middle West: Its Meaning in American Culture* (Lawrence: University Press of Kansas, 1989), 14–16, 23.

8. Oscar H. Will & Co. catalog, 1896, 1897, OWP, NDIRS; and George F. Will, *Corn for the Northwest* (St. Paul MN: Webb, 1930), 73.

9. Oscar H. Will & Co. catalog, 1908, 1917, 1918, OWP, NDIRS. Although it is clear from the context of most letters that George Will is the primary author, the letters always carried the signature of the company: "Oscar H. Will & Co." Only in 1955, shortly before he died, did George Will sign the letter with his personal name identified as president of the company.

10. Oscar H. Will & Co. catalog, 1922, 1926, 1924, 1927, 1929, OWP, NDIRS.

11. Emphasis added. Will, *Corn for the Northwest*, 21–24, 5, 11, 9. Will cites a "Biological Survey of the United States issued some years ago" which produced a "Zone Map of North America," meant to chart animals by regions or zones that "coincides so closely with the area which we have marked out as possibly corn-growing territory" (41–42).

12. Will, *Corn for the Northwest*, 140. For understanding Will's small-farm capitalist vision, see also Mary Neth, *Preserving the Family Farm* (Baltimore: Johns Hopkins University Press, 1995), 5; and Hal S. Barron, *Mixed Harvest* (Chapel Hill: University of North Carolina Press, 1997), 7–16, 194.

13. John C. Hudson, *Making the Corn Belt: A Geographical History of Middle-Western Agriculture* (Bloomington: Indiana University Press, 1994), 7, 9, 10. Moving west, Hudson notes "in 1889 more than five million bushels of corn were harvested west of the 100th meridian in southwestern Nebraska," but corn production soon retreated (148). Hudson argued, "The failure of Dent corn in dry years was more responsible than any other factor in checking the westward advance of corn/livestock agriculture" (149). Moving north, about 1880, the Corn Belt "stalled" in northern Iowa, where it took about thirty years to move fifty miles north into Minnesota (and presumably the eastern Dakotas) (152). Over the course of Will's lifetime, the Corn Belt moved slowly north, from 1890 to 1950 into Minnesota, Wisconsin, Michigan, and Indiana (155). Will argued the productivity of dent corn "began to slacken"

in the "frontier" fields of South Dakota. Individually or in combination, the "arid west," northern latitudes, and high altitudes halted "the triumphal progress" of corn growing as such agriculture had been practiced in what he called "the milder central states." See George F. Will and George E. Hyde, *Corn among the Indians of the Upper Missouri* (Lincoln: University of Nebraska Press, 1964), 22–24. See also Will, *Corn for the Northwest*, 21–24, 84–85, 148. Will noted the beneficial qualities of the seed: "extreme earliness," "unusual drouth resistance," hardiness under pressures of wind, hail, and frost, and finally, an "unusual leafiness" good for feed (146).

14. Will, *Corn for the Northwest*, 13, 14, 16, 24–26, 39, 152–53; Oliver E. Baker, "Agricultural Regions of North America, Part I, The Basis of Classification," *Economic Geography* 2, no. 4 (October 1926): 460–61. In *Making the Corn Belt* Hudson mentions Will's experiments with flint and flour corn seeds and mentions the Will Co. development of a "semi-Dent" variety but argues "the results were poor" (153).

15. Will, *Corn for the Northwest*, 134–35, 80, 26.

16. G. F. Will and H. J. Spinden, "The Mandans: A Study of Their Culture, Archaeology and Language," *Papers of the Peabody Museum of American Archaeology and Ethnology, Harvard University* (August 1906): 79–219.

17. Will, *Corn for the Northwest*, 135.

18. George F. Will, "Drought Resistant Shrubs and Plants," *North and South Dakota Horticulture* 2, no. 12 (1930): 3.

19. Oscar H. Will & Co. catalog, 1935, 1937, OWP, NDIRS. Will and many people who grew up during this period on the grasslands used the terms "drought" and "drouth" interchangeably.

20. Oscar H. Will & Co. catalog, 1940, OWP, NDIRS.

21. Geo. F. Will, "Adventures in Preserving and Improving Indian Foot Plants," *North and South Dakota Horticulture* 9, no. 7 (1936): 82; Geo. F. Will, "Trees of the Dakotas," *North and South Dakota Horticulture* 12, no. 10 (1939): 112.

22. George F. Will, "Tree Ring Studies in North Dakota," *Agricultural Experiment Station Bulletin* 338 (April 1946): 19, 23–24.

23. Will and Spinden, "Mandans"; and George F. Will, "Indian Agriculture at Its Northern Limits in the Great Plains Region of North America," *Annaes Do XX Congresso International De Americanistas* 1 (1924): vi, 203–5. Citation from the title; Will also referred to "Great Plains Area" (203), "Northern Great Plains" (204), and "northern great plains" (204).

24. C. F. Marbut, "Soils of the Great Plains," *Annals of the Association of American Geographers* 13, no. 2 (June 1923): 43 (emphasis added); O. E. Baker, "The Agriculture of the Great Plains Region," *Annals of the Association of American Geographers* 13, no. 3 (September 1923): 112–13; Joseph B. Kincer, "The Climate of the Great Plains as a Factor in Their Utilization," *Annals of the Association of American Geographers* 13, no. 2 (June 1923): 68–71; and H. L. Shantz, "The Natural Vegetation of the Great Plains Region," *Annals of the Association of American Geographers* 13, no. 2 (June 1923): 97.

25. Will's early use of the label suggests some of the same factors influenced both Will and Webb. See Walter Prescott Webb, *The Great Plains* (Lincoln: University

of Nebraska Press, 1981), 353–55, 419–20, 34, 4; 353 and 416 (100th mentioned); 32, 140, and 319 (98th line mentioned). Webb's unusual definition located the Great Plains from the Mississippi River to the Rocky Mountains and beyond (3). See also Webb's opening map, n.p.

26. George F. Will, "The Value of Historical Societies in the Plains States," *North Dakota Historical Quarterly* 11, no. 4 (October 1944): 276–77; Will, "Tree Ring Studies in North Dakota," 19, 23–24. His analysis of a 534-year tree ring record suggested "the drought period of 1922 to 1937 is one of the four longest." The total number of wet years edged out the total number of dry years, 241 to 238. The region experienced "only 13 wet periods lasting 7 years or longer," but 17 drought periods of that length.

27. See Baker, "Agricultural Regions of North America," 460–61. In separate articles he described both "The Corn Belt" (1927) and "The Middle Country Where South and North Meet" (1927), among other regions.

28. Oscar H. Will & Co. catalog, 1955: 2, OWP, NDIRS.

29. Will, *Corn for the Northwest*, 11, 70–71; Hudson, *Making the Corn Belt*, 154, 167–68.

30. Hudson, *Making the Corn Belt*, 198, 171–72, 196–98, 12–13. Hudson in *Making the Corn Belt* reports that "climates of specific localities did reward some varieties more than others" (153). John L. Shover in *First Majority—Last Minority* (DeKalb: Northern Illinois University Press, 1976) has called the post–World War II transformation in agriculture the "great disjuncture" to denote its magnitude (xiii–xiv, 148).

31. Oscar H. Will & Co. catalog, 1955: 51, OWP, NDIRS. Both mixtures had varying amounts of brome grass, yellow sweet clover, alfalfa, and wild rye.

32. Will, *Corn for the Northwest*, 11.

33. James Shortridge, *Middle West*, 21–26; and Hudson, *Making the Corn Belt*, 12.

34. Hugh Prince, *Wetlands of the American Midwest* (Chicago: University of Chicago Press, 1997), 231–33, 288, 30. Prince mentioned also the new "regular shape" aligned with the needs of new machinery (233).

35. Certainly, this proved true for people living on the eastern tall grasslands "prairie peninsula" jutting east from Iowa into Illinois and Indiana. See Edgar Nelson Transeau, "The Prairie Peninsula," *Ecology* 16 (July 1935): 423–37. Although Shortridge in *Middle West* did not analyze the Northwest specifically, his findings that the Middle West became "a general label for all parts of the interior that were characterized by a prosperous rural economy" suggests the same northern grasslands pattern (26). Still, according to Prince in *Wetlands of the American Midwest*, citing a John C. Weaver study, "the northwestern reaches of the 'corn belt,'" considered western Minnesota and eastern South Dakota in 1949, exhibited the most crop diversity "for the entire Middle West" (296).

36. Will's Bismarck Seed House catalog, 1961, cover, inside letter, 5, 7, 20, 21; and 1955 Oscar H. Will & Co. catalog, 33, 41, 49, 50, 56, 58. In perhaps deference to company history, one of the new catalog's "80th Anniversary Feature Varieties" included a picture of a corncob of the variety "Earligold Hybrid Sweet Corn," described as "one of the best for the Northwest—large eared, early, with wonderfully delicious

flavor." A few years later the catalog cover showed color photographs of a tomato developed by the state's agricultural college (now North Dakota State University) at Fargo, a hybrid cucumber, and sidewalk snapdragons, pansies, and zinnias. See Will's Bismarck Seed House Catalog, 1965, cover.

37. John R. Borchert, *America's Northern Heartland: An Economic and Historical Geography of the Upper Midwest* (Minneapolis: University of Minnesota Press, 1987).

38. The 1961 Will's Bismarck Seed House catalog refers specifically to prices linked "to 4th zone," which they suggested "approximately" conformed to their map based on state lines. Christopher Daly, Mark P. Widrlechner, Michael D. Halbleib, Joseph I. Smith, and Wayne P. Gibson, "Development of a New USDA Plant Hardiness Zone Map for the United States," *Journal of Applied Meteorology and Climatology* 51, no. 2 (February 2012): 242–43. Although the first mapped hardiness zonation systems appeared in 1927 and 1928, the USDA issued what became the standard "Plant Zone Map" in 1960, the year before Will Jr. reorganized the company. See Will's Bismarck Seed House catalog, 1961, cover, inside letter, 7, 21.

39. George F. Will had some notion of an Indigenous use and conception of northern grasslands space. See Will and Hyde, *Corn among the Indians*, 238, 34, 60, 174, 171.

40. Joy Porter, *Land and Spirit in Native America* (Santa Barbara CA: Praeger, 2012), 5, 31.

41. Basso, *Wisdom Sits in Places*, 10, 32–33, 55, 57. Basso studied the Western Apaches, but suggests "that general similarities do exist" (63) among diverse Indigenous peoples. Basso explains that landscape features often have served as centuries-old "mnemonic pegs on which to hang the moral teachings of their history" and may stand in "symbolically" for Indigenous elders who passed on cultural ideas through narrative (62, 60). See also Molly P. Rozum, *Grasslands Grown: Creating Place on the U.S. Northern Plains and Canadian Prairies* (Lincoln: University of Nebraska Press, 2021).

PART 4
Energy Landscapes

13

Energy Heartland

*How the Midcontinent Pipeline System
Fueled and Fouled the Great Plains*

PHILIP A. WIGHT

In March 1904 a stunning announcement swept the Great Plains and the U.S. oil industry. Standard Oil declared that it would construct an unprecedented pipeline system to transport Kansas crude oil to Chicago and beyond.[1] At nearly six hundred miles in length, the Kansas-Indiana line was staggeringly expensive and would give Standard complete control over the state's oil exports. The idea of such a massive pipeline elicited scoffs and jeers from many oilmen. "It is looked upon as too ridiculous a proposition to be even discussed seriously," one reporter quipped.[2] Despite the incredulity of its critics, over the next nine months Standard extended its "notoriously long arms" and constructed "the longest pipe line in the world."[3] Thanks to its sixteen-million-dollar investment, the corporation could now pump Great Plains' petroleum to its Whiting, Indiana, refinery—the world's largest—and into its eastern pipeline system that stretched all the way to New York harbor. Shortly after this new trunk line became operational, Standard spent millions more and built a parallel twelve-inch pipeline—the most capacious oil conduit then ever constructed.[4]

By constructing this new pipeline system, Standard forged a new transportation corridor that would forever change the energy geography, environment, and peoples of the Great Plains. The pipeline established a template for a century of transcontinental energy transportation that was relatively reliable, inexpensive, and invisible. It was the first among dozens of sprawling, interconnected pipeline systems that helped transform the Great Plains into an agroindustrial energy heartland. These early years of experimentation and innovation laid important social expectations concerning the flow of inexpensive fossil energy, the subterranean bounty of the Great Plains, and the possibilities for an energetic future.

As the contemporary United States and Canada face unprecedented pipeline protests, and many citizens question the ecological impacts of these energy arteries, exploring the environmental history of these infrastructures offers a timely case study. How did these extensive hydrocarbon pipelines shape the history of the Great Plains' environment and peoples? What is the relationship between the Great Plains and this energy transmission technology?

The historical geography of the Great Plains facilitated the innovation and expansion of the world's most capacious hydrocarbon pipeline system. In turn, the construction and endurance of this system had profound implications for the peoples and environment of the Great Plains. Pipelines were not simply a passive element of the petroleum supply chain; they were arguably the most important mechanism for the production, transportation, and control of hydrocarbons. Being so consequential, pipelines provide a lens to understand the changing environmental history and present controversies of the Great Plains.

While pipelines crisscross the continent, the Great Plains have a unique historical relationship with this energy-transmission technology. The United States—historically the world's most prodigious producer and voracious consumer of fossil fuels—has more pipelines than any other nation. This 2.6-million-mile pipeline infrastructure is long enough to wrap around the earth ten times and is over four times longer than the nation's interstate highway system.[5] The greatest concentration of interstate "trunk lines"—the longest, most capacious, and consequential pipeline systems—runs from and through the Great Plains and Canadian Prairies. In separate systems, these pipelines transport crude oils, refined petroleum products, and natural gas throughout the continent. Though they carry different cargos, these pipeline systems share a similar coevolution and historical geography. The totality of this expansive network throughout the Great Plains is the "Midcontinent Pipe-

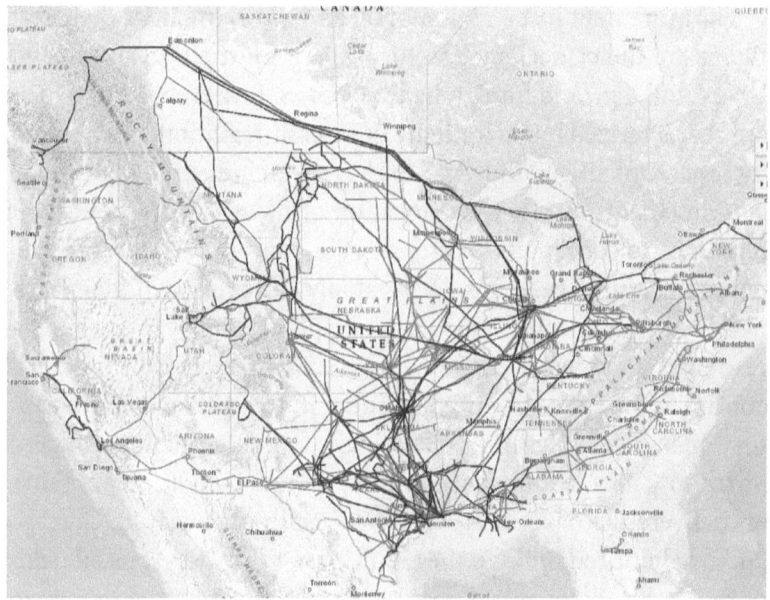

FIG. 23. Contemporary U.S. and Canadian crude-oil and petroleum-product trunk lines. U.S. Energy Information Agency, 2017.

line System." This network of vital energy arteries stretches from the U.S. Gulf Coast to Northern Alberta, spanning laterally from Wyoming to Ohio, and forming an enduring energy heartland. The energy geography of this unparalleled pipeline system is the product of geology, political economy, and culture.

During the Cretaceous Period, an inland sea teaming with prehistoric marine life dominated the Great Plains region. As this "Western Interior Seaway" receded it produced relatively flat terrain and trapped vast deposits of decaying marine life that would in time become hydrocarbons. The equatorial position of the Great Plains during the Cenozoic and Carboniferous eras also encouraged the formation of huge deposits of petroleum, natural gas, and coal.[6] Millions of years later, the receding Interior Seaway landlocked many of the largest deposits in the midcontinent, trapping them hundreds of miles from major waterways—historically humanity's easiest mode of transportation.

Far more than just a region of oil and gas extraction, the Great Plains are the critical geographical space for the transmission of U.S., Canadian, and foreign hydrocarbons. Reserves of fossil fuels are characterized by their highly uneven distribution.[7] As humanity began utilizing liquid fossil energy on an industrial scale in the late nineteenth century, the location of these reserves and their proximity to consumers became a major concern. Energy entrepreneurs structured their markets spatially and grounded their businesses geographically. The vast geographical gulf between energy resources and energy consumers gave rise to the sprawling Midcontinent Pipeline System. Beginning in the early twentieth century, plains pipelines moved landlocked midcontinent petroleum north to Chicago and south to the tidewater, where steam tankers delivered it to world markets. Six hundred miles from Chicago and five hundred miles to the Gulf Coast, the prosperous oil fields of the Great Plains relied on pipelines to facilitate the increased production and export of fossil energy. These developments transformed the Great Plains into the nexus of North American energy mobility and created today's powerful and increasingly controversial system.

The pipeline networks of the Great Plains always exerted environmental change far beyond their narrow physical footprints and wrought significant environmental consequences. First, by enabling the economic utilization of oil fields throughout the region, pipelines precipitated the growth of the petroleum industry. Oil and natural gas are not worth much at the wellhead and must be transported to market to be of significant value. Pipelines transformed the landlocked hydrocarbon fields of the midcontinent into economic reserves. Fields that lacked access to pipelines languished, but experienced rapid development once efficient overland transportation corridors were constructed. Quite simply, pipelines throttled production, and in the case of the Great Plains, unlocked enormous reserves of oil and gas for the continent's booming industrial economy. Energy corporations used pipelines to create a "geography of mass consumption" throughout the Great Plains and North America.[8]

Second, by unleashing large volumes of hydrocarbons, the Midcontinent Pipeline System fueled mechanized mobility and industrial agriculture throughout the region. These trunk lines were nothing less than a transportation revolution, on par with canals and railroads in their ability to economically move product to market. As the most efficient system for delivering large volumes of oil and gas overland, these carbon conduits became an immense force of technological momentum.[9] Midcontinent Pipelines slowly but surely enmeshed fossil fuels in the culture and political economy of the plains. By increasing access to energy for producers and consumers, driving down costs, and transporting energy virtually silently and invisibly, hydrocarbon pipelines incentivized citizens to use increasing volumes of oil and gas.

Third, the construction of the Midcontinent Pipeline System network facilitated considerable "environmental distancing" and made energy more invisible to the average consumer. The environmental history of North America is contoured by the transportation of energy (and commodities in general) over longer and longer distances. As the single most important technology for the terrestrial transportation of hydrocarbons, trunk lines facilitated the separation of producers from consumers—both geographically and psychologically. Not only were distant consumers unlikely to know where their oil and gas originated, they had little conception of the vast intercontinental network that delivered these products throughout the supply chain. Pipelines established a "pattern of portability" that linked rural resource hinterlands to urban metropolises, creating deeply imbricated national and international markets.[10] The Great Plains were at the heart of this geographical nexus, but the ever-expanding Midcontinent Pipeline System eluded the public eye. Pipelines played a powerful role in making energy invisible throughout the Great Plains and North America. Oil and gas were "best managed," according to petroleum economist Edith Penrose, "if allowed to flow continuously from the well, through pipelines, into tankers if necessary, and through refineries, unseen and untouched."[11] While railroads were larger-than-life symbols of modernity and progress, pipelines were silent subterranean conduits that rarely entered the public's consciousness but nevertheless fueled agroindustrial civilization.

The Great Plains evoke images of "amber waves of grain" and an enduring agrarianism that underlies the conception of an American heartland. Focusing on the extensive pipeline networks crisscrossing the plains reveals an alternative environmental history of the region. These pipelines suggest a region that is no less agrarian, but far more committed to industrial capitalism and mechanized agriculture than nostalgic mythologies of preindustrial farming. The modern Great Plains thrive on cheap fossil energy, seized land, and the furtive movement of hydrocarbons. Thanks to the technology of long-distance pipelines, the Great Plains are not only the breadbasket of North America, they are an energy heartland—a region of petroleum arteries, gas veins, and carbon conduits supplying the continent with powerful and perilous fossil energy.

Hydrocarbon pipelines were first utilized in the United States in 1816 when Baltimore began to produce artificial gas from coal for illumination.[12] These early iron lines constantly leaked and could only move gas short distances. "Colonel" Edwin Drake's discovery of petroleum in Titusville, Pennsylvania, in 1859 and the ensuing oil rush spurred the innovation of modern pipelines. As drillers extracted larger volumes, transportation emerged as the greatest challenge. Horse-drawn wagons riding on heavily rutted roads were slow, labor intensive, and expensive. Due to these dynamics, the price of transporting oil often exceeded its value at the wellhead.

In 1865 the entrepreneur Samuel Van Syckel laid the world's first major crude oil pipeline over five miles from Pithole to Miller Farm and its adjacent railroad line. The two-inch line had a total of three steam-powered pumps that forced eighty-one barrels of oil per hour through the line—the daily equivalent of three hundred men moving barrels for ten hours.[13] Following the success of Van Syckel's experimental line, oilmen constructed hundreds of local gathering pipelines and connected most of the wells in Pennsylvania's Oil Regions by 1866. While these narrow and short lines solved the problem of local transmission, Standard Oil's railroad monopoly dominated long-distance transportation and posed an existential threat to independent producers.

In the late 1870s a group of businessmen circumvented Standard's strangulation of Pennsylvania's Oil Regions by building a 109-mile "trunk" line called the Tide Water Pipe Line. Expensive and daring, the large-diameter pipeline began pumping oil to Williamsport in 1878. This first trunk line, argues oil historian Daniel Yergin, "was a major technological achievement, comparable to the Brooklyn Bridge four years later." Reacting to the success of Tidewater, Standard Oil soon constructed four long-distance trunk lines from the Oil Regions to Cleveland, New York City, Philadelphia, and Buffalo.[14] The age of interstate trunk lines had arrived, and at a critical moment in the expansion of the American oil industry.

On November 28, 1892, William Mills's steel drill bit hit a hydrocarbon reservoir 832 feet below Neodesha, Kansas, and introduced the Great Plains to the age of petroleum extraction. Oklahoma, or "Indian Territory" as it was then called, followed suit in 1897 when prospectors unleashed a gusher near Bartlesville. Wildcatters soon revealed the contours of the "Mid-continent field," a collection of hundreds of petroleum pools that stretched seventy-five miles wide and one hundred and seventy-five miles long. Oilmen soon brought hundreds of new wells online throughout this petroleum province. Within the first decades of the twentieth century more than thirty thousand wells penetrated the field. The oil industry considered it to be the biggest oil reservoir in the world.[15] By 1905 newspapers were regularly referring to the remarkable developments of the midcontinent, short-hand for the oil fields and their energetic bounty.

As it had done in Pennsylvania and the Lima-Indiana oil fields, Standard moved quickly to control the flow and refining of oil in the midcontinent. In 1904 Prairie Oil, Standard's local agent, built the Great Plains' first trunk line—an eight-inch line spanning 116 miles, from Humboldt to Sugarcreek, Kansas.[16] This trunk system was the first stage of Standard's ambitious line to Chicago and was "destined to become the largest in the country." Between 1905 and

1906, Standard extended this line northward to its Whiting, Indiana, refinery near Chicago, as well as southward into Oklahoma's flourishing oil pools. This sprawling system incentivized producers to increase extraction throughout the Great Plains, although they did not control the market or their destinies.[17]

Kansas and Oklahoma production increased even more after upstart Texas oil firms constructed pipelines from the midcontinent to the Gulf Coast beginning in 1907 and Standard finished a pipeline from Oklahoma to Louisiana to export Great Plains crude by tank steamer in 1910.[18] As pipeline historian Arthur Johnson argues, in conjunction with new fields, these pipelines enabled the growth of new vertically integrated firms like Gulf, Texaco, and Sun Oil that could compete with Standard in the midcontinent.[19] Even John D. Rockefeller admitted the tremendous power of these infrastructures to shape markets and spur corporate growth. "The entire oil business is dependent upon the pipe line system," he explained in 1899. "Without it every well would shut down and every foreign market would be closed to us."[20]

The ability of Standard Oil to use its pipelines to bar entry to independent producers and generate monopoly returns elicited a flood of protests from the midcontinent. The Progressive-Era federal government responded with an investigation headed by James Garfield, the son of the former president. Garfield's explosive report underscored the enormous business advantage that pipelines gave their owners and prompted the first federal regulation of these systems, the Hepburn Act of 1906. While the act began a contentious history of federal pipeline regulation, it did little over the next twenty years to change pipelines as weapons of corporate warfare that could throttle production, vertically integrate supply chains, and move enormous volumes of crude.

Standard's expansive system and the other early trunk lines were technical marvels but wrought enduring environmental consequences. Among the most obvious and alarming were ruptures, leaks, and fires. While some early lines were commonly patrolled, many trunk lines were seldom surveilled unless a major drop in pressure occurred. Periodic leaks were an accepted part of the pipelining business. In 1907 the business-friendly *Wall Street Journal* estimated that 2 percent of all oil transmitted through pipelines was lost to evaporation and leaks.[21] With hundreds of millions of barrels of crude extracted each year (166 million in 1907 alone) and the majority moved by pipeline to be refined, millions of barrels of crude likely spilled each year.[22] These leaks polluted the soil, contaminated water sources, and angered local residents.

While many leaks were small, breaches in major trunk lines could become terrifying events. On March 27, 1904, Standard's twelve-inch trunk line from the oil fields of Indiana to its Cleveland refineries (part of Standard's trunk-line system that soon would stretch all the way to the midcontinent) broke southwest of the Ohio town of Berea. A stream of oil flowed into the Rocky River and someone downstream set fire to the black slick. The *New York Times* reported that "the blaze ran backward, and the stream became a river of fire, the flames mounting up from the surface of the water ten to fifteen feet, with a huge volume of dark, black smoke above." Despite the area being wet from weeks of successive rains, the "river of fire" consumed trees along the riverbanks, fences, and nearby homes.[23] Pipelines exposed rural residents throughout nation, like those of Berea, to the ever-increasing carboniferous pollution of the industrial era.

The decades between 1911 and 1931 witnessed an extraordinary period of oil production, pipeline construction, and automobility throughout the Great Plains. The phenomenal growth of fossil fuel consumption—thanks mainly to the automobile and farm tractor—drove the innovation and expansion of pipelines throughout the region. With a stagnant domestic kerosene market, the advent of the internal-combustion engine offered a windfall for the adolescent petroleum industry. By 1909 both Henry Ford and Random E. Olds established factories with assembly lines—a crucial innovation that reduced costs and facilitated mass production. With oil emerging as the dominant motive fuel for automobiles, gasoline sales surpassed those of kerosene in 1911. With the democratization of the automobile, the distribution of gasoline more than quadrupled during the 1920s.[24] To meet the demand, interstate pipelines grew from 6,800 miles in 1900 to over 24,400 twenty years later. Because the diameter of these pipes also grew over the same period, total pipeline capacity grew even faster than mileage.[25] American mechanized mobility demanded ever-greater consumption of hydrocarbons, and pipelines both delivered this energy and were critical in entrenching a powerful new energy regime.

The transition to fossil fuels for motive energy also ushered in a new era for agriculture. While the first tractors were steam-powered from the combustion of coal, gasoline-powered models soon emerged as the industry standard. Their success wrought enormous changes for American farming communities across the plains. The year 1918 witnessed "peak horse" for the United States, as 85,000 tractors and 89,000 trucks obviated additional animal power.[26] More than ten animals disappeared for every tractor introduced. In conjunction with other equipment, these energetic behemoths resulted in a 50 percent reduction in the time required to plow and saved thirty days of labor per year. Ownership surged from 158,000 tractors in 1919 to over 827,000 a decade later, increasing "non-highway" consumption of gasoline from 1.79 to 21.7 million barrels over the same period.[27] Petroleum-fueled mechanization spurred overproduction and made large numbers of rural residents into surplus labor. More than three million people left agriculture during the decade.[28] Pipelines not only facilitated major change for farmers, they structured markets for rural oil producers.

The construction of new trunk lines highlighted a salient feature of the energy transmission technology: pipelines throttled production. Wyoming's Salt Creek field epitomized this dynamic. Oilmen discovered significant volumes of high-quality petroleum that could provide as much as 50 percent gasoline per barrel, making the field "the most valuable in the country." Yet a high-quality product meant little thousands of miles away from marketing hubs. Due to a lack of pipelines, "the market for Wyoming oil has been extremely limited and the price of crude there is far below what the oil is actually worth." Transforming Wyoming into a prosperous oil state, the *Wall Street Journal* declared in 1916, is "dependent on the building of a pipe line from the State to the big consuming centers."[29] Finally in 1924, a trunk line was constructed to transport crude out of state and across the Great Plains.[30] The case of Wyoming demonstrates that pipelines were essential infrastructures for monetizing oil fields and fueling long-term development.

Several major technological factors during this period increased the success and efficacy of pipelines and expanded the diversity of their cargos. Steel mills innovated the production of larger-diameter, higher-tensile steel pipe, which pipeliners began welding together. Additionally, powerful and reliable diesel pumps began replacing steam pumps after 1914 and became standard by 1917. These pumps could more efficiently move oil and gas at higher pressures. The 1920s also saw significant advances in pipeline technology, such as electric welding and protective anticorrosion coatings, which allowed for longer, more reliable pipelines to be constructed.[31]

Prior to these technological advancements, pipelines could not effectively move natural gas over long distances. Natural gas was a useful fuel but was most often flared or vented into the atmosphere because producers could not transport it to market. Before 1925 the longest gas pipeline was less than two hundred miles. There were no intercontinental trunk lines that could move gas from the production basins of the Great Plains to urban consumers on the East Coast.[32] This situation became especially wasteful after wildcatters discovered two gigantic natural gas fields in 1918 and 1919. In contrast to the "monopoly, shortage, and increasing prices" of the East Coast, according to natural gas historian Elizabeth Sanders, the Southwest experienced "an enormous oversupply; thousands of producers with no pipeline outlets scrambled to extract some marketable product from their leaseholds—in the process letting millions of cubic feet of gas escape into the atmosphere."[33]

This situation changed dramatically in the early 1930s when technological innovations allowed for a new generation of gas trunk lines. Three one-thousand-mile interstate natural gas pipelines were constructed from the Houghton and Panhandle gas fields across the Great Plains to Chicago, Indianapolis, and Minneapolis (and cities in between) between 1930 and 1932. These new long-distance lines enlarged the region's natural gas industry, provided fuel for distant urban consumers, and transformed Great Plains' gas supplies into a more national resource. With supply secured by pipeline, Chicago's Peoples Gas Light Company began the first major marketing of natural gas for home heating in 1931. But the Great Depression halted the growth of long-distance natural gas lines across the plains before they could reach the energy-hungry markets of the Northeast.[34]

During these same years, the precipitous deployment of product pipelines made gasoline more accessible and less expensive, further deepening the Great Plains' reliance on automobiles and farm tractors. "Product pipelines" transported refined petroleum products like gasoline, diesel, kerosene, and propane. After a series of successful experiments in the late 1920s, competing oil firms began a massive build-out of product lines across the nation. The widespread deployment of these pipelines in the 1930s increased the availability of gasoline in rural areas, made consumers' proximity to refineries less important, and decreased gasoline's cost.[35]

The largest product pipeline system in the world was the Great Lakes Pipe Line. Constructed between 1930 and 1931, the pipeline systems' multiple lines stretched like a tree over 1,500 miles from Tulsa, Oklahoma, as far north as Minneapolis, and as far east as Chicago. It supplied gasoline to major metropolitan areas such as Des Moines, St. Paul, and Kansas City, as well as rural areas in between. The sweeping line required nearly $17 million to construct and large amounts of private capital, necessitating an unprecedented joint venture between six firms.[36]

In a surprising twist, the Great Lakes Pipe Line helped Texas residents struggling with the Dust Bowl. As a drought plagued the Southwest during the summer of 1934, residents of northern Texas were desperate for water supplies. The Great Lakes Pipe Line Company happened to be conducting hydrostatic testing on a recently completed line extension. Instead of filling the line with gasoline after the water testing, the company pumped millions of gallons of potable water from Kansas City through the brand new line to thirsty residents in northern Texas. While pipelines often fouled waterways and contaminated crops, they also provided significant material benefits for Great Plains' residents facing harsh environmental challenges.[37]

Product lines were especially important to the Great Plains because the region consumed large volumes of gasoline per capita. Demand for refined products was not evenly distributed throughout the nation. Areas like the Great Plains and Midwest used far greater quantities of gasoline for farm tractors and rural automobility compared with other areas of the country. Automobiles were so popular with the region's residents that by 1936, five Great Plains states were among the top ten in the nation for car ownership as a proportion of population.[38] The region also had little use for certain petroleum byproducts like heavy fuel oil (utilized by ships), so it made sense to construct product pipelines to ship the relevant fuels directly to consumers.[39] By the 1930s shipping refined products by pipeline was roughly 70 percent less expensive than rail, a factor that drove down costs and ultimately further deepened the region's petroleum dependence.[40]

Product pipelines continued the effect of making petroleum—especially gasoline—more invisible and its environmental effects more distant. Consumers could now fill their automobiles and tractors at more locations for less money. Pipelines' ability to separate producers and consumers, like many aspects of the modern industrial economy, hid the true environmental costs of petroleum consumption. "As a result," argues historian Christopher Wells, "interwar motorists had little reason to feel any connection to the oil industry's environmentally destructive activities."[41] Widespread public recognition of these costs would not emerge until after World War II.

The exigency of World War II and the primacy of oil for the Allies' mechanized war machine precipitated the construction of two of the most consequential pipelines in American history. In 1939 planners called for a massive pipeline stretching from Texas to New Jersey to alleviate the vulnerability of the maritime shipping route between the Gulf and East Coasts. This route was vital to the Eastern Seaboard, which consumed 40 percent of the country's petroleum but produced almost nothing.[42] The outbreak of war proved planners prescient; German U-boats sank fifty-five tankers within six months, imperiling the East Coast's vital fuel supply.[43]

Reeling from these losses, Secretary of the Interior Harold Ickes approved the "Tulsa Plan" in early 1942 for a massive pipeline from Texas to the Pennsylvania Seaboard. Officially named the "War Emergency Pipeline," the two-foot-wide artery was colloquially called the "Big Inch." The impressively wide trunk line could carry five times more oil than a conventional crude line. Over eighty different private companies hired sixteen thousand workers to construct the sprawling 1,243-mile oil artery. By the end of 1943 the Big Inch was carrying 250,000 barrels per day, nearly half of the East Coast's petroleum needs and the equivalent of eighty tankers. The U.S. invasion of North Africa created additional supply shortages on the East Coast, and Ickes redressed this problem by authorizing the construction of a parallel product pipeline to the Big Inch. Slightly smaller at twenty inches, the "Little Big Inch" carried 175,000 barrels per day of gasoline, heating oil, diesel, and kerosene—each batch separated by rubber balls—from the Houston area to Linden, New Jersey.[44]

These pipelines were major technical successes that proved enormously consequential both during and after the war. The Inch Lines were the first large-diameter, long-distance pipelines—which made them the biggest in the world. Thanks to these twin arteries, Great Plains petroleum could be shipped efficiently and securely across the nation. Pipelines moved only 4 percent of the East Coast's supply in 1941, but 42 percent after the construction of the Inch Lines.[45] These new lines freed up Allied tankers to ship petroleum directly from the East Coast to Europe and beyond. Thanks in part to these lines, the United States not only became the "arsenal of democracy," but according to historian David Painter, also the "gas station of democracy."[46]

The Inch Lines provided a spectacular engineering demonstration for the postwar oil industry and were foundational for construction of the modern Midcontinent Pipeline System. The lines demonstrated that large volumes of hydrocarbons could be moved efficiently over vast distances. Their innovation established the technical and business case for the massive overland movement of crude, natural gas, and refined products. The Inch Lines proved the tremendous economies of scale possible when operating large-diameter (more than twenty inches) pipelines. Since the volume of a cylinder increases with the square of its radius, the doubling of a pipeline's diameter resulted in a quadrupling of its potential throughput. This greater throughput made large-diameter pipelines so efficient they became price competitive with historically cheaper oil tankers. But these large-diameter lines also increased the potential for more destructive leaks.

The end of the war brought a surge of pipeline construction. A historic expansion of the Midcontinent Pipeline System between the mid-1940s and 1960s tapped the oil fields of North Dakota and Alberta, transitioned East Coast cities to natural gas, and further imbricated the U.S. and Canadian petroleum economies. Like the 1920s, the massive build-out of long-distance pipelines was coterminous with unprecedented levels of energy consumption. With the phasing out of coal-powered locomotives, nearly the entire U.S. transportation sector relied upon petroleum as its motive energy. In 1946 Americans consumed an average of 4.9 million barrels of petroleum per day; by 1952 daily consumption surged to 7 million barrels. The thirty years following the end of the war witnessed a historic boom in pipeline construction, reshaping the pipeline map with up to sixteen thousand miles being constructed each year. Unprecedented U.S. oil consumption necessitated rising oil imports from other nations (the United States became a net importer for the first time in 1948), spurring new pipeline construction to bring foreign petroleum north from Houston and south from the Canadian Prairies. During these decades the pipeline industry "came of age" and the Midcontinent System matured into its modern incarnation.[47]

Among the most consequential developments of the early postwar era was construction of transcontinental gas pipelines linking the Great Plains with the U.S. East and West Coasts. Pent-up residential and industrial demand following the end of the war mixed with strong economic growth to create a twenty-year construction boom in natural gas lines. Strikes by the United Mine Workers furthermore fueled the desire of the Northeast to convert from coal to natural gas. In 1947, despite objections from the coal and railroad industries, both Big Inch and Little Big Inch pipelines were sold as "war surplus property" to the Texas Eastern Transmission Corporation and converted to natural gas. Moreover, independent gas producers built extensive new interstate gas transmission pipelines across the Great Plains and, in doing so, increased interstate natural gas transmission by 250 percent between 1946 and 1950.[48]

These new wide-diameter lines required high pressure and abundant gas to operate. This drove increased production in Texas and throughout the midcontinent.[49] Thanks in part to this tremendous build-out of pipeline infrastructure, between 1940 and 1955 production of natural gas in the United States rose from 2.6 trillion to 9.4 trillion cubic feet per year.[50] While the construction of pipelines throughout the midcontinent incentivized increased gas extraction, these new gas lines also helped efficiently utilize hydrocarbon supply. In 1947, for the first time, more gas was consumed by residential consumers than flared from wells into the atmosphere. Inexpensive gas delivered by pipeline also helped cities attract manufacturing industries. "The availability of natural gas for domestic and industrial fuel," argue energy historians Joseph Pratt, Martin Melosi, and Kathleen Brosnan, gave "an important competitive advantage over regions still dependent on coal and other fuels."[51] These gas pipelines also decreased the nation's reliance on coal. Following the construction of the 1,840-mile Transcontinental Gas Pipe Line in 1949, almost overnight New York City transitioned from the largest manufactured gas market in the nation to a negligible consumer of the coal-derived fuel.[52]

In the early postwar years, the Midcontinent Pipeline System expanded to tap important new petroleum reservoirs under the northern prairies. Following the discovery of major oil reserves at Leduc, Alberta, in 1947, Imperial Oil was forced to limit production until it could build a suitable pipeline system. From the very beginning of Alberta's oil development, constructing pipelines south to major marketing centers was an imperative for profitable and expanding production. Thus, between 1949 and 1950 Imperial Oil constructed the sprawling Interprovincial Pipeline (named Lakehead in the United States), from near Edmonton, Alberta, across the northern prairies to Clearbrook, Minnesota, and finally, Superior, Wisconsin. Newspapers marveled at the capacity of the new line, which could hold 1.8 million barrels of oil at any one time—or as they explained, enough to fill 260 of the large grain elevators that dotted the prairie.[53] Between 1953 and 1956, Interprovincial expanded the pipeline to Sarnia, Toronto, and Buffalo. In time this system—now known as Enbridge's "Mainline" system—would grow to 3,100 miles and become the longest liquid hydrocarbon transportation system in the world.[54]

Similar developments occurred south of the Canadian border. After oil was discovered in North Dakota, a corporate joint venture constructed the 1,149-mile Platte Pipeline from the state's Big Horn Basin to Wood River, Illinois, in 1952. The Platte line, according to pipeline historian Arthur Johnson, "inaugurated the new era of big-inch pipelining from the Rockies to Midcontinent refineries." The 450-mile Butte Pipeline then connected North Dakota's booming Williston Basin to the Platte system in 1955.[55] These new lines greatly expanded the Midcontinent Pipeline System and funneled large volumes of crude to and through the Great Plains.

The aggregate effect of these geographic expansions, technical innovations, and capacity additions—in conjunction with rising consumption—proved enormous. In 1950 petroleum overtook coal as the nation's leading energy source. Pipelines became the dominant mode of hydrocarbon transport throughout the United States and Canada. The liquid nature of petroleum allowed for both its easy conveyance and regular escape into the environment. "As a means of ferrying energy from point of extraction to point of use," historian John McNeil contends, "oil tankers and pipelines were both more economical and more hazardous than coal transport."[56] With the deployment of more sophisticated large-diameter pipelines after the war, spills were both less frequent but more devastating when they inevitably occurred.[57] These accidental releases were but one aspect of the petroleum supply chains' environmentally destructive nature. From oil fields, to refineries, to tailpipes, "the production and consumption of oil," Adam Rome argues, "contributed to almost all of the most pressing environmental problems of the twentieth century."[58] In the early postwar years, experts began expressing alarm over these environmental concerns, but pipelines evaded major public concern until the proposed Trans-Alaska Pipeline System in 1969.

As the postwar years ticked onward, this system of pipes, valves, and pumps rumbled around the clock, fueling the continent's industrialized agriculture and mechanized mobility. As American and Canadian energy demand increased, so too did the size and scope of the Midcontinent Pipeline System. As part of a positive feedback loop, these pipelines also increased the ubiquity of cheap gasoline and created vast social landscapes reliant on fossil fuels. The pipes laid during this era form the backbone of today's legacy pipelines that continue to pump millions of barrels of crude, natural gas, and petroleum products, despite being over sixty years old.[59] Their legacy weighs heavily upon the present. While pipelines provided unprecedented energy for residents of the Great Plains to overcome environmental challenges, these lines also carried with them oil spills, gas leaks, and numerous environmental hazards. Power and pollution were inseparable bedfellows, and their combined influence ensured the enduring transformation of the Great Plains into an energy heartland.

Notes

1. "Kansas-Indian Territory Oil Field: Remarkable Development Is Now Going On," *Wall Street Journal*, March 7, 1904.

2. "Texas Oil Production: Constant Reduction in Output," *Wall Street Journal*, April 29, 1904.

3. "The Longest Pipe Line," *Wall Street Journal*, December 24, 1904.

4. Knox Smith, "Report of the Commissioner of Corporations on the Petroleum Industry" (Washington DC: Government Printing Office, 1907), 146.

5. "General Pipeline FAQs," Pipeline and Hazardous Materials Safety Administration, United States Department of Transportation, accessed November 16, 2017, https://www.phmsa.dot.gov/faqs/general-pipeline-faqs.

6. H. E. Copeland, Amy Pocewicz, and Joseph M. Kiesecker, "Geography of Energy Development in Western North America: Potential Impacts on Terrestrial Ecosystems," in *Energy Development and Wildlife Conservation in Western North America*, ed. David E. Naugle (Washington DC: Island Press, 2011), 9–10.

7. Earl Cook, *Man, Energy, and Society* (New York: W. H. Freeman, 1976), introduction.

8. Matthew T. Huber, *Lifeblood: Oil, Freedom, and the Forces of Capital* (Minneapolis: University of Minnesota Press, 2014), 42.

9. For a discussion of "technological momentum," see Thomas P. Hughes, *American Genesis: A Century of Invention and Technological Enthusiasm, 1870–1970* (New York: Penguin Books, 1989), 470–71.

10. William R. Freudenberg and Robert Gramling, *Blowout in the Gulf: The BP Oil Spill Disaster and the Future of Energy in America* (Cambridge MA: MIT Press, 2010), 71–72.

11. Huber, *Lifeblood*, 47.

12. David E. Nye, *Consuming Power: A Social History of American Energies* (Cambridge MA: MIT Press, 1997), 95. Gas pipelines were deployed as early as 1,000 BC, when the Chinese used bamboo piping to transport natural gas for illumination. Daniel B. Luten, "The Economic Geography of Energy," *Scientific American* 225, no. 3 (September 1971): 164–78.

13. Brian Black, *Petrolia: The Landscape of America's First Oil Boom* (Baltimore: Johns Hopkins University Press, 2003).

14. Daniel Yergin, *The Prize: The Epic Quest for Money, Wealth, and Power* (New York: Simon & Schuster, 1990), 43.

15. Nigel Anthony Sellers, "Oil, Wheat, and Wobblies: The Industrial Workers of the World in Oklahoma, 1905–1930" (PhD diss., University of Oklahoma, 1994), 166.

16. Harold F. Williamson, *The American Petroleum Industry: The Age of Energy* (Chicago: Northwestern University Press, 1963), 65, 90.

17. Francis W. Schruben, *Wea Creek to El Dorado: Oil in Kansas, 1860–1920* (Columbia: University of Missouri Press, 1972), 47–48.

18. Williamson, *American Petroleum Industry*, 95–97.

19. Arthur Johnson, "The Early Texas Oil Industry: Pipelines and the Birth of an Integrated Oil Industry, 1901–1911," *Journal of Southern History* 32, no. 4 (November 1966): 516–28.

20. United States Bureau of Corporations, *Report to the Commissioner of Corporations on the Petroleum Industry: Prices and Profits* (Washington DC: Government Printing Office, 1907), 638.

21. "Eastern Oil Fields: Great Importance to Pipelines," *Wall Street Journal*, November 20, 1907.

22. "U.S. Field Production of Crude Oil," *U.S. Energy Information Agency*.

23. "Miles of Blazing River," *New York Times*, March 28, 1904.

24. Christopher Wells, *Car Country: An Environmental History* (Seattle: University of Washington Press, 2012), 174.

25. Williamson, *American Petroleum Industry*, 65.

26. Vaclav Smil, *Energy in Nature and Society: General Energetics of Complex Systems* (Cambridge MA: MIT Press, 1997), 169.

27. Williamson, *American Petroleum Industry*, 446.

28. Alan Brinkley, *Unfinished Nation: A Concise History of the American People*, vol. 2 (McGraw Hill, 2013).

29. "Wyoming Needs Pipe Line to Oil Fields: State's Position as Producer Can Be Established Only by Better Transportation," *Wall Street Journal*, June 9, 1916.

30. Arthur M. Johnson, *Petroleum Pipelines and Public Policy, 1906–1959* (Cambridge MA: Harvard University Press, 1967), 133.

31. Williamson, *American Petroleum Industry*, 91, 586.

32. Christopher Castaneda, "Regulated Enterprise: Natural Gas Pipelines and Competition for Northeastern Markets, 1938–1954" (PhD diss., University of Houston, 1990), 24.

33. Elizabeth Sanders, *The Regulation of Natural Gas: Policy and Politics, 1938–1978* (Philadelphia: Temple University Press, 1981), 24.

34. Castaneda, "Regulated Enterprise," 31–32.

35. John A. Hansen, *U.S. Oil Pipeline Markets: Structure, Pricing, and Public Policy* (Cambridge MA: MIT Press, 1983), 1. Johnson, *Petroleum Pipelines and Public Policy*, 258.

36. Williamson, *American Petroleum Industry*, 577–78.

37. "Oil Line Carries Water: New Pipe in Texas, Used to Relieve Drought Stricken Areas," *Wall Street Journal*, August 11, 1934.

38. Michael D. Green, "Automobiles" in *Encyclopedia of the Great Plains*, ed. David J. Wishart, accessed December 1, 2017, http://plainshumanities.unl.edu/encyclopedia/doc/egp.tra.002.

39. "Pipelines Push: They Expand Rapidly as Oil Companies Push into New Market Areas," *Wall Street Journal*, September 15, 1959.

40. Williamson, *American Petroleum Industry*, 575–76.

41. Wells, *Car Country*, 178.

42. Williamson, *American Petroleum Industry*, 757.

43. Christopher James Castaneda and Joseph A. Pratt, *From Texas to the East: A Strategic History of the Texas Eastern Corporation* (College Station: Texas A&M University Press, 1993), 17. Williamson, *American Petroleum Industry*, 763.

44. Williamson, *American Petroleum Industry*, 764.

45. Yergin, *The Prize*, 375–76.

46. David Painter, "Oil and the International History of the Twentieth Century," lecture at Boston University, September 2014.

47. Johnson, *Petroleum Pipelines and Public Policy*, 347–60.

48. Yergin, *The Prize*, 430.

49. Christopher J. Castaneda, "The Texas-Northeast Connection: The Rise of the Post–World War II Gas Pipelines Industry," *Houston Review* 12, no. 2 (1990): 80.

50. Gerald D. Nash, *United States Oil Policy: 1890–1964* (Pittsburgh PA: University of Pittsburgh Press, 1968), 210–11.

51. Joseph Pratt, Martin Melosi, and Kathleen Brosnan, *Energy Capitals: Local Impact, Global Influence* (Pittsburgh PA: University of Pittsburgh Press, 2014), 40.

52. Castaneda, "Texas-Northeast Connection," 93.

53. "Canadian Oil Line to U.S. to Open This Year: Product Will Travel 1,180 Miles," *Chicago Daily Tribune*, May 8, 1950.

54. Bob Eleff, "Minnesota's Petroleum Infrastructure: Pipelines, Refineries, Terminals," Research Department, Minnesota House of Representatives, updated October 2018, http://www.house.leg.state.mn.us/hrd/pubs/petinfra.pdf.

55. Johnson, *Petroleum Pipelines and Public Policy*, 358, 373.

56. J. R. McNeil and Peter Engelke, *The Great Acceleration: An Environmental History of the Anthropocene since 1945* (Cambridge MA: Harvard University Press, 2016), 21.

57. Trudy E. Bell, "Pipelines Safety and Security: Is It No More Than a Pipe Dream?," *Bent of Tau Beta Pi* (Winter 2015): 12–19.

58. Adam Rome, "What Really Matters in History?: Environmental Perspectives in Modern America," *Environmental History* 7, no. 2 (April 2002): 303–18.

59. Hansen, *U.S. Oil Pipeline Markets*, 12.

14

Places of Overburden

Strip Mining and Reclamation on the Northern Great Plains

RYAN DRISKELL TATE

The Bull Mountains of Montana lie more or less in the middle of the northern Great Plains, a remote, hard-driving area where towns come few and far between. Most Americans have never visited this rural and sparsely populated place, but many have an instinctive sense of the landscape. It's a staple of American folklore and popular myth-making—the "Old West" of cinematic imagination and Louis L'Amour frontier novels. There's an engulfing presence out here of the chiseled layers of deep time, but despite its rugged exterior, the region has always been, ecologically speaking, a thin and delicate place. The average rainfall can barely fill a two-gallon bucket, and the plateau country is easily scarred. The western novelist Edward Abbey once called this a "land of almost painful beauty"—an unforgiving environment that beckons and repels.[1]

Today, thousands of ranchers and farmers still run their herds on these prairies and brag about the surface riches: the native grass, the spring water, the open space. But beneath these western soils lay older bounties—compressed swamps of subbituminous and lignite rocks stacked in strata of former worlds. These geological formations account for about 20 percent of the world's coal reserves and half of all American coal deposits. Yet for tens of thousands of years, they played almost no role in human ways of life.[2] The Great Plains Indians, and the first whites in the region, recorded coal outcroppings and may have burned lignite for heat. But they lived without tapping the reserves of fossil fuels underground. Even after the development of the skills and knowledge to extract coal, the western mines powered railroads, front range homes, and labor wars, but never amounted to a large share of national production.³

That all changed in the late 1960s when a coal rush engulfed the region. A constellation of political and economic forces spurred the western migration of acquisitive energy firms. The labor unrest in the Appalachian coalfields and the air pollution control standards of the Clean Air Act threatened the industry's razor-thin profit margins out east. The coal companies diversified and invested their capital into the western coalfields, where the nonunion workforces and "clean"-burning coal promised new opportunity. The onset of the 1973 oil crisis only accelerated this shifting geography of coal production. As the nation's most abundant fossil fuel, coal found favor amid the political imperatives to secure "energy independence." American policymakers and industry leaders doubled down on coal as the "pivotal fuel" and "fuel for tomorrow" under the presumed threat foreign oil (and the "serfdom" of oil imports) posed to cultural predilections. By the nationalist creed "for the good of the nation" energy conglomerates rushed into Montana, Wyoming, and the Dakotas to peel back the soil and strip mine the wide and unskimmed seams.⁴

Strip mining wrought one of the greatest environmental changes to the northern Great Plains since the destruction of the bison. The titanic "earthmovers" stripped bare life's essentials and rooted out a single commodity. This brute-force exploitation of resources may, in the long run, prove more vicious than anything that has come before. The mines and power plants have become, by some measures, almost equivalent to a force of nature: they move more earth than natural erosion and rank among the largest carbon polluters on the planet.⁵ The climate scientist James Hansen warns that such operations inflict so much environmental decay they are fast becoming "death factories." By Hansen's calculations, each coal-fired power plant may bear the blame for the future extinction of four hundred species.⁶ Many scholars insist that such human alterations of the environment have created an entirely new geological epoch dominated by humanity—the "Anthropocene."⁷ There's no doubt the conquest of mass extraction has shaped the recent history of the northern plains, perhaps more than earlier ecological conquests and disasters.

But these bird's-eye perspectives, as is often the case, have distorted the realities closer to the ground. The conflict over strip mining in its early years provides an object lesson in the complexities of the region and its experiences. Back in the 1970s the region's agricultural people, who lived and labored above these coalfields, expressed little worry about the global threat of the climate crisis that captures so much attention today. What mattered most to them were the sharp and localized pains. They lived off the surface relations and did not want to lose those relationships to a mine or a power plant or a high-voltage transmission line. The ranchers prided themselves on the regional ecology, no matter how much they may have once abused it and broken it and run roughshod over it. Most fretted over what would become of their outfits if strip mines dissembled the local ecosystems on which they relied. The ranchers took the sacrifice personally and resented the ravages of the big machines, because every twinge in the environment signified something deeper: the sacrifice of "rural life for urban death."

At bottom, the ranchers of the northern plains feared the slow violence of mining that might transform their homes into places of "overburden."[8] Overburden is the industry term for the disposable ecosystem: all the soil, the plants, the rocks, and the animal life that mines tear apart to root coal from the ground. It's the Orwellian way of referring to a cultural and economic place where ranchers and farmers make their living. The ranchers feared the literal and metaphoric loss of their homes and workscapes. As the rancher Carolyn Alderson once protested to the coal firms, "Do not make the mistake of lumping us and the land all together as 'overburden' and dispense with us as nuisances."[9]

The ranchers of the northern prairies locked horns with the coal companies throughout the 1970s. They banded together to build political organizations and safeguard their psychic wages in the somatic energies stored away in the grass and cattle at the surface. Most kept their politics local. They focused on the small practical and perceptual changes in their lifeworlds—the subtle, but no less significant, ways that fossil-fuel modes of production heaved up and ruined the grass and air and water. They pushed for state and federal "reclamation" laws to protect cattle country from the worst excesses of strip mining. These ranchers failed, in the long term, to stop the gore of development, but their story reminds us how much local peoples working together to manage and protect their beloved place can accomplish in the age of climate crisis. The full-throated screams about humanity's "eleventh hour" will never compare to the defense of parochial nature—the instinctive sense to protect what's near.[10]

Reclaiming the West

The surface mines in the American West once operated under the general presumption that strip mines would become sacrifice areas. As far back as the early twentieth century, the nation's coal operators conceded that strip mining was destructive to the earth "unless carefully engineered and controlled." Appalachian writer and activist Malcolm Ross first criticized the practice in a close examination of the "bungling and bloodshed" of coal mining in West Virginia and Kentucky, but the American public took little heed until strip mining emerged as a political topic during the 1960s.[11] The high visibility of the operations opened them to criticism by local residents, critical journalists, and watchdog groups. The federal government reported on the mass disturbance of the practice in the mid-1960s and found forests and watersheds and entire communities laid to waste. The country's newfound awareness turned strip miners into proverbial rapists, polluters, and exploiters.[12]

Stewart Udall, the secretary of the interior, recommended Congress step in to protect the public interest.[13] The remedial work of mining became more involved in the years that followed. The National Environmental Policy Act, which President Richard Nixon signed in 1970, shifted the focus of environmental law from pollution controls to protection of American "ecology." The bill empowered environmentalists in the policymaking process through the far-reaching, but once little noticed section, of the environmental impact statement. Afterward, coal permit applications required a wealth of scientific inventories about proposed mine sites and their postmining use.

As in Appalachia, many states in the northern plains passed "reclamation" laws, toothless though they were, amid these awakened public sympathies for environmental protection. After stripping the land, the coal companies now had to "reclaim" it: clean it up and put it back to the way it was before. The highest standard of "reclamation" returned the land to the same or better conditions (at least in theory). These techniques launched a series of intensive experiments in environmental engineering. The companies needed to refill the mined holes with rock and dirt, bulldoze the terrain into rolling hills, cover them with topsoil, reseed them with a mix of grasses and shrubs, rebuild the hydrological functions, and then leave behind a revegetated ecosystem.

The coal developers shaped these early regulations to protect their interests. They worried about getting "boxed in by politicians" who might "regulate us to where we can't operate efficiently."[14] In Wyoming the operators ensured restoration fell to their oversight and discretion. The companies recovered and revegetated the coal seam only "if practicable"—that is, after they determined the feasibility of reclamation based on a cost-benefit analysis. In Montana and North Dakota the operators had to return the land to "useful production"—meaning, to some degree of revegetation for grazing or crop harvest, lakes or ponds, wildlife refuge, or recreation or industrial sites. But after a few seedings an area was considered "reclaimed" even if nothing could grow on it. To make matters worse, none of the states dealt any major penalty for failures to comply.[15]

The science behind reclamation was rough and experimental in these years. Most knowledge of reclamation came from intermittent academic studies from the 1950s and the slim contract work of the surface mine industry. There were no long-term experiments in shaping and revegetating the western lands. "We're suffering from a disease that can be terminal if it isn't controlled," said Montana rancher Carolyn Alderson, "—it's called *lackadata*."[16] The National Academy of Sciences doubted the proposition of reclamation altogether. Their report on strip mining read: "Surface mining destroys the existing natural communities completely and dramatically. Indeed, restoration of a landscape disturbed by surface mining, in the sense of recreating the former conditions is not possible." *Fortune* magazine opined that "the land might simply have to be written off."[17] "At times it seems that we are being consumed by industry," said Wyoming rancher Roger McKenzie, "while we are studying how, when, where, and even if we should be consumed."[18]

The coal companies prepared showcase plots or "reclamation sites" to demonstrate their good faith. "The people that see our reclamation are proud of it," said Albert Caskey, the foreman of Peabody Coal Company's Big Sky mine near Colstrip. "Is strip mining hurting the earth?" he asked rhetorically, "No, I don't think so. We are creating the earth. We put the earth back better than it was before. Yes, better than it was—and flatter!"[19] The region's reclamation managers experimented with grass seedlings and rock formations to provide the appearance of natural range. They told most ranchers that cattle could graze there within five years.[20] Of course, ranchers remained skeptical of feel-good corporate promises. "This is delicate country," said one ranching group from Wyoming. "The reclamation looks great—now. But after a couple of drought years and heavy grazing, it could be right back to moonscape."[21] "The point is," Montana rancher Ellen Pfister explained, "this land is so fragile, no one knows, yet, if it can be reclaimed."[22]

"It's Just Grass and Water"

Strip mining provoked controversy, in part, because ranchers on the western plains prized a particular set of connections to the grass, water, animals, and people.[23] "You were making a living off the land, off the surface," Ellen Pfister explained to me, "off the grass and the water, if you could develop it."[24] The coal companies treated the energy of the grasses as inferior to the energy of coal deposits. Most ranchers could not believe cattle ranching country and coal country could ever coexist. Any attempt to harness the region's coal energy precluded other uses of the land and water. "Mining and cows don't mix," rancher Wallace McRae put it bluntly: "Besides, we all eat grass, in the form of beef," he continued, "and there is no way we can eat coal."[25]

These surface resources mattered to these ranchers because they served their interests as capitalists. In the ranching business, cattle are the principal means for accumulating wealth. The very term *cattle*, as the historian Ted Steinberg reminds us, comes from the same etymological roots as *capital*, the common "stock of life." But cattle can only store wealth if it is properly fed on the energies stored in grass and water at the surface. "On my ranch," McRae said, "I really grow energy, that's what grasses and cows really are. Energy." He continued, "In my grass there is as much needed energy as there is energy in the coal beneath it."[26]

The control of sustainable grasslands, and the precious water supplies on which they depend, was a political enterprise. Since the heyday of the Cattle Kingdom in the 1880s, ranchers' political might grew in tandem with their control over these ecosystems. The first cattle boom (the stuff of cowboy myth and legend) brought a stampede of white men, stock, and capital onto the rangelands. The big-time cowpunchers shunted aside the thinning herds of bison and the Great Plains Indian tribes, who they stripped of their ecological homelands. Three generations of ranchers maximized their grassland holdings. They took the best lands they could find and expanded their private holdings in this inland empire by force and violence, whenever necessary. The cattlemen configured the rangeland in the most productive way possible to harness the exchange value of grass. They built an industrial ecosystem based on fossil fuels that forged the metal goods and tools that they needed to cultivate these "barren" plains for domestic and international market.[27]

The cattle barons propped up their political authority through the control over the native grasslands. The price for beef remained stubborn and low even when times were good. The ranchers expanded to keep their operations viable: they spread out their acreages and bred up Texas longhorns with barnyard stock. The hoofs, teeth, dung, and piss of the bred-up bovines remade the region's groundcover (often for the worse). As new heavy breeds fattened quickly, they thinned out the buffalo and grama grasses in vast stretches. The invasive and exotic species, like cheatgrass, propagated in its place. The Bureau of Land Management conducted a study of the grass in 1980 and recorded 170 million acres in "fair, poor, or bad condition."[28]

The ranchers in the late twentieth century ran their herds on the native grasslands that remained: western wheatgrass, green needlegrass, needle-and-thread grass, Sandberg bluegrass, and blue bunch grass. These native grasses overlaid about 60 percent of the coal reserves in the region, the most of any ecosystem. Local cattlemen boasted that their herds could be raised for market without ever seeing the inside of a feedlot. "This land, as it stands," Ellen Cotton said, "is more valuable than the coal underneath it. Cattle can grow to good weight here without needing to be fed any grain. There's hardly any other place in America like this."[29] To be sure, most ranchers fattened and flavored the cattle with grains, but the ownership of western rangeland often came second to securing what the historian Patricia Limerick calls the "property in grass."[30]

Strip mining reorganized these natural energy systems and posed drastic consequences for cattle country. The big machines uprooted the grasslands and peeled back six to twelve inches of vegetation and topsoil ("overburden"). These soils, often rich in decaying organic material and microbes, supplied most nutrients for plant growth. The big machines dumped the overburden into a mixed-mash of landfill called "spoil." These spoil banks buried surface materials under mounds of rock and dirt that had never before supported life. The haphazard treatment of the overburden destroyed the structure of the topsoil: the texture, the moisture, and the "sweetness" or "sourness" of the chemical makeup. The whole process reduced the long-term carrying capacities for livestock. As a coal company geologist put it: "To think that we can level the lands and eventually have fields of grass belly deep to a tall steer is unrealistic, of course."[31]

The ranchers worried, too, about the threat they couldn't always see: the so-called "hidden" problem of water. The sudden boom in coal strip mining hastened a new era of fierce quarrels over the possession of the region's scarce water resources.[32] The plains, even now, remain dependent on the open-course creeks and rivers of the Upper Missouri Basin. "If you don't have water to go with your grass out here," said rancher Ellen Pfister, "you may as well go to Arizona or sell the place. It doesn't work without water."[33] Whereas in Appalachia, water contributed to much of the wreckage from strip mining—the acid drainage, the erosion, the sedimentation—in the northern plains, water was scarce and the most severe problem was maintaining the hydrologic function. The region's alluvial valleys like the Tongue River valley provided the lifeblood of many ranching operations. Most ranchers worried that coal corporations might change the natural drainage patterns, causing dried-out springs and wells in some places and washouts and floods in others.

The coal seams, and some sandstone layers above them, were also the most prized aquifers in the region. They provided a kind of underground pipeline system for stores of "fossil groundwater." The Madison Aquifer, a bowl-shaped reservoir twelve thousand feet below the surface, held one billion acre-feet of water by some measures, where an acre-foot is about 325,000 gallons. The blasting of rock scrambled these geological layers of deep time and opened fissures and cracks within the coal seams that made multilayered aquifers run together. The ranchers referred to strip mining as "aquifer removal"—a permanent demolition of the precious underground hydrologic functions.[34]

On top of it all, coal companies required so much water for mining and power generation that some agricultural producers feared the sheer competition for access. The coalfields required more water to operate than half the residents of New York City. As a result, coal companies lobbied federal and state governments to reroute water courses and channels to better serve their interests.

The Bureau of Reclamation contracted with fourteen companies and promised to build them a network of aqueducts and hundreds of miles of buried pipe. The water would come from existing reservoirs and half a dozen new ones—with as much as 3.2 million acre-feet from the Yellowstone River and its tributaries alone.

What would coal companies leave behind for the rest? "If they go on strip-mining," rancher Ellen Cotton said, "they don't really know if they are spoiling our water supply." The mines already drained waterwaste into the mine pits and contaminated the runoff and polluted the ground with toxic materials. Groundwater studies found such high concentrations of minerals and sodium that the water proved to be useless for irrigating vegetation and grazing stock. The groundwater closest to the surface was often "real bad" according to rancher Digger Moravek from Wyoming. Bill Schneider, a local biologist, summarized the problem before a public hearing: "We are going ahead with strip mining without knowing positively if the land's original productively and diversity can be restored. We're involved in a game of chance without knowing the odds. Should we take the gamble?"[35]

"Lipstick on a Corpse"

The lack of certainty about the long-term prospects of reclaimed land opened the door to competing claims about the region's patterned ecology. Most ranchers argued that reclamation was impossible. They pointed to the environment and its history: earlier generations of homesteaders had sliced the native grasses and plowed up the topsoil for wheat and killed off the palatable native grasses. Almost a half-century later, the land still bore the telltale scars of their blade.[36] If a homesteader with an old plow could carve out such irrevocable damage to the native grasslands, then how did coal companies seriously propose strip mining an entire ecosystem and reassembling it without consequence? "We've been assured that the land can be restored," Bob Tully told reporters visiting his ranch, "but this mining has been going on out here since 1969, and the fact is that land hasn't been restored to the extent that a rancher can be certain it can be economically feasible to use it for agriculture again, and that's the only criterion that really counts. This kind of talk from these big mining companies really burns me up."[37]

The pride and practice of ranch work had imparted to these ranchers a sophisticated knowledge of the region's environmental history. They knew native grasses from perception and experience of craft. They grasped the sciences of botany and animal husbandry through traditions passed down and formal educations. Older ranchers schooled their sons and daughters in the practices and customs of ranch life. Many up-and-coming ranchers were also formally educated in these years, earning practical bachelor of science degrees, and with a landwise squint could discern the grazing systems and recent weather and climate patterns from the condition of the grass.[38]

Early reclamation procedures, though, offered little guidance about how to restore the surface productivity of the grass. The rancher Wallace McRae complained to state officials that there was no "assurance" that the land would return to productivity. Another rancher said reclamation "looks good" to the passerby "but the cattle won't eat it most of the year and there's no way it can [be] economically feasible as a ranch ever again."[39] "I hope we can give the nation the energy it needs," said rancher Leo Farley. "But we don't want to lose our air and water and be left with a hole in the ground."[40] The coal companies expressed their own uncertainties in private correspondence. Westmoreland Coal Company found that "within the first few years following vegetation establishment, species diversity would decline further as perennial grass species become dominant and crowd out less competitive species. This would tend to reduce livestock carrying capacity." Another corporate report read: "Successful short-term vegetation establishment does not necessarily presage long term success."[41]

The ranchers claimed that the size and growth of perennial native grasses provided the most reliable indicator of reclamation. "Native grasses are the key to whether or not the land has been restored to a balanced condition," said Bob Tully. During these postwar years range managers used the concept of "increasers" and "decreasers," based on how different plants responded to grazing. The ranchers needed plants that both thrived and withered for their long-term grazing patterns and cycles.[42] But coal companies were well aware of their limitations at seeding native grassland. So they prioritized aesthetics instead. One scientist from the University of Montana testified to a public hearing that "just because someone is able to reclaim an area for 1 year or 2 years and say, 'See, here is a nice, pretty picture, and here is vegetation that is successful,' that does not mean that that vegetation is adapted to the extremes of conditions that one could expect."[43] The "idea was they were going to plant these domesticated hay grasses on it and fertilize them and sprinkle them," rancher Ellen Pfister told me, "and it would just be better than you could ever believe. Well, it didn't really work."[44]

Some ranchers compared reclamation techniques and procedures to putting "lipstick on a corpse." The heavy inputs of fertilizer and irrigation camouflaged the ugliness: "that kind of restoration looks good now," said Bob Tully, "to someone who doesn't know cosmetic when he sees it."[45] Carolyn Alderson liked to joke about reclamation: "it's a little like a plastic surgeon saying, 'Say! With a little work, I could really make a beautiful woman out of your wife!'"[46] The rancher Ed Dobson traveled the country to present exposés of corporate malfeasance: "they don't say they hauled in 6 inches of topsoil, used 100 pounds of nitrogen per acre and 60 pounds of phosphorus and seeded with 160 pounds of seed per acre."[47]

These ranchers questioned whether reclamation officials held any true commitment to maintaining the integrity of the ecosystem. They pointed out that most reclamation took place in the high-visibility areas, and lands tucked back from the highway remained unreclaimed. The loose talk of company men also fueled the ranchers' suspicions. One executive from the Big Horn Coal Company told a reporter, "I don't know what these ranchers are hollering about anyway. This land isn't good for anything. My own personal opinion, you could give it all back to the Indians." The public relations director for Consolidation Coal Company once wrote that land in the northern plains would "be richer for having been strip mined." Another coal executive admitted outright: "You know, when it comes to reclamation, I say we can do it, and you say we can't, and when it comes right down to it, neither one of us knows what we're talking about."[48]

At best, these reclamation procedures demanded a radical simplification of the landscape. Landscape surveys and reports prepared by teams of consulting scientists, engineers, and technicians were always something of a cartographer's fiction—an audit of an environmental unit and its equilibria that had been superimposed on the natural world. These studies took little account of history: the chance that in the future, as in the past, the seasonality of rainfall, wind, temperature, humidity, seeding, and animal habits might fall below "average" and fail to reproduce the controlled variables of their studies. The very idea that industry could tear apart the earth and reassemble it ignored the ecological collisions that transpired in the process of industrial development. There was no ignoring the fundamental transformations of earth when it changed, at the industry's hands, from ecosystem to overburden.

Resource Councils

The environmental horrors in the Appalachian coalfields provided western ranchers with a vivid illustration of what could happen with unregulated strip mining. The treatment of the people and place in the eastern coalfields as the "Other America" unnerved ranchers who feared the exploitation of their own living and working environments. "We were horrified because we knew what they would do," remembered Ellen Pfister. "When I was 15, my mother took me to Pennsylvania to see my great-grandfather's farm. We got out there. It was just a pile of rubble. I thought it was a pretty awful way to treat land."[49]

The ranchers needed more than righteous indignation to stop the environmental threat of strip mining. They built new political organizations in the 1970s to safeguard their proprietary interest in these lands. They expressed urgency over the need to protect their near and close and dwelt-in places, which rose from their growing sense, like many Americans in the 1970s, that personal experiences were political. Their personal perspectives should not be belittled or insulted for their NIMBYism ("not in my backyard"). These ranchers understood their private struggles against the energy business were a collective endeavor—a last-ditch effort to save their homes and workscapes from the claws of the big machines. They organized new statewide political organizations to protect their grasses and ways of life: the Northern Plains Resource Council in Montana, the Powder River Basin Resource Council in Wyoming, the Dakota Resource Council in North Dakota.

These regional coalitions brought together an unlikely alliance of familiar foes of ranchers and environmentalists.[50] They hired young staffers that reflected the stakes of the conflict (local ranchers who had family ties in the fight and college students who had come of age in the counterculture). In fact, the chairman of the Montana Power Company, George O'Connor, said he only began to worry about the opposition when he saw "young long-haired liberals teaming up with old conservative ranchers."[51] While most ranchers weren't willing to be bossed by self-righteous young people, they recognized the need to broaden their movement.

These staff compared their early work to "putting out brush fires"—racing from one catastrophe to the next. Their political maneuvering, haphazard as it may have been, beat everyone's wildest expectations. As historian Cody Ferguson has shown, these groups expanded their membership and turned out their members for every coal symposium and public hearing in the region. They lobbied the region's probusiness "cowboy" interest groups and stockgrowers associations to endorse stronger strip-mining regulations. They built bipartisan support through motions on the floor of the state party conventions. In Montana, both the Democratic and Republican parties endorsed planks to provide "adequate protections" for landowners and proper reclamation procedures. The state's ranchers even redrafted the coal mine reclamation bill. They read through all relevant state and federal legislation and then wrote their own, which required coal companies to prepare mine plans with in-depth descriptions of premining conditions and restoration procedures. The rancher Bob Tully liked to joke that the ranchers and staffers drafted the legislation "in the proverbial smoke-filled room."[52]

The homebrewed law sealed the ranchers first taste of victory. The Northern Plains Resource Council in Montana handed legislation over to Dick Colberg, their friend in the state legislature. He was a backbencher, but like a seasoned professional, he folded the legislation almost verbatim into the preferred bill moving through the senate. Montana's strip-mining legislation, signed by Governor Thomas Judge in March 1973, became one of the strongest of such bills in the country. "It was pretty incredible what we got done," Steve Charter, an initial staffer, told me. "At the time, we didn't really appreciate what we were doing or how hard that is."[53]

The fast success in Montana spurred the expansion of rancher's "resource councils" throughout the region. Bill Barlow, a rancher from near Gillette, Wyoming, and several of his neighbors gathered at a local barn and chartered the Powder River Basin Resource Council that very year.[54] The Dakota Resource Council organized later in the 1970s and took their turn lobbying for tougher protections for landowners and the environment. Together these resource councils provided a clearinghouse of information and helped, as one rancher put it, "get the right people in touch with each other."[55]

The coal boom accelerated on the northern plains in the years that followed. The region soon began producing more coal than the northern and southern Appalachia coalfields combined. The ranchers' oppositional politics would take new forms as the years progressed. Their fortunes waxed and waned. The resource councils soon expanded their networks into environmental circles. The local chapters of the Sierra Club, local wilderness associations, the Environmental Defense Fund, the Natural Resources Defense Council, and the *Whole Earth Catalog* provided funding and support. But most ranchers, still a conservative bunch, remained leery of these outside liberals and "wild eyed, fuzzy headed environmentalists."[56]

Over time, the ranchers learned to tolerate the big environmental organizations, but they remained anchored to the basic essentials of agriculture: land, air, and water. They never forgot that the origins of coal opposition took root in the places of "overburden"—where microenvironments of grass and water bound regional identities and ways of life to the land. The sheer size and scale of these strip mines epitomized for many the disheartening spectacle of humanity living on borrowed time. The Sierra Club has bemoaned the strip mines as the "most massive industrial development of a rural area within a short period of time that has ever occurred in this country."[57] But the ranchers remained reticent about seeing themselves as anything but agriculturalists: "this doesn't make us environmentalists," wrote Bill McKay Jr., the former head of the Northern Plains Resource Council in 1978. "We're still ranchers and farmers."[58]

The story of these ranchers in their David versus Goliath fight against Big Coal provides a lesson for us all in a moment of climate uncertainty. They rooted their fight in their dwelt-in places, which provided the organizing principle for their collective action. Their grassroots politics against the big machines literally began with the grass. Perhaps only loyalty to a place, even one cast off as "overburden," can bring ornery rugged individualists together to claim collective stewardship for the Great Plains ecology.

Notes

1. Edward Abbey, "The Second Rape of the West," in *The Journey Home* (New York: Penguin, 1977), 181.

2. Robert A. Wright, "Revival of Coal Mining in Energy Crisis Divides West" *New York Times*, April 2, 1973, 55. James S. Cannon, *Mine Control: Western Coal Leasing and Development* (New York: Council on Economic Priorities, 1978), 109; National Academy of Sciences, *Coal as an Energy Resource: Conflict and Consensus* (Washington DC: National Academy of Sciences, 1977), 35.

3. In 1965 only 4 percent of U.S. coal came from Western mines. U.S. Department of Energy, Energy Information Administration, *Coal Data: A Reference* (Washington DC: Energy Information Administration, 1989), 15. On early Western mines, see Robert A. Chadwick, "Coal: Montana's Prosaic Treasure," *Montana: The Magazine of Western History* 23, no. 4 (Autumn 1973): 18–31; Richard White, *"It's Your Misfortune and None of My Own": A New History of the American West* (Norman: University of Oklahoma Press, 1991), 256–57.

4. Ben Franklin, "Coal Rush Is On as Strip Mining Spreads into West," *New York Times*, August 22, 1971, 1, 49; Thomas Bass, "Moving Gary, Indiana to the Great Plains:

The Oil Companies Head to the Prairies," *Mother Jones*, July 1976; On "energy independence" see Meg Jacobs, *Panic at the Pump: The Energy Crisis and the Transformation of American Politics in the 1970s* (New York: Hill & Wang, 2016). For "fuel of tomorrow" see quote from Lester B. Lave in Stuart Diamond, "King Coal's Bid for Comeback," *New York Times*, July 14, 1984. For "pivotal fuel" see quote from Federal Energy Administration chief John Sawhill in "Bringing Back Coal," in *Morgan Guarantee Survey* (New York: Morgan Guaranty Trust Company, July 1974). For "serfdom" of oil, see Emma Rothschild, "Illusions about Energy," *New York Review of Books*, August 9, 1973, 29–34.

5. John McNeil, *Something New Under the Sun: An Environmental History of the Twentieth Century World* (New York: W. W. Norton, 2001), 32.

6. James Hansen, "Coal-Fired Power Stations Are Death Factories. Close Them," *Guardian*, February 14, 2009.

7. There is a large literature on "strip mining" coal, mostly focused on Appalachia. See Chad Montrie, *To Save the Land and People: A History of Opposition to Surface Coal Mining in Appalachia* (Chapel Hill: University of North Carolina Press, 2003).

8. For "slow violence," see Rob Nixon, *Slow Violence and Environmentalism of the Poor* (Cambridge MA: Harvard University Press, 2013).

9. "'We Intend to Win': Rancher, Housewife, Young, Old Speak Out to Defend Their Land," *Sheridan Press*, October 26, 1972. For "workscapes," see Thomas Andrews, *Killing for Coal: America's Deadliest Labor War* (Cambridge MA: Harvard University Press, 2008).

10. This essay builds on the approach of anthropologist Tim Ingold and historian Michael Stewart Foley, who both emphasize the vitality of local politics. Ingold calls this "local ontologies of engagement" and Foley calls this "front-porch politics." See Tim Ingold, *The Perception of the Environment* (New York: Routledge, 2011), 216; Michael Stewart Foley, *Front Porch Politics: The Forgotten Heyday of American Activism in the 1970s and 1980s* (New York: Hill & Wang, 2013). This is also clear in the recent historiographic turn back to small scale and human terms among environmental historians. See, for instance, Thomas Andrews, *Coyote Valley: Deep History in the High Rockies* (Cambridge MA: Harvard University Press, 2015). Jared Diamond has argued that Montana is an example of a society living at its "eleventh hour." See Jared Diamond, *Collapse: How Societies Choose to Fail or Succeed* (New York: Viking Press, 2005).

11. Genevieve Atwood, "The Strip-Mining of Western Coal," *Scientific American* 233, no. 6 (December 1975): 23–29; Linda Branch and Christy Fischer, eds., "Coal Development: Collected Papers Volumes 1 and 2" (papers presented at Coal Development Workshops in Grand Junction CO, and Casper WY, sponsored by the Bureau of Land Management, July 1983), 1290; Daniel Philip Wiener, Joseph Mohbat, John DiStefano, and Ron Lanoue, eds., *Reclaiming the West: The Coal Industry and Surface-Mined Lands* (New York: Inform, 1980), 33, 39; Malcolm Ross, *Machine Age in the Hill* (1933; repr., London: Forgotten Books, 2016), 3; Thomas Pew, "Specter of American Wasteland," *Horticulture*, August 1977, 44.

12. Cody Ferguson, *This Is Our Land: Grassroots Environmentalism in the Late Twentieth Century* (New Brunswick NJ: Rutgers University Press, 2015), 126.

13. Ferguson, *This Is Our Land*, 126.

14. Stan Steiner, *Vanishing White Man* (New York: Harper & Row, 1976), 47.

15. Sandra Muckelston, "Strip-Mining Reclamation Requirements in Montana: A Critique," *Montana Law Review* 32, no. 1 (Winter 1971): 7.

16. National Academy of Sciences, *Rehabilitation Potential of Western Coal Lands: A Report to the Energy Policy Project of the Ford Foundation* (Cambridge MA: Ballinger, 1973), 2–3; K. Ross Toole, *The Rape of the Great Plains* (New York: Little, Brown, 1976), 148.

17. Toole, *Rape of the Great Plains*, 150; Steiner, *Vanishing White Man*, 258.

18. Steiner, *Vanishing White Man*, 254.

19. Steiner, *Vanishing White Man*, 46–47.

20. Pew, "Specter of American Wasteland," 46; Toole, *Rape of the Great Plains*, 148; Mike W. Edwards, "Should They Build a Fence Around Montana?," *National Geographic*, May 1976, 112.

21. Bill Richards, "Powder River Basin: New Energy Frontier," *National Geographic*, February 1981, 112.

22. Calvin Kentfield, "New Showdown in the West," *New York Times*, January 28, 1973, 252.

23. Wallace McRae, *It's Just Grass and Water: Poems* (Helena MT: S. Higgins Press, 1977).

24. Ellen Pfister, interview with author, Roundup MT, August 11, 2017. Notes are in author's possession.

25. Stan Steiner, *Ranchers: A Book of Generations* (Norman: University of Oklahoma Press), 119, 225; Sally Jacobsen, "The Great Montana Coal Rush," *Bulletin of Atomic Scientists* 29, no. 4 (April 1973), 39.

26. Ted Steinberg, *Down to Earth: Nature's Role in American History* (New York: Oxford University Press, 2012), 129; Jeremy Rifkin, *Beyond Beef: The Rise and Fall of the Cattle Culture* (New York: Plume, 1992), 28; Wallace McRae as quoted in Steiner, *Ranchers*, 225, 119.

27. Robert V. Hine and John Mack Faragher, *The American West: A New Interpretative History* (New Haven CT: Yale University Press, 2000), chap. 10.

28. Richard Manning, *Grassland: The History, Biology, Politics, and Promise of the American Prairie* (New York: Penguin, 1995), 133; William Cronon, *Nature's Metropolis: Chicago and the Great West* (New York: W. W. Norton, 1991), 211–13; Steinberg, *Down to Earth*, 131; Wiener et al., *Reclaiming the West*, 49.

29. U.S. Department of the Interior, Water for Energy Management Team, *Report on Water for Energy in the Northern Great Plains Area with an Emphasis on the Yellowstone River Basin* (Denver: Water for Energy Management Team, 1975), IV-8; Teresa Jordon, *Cowgirls: Women of the American West* (Lincoln: University of Nebraska Press, 1992), 96; Pew, "Specter of American Wasteland," 44.

30. Patricia Nelson Limerick, *Legacy of Conquest: The Unbroken Past of the American West* (New York: W. W. Norton, 1987), 71–72; Steiner, *Ranchers*, 119.

31. For a guide to the scientific inquiries into the ecological impacts of coal strip-mining in the northern Great Plains, review Sally Ralston, David Hilbert, David Swift, Barbara Carlson, and Lieta Mengies, *The Ecological Effects of Coal Strip Mining: A Bibliography with Abstracts* (Washington DC: Fish and Wildlife Service, U.S. Department of Interior, 1977). "Sweetness" and "sourness" are references to soil acidity; see E. Brohard, "Strip Revegetation" *Coal Age* 67, no. 3 (1962): 64–65.

32. Wiener et al., *Reclaiming the West*, 162–63.

33. Pfister, interview.

34. P. H. Rahn, "Ground Water in Coal Strip-Mine Spoils, Powder River Basin," in *Proceedings of the Fort Union Coal Field Symposium*, ed. W. F. Clark (Billings: Eastern Montana College, 1975), 3:348–61; Rick Bass, "High Plains Poison," *Sierra*, March/April 2010, 38; Janet Marinelli, "Home, Home on the Range," *Environmental Action* 12, no. 4 (October 1980), 4–11.

35. Pew, "Specter of American Wasteland," 46; Marinelli, "Home, Home on the Range."

36. Edwards, "Should They Build a Fence?," 628; Toole, *Rape of the Great Plains*, 133–35; Steiner, *Ranchers*, 228.

37. Jordon, *Cowgirls*, 98.

38. Merton J. Reed and Ronald Arnold Peterson, *Vegetation, Soil, and Cattle Responses to Grazing on the Northern Great Plains Range*, Technical Bulletin No. 1252 (Washington DC: U.S. Department of Agriculture, 1961), 24–25, 26, 42, 46; Michael Parfit, *Last Stand at Rosebud Creek: Coal, Power, and People* (New York: Dutton, 1980), 16–18; Manning, *Grassland*, 134–35.

39. Statement of Wallace McRae of Forsyth, Montana, *Environment and Mining Hearings* 51 (1973), 1566; Pew, "Specter of American Wasteland," 46.

40. Grace Lichtenstein, "For Montana Rancher, Strip Mining Has Lost the Allure of 1968," *New York Times*, April 19, 1975, 14.

41. Montana Department of State Lands, Westmoreland Resources, Inc., Final Environmental Impact Statement, Absakloa Mine, Big Horn County, Montana, December 1979, III-15, Little Big Horn College, Crow Indian Reservation, Westmoreland Papers, box 4.

42. Manning, *Grassland*, 134–35; Pew, "Specter of the American Wasteland."

43. Toole, *Rape of the Great Plains*, 148.

44. Pfister, interview.

45. Toole, *Rape of the Great Plains*, 144.

46. Kentfield, "New Showdown in the West."

47. Toole, *Rape of the Great Plains*, 144, 149; Pew, "Specter of American Wasteland," 46.

48. "Strip Mine Hearing Set," *Billings Gazette*, May 30, 1971; John Kuglin, "Divided Roundup Area Argues Strip Mining," *Great Falls Tribune*, June 19, 1971; Kentfield, "New Showdown in the West."

49. Pfister, interview.

50. Marinelli, "Home, Home on the Range," 5.

51. Anne Goddard Charter, *Four Dollars and Sixty Cents Short: The Battle of the Bulls* (Roundup MT: Stonehouse, 1993), 42.

52. Ferguson, *This Is Our Land*, 49–52.

53. Steven Charter, interview with author, Shepherd MT, August 10, 2017.

54. "Family Values: A Rancher and Her Children Take on Big Energy," *Sierra*, May/June 2006, 16.

55. Ferguson, *This Is Our Land*, 38, 48.

56. Wallace McRae as quoted in James Robert Allison III, *Sovereignty for Survival: American Energy Development and Indian Self-Determination* (New Haven CT: Yale University Press, 2015), 82.

57. Ben Franklin, "Coal Strip Mining in West Facing Obstacles" *New York Times*, March 24, 1975, 20.

58. Ferguson, *This Is Our Land*, 68.

15

Encountering Oil Cultures in a Prairie Town

JONATHAN PEYTON AND MATTHEW DYCE

Consider the strange case of August Fontana. In late 1954 he sued the government of Canada for fraud, alleging the Crown's representatives had unlawfully appropriated his entitlement to mineral oil rights on his farm. Fontana's land was adjacent to the town of Virden, about sixty miles from the North Dakota border, in the prairie wheat fields of southwest Manitoba. Fontana, an eighty-eight-year-old pensioner, had sold his 320-acre property for $9,000 to the federal government in 1940 so that the state could build an air force training facility during the Second World War. An Italian immigrant, he sold his land for "patriotic purposes" during a precarious time for the Commonwealth, as his lawyer claimed, and was told that the government did not want the mineral rights. The airfield, claimed one commentator, "gave Virden its send off towards prosperity."[1] Yet in 1954 the state sold the oil rights to Gulf Oil for $200,000. His lawyers appealed for restitution from the state, arguing largely on moral grounds, but he lost in the courts and on appeal. Fontana's case became a mini–cause célèbre in Virden, with two hundred residents signing a petition on his behalf and the local member of Parliament making a special appeal to cabinet. Fontana lost in the courts, and not long after died penniless at a hospice in town. His name was soon forgotten.

Juxtapose Fontana's curt parliamentary and juridical dismissal with the narrative built around the McIvor family. In 1881 Kenneth McIvor arrived in Manitoba direct from the Isle of Skye in Scotland. He benefited from the homesteading rules established by the Canadian state to attract just this type of settler to the recently "opened" Western interior: establish residence (six months out of every year over three years), cultivate a portion of the land, build a domicile, and the land was yours. McIvor, one of the earliest settlers to the area, worked the land well and developed a substantial and unusually prosperous farm. He grew wheat, rapeseed, and market vegetables, likely raised livestock, and was indifferent to what lay beneath his property. Three quarters of a century later, his grandsons, Hart and George, had other notions of the value of the McIvor homestead. The grandsons had learned the drilling trade and formed the McIvor Drilling Company in Alberta. During a lull in contracts, they decided to drill a shallow well on the property, which was still in the family. By accident or by hunch, Hart and George found the first flowing oil in Manitoba, touching off a sequence of events that would produce a small but persistent oil economy in the area.[2]

These stories are symbolic of the experience that many in the Great Plains endured. August Fontana's story is little different from countless others who eked out, found, and many times lost prosperity in the Canadian prairie west. In legal history, it developed precedent that provincial and federal governments held title to unsecured mineral rights, and that municipalities conversely did not own subsurface rights. In economic terms, it secured a tidy profit for Gulf Oil who began production in earnest. As local history, it helped submerge the story of August Fontana beneath other narrative layers that the town would soon embrace. Conversely, the McIvor family story is one of those just-so stories that proves the possibility of all those overnight riches narratives that oil cultures often rely upon.

Taken together they illustrate the vast gulfs that loomed between poverty and wealth in a resource frontier. Yet the stories are similar in important ways. Each describes the transition from farming to oil production, detailing the new ways that people related to the idea of wealth coming from the earth. Both families saw the complete inversion of the definition of property in the Virden area, from an aboveground agricultural economy of wheat and cereal grains to an economy based on the subsurface value of oil. In this respect, Virden in the postwar years was not unlike a host of other locations that have experienced similar inversions across the globe, where the discovery or abrupt change in the value of the physical environment is marked by the appearance of a new definition of "resource," new markets and transportation pathways, and conflicts over rights as old definitions of ownership and responsibility were replaced by new ones.

The two stories highlight the cultural and historical ambivalence wrought by extractive economies on the Prairies, and by oil in particular. In the American context, Frederick Buell has described oil stories as narratives that waver between exuberance and catastrophe.[3] In his telling, energy histories must be "entwined with changing cultural conceptualizations and representations of psyche, body, society, and environment . . . correlated not just with changing material cultures, but with symbolic cultures as well."[4]

These American oil stories, from places like Texas and Oklahoma (and now Pennsylvania and North Dakota), are stories of fantastic wealth, of "black gold" and self-made entrepreneurial triumph. But they are also stories of despair, of coastal and riparian habitats ruined, and of the individual hubris that produces oil in adversarial environments (allowing oilman Daniel Plainview in the 2007 film *There Will Be Blood* to proclaim, "I drink your milkshake!"). And, latterly, they are stories of murder, theft, and state impunity.[5] These multiple oil narratives, as characterized in the introduction to this volume, reflect increasingly polarized environmental, economic, and cultural relations. These narrative tropes also characterize the Canadian Prairies, especially in debates about the perils and possibilities of development in the oil/tar sands in Northern Alberta. Yet we argue in this chapter that smaller extractive economies, in places like southwestern Manitoba, have produced more mundane, even ambivalent, cultural feedbacks. "Oil cultures" in Manitoba are characterized less by Buell's exuberance and catastrophe than by accommodation, adaptation, small profits, ambiguous environmental legacies, and considerable state intervention.[6] We test these ambiguities with two resource "encounters": a conventional history of the development of an oil economy in Manitoba in the latter half of the twentieth century and a more detailed, speculative investigation of the oil cultures of Virden, Manitoba, the town at the center of the small provincial oil economy since the 1950s. Although we deal in this chapter with very different regional and national contexts, we find many similarities with other essays in this energy section—energy encounters produce peoples' sense of place and, even more directly, frame social relations with the natural world.

Encounter 1: A Short History of Extractive Progress

The story of hydrocarbons in Canada is often told as an Albertan story, following a narrative trajectory that builds upon early extractive failures to arrive at the "eureka" moment of the 1947 gusher at Leduc, followed by the growth of a conventional oil industry and, eventually, the successful development of the Athabasca tar sands.[7] Smaller, more localized hydrocarbon economies are often presented as adjunct or peripheral to this Albertan narrative. Yet most hydrocarbon economies, particularly on the prairies, follow a similar pattern. The southwestern corner of Manitoba has a long relationship with the oil industry, shaping the economy and working culture of the region alongside its foundational agricultural economy. Standard accounts of Manitoba oil begin in the 1950s in and around the town of Virden, but oil exploration in the province actually dates to 1877, when the first well was drilled by the Manitoba Oil Company near Dauphin. Shallow wells, drilled variously around the province's southwest, produced more geological information than actual oil. Deeper wells of up to 1,500 meters were drilled in the years between 1930 and 1950, though none produced more than small "shows."[8] Much of the early drilling was, as described disdainfully by the province's chief geologist in 1951, undertaken "on assumed structures or by non-scientific methods."[9]

In the midst of a developing exploration economy in the southwest, the provincial government passed the first oil and gas legislation in 1947, and in the same year the Brandon Exploration Company was issued the first oil and natural gas reservation numbers. Even in these early years, there were strong international ties between oil companies.[10] Prominent multinational companies had the capital to fund exploratory endeavors. This investment, as was usually the case in developing oil economies, shaped local conditions to favor industrial relations.[11] It was not the provincial or federal governments, but rather, multinational capital and expertise that pursued the first geophysical surveys in the province. The California Standard Oil Company began this practice in 1947, using seismic surveys and some gravity meter surveys to begin a sustained, scientific, and measureable exploration of Manitoba's geological endowments.[12] A few years later, in 1951, Cal Standard (parent company to the Brandon Exploration Company, and now known as Chevron) drilled the first successful commercial oil well in the province, located fifteen kilometers west of Virden, in the Williston Basin. That same year the Daly Field, located directly west of the Virden area, was proven viable for exploration, and in 1952 seventy-three successful wells were drilled.[13] New oil fields followed in quick succession: Tilston and Waskada in 1952; Virden, Lulu Lake, and Whitewater in 1953; Pierson in 1954; West Butler in 1955; and Kirkella in 1957.[14] Provincial oil production statistics skyrocketed: 11,000 barrels in 1951; 107,000 barrels in 1952; 656,000 barrels in 1953; 2,148,000 barrels in 1954; and 4,145,000 barrels in 1955.[15]

The introduction of drilling in the province kick-started a small but lucrative oil industry. In short order, Manitoba's first crude oil pipeline gathering system was installed in the Daly Field, centered on the agricultural hamlet of Cromer, which became a transportation hub for oil traveling by pipe and rail. By 1955 a total of 554 wells were producing 658,789 cubic meters of oil, and over 1,500 wells were active by the end of the decade.[16] Oil exploration and production steadily increased in the 1960s, although the number of new wells steadily decreased, presaging future difficulties. Oil production peaked in 1968 at 986,023 cubic meters, a substantial figure in an economy of Manitoba's size.[17] Yet the 1968 peak was chimerical, followed by a stagnant decade that saw the oil economy sink into entropy. Years of single- and double-digit well starts became the norm.[18] Indeed, this downturn may have been heralded by a massive spill in 1967, near the town of Glenboro, when Line 3 of the Interprovincial Pipeline failed during a pressure test, releasing over five million liters of crude oil onto the bare ground, to date the second largest "on-shore" oil spill in Canada.[19] Outside of the local context, the spill was hardly newsworthy, but for the farmers and "oilmen" of the province's southwest it was a reminder of the capricious nature of extractive economies, at once profoundly global and intensely local.

In the 1970s oil's capricious development continued. Shifting oil fortunes turned auspicious again following Shell's declaration of a deep oil find in neighboring North Dakota in 1977.[20] As a result Manitoba's oil patch, which has to a large extent followed exploration and investment patterns instigated by its southern neighbor, began attracting interest and investment from multinational energy companies. This interest peaked in 1981, with the discovery of the Lower Amaranth Formation at Waskada.[21] Manitoba's second oil boom began, with over a thousand wells drilled before the end of 1985. More robust oil and gas legislation accompanied the increase in drilling, particularly as conflict developed between local stakeholders and the companies operating in their midst. In 1983 the Manitoba Surface Rights Act created a board to mediate drilling and leasing conflicts between petroleum companies and landowners.[22] The Surface Rights Act created a legal regime for landowners to negotiate details about reimbursement, well location, and expectations from drilling companies. The act has profound limitations that revolve around what it is to be a surface-rights versus a mineral-rights owner, alongside the built-in power imbalances that put farmers and landowners in a dependent but sometimes adversarial relationship with government and oil and gas companies.

The industrial growth of the early 1980s oil boom was short-lived. This was perhaps inevitable, given the "cyclonic" nature of resource development experienced in so many Canadian resource towns and so many "boomtowns" across the continent.[23] The geopolitics of international oil economies had direct effects on the productivity of southwest Manitoba's oil fields. In the 1970s and early 1980s, OPEC (Organization of the Petroleum Exporting Countries) nations sought to manipulate oil markets by withholding production, orchestrating then record-high markets for oil through unified petroleum pricing and production in member countries. The ebb and flow of oil markets then reached a nadir in 1986, when a major market crash caused oil prices to collapse, leading to a massive glut of petroleum products, further exacerbating price decreases and corresponding production complications.[24] This 1986 crash had global repercussions, including in Manitoba's oil patch. The price of oil fell by 46 percent locally, grinding the local industry to a virtual standstill.[25] The massive decrease in oil prices meant Manitoba's industry would need time to recuperate from the oil depression. Provincial oil infrastructures were also reorganized for geographical proximity and logistical convenience at this time. The Shell Canada refinery in the St. Boniface neighborhood in Winnipeg was closed and replaced by the concentration and upgrading of facilities at Cromer, where all Manitoban oil would be collected (by truck or by pipe) and sent through the continental pipeline system to refineries in the United States or Eastern Canada.

In spite of the dour economic forecasts in the wake of the OPEC oil crisis, there was promise on the horizon for Manitoba's oil industry. In 1985 it was discovered that the Bakken Formation, more recently heralded as North Dakota's economic savior and the solution to the United States' perennial domestic energy security crisis, produced oil in the Daly Field in Manitoba.[26] The Daly Field is located in the northeastern regions of the Bakken Formation, directly west of the town of Virden, which had maintained its position as the primary oil service center in the province. The formation was large and accessible; it has been active to the present. By 1992 the Virden and Daly Fields accounted for almost 60 percent of the province's oil production. The province's eleven recognized oil fields had produced 184 million barrels of oil from 3,800 wells. It was a sizeable component of Manitoba's economy, roughly 6–8 percent in most years. Yet there was considerable scope for future development; deeper horizons had not been adequately surveyed. These deeper-lying deposits had been exploited elsewhere, and deep-drilling incentive programs would further embolden extractive economies in the province.[27]

Economic viability was at least partially explained by advances in production technology, what industrialists and oilmen like to call "innovation." Around this time the combined technologies of horizontal drilling and multistage hydraulic fracturing (fracking) were introduced in the province, importing an emblematic "brute force technology" capable of dramatically scaling-up hydrocarbon production.[28] Prior to the introduction of multistage fracking, drilling in the province was limited to subsurface depths of about 1,000 meters, primarily interventions into the Mississippian Lodgepole and Mission Canyon Formations located between 600 and 1,050 meters deep. An "oil culture" was already well-established in the region; fracking technology simply amplified its discursive weight and technological potential while underscoring the profound ambiguities that follow in the wake of oil. The new drilling technologies introduced in the 1980s allowed for much deeper drilling capabilities, while horizontal drilling allowed operators to direct wells into previously inaccessible areas.

Hydraulic fracturing is usually presented as a new technology, or as a radical improvement of existing technology, an intervention that can open up new subsurface strata for exploitation. This narrative frame reflects one of the central themes of this book, that of technological adaptation, although in this case adaptation was the result of a desire to exploit a new resource rather than a response to catastrophic events or environmental change. Adaptation implies change over time; in Manitoba, as elsewhere, the practice of fracking should be historicized. A historical approach can show both how the case for fracking as a technological adaptation develops and how the geological base of knowledge that the technology requires is produced by the state and extractive interests. The injection of pressurized solutions into wells has been practiced in Manitoba since the 1950s; it is simply the scale of the endeavor that is different. Those working in and around the oil patch often relate the likely apocryphal story suggesting southwest Manitoba was the site of Halliburton's first successful frack.[29] Modern fracking is also contingent on the geological knowledge that was being generated by the early "unsuccessful" dry wells of the 1930s and 1940s. As provincial chief geologist (and former Cal Standard managing supervisor) J. D. Allan had it,

> Petroliferous shales have been known in Manitoba for many years. Some of these shales will burn when placed on a fire, but extensive sampling and laboratory investigation by the Mines Branch, Ottawa, in 1923, indicated that the highest recovery that could be obtained by distillation was about 7.5 gallons of petroleum per ton of shale. This amount of oil could not be recovered economically at present, however, the shales could be source beds of oil which may have been driven out of them by pressure and movement into favourable reservoir structures.[30]

Allan was inadvertently anticipating modern fracking economies, hinting at the combination of technological aptitude and economic feasibility that modern oil plays require. Indeed, the particular geological conditions that allow for fracking in the modern era are often based on the haphazard collection of geological knowledge of previous nonscientific regimes. Viewed as a historical process, fracking might be framed as simply a product of the technological innovation required by the geology of that particular place. Indeed, fracking (by any other name) was common as well productivity declined in the 1960s. Oil companies operating in the major fields around Virden began to cooperate on secondary "assisted recovery operations." These companies, operating under the technical direction of Chevron, implemented the practice of "waterflooding," where water is forced into oil laden rock pores to flush the oil into the well bore.[31] Fracking has always been present in Manitoba's oil economy; it is the scale capabilities that have transformed in recent years.

Horizontal drilling ramped up Manitoba's oil production. The technology was available in the 1980s, but the real impacts of fracking were not felt until the 2000s. The production benefits of fracking technology have carried over to current drilling practices. Most of the drilling now occurs in the Williston Basin, which encompasses the Bakken Formation, connecting southwestern Manitoba, southern Saskatchewan, North and South Dakota, and Montana. Well production capabilities dramatically increased oil extraction. Horizontal wells have also proven to be more productive than vertical wells in the province, producing approximately 3.8 cubic meters per day compared to 1.91 cubic meters per day.[32] This meant Manitoba had a much larger potential, and the drilling economy was revitalized with record-breaking extraction figures the result.

In 2009 it was estimated that with fracking technology there was approximately 9.5 billion cubic meters of oil recoverable in the province. The height of the global frenzy around the new oil and gas economy in 2012 was also a record-breaking year for drilling in Manitoba with almost three million cubic meters of oil produced. This positive industrial trend continued in 2013 with 530 new wells drilled, 498 of them horizontal. The total production for the year reached just over three million cubic meters, with approximately eight thousand cubic meters of oil or over fifty thousand barrels produced each day. These drilling numbers held for a few years after the downturn that began in 2014; more recent drilling statistics have the number of new wells drilled at under 300 per year, and as low as 62 in 2016.[33]

In 2015 the price of oil fell dramatically due to several factors, not least the massive amounts of oil being produced through fracking technology domestically in the Bakken Shale and similar formations both in North America and elsewhere. In effect, the boom created by the implementation of new fracking technologies produced the conditions that have resulted in reduced prices and supply gluts, exactly the phenomena that threatens the health and capacity of the oil industry and the well-being of workers in the Bakken. The impact of the depression in price and production is being felt presently, and is evident in the communities of southwest Manitoba.[34] Oil's historical ambivalence often manifests in the present.[35]

Encounter 2: A Public History of Oil Cultures

Virden is oil country. The early years of exploration and the discovery of oil have stamped the legacy of oil production on the landscape of Virden. Visible markings of the industry's presence and history can be found throughout the region, especially in the unofficial "Oil Capital" of Virden. The local junior hockey team is the Virden Oil Capitals (official team slogan, "Powered by Energy"), while the senior team has long gone by the "Oil Kings" moniker. The senior baseball team used the comparatively simple name "Oilers," a name currently carried by all town youth baseball teams. Roughnecks and locals mix at The Oil Drop Saloon, a local watering hole. Oil companies sponsor social and education programs, the new recreation center, the annual rodeo, and the music and arts festival. Oil is central to public life.

Older vertical wells can be seen bobbing next to high-tech and high-impact fracking pads. The community identifies with its oil history, displaying the first oil pump jack outside of the Virden Tourism Information Center in the center of town. This industrial heritage pride is strengthened by the memories of many families that have worked within or have leased to the industry for generations, adding personal narratives that bolster a cultural collective identity built around oil extraction in the area. In many respects, Virden's oil culture reflects the conventions seen in any North American resource town. Yet the historical record can show ambivalences that creep through the cracks of the current regime of social license, community engagement, and corporate social responsibility.

In late 1954 it was confirmed that Virden had oil under its streets. The town was already the regional center of the provincial oil economy and had already experienced some of the economic prospects and social dislocations that accompany oil. Virden's economy had been previously built around grain, but most locals greeted the possibility of a "two-crop economy" with a cautious optimism; or at least, as one commentator had it, the notion that the town was potentially rich was "accepted philosophically" by residents as they saw "the sticky oil saturating the fertile black earth." Virdenites had "taken the boom with dignity," and many expressed a simple equanimity at oil's prospects for the town.[36] Even the mayor, challenging the image of the small town booster, suggested, "we're not counting any chickens."[37]

It was left to the oilmen to trumpet oil's potential, a potential that was embedded in the lack of geological knowledge about southwest Manitoba. For Cal Standard's man on the ground, optimism could be found in the fact that, "we are only beginning to understand how or why there is oil under Virden. . . . Manitoba has a great future in oil here for a long time." B. A. Oil's representative developed a similar rationale: "Oil potentialities in this area have only been scratched."[38] The first well within the town's limits was drilled in January 1955. In total sixteen wells were drilled, one for each legal municipal subdivision, all of them "steady producers of high grade oil."[39] By the end of March 1956, these wells had produced 250,000 barrels.[40] This drilling frenzy also produced other resources, if inadvertently, as in 1956 when drillers on the southern town limits found water instead of oil. The accidental water resource flowed from its aquifer for weeks before it was successfully harnessed and connected to municipal supplies.[41] Oil's "potential" was persistent, dragging Virdenites through the down years of the 1960s and 1970s. In Manitoba's oil patch, potential hinged equally on technology and geology. By 1979 "new seismic techniques" allowed drillers "to better pinpoint potential oil reservoirs down to 14,000 feet . . . opening up the possibility of economically draining Manitoba's remaining shallow reserves—and tapping potential resources deep beneath existing wells."[42] Potential was also contagious, helping to secure investment capital. As one economic analyst from Winnipeg suggested, "There's lots of potential—our wells are not only shallow, but there haven't been many drilled yet."[43]

Oil also produced a sense of social solidarity, largely built around the safety of gender norms, exemplified most directly by the Oil Wives Club (OWC). If the oil patch was produced as a masculine space, social relations were gendered female; the OWC "adds to the social life" of the town.⁴⁴ Formed in 1953, and active until the mid-1970s, OWC was a community service organization that developed a sense of civic engagement in a town that was growing rapidly with the ever-changing influx of itinerant oil families. OWC raised funds for local youth, service, and civic "improvement" organizations like the Boy Scouts, Cub Scouts, and Girl Guides, most notably assisting in fundraising for the new recreation and community center (recently replaced with funding from contemporary corporate oil actors). In 1956 OWC also "saved" the municipal library by fundraising and by establishing a volunteer committee to replace the librarian that, paradoxically in the midst of an oil boom, the town could no longer afford.⁴⁵

This cautious optimism was tinged with a sense of anxiety about how oil prosperity was changing the dynamics of the town. New community services were installed, thrusting Virden into modernity: water and sewer services, the community center, paved roads, newer service and industrial developments out by the new transnational highway that bypassed the town. Indeed, a keen observer today could trace Virden's oil boom in its vernacular architecture: many "downtown" buildings are constructed with the faux brick composite common to 1950s suburban and commercial buildings. The town "modernization" received mixed reactions; some residents and newcomers were excited for the aesthetic and quotidian improvements, while others lamented the fading moments of an idyllic and referential rural existence, ruing the loss of the "charm and dignity" of the old downtown shop facades.⁴⁶

Two episodes from the mid-1950s illustrate the tensions at the heart of the anxiety expressed by Virdenites. In 1955 Virden witnessed the demolition of the old livery barn, one of the first buildings erected in town. Flush with newfound oil revenues, "speculative eyes" began proposing alternative developments for the site. A hotel and a new school were mooted, before it was decided to build a two-story office block to house a host of private and government offices that had been necessitated by the boom. And, in a poetic convergence of history and present, it was decided that the stones from the barn would be used as a foundation for a new gas station and garage to be built near the highway.⁴⁷ Living amid oil was one thing, but managing it and maintaining the services of the town were another. At the same time, Virdenites were forced to contend with space in a way that they never had before. They came face to face with the impermanence of oil cultures as they struggled to deal with the problem of "trailerites," the itinerant oil families and rig workers that actually did the work of extraction. Parking in town became an issue as trailers clogged the streets, while many residents rented front and backyard space to trailers. By the later years of the 1950s, the trailer problem was so acute that the park was converted into a trailer camp, while town officials solicited the opening of a trailer court, complete with water and sewage services, on the outskirts of town.⁴⁸

Much of the anxiety was also manifest around concerns about the longevity and ephemerality of the oil economy. There was a constant tension between optimism and uncertainty in Virden. The figure of Steve Hegion is illustrative here. Hegion was one of the original oilmen in Virden, moving there in 1954, prospering as a consulting geologist through the original regional drilling campaign. But by 1961 his optimism was directed at resource diversification. He suggested that "all we need is someone to realize the area's potential": the boom years would return, but this time it would be based on salt, gravel, potash, and helium.⁴⁹ Simultaneously, in his role as president of the chamber of commerce, he was already trying to allay fears of decline through the promotion of secondary recovery programs, the prospects of further drilling, and a modernist faith in a productive future: "There are new promising areas to be explored and I know that when present wells dry up new finds will be made. That's the way it has always been."⁵⁰ In 1971 Hegion was elected mayor on a platform not based on enticing oil to the region, but rather manufacturing. An oil economy would continue, Hegion claimed, but drilling would slow because of interference from the federal government, and Virden would rebrand itself as a "satellite industrial community" to nearby Brandon. Later in the decade Hegion confirmed that Virden would never again "attain the position of an oil boom town."⁵¹ Yet the North Dakota strike of 1977 changed Virden's position once again, allowing Hegion to be "quite confident" of further drilling success in the region. The area's potential would entice drillers and investment capital, while new technologies and geological knowledge, alongside a reimagined deep-drilling royalty structure, would reinvigorate the oil economy: oil companies would "naturally drill to the lower horizons . . . there are indications of possible oil to be found at lower depths. It's quite likely they'll be drilling deeper."[52] Hegion's "possible oil" again hints at some of the tensions that oil's invisibility and impermanence brought to the community.

Oil anxieties were also marked by the fact that most Virdenites profited only modestly from oil. As one commentator had it, the "boom brings no 'killings'"; there were no oil barons, no instant millionaires, in the streets of Virden.[53] It was as though the physical signs of development could not be trusted, partly because their source could not be seen. There was massive population growth from 1,700 to 3,000 and beyond in only a few years at the outset of the boom. Yet in 1955 municipal voters rejected a tax increase to fund the construction of a new school. This may be explained by rural fiscal conservatism, but an anxiety at an uncertain oil future also appears periodically in Virden. We can read this tax rejection against the assertion in the early 1960s that Virdenites were "too busy to worry about [a] decline."[54] The middle ground between optimism and uncertainty is rich with analytical possibilities in oil histories.

The same middle ground also exposed deep-seated tensions embedded in the local vs. provincial/metropolitan dynamic that has often characterized Manitoba's social and environmental history. Anxious commentators, columnists, op-eds, and community members remarked consistently about the changing social dynamics of the town, particularly as improvement to social services lagged behind the pace of change. On top of the trailerites problem, Virdenites also had to contend with rising commercial and residential rents, an insufficient housing stock, rising prices in local stores, and persistent problems in the local school, where the rising population made it impossible to plan for student numbers, taxing the already stretched space capabilities of the school building. The influx of "young men" was also cause for concern. Mayor Dave Reid hoped to provide "proper places" for drillers and rig workers to enjoy their leisure but admitted to a lack of resources.[55] The increased population and the new industrial horizons also exacerbated pressure on existing infrastructure. The sixteen oil wells within the city limits meant that the town badly needed new fire equipment in case of an emergency, as well as new saltwater disposal systems and new regulations on protection structures for the wellheads that dotted town landscapes. Road maintenance was also a hot-button topic. Oil trucks and heavy equipment coursed directly through town. Dust was thick through town in the summer months, regional roads were often disheveled, and some residents took to oiling the roads themselves before paving programs were established.

The socioeconomic and infrastructure issues that followed oil into Virden were aggravated by the fact that the town itself could not pay for solutions. Royalties from oil were not all collected by the municipal government, as a complex property regime determined before the advent of the oil economy meant that the province held a large percentage of the oil revenues, even those earned from oil directly under Virden's streets.[56] The municipality also could not tax many of the oil newcomers, because they were not permanent residents, or because they lived in "unofficial" housing like trailer camps or front yards. Yet the municipality was responsible for providing all services to both locals and itinerant workers. This question of taxation, responsibility, and jurisdiction lies at the heart of the historical ambivalence around oil in the Virden area. In June 1955 this ambivalence came to a head, where the standard complaint became that the province got all the money, while the town had to pay for services. As one commentator put it, amid the plenty of an oil economy, "Virden has become the beggar, eating the crumbs that fall from the rich man's table."[57]

Conclusion: All That (Historically) Glitters . . .

The ambivalence that surrounds the development of oil is revealing in Virden. The cultural geography of the landscape represents oil as an everyday feature of Virden. It is built into the very fabric of the town—parks overseen by decommissioned derricks, the hockey team "Oil Capitals," and golfers who must play around a pump jack hazard (right between the first and third fairway) before they can retire for a drink at The Oil Drop Saloon. Virdenites engage the landscape to develop a regional narrative that equates oil with progress, permanence, and wealth. The contemporary boom in fracking (which has been destabilized in recent years) is persistently read through oil as a story about the value and inevitability of a "boom," one that will produce a hydrocarbon security that will take Virden back to prosperity or bring new connections the town desperately needs. Old-timers that remember the "mosquito-like oil pumps [that] suck wealth from the ground" may harbor nostalgia for those halcyon oil days of the 1950s.[58]

Yet we insist that a careful revisiting of the history of oil in Canada and an analysis of its arrival in Virden reveals anything but a stable process. Rather, the oil boom brought disparities of wealth and poverty, raised uncertainty about ownership and the provision of services, and upset the social fabric of place, requiring people to make new choices about the meaning of their town. Anxiety about the socioeconomic influence of itinerant communities, concerns about moral degradation, and the legal wrangling between locals and international capital that characterizes the fracking economy in North Dakota and southwest Manitoba is conditioned powerfully by the previous oil exploration encounters. Out of the wells flowed not only wealth and opportunity, but new kinds of social relationships, new stories about the town. As the inversion of the landscape, oil replaced the permanence of wheat—making it "historical"—and assuming the regularity and assurance attributed to the meaning of that resource. The contemporary fracking boom in Manitoba thus relies on an imaginary historical geography created by oil, one that sees petro-capitalism reassuring itself of its permanence and stability. As one local wag had it on the eve of Virden's entry into the oil economy, "Oil is a city slicker come to town. It may be all right. It may slip out tomorrow taking all the money and leave only shattered dreams."[59]

Notes

1. Peter Hendry, "Prosperity Changes the Face of a Town," *Winnipeg Tribune*, June 26, 1953.
2. J. G. Cowan, "Manitoba's Black Gold," *Canadian Geographical Journal* 53 (September 1956): 84–93.
3. Frederick Buell, "A Short History of Oil Cultures: Or, the Marriage of Exuberance and Catastrophe," *Journal of American Studies* 46, no. 2 (May 2012): 273–93.
4. Buell, "A Short History of Oil Cultures," 273.
5. David Grann, *Killers of the Flower Moon: The Osage Murders and the Birth of the FBI* (New York: Doubleday, 2017).
6. The designation "oil cultures" is prevalent in the developing field of energy humanities. See Ross Barrett and Daniel Worden, eds., *Oil Culture* (Minneapolis: University of Minnesota Press, 2014).
7. The literature on the history of oil in Canada is surprisingly small, but see Paul Chastko, *Developing Alberta's Oil Sands: From Karl Clark to Kyoto* (Calgary: University of Calgary Press, 2004). Those looking for a more comprehensive treatment of Canada's energy history should consult Ruth Sandwell, ed., *Powering Up Canada: The History of Power, Fuel and Energy from 1600* (Montreal: McGill-Queen's Press, 2017).
8. J. Donald Allan, "Exploration for Oil and Gas in Manitoba," *Canadian Oil and Gas Industries* 4, no. 6 (June 1951): 34.
9. Allan, "Exploration for Oil and Gas in Manitoba," 33.
10. Paul Chastko, "Anonymity and Ambivalence: The Canadian and American Oil Industries and the Emergence of Continental Oil," *Journal of American History* 99, no. 1 (2012): 166–76.
11. For a sustained discussion of the transnational movements of technology, labor, geological knowledge, and extractive expertise in development energy economies, see the chapters in Joseph Pratt, Martin Melosi, and Kathleen Brosnan, eds., *Energy Capitals: Local Impact, Global Influence* (Pittsburgh PA: University of Pittsburgh Press, 2014).
12. Pratt, Melosi, and Brosnan, *Energy Capitals*, 34.
13. Andrew Galarnyk, *Oil in Manitoba*, Mineral Education Series (Winnipeg: Department of Mines and Natural Resources, 1987), 6.
14. Galarnyk, *Oil in Manitoba*, 6.
15. Cowan, "Manitoba's Black Gold," 91.
16. Galarnyk, *Oil in Manitoba*, 6; "Manitoba 2008 Oil Activity Review," in *Seventeenth Williston Basin Petroleum Conference* (Regina: Saskatchewan Ministry of Energy and Resources, April 26–28, 2009), 26–28.
17. Galarnyk, "Oil in Manitoba," 7.
18. "Manitoba 2008 Oil Activity Review," 31–32.
19. Sean Kheraj, "The Biggest Oil Pipeline Spills in Canadian History," ActiveHistory, July 23, 2015, http://activehistory.ca/2015/07/the-biggest-oil-pipeline-spills-in-canadian-history/.

20. Julia LeFever, "History of Oil Production in the Bakken Formation, North Dakota," in *Guidebook to Geology and Horizontal Drilling of the Bakken Formation* (Billings: Montana Geological Society, 1991), 3–17.

21. Harvey Young, "Mining and Extractive Industries in Manitoba," in *The Geography of Manitoba: Its Land and Its People*, ed. John Welsted, John Everitt, and Christian Stedel (Winnipeg: University of Manitoba Press, 1996), 246.

22. Manitoba Petroleum Branch (2015). http://www.gov.mb.ca/iem/petroleum/.

23. See, for instance, Arn Keeling, "'Born in an Atomic Test Tube': Landscapes of Cyclonic Development at Uranium City, Saskatchewan," *Canadian Geographer* 54, no. 2 (2010): 228–52; Arn Keeling and John Sandlos, "Environmental Justice Goes Underground: Historical Notes from Canada's Northern Mining Frontier," *Environmental Justice* 2, no. 3 (2009): 117–25.

24. Robert Mabro, "OPEC and the Price of Oil," *Energy Journal* 13, no. 2 (1992): 1–17; Timothy Mitchell, *Carbon Democracy: Political Power in the Age of Oil* (New York: Verso Books, 2011).

25. Galarnyk, "Oil in Manitoba," 14.

26. Young, "Mining and Extractive Industries in Manitoba," 246.

27. Young, "Mining and Extractive Industries in Manitoba," 249.

28. Mary Agnes Welch, "Fracking on the Rise in Manitoba," *Winnipeg Free Press*, July 2, 2013; Mary Agnes Welch, "Manitoba Oil Patch Top Polluter," *Winnipeg Free Press*, September 16, 2013. Fracking involves the injection of fluids—water, a proppant (usually silica sand), and a proprietary mixture of chemicals—under massive pressure to break or "fracture" shale, releasing oil and gas that is collected at the surface. For an extended illustration of "brute force technologies," see Paul R. Josephson, *Industrialized Nature: Brute Force Technologies and the Transformation of the Natural World* (Washington DC: Island Press, 2003).

29. The company claims its first frack occurred simultaneously in Oklahoma and Texas in 1949. See http://www.halliburton.com/en-US/ps/stimulation/fracturing/default.page.

30. Allan, "Exploration for Oil and Gas in Manitoba," 35.

31. Jean L. Whiteford and Edith A. Moody, eds., *Virden Review 1957–1970* (Brandon MB: Leech, 1970), 44.

32. Manitoba Petroleum Branch (2015). http://www.gov.mb.ca/iem/petroleum/.

33. Manitoba Petroleum Branch (2020). https://www.gov.mb.ca/iem/petroleum/stats/index.html.

34. Bartley Kives, "Oil-Industry Slowdown in Manitoba," *Winnipeg Free Press*, July 25, 2015; Welch, "Fracking"; Brian Zinchuk, "Manitoba Expects Significant Decline in Activity: Drilling Down Substantially," *Pipeline News*, June 8, 2015, http://www.pipelinenews.ca/features/drilling-exploration/manitoba-expects-significant-decline-in-activity-1.1953491.

35. Those interested in the social and environmental relations produced by fracking in Manitoba should see Kaela Mae Hlushko, "Fracking Futures: Political-Ecological

and Socioeconomic Realities in Southwestern Manitoba's Oil Field" (master's thesis, University of Manitoba), 207.

36. Frank Rutter, "V-Day at Virden—Black Gold in the Streets," *Winnipeg Tribune*, December 22, 1954.

37. "Virden's Wallet: 16th Well Drilled," *Winnipeg Tribune*, November 2, 1955.

38. Quoted in "Virden's Wallet."

39. "Virden's Luck," *Winnipeg Tribune*, December 1956.

40. Cowan, "Manitoba's Black Gold," 92.

41. "$3,000 Down Drain," *Winnipeg Tribune*, December 15, 1956.

42. Marianne Tefft, "Virden's Oil Again Pulls Well-Drillers," *Winnipeg Tribune*, August 10, 1979.

43. Quoted in Tefft, "Virden's Oil."

44. Mrs. Ewen MacDonald, "Nomadic Housewife Says: It's No Longer a 'First-Name Town,'" *Winnipeg Tribune*, October 23, 1954.

45. "Saved by the Belles," *Winnipeg Tribune*, May 24, 1956; Anne Anderson, "Town's Active Oil Widows Help Virden and Have Fun," *Winnipeg Tribune*, October 21, 1955.

46. "Doesn't Look the Same: Mixed Feelings Greet Virden Modernization," *Winnipeg Tribune*, June 18, 1955.

47. Anne Anderson, "'Sore Thumb' Clears Way for Progress," *Winnipeg Tribune*, April 19, 1955.

48. Anne Anderson, "Parking Space Is a Big Problem for Trailerites," *Winnipeg Tribune*, April 13, 1954.

49. "New Resources Could Spur Virden's Growth," *Winnipeg Tribune*, March 13, 1961.

50. Jim Hayes, "Virden People Too Busy to Worry about Decline," *Winnipeg Tribune*, December 19, 1961.

51. "Virden Boom Rated Unlikely," *Winnipeg Free Press*, 1979.

52. Paul Moloney, "Major Manitoba Oil Find 'Coming,'" *Winnipeg Free Press*, September 14, 1979.

53. "Boom Brings No 'Killings,'" *Winnipeg Tribune*, October 23, 1954.

54. Hayes, "Virden People Too Busy."

55. Dave J. Reid, "We Still Want More Industry," *Winnipeg Tribune*, October 23, 1954.

56. "Poor Little Rich Girl," *Winnipeg Tribune*, January 7, 1955.

57. Anne Anderson, "Virden's Oil: Does It Enrich the Province—but Impoverish the Town?," *Winnipeg Tribune* June 18, 1955.

58. "Boom Brings No 'Killings.'"

59. "Boom Brings No 'Killings.'"

16

Blows Like Hell
The Windy Plains of the West

JULIE COURTWRIGHT

Ferdinand Van Ostrand, New York native and nineteenth-century western trading agent, hated the Great Plains wind. Actually, hate was entirely too mild a word. He *loathed* the Great Plains wind. He obsessed over it, cursed it, taunted it, and assigned it its own malevolent personality. Stationed at Fort Berthold in northwestern Dakota Territory, beginning in 1869, Van Ostrand had ample occasion to nurse his hostility, and to purge into his diary. "After we left there the wind came up and blew like h—l and still does," he wrote in April. In May: "Windy as the d—l"; August: "This is the windyest [*sic*] place I have ever struck—an opinion which I formed a long time ago"; September: "the wind has blown spitefully all day"; October: "Since about 10 a.m. the wind has blown fearfully and the dust has choked and blinded everyone. Tonight is dark and tempestuous"; March: "These infernal high winds . . . favor us with their manifold discomforts. . . . A description of the weather for one day answer[s] for all [just] about, windy. . . ."

A practical as well as emotional problem, the wind often affected life and work at the fort. Storms ripped the roofs off of barracks and destroyed other property. Daily wind was sometimes so powerful that it interfered with river crossings and forced boats to make detours or alternate landing plans. Cold wind chilled sleeping quarters while hot wind shriveled vegetable gardens. In October 1871 the men, irked by their constant daily exposure, unofficially renamed their fort in the wind's honor. Fort Berthold became "Fort Blowhard." They even carved the new name on a log at the camp's edge, identifying to all who entered the most troubling environmental feature of the northwestern plains. "We give witness to the fact that it is no misnomer," the trader concluded of his newly christened home. Less than two years later, an early and unexpected death from pneumonia granted Van Ostrand permanent solace from the relentless gales that haunted him. His colleagues sent his body back to the less blustery East for burial.[1]

Although the beleaguered New Yorker believed North Dakota gales to be absent of redeeming qualities, they are, in fact, a nuanced environmental force, capable of shaping human lives, economies, thoughts, and cultures in a variety of complex ways. Wind has meaning. It comes from somewhere else and links humans to the rest of the world—often the first and most automatic way to connect with unseen places. It brings smells and sounds and shapes from over the horizon and a way to feel something that is *beyond*.

The human/wind connection is current but also historical. Because people in the past also felt and interpreted wind, it unites us with a different *beyond*—across time as well as geography. Much like today, wind tormented and fascinated people in the past. It inspired stories, shifted economies, soothed the frightened, and terrified the vulnerable. Human interactions with the wind, as with other regional environmental characteristics, helped cultivate a sense of place, a familiar attachment, or even an innate *knowing* of a space, a knowledge more sensory than overtly intellectual. As an intellectual topic, the study of wind traditionally falls under the purview of meteorologists and other scientists, but the secularization of nature, as historian Dan Flores noted, has caused us to neglect the gamut of meaning within the natural world in favor of compartmentalizing it as a collection of resources. Wind is at the forefront of discussions about current and future energy, but in its uncompartmentalized entirety wind has a past and a present that is more than scientific or economic, two of the most common ways that scholars connect humans to environment. "Our reactions to landscape," Flores concluded, "have also been aesthetic, creative, mythic, and entirely sensual."[2]

Studying human reactions to landscape places wind in historians' wheelhouse, particularly those intent on using the senses as a way to access history. As they do today, touch, sight, smell, hearing, and taste guided human action and emotion in the past. As sensory historian Mark M. Smith has intuited, "The history of the senses ... urges us to think expansively about the past and helps explain not only why we know what we know but why we do not always understand as fully as we might why we know what we know."[3] In other words, sensory history helps explain why *feeling* the wind (in both a literal and emotionally intelligent way) connects humans to the Great Plains.

The history of wind, therefore, is more than a history of an energy resource or a transporter of dust in the 1930s.[4] Wind is energy with nuanced meaning that shapes human lives, both literally and figuratively. It is powerful but simultaneously intangible and ephemeral. It is relief and danger, sustaining and devastating. It is movement—almost (but not quite) intangible mobility—that transcends the turning of wind turbines, which, while vital, are just one part of the story. Wind is not *on* the plains but is *above* the plains and even *encompasses* the plains. Wind is energy that humans not only harness but experience. It blows over fields, aids in transportation, assists evolution, shapes architecture, shifts politics, and contributes to human identity. Wind is powerful in so many ways.

Of the thirty-four windiest places in the United States, according to data compiled between 1984 and 2015 by the National Oceanic and Atmospheric Administration (NOAA), twenty-one, or 61 percent, are on the Great Plains. These include cities on the high plains—like Amarillo, Texas, or Cheyenne, Wyoming—as well as more eastern tallgrass places such as Wichita, Kansas, and Fargo, North Dakota. Locations also span the length of the region, with the northern, central, and southern plains all represented. Windiest locations not on the plains are, with only two exceptions, coastal or island cities. Alaska is the most heavily represented state, giving the Northwest six slots on the top thirty-four list. The South claims two slots, both in coastal Texas, while the Southwest, Northeast, and Midwest take one each. Finally, Hawaii, in the Central Pacific, claims two windy locations. The Great Plains, however, with twenty-one cities on the list, far outpaces any other section, making it the windiest region in the country.[5] In Dodge City, Kansas, named the windiest city more than once by the National Climatic Data Center in North Carolina (now NOAA), citizens claimed that "newcomers are rather astounded by it, [but] old-timers take it in stride." Wind in Dodge is a "way of life."[6]

This windy existence is also a constant source of curiosity to those traveling through the region, yet another indicator of the force's authority. Visitors *notice* the Great Plains wind. In August 2012 a blogger did a study of words associated with each of the fifty states. Using Google, she tracked the top four most common words searched when linked with individual state names. "Windy" was the number one word associated with Kansas, Montana, South Dakota, and Wyoming. It ranked number two in Oklahoma, Nebraska, and Minnesota, number three in New Mexico and North Dakota. Of the states that touch the grassland, only in Colorado, Texas, and Iowa did "windy" not make the top four. Perhaps even more significant, the term made the top four in nine out of twelve Great Plains states—core or peripheral—but nowhere else. "Windy" did not make the top four searched terms in any other state outside the region.[7] According to these results, Google users associate wind with the Great Plains just as heavily as NOAA and the old-timers of Dodge City. On July 6, 2013, Ree Drummond (a.k.a. The Pioneer Woman), popular blogger and native Oklahoman, sent a brief observation to her followers via Twitter: "Oklahoma is windy. Times a thousand."[8]

All this wind has great potential as a source of sustainable energy, and historians who have worked on wind have focused on the technological ins and outs as well as the controversy over and benefits of wind power.[9] Great Plains peoples, however, have contended with the near incessant blowing and shared their history with it for as long as humans have lived in the place. The human-wind connection stretches back long before the area became home to the largest regional concentration of wind turbines (over twenty-five thousand) in the country.[10] A shared history means that regional identity and the value of place are inexorably tied to wind. A near perfect wind environment, with few trees and even fewer topographical impediments, the Great Plains wind is special. Ask anyone who has ever lived there, or just stopped for gas along I-70. As early as 1857 an Omaha, Nebraska, writer, reporting on a town fire in March, noted that when the blaze started "the wind was blowing at the time, as only a Nebraska wind can blow."[11]

Even the tools of wind energy conversion are far older than the current turbine debate and are contributors to plains identity. Windmills have dotted the landscape since Euro-American settlement began, and beyond their practical uses, served as a visible touchstone within the big space—a bit of vertical in a horizontal landscape. Windmills, fastened to the earth while spinning in the sky, simultaneously announced in the nineteenth century up to the present day, "I am here," and "this place is energetic and mobile." Because windmills brought much-needed water to the surface, they were a key technology that helped Great Plains peoples survive and succeed in an unpredictable climate. They did so by utilizing a plentiful resource (wind) to provide a scarce one (water).

Wind is a dominant characteristic of the Great Plains region, a part of people's stories. It has been a resource and a hindrance, its potential to do both harm and good debated long before the twenty-first century. More than an energy source, daily wind and crisis wind were and are a critical part of regional identity, a ubiquitous presence, the meaning of which shifts from moment to moment depending on circumstance, adaptation, and viewpoint. The import of wind, in fact—its contribution to sense of place and the emotional and sensory weight it carries—is every bit as volatile and intangible as the force itself. Wind's journey through history, and plains peoples' interactions with it, is an important way to connect the plains environment and its future with its past.

While American Indians, long familiar with the region's wind, included it in religion and lore, newcomer settlers of the mid-nineteenth century also realized the ubiquitous presence and strength of the force quite early.[12] The plains hosts an enormous

FIG. 24. An Aermotor windmill pumping water into a reservoir in Finney County, Kansas, ca. 1895. Kansas State Historical Society.

variety of winds, from powerful straight-line, blisteringly hot, numbingly cold, dusty, and tornadic winds to daily wind—so prominent that newly settled residents wrote to warn others back east that they should literally brace themselves against the gales and "make up their minds to stand a great deal," if they thought they wanted to live in the region.[13] In 1855, near the beginning of the Euro-American migration into Kansas, the editor of the *Herald of Freedom* observed that "the only objection we have found to the climate in Kansas, thus far, is the heavy winds." The winds might blow in Pennsylvania and Ohio too, the editor continued, but in Kansas "it occurs oftener, and is longer protracted." An early settler in droughty, flat, grasshopper-infested, prairie fire-plagued Kansas, therefore, noticed the *wind* before any other environmental characteristic for which the territory later became known. After two more months of experience, the editor was ready to "confess that we have felt more inconvenience from the wind and dust, since our arrival in Kansas, than from any other source." Settlers who could not handle the inconvenience, or find ways to deal with it, "will go out of the Territory complaining it is the worst climate they ever knew."¹⁴ W. E. Lovejoy, riding into Dakota in 1878, observed that it was not settlers, but the wind itself, a "fierce northwest zephyr," that, to him, "seemed in an awful hurry to get out of the country." Lovejoy's first impression of Dakota Territory, therefore, was not its vastness, nor its agricultural potential, but its fast and furious wind.¹⁵

Along with the Kansas editor's irritation, Lovejoy's astonishment, and Van Ostrand's anger, the blowing inspired other emotions. The dime novel publisher, Erastus Beadle, on an adventure trip to the central plains, thought the wind unsettling. He wrote a letter to his children, telling them he was truly on the "wild prairie," where "the wind blows a hurricane and shakes this frail cottonwood building, creeping in to every crevice, rattling my paper as I write."¹⁶ In 1855 a Kansas Territory booster admitted feeling lonely as he lay in his bed, listening to the sound of the wind outside his cabin.¹⁷ Mary Dyck of Hamilton County, Kansas, in a Dust Bowl diary that features wind, or its rare (and therefore notable) absence in nearly every entry, assigned emotion not to herself, but to the crying outside. "Wind howled today[.] It sounded very sad," she wrote in June 1937.¹⁸ Still other writers found pleasure, or even comfort from the wind's sound. A newspaper writer fondly called the wind "a musician at birth" that finds a crevice in a window, "sighs over it and goes up and down the scale upon it."¹⁹

Writers publishing beyond newspapers, Twitter (in the case of blogger Ree Drummond), and their own letters and diaries have used the wind to tell their sensory stories about the Great Plains. Willa Cather, in *My Ántonia* (1918), perfectly captured the relentlessness and majesty of the Nebraska wind's sound. In spring, "the wind shook the doors and windows impatiently, then swept on again, singing through the big spaces," while in winter it "moaned over the prairie." While singing, moaning wind served as a long-term agent of erosion on rock and dirt—witnessed by Mary Dyck during the Dust Bowl of the 1930s—Cather focused on its temporary, and more beautiful, visual effect. "All about us the snow was crusted in shallow terraces, with tracings like ripple-marks at the edges," she wrote, "curly waves that were the actual impression of the stinging lash in the wind."[20] On a landscape that observers frequently described as "empty," the wind made its mark, a force so influential that it imprints itself onto the landscape in both fleeting and enduring mediums.

Although not technically a native, Cather knew Great Plains wind and incorporated it into her work. Perhaps the novel most overtly tied to the perception of Great Plains wind, however, was Dorothy Scarborough's 1925 book *The Wind*, which caused a historical storm following its publication. The main human character in the book is Letty Mason, representing all women forced to be pioneers, and the hardships they encountered on the plains. At the beginning of the novel, Mason moves from Virginia to Texas, where she encounters The Wind, a fully developed antagonist in the story, a demon intent on driving Mason insane.[21] Often credited as one of the first novels to depict negative features of the American West, *The Wind* revolves around themes like boredom and deprivation, and, as Scarborough wrote in her first sentence: "the wind was the cause of it all." Winds were "the enemies of women," cruel and unrelenting, "trying to wear down their nerves by attrition, and drive them away. . . . How could a frail, sensitive woman fight the wind?" It was, Scarborough wrote, her "demon lover."[22]

Scarborough's emphasis on the reaction of *women* to the wind reflected a well-established trope in Western history and myth. Because of their supposed fragility, women who lived on the harsh plains were thought to be more susceptible to insanity than men. Their minds and sensitive natures could not tolerate the open, treeless, monotonous, and above all, windswept, environment, and they simply broke down. "The wind *alone* drove some to the verge of insanity and caused others to migrate in time to avert the tragedy," historian Walter Prescott Webb argued in 1931.[23] Scarborough used a long-established and biased assumption about the way women reacted to the Great Plains to advance her story, and, in the process, reinforced for the book's readers not only the influence of the wind on the emotional health of residents, but its status as a force that only plains insiders—largely male—could understand and combat. Hardened (read less feminine) plains women might stand a chance against the wind, but weak outsiders, especially female, such as Letty, were no match.

While gender issues are the obvious point of analysis for modern readers of *The Wind*, it was, interestingly, not that subject that concerned early twentieth-century Texans. Because Scarborough's book was originally published anonymously, and because it portrayed West Texas as a harsh, unforgiving, environment, readers assumed that *The Wind* had been written by an outsider. They considered it a "brutal and unwarranted attack . . . on the land they loved." West Texans launched a hate campaign against the book and its unknown author, teasing out supposed historical errors, claims of geographical and cultural ignorance, and even "incorrect cowboy lingo." Scarborough refuted the attack, first anonymously and then openly. She argued that her book was a novel, not history, and therefore need only capture the "essential truth," as opposed to actual truth, of a place. In 1928 Metro-Goldwyn-Mayer turned *The Wind* into a movie starring Lillian Gish. To recreate Scarborough's version of the Texas wind, movie makers used eight airplane propellers to blast sand and sulfur onto Gish, who called the job "one of my worst experiences in film making."[24]

Both Scarborough, a Great Plains native at birth, and Cather, a nonnative who *became* native through experience and reflection, understood the region, in part, through the wind. Both women, long before they wrote about the force, felt, smelled, tasted, heard, and saw it, so that for them, and for all Great Plains peoples, the wind felt like home, for better or for worse. On his first day after moving to Oklahoma, a newcomer encountered a gas station employee who asked him if he had found a house to live in that had a hole in it. "Why?" inquired the newcomer. "So you can stick a crowbar through the hole to test the wind," the Oklahoman advised. "If the crowbar only bends, it's safe to go out. If it breaks, you better stay in."[25]

Although daily wind is a long-term trial, it is crisis wind that garners headlines on the plains, and because it causes the most drama, it most obviously influences culture. Storms, winter blizzard and spring thunder alike, amazed historical residents with their wind-driven power, and the resultant property damage and cost in human life reinforced the impression. Spring on the Great Plains is tornado season, the storms so prominent, the watches and warnings so familiar, the anniversaries of historic past storms so well-known, that the experience has become part of the place. Jokes fly about seasoned plains people who treat stormy nights as lawn chair entertainment, but the possibility of total destruction is always there, the unimaginable, yet possible, fueling the nervous energy and the laughs. "The tornado predicted for Sheridan to-day fails to materialize so we live on," joked Edith Clark of Wyoming in 1913.[26]

Euro-American tornado culture on the plains originated in the nineteenth century, when newcomers confronted the large numbers of twisters that formed on the grasslands and quickly realized, as one Kansas writer did in 1881, that "cyclone caves" were more necessity than luxury.[27] In 1887 a group of Women's Christian Temperance Union ladies gathered on a lawn in David City, Nebraska, for a party, when a tornado moved through the area. "Several of them were picked up by the wind and carried short distances," the news reported, although they were not seriously injured. "All is confusion and no reliable news," concluded the journalist about the rest of the town's fate.[28]

Rumors, stories, misinformation, and an inability to predict the storms added to the uncertainty. An out-of-season tornadic storm hit Wichita, Kansas, in October 1894, destroying thirty houses and barns and uprooting hundreds of trees. "For twenty years Wichita has felt easy about tornadoes," the press noted, "on account of an Indian legend, which said none ever visited or would visit us."[29] Fear of possible death and destruction from a tornado inspired plains residents to invent myths that explained why the places they lived were protected from the twisters. At Wichita two rivers came together, which somehow safeguarded the city. At Topeka, Kansas, Burnett's Mound, a hill on the southwest side of town, split the winds and prevented tornadoes from entering the city. Added to this myth was a story about several Potawatomie Indians who were killed by a tornado and buried at the base of Burnett's Mound. Thereafter, the Great Spirit protected the area from tornadoes. On June 8, 1966, Topeka's Burnett's Mound myth took a hit (so to speak) when an F5 tornado crossed the mound, demolished parts of the city, and killed eighteen people.[30]

Tornadoes are more common on the central and southern plains than they are in the north, but the odds went against Fargo, North Dakota, on June 20, 1957, when a massive tornado "smashed" the northern part of the city, killing at least eight people, five of whom were children from the same family. Because the storm struck early on a summer evening, daylight afforded a better than average view of the funnel. "First it was just a swirl of dust and leaves—then everything began to fly," said Dr. R. M. Slominski, who rode out the storm on his basement floor with his wife and four children. When he emerged, Slominski said, he could not believe what he saw—destruction everywhere, and "not a tree standing, most snapped by the swirling wind at a four-foot height." At some point the tornado on the ground lifted back into the air and resumed its status as a funnel. Victims could see it off to the east for at least thirty minutes longer, a "snake of wind mov[ing] slowly away."[31]

Although an ill-advised tradition, tornado culture indicates to some modern plains residents that because they are experienced plainsmen, they must not capitulate to fear and take shelter in their basements or other protected rooms. In the early days of settlement, the best wind-protected houses on the plains were, conveniently, those made of readily available sod, which were the least drafty. After learning about the intensity of regional wind, those in the know advised that people should continue to live in their sod structures until sawmills could provide boards that could be fitted together tightly enough to keep the wind out.[32] Even after frame houses began to replace sod or dugout, families still used their old houses as storm shelters. Because people were frightened of cyclones, houses with "storm caves" were more desirable than those without and brought a higher rent.[33] Even during his first March (the windiest month) in Kansas, the editor of the *Herald of Freedom* promoted a particular type of roofing "for use in localities much exposed to the wind. It is durable, and must come into general use in Kansas."[34]

In addition to speed and turbulence, wind temperature shaped lives, emotions, economies, and landscapes. One cold night in November 1860, the *Omaha Nebraskian* aptly described the north wind as "keen as a razor and cold as an ice-berg."[35] In the cold, wind can make the difference between death and life. A notable example is the "Children's Blizzard" of January 12, 1888, which killed almost three hundred Nebraska and Iowa children on their way home from school due to its sudden onset and extreme wind chill. "Cold . . . can kill without wind," author David Laskin wrote of the tragedy, "but it takes longer."[36]

Hot winds are particularly destructive to agriculture on the plains and prairies and are frequently linked to crop failure. In 1878 an optimistic plains booster argued that "hot winds of the early years," while admittedly an initial serious drawback to plains agriculture, had gone the way of the drought and would no longer be a problem. As rain followed the plow, an old theory that claimed plowing land would create a wetter climate, excessive moisture would negate the wind's effects, and farmers had nothing more to fear.[37] As with myths that reassured believers of their safety from tornadoes, plains peoples desperately wanted promises that hot winds, which could be every bit as destructive as other forms of crisis wind, would not hurt them, a yearning based more on emotion than intellect. The booster's 1878 claims about the disappearance of hot winds would doubtless have come as a shock to later farmers like Mrs. John Dorchester, who, with her husband, watched their corn and cotton wilt in 1911. In 1894 Carrie Gable and her husband left Nebraska and settled in Oklahoma, where they expected to grow corn as they had up north. That first year, however, several days of hot winds burned them out just as the crop reached the roasting ear stage. "My plans for canning a lot of corn were blasted," Gable said of the southern plains wind. The couple was forced to reevaluate their future farm plan as a result.[38]

Of course during the 1930s, wind and dust were always on farmers' minds. Western Kansas landowner Ray Garvey, living in Wichita, exchanged hundreds of letters with his farm manager and partner, John Kriss, near Colby, during that decade. Handling a mammoth wheat operation like G-K Farms in the midst of the Dust Bowl required an endless exchange of ideas and plans. Wind was at the center of virtually every agricultural problem the men experienced. Not surprisingly, there was too much of it and too little moisture. Kriss complained of electricity in the wind that singed the wheat, wind that "doesn't stay in one direction long enough to blow up a rain," and neighbors who refused to plow in a way that might alleviate some of the blowing's influence. Each February Kriss began to dread the windy spring to come. He and Garvey debated about how best to plow and often felt their conservation strategies were moderately effective. "G-K Farms stuff wasn't moving," Kriss wrote of their soil after a wind event in January 1935. "Our deep furrow drilling has been holding it pretty good so far." Still, bad days happened. "We haven't much of anything to brag on in the way of wheat now," Kriss informed Garvey in May 1937. "The drying effect of the wind was as bad as the dust on the wheat.... Yesterday was the bluest day I have had for a long time."[39]

Crisis wind received the most attention on the plains, but the constant, daily wind, with very few wind blocks to get in its way, blew in its own set of challenges. "I remember it as being always windy, either hot or cold," Mattie Medlin mused about her Oklahoma home. In 1895 J. M. Armfield moved north from Texas onto Cheyenne and Arapaho lands. There he found "the hardest, most constant wind I have ever seen anywhere."[40] Further north, rancher William Sewall revealed Dakota Territory's blustery reputation in a letter to his brother. "We had one of the winds that you hear people tell about out west," he noted of that day in 1886.[41] The wind was almost always blowing, so it was almost always a consideration.

The eternal winds might chip away at a person's good humor, or it might augment it, as soon as that person accepted perpetual wind as a fact of life. Maintaining a sense of humor about the wind, in fact, is doubtless a benchmark to becoming native. Numerous jokes and amusing stories circulated about the near daily blustery conditions. "'Does the wind blow this way here all the time?' asked the ranch visitor in the West. 'No mister,' answered the cowboy; 'it'll maybe blow this way for a week or ten days, and then it'll take a change and blow like hell for a while.'"[42] One night, as a storm blew outside, a farmer shut his doors and windows and went to sleep. In the morning, there were several inches of sand in his bedroom. He'd forgotten to plug the keyhole.[43]

A good humor helped some plains residents to carry on despite the ridiculousness of daily wind. "*Very windy!*" Edith Clark, of Wyoming, remarked to her diary at the end of May 1908. Still, she and a friend ventured to town. "At about three o'clock Blanch & I tie our hair down & our heads on & start for a cross-country walk in the wind."[44] In Devils Lake, North Dakota, daily wind took its toll on Mabel Mitchell's garden. A diarist of the 1910s, Mitchell noted the direction and speed of the wind in nearly every entry. "Strongest wind of [the] season," Mitchell wrote on August 10, 1907. "Blew corn, beans, and most all of [my] garden to the ground."[45] Soon after moving to Oklahoma after the land run, A. J. Gummow made a winter trip back to Kansas to haul straw for his farm. The wind blew so hard during his two-day journey that little of the unbaled straw made it home with him. It blew out of his wagon and scattered across the prairie, making his trip an exceedingly unproductive one.[46] Finally, although 1930s Kansas farmwife Mary Dyck had many reasons to dislike the wind, she became particularly annoyed when the static "lectricity" it carried kept her from hearing her soap opera stories on the radio. "Its [sic] very lonesome when we cant [sic] have much Radio," she wrote.[47]

As annoying as the wind often was, as destructive as it could be, it was also a fact of life on the Great Plains. It inspired plenty of complaints, frustration, and even anger, but ultimately the wind remained. As long as it did, many people grudgingly admitted, they might as well use it, laugh about it, and occasionally focus on the positive things about living in a wind environment. Crises, such as dust storms and tornadoes, happen, but the plains region is more than a sum of its wind-driven historical or current disasters.

One example of the wind's positive historical effect was its influence on the periodic swarms of grasshoppers and locusts that visited the grasslands, creatures that ate everything in sight, wreaking economic, social, and psychological havoc wherever they went.[48] Farmers in the nineteenth century used poison and tried scores of ways to deter them, but ultimately, it was the wind that mattered most. "The Hoppers are going S.W. but as the wind don't blow much they go pretty slow," noted Minnesota farmer Sylvester Pound in his 1876 diary. They "have flew to the south West all day & I guess about as many lit as there was flew away[.] They have destroyed the crops very badly down in the valey [sic]."[49] Low places protected from the wind, therefore, were especially vulnerable to hoppers. Even the wind-hating trader, Ferdinand Van Ostrand, found redeeming features in a brisk breeze that blew the hoppers away. "The grass hoppers or locust came today in good earnest," he wrote in July 1871. "About noon they were swarming at every stop. . . . They soon found the garden. . . . If they remain a few days—good-bye to the Indian corn." In the next entry, however, Van Ostrand noted that a "high wind has prevailed all day and it has retarded the movements of the grass hoppers. . . . The damage as yet has not been great."[50]

Particularly in the spring, plains residents expected high winds. The blows were a significant problem for farmers, but ranchers felt less hardship—yet another element of the farmer/rancher divide in the region, another way in which the two rivaled economic groups used the environment differently. "We got our March winds in May," the *Daily Yellowstone Journal* out of Miles City, Montana, commented in 1887. But "what matters it if the wind does blow a gale during twelve or twenty-four hours[?]" In an area dominated by ranching, there were no crops to worry about, the cattle kept eating, and the wind, in fact, cleaned the fleece of wooly grazers. "Tho' all the world kicks over the state of the weather," the editor concluded, "we in Montana can well afford to say with the poet: 'Blow yet winds, and ye tempest roar.'"[51]

Windmills, dotting the plains since Euro-American settlement began, also tell an optimistic story of adaptation to the cantankerous prairie/plain environment. "A windmill is much needed at Lawrence," a writer remarked about the Kansas Territory town soon after its founding. "The scarcity of water power, and the abundance of wind which is always felt on the high grounds, seem to render that sort of machine a necessity in Kansas."[52] In semiarid country, the plentiful resource, wind, not the scarce, water, milled grains.[53] As windmill design improved in the mid-nineteenth century, people interested in pushing settlement onto the plains saw an intimate connection between the developing technology and the very foreign, large, open, and windy grassland environment. "In Kansas, these mills are to perform a great service in our future history," the *Herald of Freedom* prophesied in 1857, a century and a half before power companies began constructing giant wind farms on the landscape. "The country seems peculiarly adapted to their use."[54] Recognized and adopted in an earlier century, Great Plains peoples continued to adapt and expand the partnership between technology and the wind.

In the twentieth century, some rural residents first gained access to electricity with a windcharger installed on their farms. John Nesbit was born in South Dakota in 1912 and immigrated to Montana with his father in 1916. They settled on the newly opened Fort Peck Indian Reservation lands in the northeast part of the state. Without electricity until about 1949, the Nesbits installed and used a windcharger for at least three years before power from the electric co-op reached them. The wind powered lights and tools that the farmers used for work around their homestead. This was useful, as Nesbit remembered that the progress of the co-op electricity installation was slow. It reached farms within three miles of the Nesbit land, but nevertheless took another two years to get to them. In the meantime, wind powered their work and home life.[55]

Windmills and turbines are the most obvious intersection between technology and wind, but innovators have used other kinds of technology both to utilize the wind's energy as well as to overcome its formidable presence on the Great Plains. The wind's movement, in particular, symbolized freedom. "Let men think and act *free as air* on these grand garden plains of the mighty West," a nineteenth-century enthusiast wrote. "You who long for freedom,

FIG. 25. Lesley's wind wagon. Kansas State Historical Society.

come to Kansas."[56] Perhaps it was that freedom, felt on the wind, that inspired multiple innovators (or crackpots?) to build prairie schooners—wind-propelled wagons designed to blow several passengers to the west, overland across the plains to the Rocky Mountains and back.[57] Although the idea of *blowing* across the inland sea of grass is somewhat laughable today, the impulse that drove the prairie ship designers is not unfamiliar. Use an available resource, control it, and harness its power. What better way for humans to connect with the movement and strength that the wind brought to the landscape than to cause it to literally propel them across the big space? History demonstrates that the spirit of a place, as Flores noted, is as dependent on human imagination as it is on landscape, a sentiment capably revealed by the prairie schooner.[58]

Taking the impulse that drove inventors to develop the prairie schooner further, in Wichita, Kansas, aviation emerged as a dominant pastime and then industry in the twentieth century. In many ways, high and unpredictable winds were an obstacle to the city's emergence as an aviation center. It was not logical for one of the windiest cities in the country to earn the nickname "Air Capital" in honor of its dominance in aviation, but an "air-mindedness" nonetheless emerged among Wichita's citizens. In a place with a sky that was impossibly big and open, noted historian Craig Miner, it seemed more natural to look up than anywhere else. Recognizing that the air-minded impulse was good for business, and perhaps sensing the freedom of movement within the wind again, Wichita boomers argued that environmental characteristics such as open, relatively flat ground, peerless visibility, and a lack of fog were enticing enough to overcome the city's wind problem. Even if Wichita's wind averages would never decrease, airplanes would improve and pilots would learn to adjust over time.[59] After all, if a pilot could learn to fly in Kansas wind, he or she might fly anywhere.

Early aerial performer Roy Knabenshue learned a hard lesson about the Kansas breezes in 1908, when his flight demonstration rapidly shifted the attention of spectators from the air back down to the earth. Wichitans invited Knabenshue to a local fair to demonstrate his 150-foot-long airship, which he had flown successfully in New York and other locations around the country. City leaders wanted Knabenshue to fly his dirigible from a starting point on Ackerman Island, in the middle of the Arkansas River, to the downtown city building, a distance of about half a mile. The wind, however, proved too much for Knabenshue's contraption, which stayed anchored and windbound for most of the fair. Eventually, the pilot made several attempts, all failures, and the final "flight" ended with a crash, injuring both man and machine. Although the quality of the gas inside the balloon contributed to the difficulties, the wind was the primary issue, and as Knabenshue loaded the fractured pieces of his invention on the train for shipment back East, wind-wise locals advised that he avoid demonstrations on the prairies in the future.[60]

Despite Knabenshue's less than auspicious start, other aviation pioneers, such as Albin Longren, "The Wizard of the Air," and Clyde Cessna, had more success flying in Kansas wind. Both men did aerial demonstrations, promoting Kansas aviation as entertainment. Cessna was known for actually flying his latest inventions from his Kansas home rather than hauling them to fair locations via train. By 1916, according to Miner, aviation was a "Kansas activity," and pilots began to move their business away from entertainment and toward industry.[61] Starting in the 1920s with Laird and Cessna, then transitioning to Travel Air, Stearman (later Boeing), Beech, and, a latecomer in the 1960s, Lear Jet, Wichita originated or hosted several big-name producers as well as numerous others whose names are not as recognizable. As early as 1929, the city produced 26 percent of United States commercial aircraft, totaling one thousand planes.[62]

The history of regional wind reveals multiple dualities. Great Plains wind is a torment, a primary cause of hardship in a difficult environment, challenged only by drought for influence and effect. Wind blows bone-chilling, dangerous, cold one day, and the next (almost without exaggeration), acts as a furnace, withering crops and everything else that draws breath. It produces destructive tornadoes—occasionally inspiring National Weather Service predictions so alarming that your mother, who lives in Kansas, phones to tell you, only half-jokingly, that "it's been nice knowing you"—as well as terrifying straight velocities, which, at speeds such as eighty-seven miles per hour recorded in Kansas in 2014, are strong enough to knock a freight train right off its tracks.[63] And yet (and here's where the first duality comes in), while wind is at best an annoyance and at worst a calamity, many observers, from inside and outside the region, both professional and layperson alike, have argued, past and present, that *controlled* wind is the region's salvation. How to cure the plains in the 1930s? Plant trees as windbreaks. How to fix the plains in the 2010s? Build wind farms. How deliciously ironic, historian Elliott West has speculated, if the economic salvation of the region was the "distilled essence" of that which had originally been an obstacle to Euro-American settlement.[64]

While the duality of wind can produce either economic/environmental destruction or economic/environmental potential, a second duality is sensory and emotional. Wind on the plains is maddening. Its forceful and unrelenting presence makes life harder for humans. It destroyed Mabel Mitchell's garden in 1907 and angered Ferdinand Van Ostrand in 1871. It has made it almost impossible for plains residents, past and present, to have a good hair day.[65] And yet, the Great Plains wind *belongs* to the region. It turns snow into sculpture and carries heavenly smells from a bakery to the other side of town. Great Plains wind connects current people to the past. It is constant but continually reimagined by the humans who experience it. Few modern Great Plains women hang their laundry on an outside line to dry, but can nevertheless understand how the first piece of wet clothes that Elsie Riney hung out in Liberal, Kansas, in 1934, was already completely dry and ready to be taken down by the time she clothes-pinned the last garment in her basket to the line.[66] Often seen as a series of calamities, the history of wind and indeed the *presence* of wind on the Great Plains means more than potential crisis. Wind is a resource and a connector, not only to landscape but to people, how they used the land, and how they felt about it.

Ubiquitous wind, therefore, might be a help or hindrance on the Great Plains—a settler's greatest ally or worst enemy or some nebulous point in between. Always present, always volatile, always influential, the wind was and is a defining feature of the region. An important energy source both in the past and present, wind's power is not, however, limited to the tangible—the electricity it might produce or the water it might move. Wind had other powers as well—the ability to influence the people of the plains on several levels—emotional, physical, and economic among them. It shaped identities and created stories. Therein lay its power and significance to history and yet another type of salvation for the identity-starved Great Plains. Reporting on a hot windstorm in Kansas Territory in 1860, an editor described a "gust of air ... so hot that we at first supposed some building close by must be on fire, and rushed to the window to ascertain." He found, however, that there was no fire heating the wind—just the wind alone. "It was nothing but the air," the plains newcomer wrote, "but such an air!"[67]

Notes

1. Ferdinand A. Van Ostrand Diary, May 7, July 31, August 28, September 22, October 4, October 11, 1871, and March 22, April 30, June 23, 1872, MS 10007, State Historical Society of North Dakota, Bismarck ND. Van Ostrand wrote so often about wind in his diary that there are too many to include in this text.

2. Dan Flores, "Spirit of Place and the Value of Nature in the American West," in *A Sense of the American West: An Environmental History Anthology*, ed. James E. Sherow (Albuquerque: University of New Mexico Press, 1998), 32–35.

3. Mark M. Smith, "Still Coming to 'Our' Senses: An Introduction," *Journal of American History* 95, no. 2 (September 2008): 379.

4. See Robert W. Righter, *Wind Energy in America: A History* (Norman: University of Oklahoma Press, 1996) and T. Lindsay Baker, "Irrigating with Windmills on the Great Plains," *Great Plains Quarterly* 9, no. 4 (Fall 1989): 21–30.

5. "These are America's windiest cities, from San Francisco to Galveston," March 1, 2019, https://www.usatoday.com/picture-gallery/travel/experience/america/2019/03/01/americas-windiest-cities-california-texas/3026812002/. All thirty-four cities on the list had an average annual wind speed of 10.5 miles per hour or more between 1984 and 2015.

6. "Magazine's Answer Blows in Dodge Wind," *Hutchinson News*, May 4, 1983.

7. Renee DiResta, "Why Are Americans So . . ." *No Upside* (blog), August 7, 2012, http://blog.noupsi.de/post/28896819324/why-are-americans-so. See also Chris Cillizza, "What We Think about the 50 States—In 1 Map," *The Fix* (blog), *Washington Post*, August 16, 2012, http://www.washingtonpost.com/blogs/the-fix/wp/2012/08/16/how-we-think-about-the-50-states-in-1-map/.

8. Ree Drummond, @thepioneerwoman, tweet via Twitter, July 6, 2013.

9. Interested parties debate the placement of the giant wind farms as a potential source of sustainable, clean, power, and as an economic boon for landowners, but skeptics argue that the addition of numerous turbines to the landscape disrupts a place that depends on openness, space, and long horizons to maintain its regional character.

10. American Wind Energy Association, "U.S. Wind Energy State Facts," accessed May 1, 2017, https://www.awea.org/resources/fact-sheets/state-facts-sheets.

11. *The Nebraskian* (Omaha), March 18, 1857.

12. Righter, *Wind Energy in America*, 4.

13. Solomon Kious to editor, *Macomb Journal*, May 22, 1879. Misc. Kious Manuscript Collection, Kansas State Historical Society, Topeka KS.

14. *Kansas Herald of Freedom* (Wakarusa), January 20, 1855, and April 21, 1855.

15. "Early Days in Dakota Territory," box 3548B, folder 1, W. E. Lovejoy Manuscript Collection, South Dakota State Historical Society, Pierre SD.

16. Erastus F. Beadle, *Ham, Eggs, and Corn Cake: A Nebraska Territory Diary* (Lincoln: University of Nebraska Press, 2001), 24.

17. *Kansas Herald of Freedom* (Wakarusa), May 26, 1855.

18. Pamela Riney-Kehrberg, ed., *Waiting on the Bounty: The Dust Bowl Diary of Mary Knackstedt Dyck* (Iowa City: University of Iowa Press, 1999), 71. Entry is dated June 16, 1937.

19. *Kansas Herald of Freedom* (Wakarusa), November 14, 1857.

20. Willa Cather, *My Ántonia* (Boston: Houghton Mifflin, 1918), 53, 64.

21. Sylvia Ann Grider, "Forward," in *The Wind*, ed. Dorothy Scarborough (Austin: University of Texas Press, 1979), v.

22. Grider, "Forward," xvi; Scarborough, *The Wind*, 1–4.

23. Walter Prescott Webb, *The Great Plains* (Lincoln: University of Nebraska Press, 1981), 506. Emphasis added.

24. Grider, "Forward," v–vi, x–xiii.//
25. Robert A. Rundstrom, "Comments" (Great Plains Environmental Workshop, University of Oklahoma, Norman OK, May 22, 2017).//
26. Edith K. O. Clark Collection, April 6, 1913, box 1, collection 12580, American Heritage Center, University of Wyoming, Laramie WY.//
27. *Atchison Daily Globe*, October 11, 1881.//
28. *Atchison Daily Globe*, July 30, 1887.//
29. "A Tornado at Wichita," *Leavenworth Herald*, October 6, 1894.//
30. Thomas P. Grazulis, "Burnett's Myth Blown Away 35 Years Ago," *Topeka Capital-Journal*, March 11, 2001.//
31. *Climates of the States: South Dakota* (Washington DC: U.S. Department of Commerce Weather Bureau, 1960), n.p.; "Fargo Tornado 6-20-57," clippings in box 60, collection no. 10691, Roy P. Johnson / Louis Pfaller Collection, State Historical Society of North Dakota, Bismarck ND. Clippings are unidentified but are likely from the *Fargo Forum* editions of June 21, 1957, and dates following.//
32. "Interesting Letter," *Kansas Herald of Freedom* (Wakarusa), February 24, 1855.//
33. Thomas A. Edwards, interviewed by Ida B. Lankford, June 8, 1937, Indian-Pioneer Papers, vol. 27, interview ID 4398, University of Oklahoma, Western History Digital Collection, https://digital.libraries.ou.edu/whc/pioneer/paper.asp?pID=1401&vID=27.//
34. "Material for Houses," *Kansas Herald of Freedom* (Wakarusa), March 10, 1855.//
35. *Omaha Nebraskian*, November 24, 1860.//
36. David Laskin, *The Children's Blizzard* (New York: HarperCollins, 2004), 6, 184.//
37. Walter Kollmorgen, "Rainmakers on the Plains," *Scientific Monthly* 40, no. 2 (February 1935): 147.//
38. Mrs. John M. Dorchester, interviewed by Maurice R. Anderson, October 20, 1937, Indian-Pioneer Papers, vol. 25, interview ID 8970, University of Oklahoma, Western History Digital Collection, https://digital.libraries.ou.edu/whc/pioneer/paper.asp?pID=1855&vID=25; Mrs. Carrie Gable, interviewed by Augusta H. Custer, August 22, 1937, Indian-Pioneer Papers, vol. 33, interview ID 8526, University of Oklahoma, Western History Digital Collection, https://digital.libraries.ou.edu/whc/pioneer/paper.asp?pID=2116&vID=33.//
39. John Kriss to Ray Garvey, March 23, 1934, box 6, folder 11; January 17, 1935 and April 12, 1935, box 7, folder 12; February 13, 1936, box 8, folder 3; February 23–24, 1937, May 24, 1937 and May 28, 1937, box 9, folder 17, Olive White Garvey and Ray Hugh Garvey Papers, Manuscript Collection no. 809, Library and Archives Division, Kansas State Historical Society, Topeka KS.//
40. Mrs. Mattie Kemper Medlin, "Short Sketch of Living in a Dugout in Indian Territory," interviewed by Hazel B. Greene, July 20, 1937, Indian-Pioneer Papers, vol. 35, 486–91, Oklahoma State Historical Society, Oklahoma City OK; J. M. Armfield, interviewed by Ida B. Lankford, June 22, 1937, Indian-Pioneer Papers, vol. 3, interview ID 4541, University of Oklahoma, Western History Digital Collection, https://digital.libraries.ou.edu/whc/pioneer/paper.asp?pID=142&vID=3.

41. William W. Sewall to "Brother," April 21, 1886, box 1, William W. Sewall Papers, MS 10072, State Historical Society of North Dakota, Bismarck ND.

42. Webb, *The Great Plains*, 22.

43. John O. Talley, interviewed by Merrill A. Nelson, April 5, 1937, Indian-Pioneer Papers, vol. 89, interview ID 1200, University of Oklahoma, Western History Digital Collection, https://digital.libraries.ou.edu/whc/pioneer/paper.asp?pID=5749&vID=89.

44. Edith K. O. Clark Collection, May 31, 1908, box 1, collection no. 12580, American Heritage Center, University of Wyoming, Laramie WY.

45. Mabel Harwell Mitchell Papers, August 10, 1907, folder 1, box 1, MS 10907, Historical Society of North Dakota, Bismarck ND.

46. Mr. A. J. Gummow, interviewed by Robert W. Small, November 27, 1937, Indian-Pioneer Papers, vol. 27, p. 69, Oklahoma State Historical Society, Oklahoma City OK.

47. Riney-Kehrberg, *Waiting on the Bounty*, 42, 45.

48. See Jeffrey A. Lockwood, *Locust: The Devastating Rise and Mysterious Disappearance of the Insect That Shaped the American Frontier* (New York: Basic Books, 2004).

49. Sylvester J. Pound Diary, July 23–24, 1876, Small Manuscripts Collection, MS 24000, State Historical Society of North Dakota, Bismarck ND.

50. Ferdinand Van Ostrand Diary, July 25–27, 1871, MS 10007, State Historical Society of North Dakota, Bismarck ND.

51. *Daily Yellowstone Journal*, May 7, 1887.

52. "News from Kansas," *Ripley* (OH) *Bee*, March 31, 1855.

53. J. M. Armfield, interviewed by Ida B. Landford, June 22, 1937.

54. *Kansas Herald of Freedom* (Wakarusa), January 3, 1857.

55. John Nesbit, interviewed by Frank Quivik, July 1, 1998, Sheridan Electric Co-op Oral History Project, Collection OH 2186, Montana State Historical Society, Helena MT.

56. *Kansas Herald of Freedom* (Wakarusa), March 31, 1855. Emphasis added.

57. One prairie ship was built by Mr. Thompson in 1855. See *Bangor* (ME) *Daily Whig & Courier*, March 10, 1855.

58. Flores, "Spirit of Place," 37.

59. Craig Miner, *Wichita: The Magic City* (Wichita: Wichita-Sedgwick County Historical Museum Association, 1988), 149; Frank Joseph Rowe and Craig Miner, *Borne on the South Wind* (Wichita: Wichita Eagle and Beacon, 1994), 2.

60. Miner, *Wichita: The Magic City*, 109.

61. Rowe and Miner, *Borne on the South Wind*, 32–41.

62. Miner, *Wichita: The Magic City*, 154, 160, 165, 178, 208.

63. The author's mother has made that phone call more than once; *Hutchinson* (KS) *News*, May 7, 2014.

64. Elliott West, "Trails and Footprints: The Past of the Future Southern Plains," in *The Future of the Southern Plains*, ed. Sherry L. Smith (Norman: University of Oklahoma Press, 2003), 40.

65. Trust me. I have personal experience.

66. Pamela Riney-Kehrberg, interview by author, December 17, 2017.

67. "Extraordinary Phenomenon," *Freedom's Champion* (KS), July 14, 1860.

CONTRIBUTORS

Jacob A. Blackwell earned his MA in history at the University of Oklahoma, where he currently is pursuing a master of education degree.

Kathleen A. Brosnan is the Travis Chair of Modern American History at the University of Oklahoma.

Clint Carroll is an associate professor of Native American and Indigenous Studies at the University of Colorado, Boulder.

George Colpitts is a professor of history at the University of Calgary.

Julie Courtwright is an associate professor of history at Iowa State University.

Matthew Dyce is an associate professor of geography at the University of Winnipeg.

Mary Hagen Erlick is a doctoral candidate in anthropology at Utah State University.

Brian Frehner is an associate professor of history at the University of Missouri–Kansas City.

Kacy Hollenback is an assistant professor of anthropology at Southern Methodist University.

Michael J. Lansing is an associate professor of history and department chair at Augsburg University.

Brenda Macdougall is an associate professor of geography and holder of the chair in Métis Research at the University of Ottawa.

Leila Monaghan is a senior lecturer in anthropology at Northern Arizona University.

Joshua Nygren is an assistant professor of history at the University of Central Missouri.

Jonathan Peyton is an associate professor in the Department of Environment and Geography at the University of Manitoba.

Christopher Roos is an associate professor of anthropology at Southern Methodist University.

Molly P. Rozum is associate professor and Ronald R. Nelson Chair of Great Plains and South Dakota History at the University of South Dakota.

Nicole St-Onge is a professor of history at the University of Ottawa.

Geneviève Susemihl is an assistant professor for cultural and media studies at Kiel University, Germany.

Ryan Driskell Tate is an Alan K. Simpson Fellow in Western Politics at the American Heritage Center, University of Wyoming.

Michael Weeks is a lecturer in history at Utah Valley University.

Philip A. Wight is an assistant professor of history at the University of Alaska, Fairbanks.

Natale A. Zappia is an associate professor of history and director of the Institute for Sustainability at California State University, Northridge.

María Nieves Zedeño is a North American archaeologist at the University of Arizona.

INDEX

Page numbers in italics indicate illustrations. Page numbers appended with a t indicate tables.

aboriginal people, 95, 266
accounting: about, xxiii, 92; benefits of, 140–41; and daybooks, 141–44, 153n3; double-entry, 138–42, 152, 153n3; and environmental imagination, 138, 140; Hudson's Bay Company, 139, 140, 141; and inventory of goods, 141, 143; seeing bison through, 145–49; as a technology, 139
agricultural economy, xxv, 321, 323
agricultural enterprises, 163, 164, 165, 168, 171
agricultural landscapes, 13, 199n2, 266, 267, 270
agricultural production, xxv, 182, 190, 253
agricultural seeds, 253, 269
agriculture: about, xxiv, xxv; changes brought to, 157–58; commercial, xxv, 256, 260, 270; defined, 11–12; and fossil fuels, 288; and hot winds, 351; policy related to, 245; settler society, xxv, 255, 271; "slash-and-burn," 12; as source of regional identity, xxv; and technology, xxv
Amendment 14 (Colorado), 171
American Museum of Natural History, 42
animals: about, xix–xxx; Arapaho, 33t; Cheyenne, 32t, 35t; and Indigenous people, 83n40, 116–17; inventory of, 146, 148; migration of, 8; Native theology tenets of, 118; into new abstract unit, 150–51; nonhuman, 114, 115, 119, 123, 129; stories related to, 123–30; and understanding of society, 117. *See also* Cherokee society
"An Incident with a Deer," 126–28

anthropogenic fires, 49, 50, 60, 61, 62
"A Pit Panther," 123–24
aquifers, 157, 170, 172, 308, 331
Arapahos, 18, 32–33, 36, 41–44
archaeological artifacts, 77–78
aridity issue, 203, 208, 210, 220, 260, 267
Assiniboine Rivers, 97–99, 110n23, 110n27, 112n42, 143

Beef Belt, 159, 165, 168, 172
Bell, James Ford, 235–36, 238–39, 241–45
Bellvue Lab, 187, 195, *197*, 198
Berger, Jacques, 95, 96, *97*, 101, 111n35
Berger, Pierre, *100*, 101–3
Big Inch pipeline, 292, 294
bison: about, xix, xx; abstracting, 149–51; through accounting, 145–49; at center of spiritual world, 52; disappearance of, xxiv; jump sites, *57*. *See also* bookkeeping
bison commodification, 19, 20, 144
bison hunting, xxiii, xxiv, 14–15, 48–62, 89
bison processing, 5, 20, 21
black fallow, 205, 208, 211, 216
Blackfoot tribe: about, 35, 41; and bison hunting, 54; description of, 82n17; fire used by, 50–54, 60–61; and Head-Smashed-In Buffalo Jump, 69; interpretive center for, 74–76; and pyro-technology, 56–58
bookkeeping: about, xxiii, xxiv; double-entry, 138–42; as a technology, 139. *See also* accounting

365

Botsch v. Leigh Land Company (Nebraska, 1975), 168
bran and germ, 232, 233, 239, 246
bread flour, 232, 233, 235, 238, 239
breakfast cereals, 231–32, 236, 238–40, 246, 247
Brookover Feed Yard of Garden City, Kansas, 163–64
buffalo hunting, 34, 36–37, 72–76
buffalo jumps, 67–70, 72, 74–75, 77–78, 80n12
Bull Mountains of Montana, 300
Bureau of Agricultural Economics (U.S. Department of Agriculture), 189, 193, 194
Bureau of Agricultural Engineering (U.S. Department of Agriculture), 181, 183, 194
Bureau of Reclamation (U.S.), 179, *188*, 189, 193–94, 198, 309
burners and builders, 10, 11, 16, 18, 20, 21
Burnett's Mound, 349, 350

Campbell, Hardy Webster, 205
capillary action, 205, 206
capitalism, xiv, 248n9, 251n41, 284
cash crops, 181, 259
Cather, Willa, 346, 348
cattle feeding, 156–64, *159*, 167–69, 172–73
charcoal rich deposits, 57, 59, 60, 61
Cherokee culture, xxiii, 122
Cherokee Nation, 114, 119, 131
Cherokee relationships, 83n40, 115, 123, 129
Cherokee society: about, 114–16; and animal stories, 123–30; conclusion about, 131–32; environmental history, 116–19; and human-animal sociality, 116–19; and migration/removal, 119–23, 130; and nonhuman animals, 114, 115, 119, 123, 129; and Osages, 8, 9, 10, 120–22; and place-names, 121, 122; and western lands, 119–22, 129
Cheyennes, 31–34, 36, 40–41, 44
"Children's Blizzard" (1888), 351
Clean Water Act of 1972 (U.S.), 162
climate change, xiii, 7, 14, 132
climate crisis, 302, 303
coal companies, 301, 302, 304–11, 313
coalfields, 301, 302, 308, 312, 314
coal reserves, 300, 307
cold cereals, 237, 238, 239, 240, 246

colluvial deposits, 57, 58
Colorado, cattle feeding in, 164
Colorado Agricultural College (CAC), 181, 183, 187, 195
Colorado-Big Thompson Project (C-BT), *188*, 189–94, *191*, 196, 198
Colorado-Big Thompson Transmountain Diversion Project, 182
Colorado River, 188, 190
commercial agriculture, xxv, 256, 260, 270
commodity prices, 234, 259
common law, 157, 160, 172
communal hunting, 50, 54, 55, 62, 66, 73
Confined Animal Feeding Operation Act (Oklahoma, 1997), 170
conservation and preservation, 184, 200n9
conservation-industrial complex, xxv, 203–5, 207, 213, 221n6
conservation tillage: about, 202, 203; and farming, 218, 219; and herbicides, 216–17; limited popularity of, 217–18; origin of, 210; proponents of, 210; rise of, 204–5, 214, 221n3
Constipation: How to Fight It (Kellogg), 237
Contact Period, 35, 54
Continental Divide, 182
Cook, W. H., 148, 149
Corn Belt, 156, *159*, 168, 258–59, 266
Corn Flakes, 237, 239
Corn for the Northwest (Will), 258, 260
corn hybrids, 264, 265
Coronado, Francisco Vásquez de, 3–5, 8, 15
crisis wind, 344, 348, 351, 352
crop failure, 264, 351
crop residues, 202, 206, 208, 215, 217
crude oil, 279, 280, *281*, 284, 324
cultural change, xxiii, 115
cultural geography, 15–20
cultural heritage, 68, 71, 77, 79–80, 97
cultural landscapes, 66, 67
cultural relationships, xx, 66, 322
cultural technologies, 118, 130

daily wind, 344, 352, 353
Daly Field, 324, 326
daybooks, 141–44, 153n3
deer, stories related to, 126–30
deerskin trade, 115, 119

dent corn, 258, 259, 272n13
diaries. *See* post diaries
dietary fiber. *See* fiber-rich diet
Dill v. Excel (Kansas, 1958), 167
ditch companies, 185, 187
dog travois, 34, 36
double-entry accounting, 138–42, 152, 153n3
Down to Earth (magazine), 217
drive lanes, 72, 73, 74
droughts, xv, xviii, 8, 208, 234, 261–63
Drummond, Ree, 346
dryland farming, 203, 205, 210, 211, 259, 266
duckfoot cultivator, 206, 207, 209
Duley, Frank L., 202–4, 207–13, 220, 221n2, 224n37
Dust Bowl: about, xv, 157; and conservation efforts, 208; and Great Lakes Pipe Line, 290–91; and heavy winds, 346, 352; historiography about, 222n8; and stubble mulching, 204
Dust Bowl: The Southern Plains in the 1930s (Worster), xiv
dust mulch, 206
dust storms, 202, 204, 208, 223n27, 353
dyspepsia, 231, 236, 237, 238, 245, 246

ecological changes, 6, 14
ecological disasters, xiii, xvii
economies of scale, xxiii, 157, 293
ecosystems, xviii, xix, 302, 306–7, 311–12
ecotone, 15, 22n9
El Turco, 4–5, 7–8
empowerment theory, 84n63
energy: about, xviii–xx; consumption, 287, 288, 291, 293, 295, 296; and strip mining, 307–8; technology related to, 280, 288; wind, 343–44, 359
environment: about, xiv, xv; constraints related to, 92, 266; human adaptation to, xix, xxii, xxvii, 157; Indigenous perspectives, 116–19; policy for, 115, 131, 132; regulations for, xxiii, 157, 162; and strip mining, 301–2, 312–13
environmental changes, xxi, 117, 160, 282, 301, 327
environmentalists, xvi, 217, 304, 313, 314, 315
equestrian revolution, 6, 7
erosion and runoff, 206, 215, 224n32

erosion control, 207, 210
ethnogenesis, 8, 91, 105
Excel Packing Company, 167
extractive economies, 322, 325, 327
extractive progress history, 323–29

family farms, 94, 255, 271
farming: about, xiv, xxvi; and cash crops, 181, 259; and conservation tillage, 218, 219; diversified, 258, 259, 267; and heavy winds, 354; industrial, 269; large-machine, 259–60; resistance to, 98; and water management, 184, 187, 194, 195. *See also* agriculture; stubble mulching
feedlots: about, xix, xxiii, 156; adaptation to environment, 157; as agricultural enterprises, 163, 164, 165, 168, 171; defined, 160; in Great Plains, 160; hostility toward, 166; and landowners, 167; lawsuits against, 163–67; licensing procedure for, 160–61; map of, *158*; offensive odors caused by, 156, 157, 160, 166–71; operators, xxiii, 157, 160–62, 169–72; pollution caused by, 160, 161, 162, 163, 165, 166; regulations for, 161–63, 167
fiber-rich diet, 231, 236, 237, 240, 245
Fidler, Peter, 145, 146
Fields v. Anderson Cattle Company (Kansas, 1964), 163, 165
fire(s): about, xvi, xxii; anthropogenic, 49, 50, 60, 61, 62; conclusion about, 62–63; demonstration of setting, *53*; grassland, 48, 49; occurrence of, 59–62; origin of, 49; prehistoric, 49; role of, 56; uses of, 48–54, 60–61
flint corn, 257–59, 260, 265, 266, 273n14
flooding, xviii, 8, 26n45, 57
flour industry, 230, 233, 238, 247
flour mills, 231, 234–36, 242–44
Fontana, August, 320–21
food frontiers, 15, 16
food production, xxv, 9–10, 12, 14–16, 18, 25n32
food systems: about, 6; bison-dominated, 20; and breakfast cereal, 247; emerging, 231, 232, 244; historicizing, 11–15; and Little Ice Age, 8; Maxi'diwiac, 17; monocultural and polycultural, 14

Index 367

Fort Carlton, 147
Fort des Prairies region, 95, 97–99, 101, 103, 105
fossil fuels, 243, 280–83, 287–88, 300–301, 306
fracking. *See* hydraulic fracturing
fur-trade, 89, 90, 91, 95, 104–5, 138–39

garden seeds, 269–70
Garland Grain Company, 165–66
Gee v. Dinsdale Brothers (Nebraska, 1980), 168
General Mills, 231, 243–47
globalization, 9, 16
global warming, 9, 48
grasses, xviii–xix, xxvi–xxvii, 13, 14, 17, 36, 44, 49, 220n1, 256, 304, 305–7, 309–12
grasslands: about, xiv, xvi, xxv, 15, 19, 220n1; and droughts, 261–63; and environmental limitations, 256; fescue, 59, 62; fire, 48, 49; "New Northwest" region of, 256–57; and ranching, 305–7; and settler society agriculture, 255; and strip mining, 305–6; and stubble mulching, 220
grass management, 13, 14
gratis transactions, 144
Great Depression, 189, 192, 244, 245, 290
Great Lakes Pipe Line, 290
Great Plains: about, xiii–xvii; aridity issue, 203, 208, 210, 220, 260, 267; Beef Belt, 159, 165, 168, 172; boundaries issue, 7–20, 262–63, 267; and cultural geography, 15–20; culture area, 31, 69, 73; economic interactions in, 20–21; horses' presence throughout, xxii; "hottest chronology," 6, 7; Indian War, 30, 37; Indigenous people, 31; map of, *xxix*; Métis hunting brigades, 89–93, 103, 105; and military records, 37–41; and oil economy, xxv, xxvi, 321, 323, 324, 333–36; and petroleum deposits, 281; productive landscape of, 5; as region, xvii–xviii; removing "prehistory" from, 7–11, 22n9; semiarid, 215, 217, 260, 267; spring on, 349, 354; territory and resources, 30–31; tornado culture on, 349–50. *See also* feedlots; pipeline system; wind
The Great Plains (Webb), xiv, 263, 264
Great Plains Pasture Mixture, 266–67
groundwater, 171, 308, 309

hard spring wheat, 231, 232, 234, 242
Head-Smashed-In Buffalo Jump, 67–72, 74–78, 81n10
Hegion, Steve, 333–34
Hepburn Act of 1906 (U.S.), 286
herbicides, 210, 216–20
herding, 10, 14, 15
heritage sites, xxiii, 66–69, 71, 76–80, 81n9
Hidatsas, 10, 15–19, 34
homebrewed law, 314
horizontal drilling, 327, 328
horses, xxii, 6, 28
Horsetooth Reservoir, *197*, 198
hot winds, 255, 340, 351
Hudson's Bay Company's (HBC), xxiii, 54, 89, 97–99, 139–41, 152
human migrations, 6, 15
hunter-gatherers, 9, 11, 12, 18, 35, 49
hydraulic fracturing, xviii, xxvii, 327–30, 336, 338n28
hydrocarbons, 280–84, 288, 293, 295, 323, 335

Inch Lines pipeline, 292, 293
Indian women: about, 28; artwork by, *42*, *43*; and awareness of environment, 41; conclusion about, 44–45; mobile lifeways of, 29–30, 37; and perceptions of world, 41–44; responsibilities of, 29; shelters built by, 40; with travois, *37*
Indigenous buffalo hunting, 72–74. *See also* Indigenous hunting
Indigenous empowerment, 79–80, 84n63
Indigenous food systems. *See* food systems
Indigenous hunting, xxiii, 116, 117, 143
Indigenous people: about, xix, xx, xxii, 68; and animals, xxiv, 83n40, 116–17; and archaeological artifacts, 77–78; and cultural heritage, 79, 80; Great Plains, 31; and heritage, 67; and places and landscapes, 71. *See also* aboriginal people; Arapahos; bison; Blackfoot tribe; Cherokee society; Cheyennes; Hidastas; Keetoowah; Métis hunting brigades; Piikani
Indigenous women, 147, 253, 255, 258, 266, 269–71
industrial agriculture, xxv, 203, 214, 218–19, 221n4, 283
industrialization, xvi, xx

Interprovincial Pipeline, 295
irrigation companies, 179, 181, 184, 187–89, 192, 193
irrigation engineers, 181–85, 189
irrigation infrastructure, 179, 192

Judith Basin hunting brigades, 92–93, 103, 106–7
Judith Basin petition, 101, 104, 106
jumps. *See* kill sites

Kansas: aviation pastime in, 356–59; cattle feeding in, 160–61, 163–64, 167
Keetoowah, 129, 135n30
killing cliffs, 74–76
kill sites, 51, 55, 59–61, 68, 69
Kirikurus, 3–5, 15, 21n3

landowners, 152, 167, 206, 313, 325, 360n9
landscape assemblage, 34–37, 43, 44, 45n6
Leigh Land Company, 168
lightning strikes, 12, 25n32, 25n35, 48
Little Bighorn, 37–41
Little Big Inch pipeline, 292, 294
Little Deer (AWI USDI) story, 128–29
Little Ice Age, 7–9, 13–14, 20, 23n17
Livestock Waste Management Act (Nebraska, 1998), 171

maize production, 8, 9, 14–16
Malin, James, xiv–xv
matrilineal clan system, xxiii, 114, 123
Maxi'diwiac, 16–18, 21
McIvor family, 320–21
McNary-Haugen Act, vetoed, 245
meatpacking firms, 158, 233
Meat Producers, Inc., 166–67
medicine bundles, 76, 78
Métis hunting brigades, 89–93, 103, 105
Midcontinent Pipeline System, 280, 282–83, 292–96
Miles, Nelson, 92, 93
military records, 37–41
mineral rights: about, 320; and August Fontana story, 320–21; conclusion about, 335–36; and extractive progress history, 323–29; and hydraulic fracturing, 327–30, 336, 338n28; and McIvor family, 320–21; and oil anxieties, 334–36; and oil cultures, 322–23, 327, 330–35; and oil drilling, 325–26; and OPEC crisis, 326–27; taxation issues, 334
mobility issue, xxii, xxiii
mounted hunting, xxii, 54
Moving Robe, 39, 40

National Environmental Policy Act (U.S., 1970), 303
National Oceanic and Atmospheric Administration (NOAA), 342, 343
native grasses, 220n1, 300, 307, 309, 310
natural gas, 280–82, 289–90, 293–94
Nebraska, cattle feeding in, 162–63, 168–69
Nebraska Environmental Protection Act (1971), 162
Neuhoff Brothers Packers, Inc., 156, 157, 165
New Deal program, xiv, xviii, 189, 225n40
Noble, Charles S., 206, 207
Noble Blade, 207, 223n27, 223n28
nomadic lifestyle, 30, 31, 72, 103
nonflour products, 231, 239, 244
nonhuman animals, 114, 115, 119, 123, 129
non-Indigenous groups, xxiii, xxiv, xxx, 72, 152
Northern Colorado Water Conservation District, 193
northern plains: about, 17, 30, 35; agricultural adaptation to, 256; buffalo hunting on, 72–74; and droughts, 261–63; high birth rate, 105; social purposes in, 73. *See also* Great Plains
North West Company (NWC), 95–98, 101–5, 109n12, 110n21, 111n34, 153n3
no-till technology, 202, 217, 219

Ogallala Aquifer, 157, 170, 172
oil boom, 325, 332, 333, 336
oil crisis, xxvi, 301, 326
oil cultures, 320–23, 327, 330–35
oil drilling, 321, 323–29, 331, 333–35
oil economies, 321, 323–25, 330, 333–36
oil extraction, xvi, xxvi, 329, 330
oil fields, xvi, 282, 285, 287, 293, 326
oil industry, 285, 291, 292, 323–24, 329
oil leaks and spills, 286–87, 325
oil patch, 325, 326, 331
oil production, 287, 321, 324, 326, 328–30

oil reserves, 282, 294
oil rights. *See* mineral rights
Oil Wives Club (OWC), 331–32
Oklahoma, cattle feeding in, 161–62, 164–65, 169–70
Oklahoma Cattlemen's Association (OCA), 161, 162
Oklahoma Feed Yards Act (OFYA) (1969), 161, 162, 169, 171
Oklahoma Swine Feeding Operations Act (2005), 171
OPEC oil crisis, 219, 326–27
Osages, 8–10, 120–22
Oscar H. Will & Co., *254, 257,* 260–61, *264, 267, 268*

packaged cereal, 238, 239
panthers, stories related to, 123–25
Parshall, Ralph, 182–96
Parshall Flume, *183,* 184–88, *194, 196*
patch burning, 60, 61, 62
Pembina region, 97–99, 101–2, 105, 107, 112n38
Piedmont region, 180–81, 183–84, 189, 193, 201n24
Piikani, 35, 70, 76–78, 82n17
Pillsbury Flour Mills, 236, 242
pipeline system: about, 280; construction of, 280–81, 293–95; deployment of, 290; and environmental costs, 291; geography of, 281; growth in, 287–88; hydrocarbons, 280–84, 288, 293, 295; infrastructure, 280–81, 294; networks, 282, 284; success of, 289; trunk lines, 280, *281,* 283–89, 292; and "Tulsa Plan," 292; and World War II, 291–92
places and landscapes, 70, 71
plague, 8, 24n19, 147
Plains groups. *See* Indigenous people
Plains Métis hunting brigades: about, 89–90; and ancestral generation, 94–99, 101–3; background, 90–92; conclusion about, 106–7; and Judith Basin hunting brigades, 92–93, 103, 106–7; kinscapes for, 94, 103–6; marital alliances among families of, 101–4, 111n32; rise of, 103; as source of wonder, 106
plant residues, 211, 213
plants: about, 5, 8; Arapaho, 33*t*; Cheyenne, 32*t*, 35*t*; and ecotone, 15; evolution of, 12–13
Platte Pipeline, 295
plow agriculture, 208, 219
The Plow That Broke the Plains (movie), 202
pollution: agricultural, 217; air, 301; controls related to, 163, 169, 303; feedlots-related, 160, 161, 162, 163, 165, 166; levels of, 166
post diaries: and daybooks, 142–44; in double-entry accounting, 140–42; John Pruden, 147–48; Peter Fidler, 145; W. H. Cook, 148–49
post-removal era, xxiii, 115
Powell, John Wesley, xiii, 263
prairie fires, 48–62
prairie landscapes, 15, 28–29, 31, 34, 37, 91
"Prairie Plains," 263
prescribed burning, 8, 10, 12, 25n31, 55
prima facie evidence, 161, 171
processed foods, 233, 241, 246
Pruden, John, 147, 148
pyrogenic landscapes, 10, 13
pyrogenic management, 12, 13
pyro-technology, 56–58

radio advertisements, 240, 241
radiocarbon dating, 57, 58, 59, 61
rainfall, xiii, 208, 210, 234, 261, 300
ranching business, xix, 305–9, 354
"reclamation" laws (U.S.), 303, 304
reclamation officials, 305, 311–12
reclamation procedures, 310, 311, 312, 313
"reclamation sites," 305, 309–12
Red River carts, 91, 97, 103, 105
Red River Colony, 98, 101, 105, 107, 108n5
Red River Settlement, 99, 101, 112n36
Red River Valley, 97, 99, 101, 110n23
regionalism, xvi, xvii, xx
relational continuity, 114, 116, 118, 123–32
resource councils, 312–15
resource management, 49, 131
Russel, J. C., 202–3, *209,* 210–13, 220, 221n2, 224n37

sacred skulls, 74–76
Sand Creek Massacre, 37–41
sand traps, 195, 196
Saskatchewan District, 97, 98, 99, 101, 151, 155n30

Scarborough, Dorothy, 347, 348
seed varieties, 265, 269
semiarid plains, 215, 217, 260, 267
settler colonialism, 115, 118, 253, 255, 257
settler society, xxv, 253, 255–56, 258, 260, 269–71
sheet erosion, 207, 224n32
Shell Canada refinery, 325, 326
Sierra Club, 314, 315
Silent Spring (Carson), 217
snowpack, 179, 181, 182, 194
soil blowing, 206, 211
soil conservation, 203, 204, 211, 218
Soil Conservation Service (SCS), 202, 206–8, 214, 221n6, 223n29
soil moisture, 202, 203, 205, 206, 215, 216
southern plains, 231, 241–43, 245, 350, 351
South Platte, 180, 181, 182, 192
spring coulee bank profile, *58*
spring wheat, 231, 232, 234, 241, 242
Standard Oil Company, xxvi, 279, 284, 285, 286, 324
state-sponsored science, 180, 187
St. Lawrence Valley, 94, 95
The Stomach: Its Disorders, and How to Cure Them (Kellogg), 237
storms, 349, 350
strip mining: about, 301; conflict over, 302; and energy systems, 307–8; and environment, 301–2, 312–13; and grasslands, 305–6; and overburden, 302, 315; as political topic, 303–4; and ranching, 305–9; and reclamation laws, 303–4; and "reclamation sites," 305, 309–12; and resource councils, 312–15; and surface mines, 303–5
stubble mulching: about, 202; commitment to, 211; and dryland farming, 203, 205, 210, 211; and Dust Bowl, 204; and grasslands, 220; public-private collaboration for, 212–15; and soil conservation, 203; spread of, 214, 215; support for, 211–12; as technological adaptation, 203, 210; total acreage, 227n78
subsistence hunting, xxiii, 68, 120
subsurface-tillage, 202, 211, 212, 226n59
summer fallow, 205, 206, 208, 212, 216, 259
surface mines, 303–5
surface residues, 207, 210, 216

Surface Rights Act (Manitoba, 1983), 325
synthetic herbicides, 216, 219

tallgrasses, 263, 269
technology: about, xv, xvi; accounting as a, 139; and agriculture, xxv; defined, xxi; energy-related, 280, 288; example of, xxvi; faith in, xxv; poem about, 220; role of, xxvi; transformation from, xxvi–xxvii. *See also* stubble mulching
Terminal Pleistocene, 59
Texas, cattle feeding in, 165–67
Texas Water Quality Board, 162
There Will Be Blood (movie), 322
till-planting, 215, 216
Timber Culture Act (U.S., 1973), 257
tipis, 29, 33*t*, 36, 40–44
tornadoes, 349–50
trade, 3, 6, 9, 20
trading posts, 138, 152
trailer camp, 333
transportation corridor, xxvi, 279, 282
travois: benefit of, 41; description of, 28; dog, 34, 36; horse, 28, 34; travel by, 34–37; women with, 37
tree ring studies, 263, 274n26
tribal governance, 122, 131
tribal religions, 134n16
trunk lines, 280, *281*, 283–89, 292
"Tulsa Plan," 292
turbines, 343, 355
Two Medicine River, 50, 54–60, 62

Ugewaleda, 121–22, 130, 136n37
"The Underground Panthers," 124–26
urban centers, 8, 9, 11, 15–17, 26n45
U.S. Timber Culture Act, 257

Van Ostrand, Ferdinand, 340, 341, 346, 354, 358
vertical wells, 329, 330
Virden, oil culture of, 330–35
Vore site, 19, 20
vortex tube, 195, *196*
voyageurs, 94–95, 102–3
V-sweeps, *209*, 213, 216, 217, 225n42

Washburn-Crosby Company, 230–31, 234–43

Index

371

Washita attack, 37–41
water diversion, 180, 184, 193
water management, 184, 187, 194, 195
water measurement, 186, 187
water resources, xxviii, 179, 308, 331
water rights, 179, 180, 181
watersheds, 179, 182, 192, 303
water supplies, 167, 189–90, 196, 290, 306, 309
water users, 189, 193, 201n24
Webb, Walter Prescott, xiv, xvi, 263, 347; and agricultural regions, 264; and land regions, 265
weeds, 198, 206, 209, 216
western lands, 119–22, 129, 265, 304
wheat farming: about, 230–31; and bran and germ, 232, 233, 239, 246; and bread flour, 232, 233, 235, 238, 239; and breakfast cereal, 231–32, 236, 238–40, 244, 246, 247; and commodity prices, 234, 259; and corporate mergers, 236; and flour mills, 231, 234–36, 242–44; and hard spring wheat, 231, 232, 234, 242; and hydromechanical power, 235; and nonflour products, 231, 239, 244; and southern plains, 241; and wheat monoculture, 230, 232, 234, 236, 242, 245; and wheat rust, 234, 235, 241
Wheaties cereal, 230–32, 239–40, 244, 246–47
white flour, 230, 231, 233, 242

White Horse Plains (WHP), 98, 99, 105, 107
white settlers, 6, 260
Wilkie, Judith, 92, 101, 102
Will, George F., 253, 255–58, 271
Will, Oscar H., 253, 256
Will's Bismarck Seed House, 268, 269, 270, 274n36, 275n38
wind: about, 340–41; and aerial demonstrations, 357–58; controlled, 358; crisis, 344, 348, 351, 352; daily, 344, 352, 353; and Dust Bowl, 346, 352; as energy source, 343–44, 359; erosion, 206, 208; as fact of life, 353; and farming, 354; farms, 355, 358, 360n9; history of, 342; hot, 351; human interactions with, 341, 343; multiple dualities of, 358–59; positive effect of, 354; reaction of women to, 347–48; sense of humor about, 352–53; turbines, 343, 355; and windiest places in United States, 342–43
The Wind (movie), 348
The Wind (Scarborough), 347, 348
windmills, 344, 345, 354, 355
wind-propelled wagons, 356
Wind River Reservation, 42
winter wheat, 231, 241, 242
World Heritage Site, 67, 68
World War II, xvi, xix, 212, 213, 291, 292

Ysopete, 3, 4, 7

zoning regulations, 161, 163, 167

www.ingramcontent.com/pod-product-compliance
Lightning Source LLC
Chambersburg PA
CBHW031845220426
43663CB00006B/498